Praise for *The Store in the Hood*:

"This is a fascinating study, offering fresh insights in a lucid style, from a master sociologist with a keen sense of history." —**Reed Ueda**, Tufts University

"The story of ethnics and enterprise captures both the American dream and the American nightmare, since the same people who seem to be pulling themselves up by their bootstraps, seem to also find themselves in conflict with their neighbors and customers. Steven J. Gold revisits this American perennial, telling a surprising story about the conflicts both engendered and avoided by the past century's waves of ethnic entrepreneurs." —**Roger Waldinger**, University of California, Los Angeles

"*The Store in the Hood* is a comprehensive study of conflicts between immigrant merchants and customers throughout the U.S. during the twentieth century. . . . This book develops a more nuanced understanding by exploring merchant/customer conflicts over the past hundred years across a wide range of ethnic groups and settings. Utilizing published research, official statistics, interviews, and ethnographic data collected from diverse locations, the book reveals how powerful groups and institutions have shaped the environments in which merchant/customer conflicts occur."—**Community and Urban Sociology Section (CUSS) Newsletter: American Sociological Association**

THE STORE IN THE HOOD

A Century of Ethnic Business and Conflict

Steven J. Gold

ROWMAN & LITTLEFIELD PUBLISHERS, INC.

Lanham • Boulder • New York • Toronto • Plymouth, UK

Published by Rowman & Littlefield Publishers, Inc.
A wholly owned subsidiary of The Rowman & Littlefield Publishing Group, Inc.
4501 Forbes Boulevard, Suite 200, Lanham, Maryland 20706
http://www.rowmanlittlefield.com

Estover Road, Plymouth PL6 7PY, United Kingdom

British Library Cataloguing in Publication Information Available

Library of Congress Cataloging-in-Publication Data

The hardback edition of this book was previously cataloged by the Library of Congress as follows:

Gold, Steven J. (Steven James)
  The store in the hood : a century of ethnic business and conflict / Steven J. Gold.
    p. cm.
  Includes bibliographical references and index.
  1. Minority business enterprises—United States—History. 2. Small business—Social aspects—United States—History. 3. Customer relations—Social aspects—United States—History. 4. United States—Race relations. I. Title.
  HD2358.5.U6G65 2010
  338.6'4208900973—dc22   2010014670

ISBN: 978-1-4422-0623-6 (cloth : alk. paper)
ISBN: 978-1-4422-0624-3 (pbk. : alk. paper)
ISBN: 978-1-4422-0625-0 (electronic)

Printed in the United States of America

CONTENTS

PREFACE

Much of my sociological work has described immigrant groups who have used self-employment as a means of making a life in a new society. I have undertaken this project to develop a broader understanding of ethnic entrepreneurship. While self-employment permits some individuals and groups who confront significant obstacles and have few resources at their disposal to survive and even thrive in American society, at the same time, running a small business can be very difficult, exacting significant human and financial costs from merchants, customers, and the local community. While my awareness of the conflicts surrounding small businesses has been shaped by sociological research, it is also a product of my biography.

Both sets of my grandparents, Jewish immigrants from Eastern Europe, were self-employed in the first half of the twentieth century. My mother's family was unsuccessful and returned to wage labor in the garment industry when their business failed. In contrast, my father's family ran a series of small food enterprises.

An inveterate storyteller, my father often described what it was like to grow up in a grocery store. While these enterprises supported his family during the Great Depression, the life that he described was quite difficult. Living behind their market, his family had little privacy and, because they needed income, felt obliged to serve customers at all hours of the day and night.

As immigrant Jews in a Catholic neighborhood, the family had to endure customers' hostility. My father described being bullied by his classmates on the way to and from school, their way of exacting revenge from a family that was both different from them and able to pocket some of their hard-earned cash. The taunting was especially harsh when neighborhood children saw him in the company of Hassidic relatives who dressed in the same manner that they had in Eastern Europe. It only stopped after my grandmother paid a burley Irish boy to escort him to class.

My father loved to share stories about his childhood with my brother and me, but there was little nostalgia in his tales. The reason he told them to us was to contrast his own arduous childhood with the much more privileged existence that we were able to enjoy because my mother and he had been able to leave small business behind, attend college, and pursue professional occupations. When we brought home unimpressive report cards, he would remind us with an air of resignation that our opportunities for rewarding careers might slip away, forcing us to spend our lives selling shirts or insurance.

As the years passed, I had many opportunities to reflect on these lessons because I repeatedly found myself close to instances of explosive conflict between ethnic merchants and their customers: I lived just outside of Cleveland during the 1966 uprising and recall the long line of national guardsmen driving past my elementary school on their way to the Hough area. I was visiting my grandmother in New Haven in the summer of 1967 when the killing of a customer by a shopkeeper catalyzed a spate of unrest. I moved to New York City just in time to witness the looting that accompanied the power failure of July 1977, and I lived in the Los Angeles area during the 1992 uprising that followed the acquittal of the police officers whose beating of Rodney King was captured on videotape.

My awareness of these conflicts directed me to the sociological study of immigration, race, and ethnic entrepreneurship. Having absorbed my dad's reflections on the human dimension of merchant-customer conflicts made me unsatisfied with academic studies that treated the topic in a simplistic manner, either idealizing self-employment as a cure-all for social and economic problems or condemning it as a form of exploitation.

My dad's message about immigrant businesses in poor communities is that, while being a proprietor allows some people to earn a living, it also involves costs, including social conflict, for merchants, customers, and the surrounding community. When experts prescribe ethnic entrepreneurship as a strategy for alleviating the problems of disadvantaged groups and communities, they disregard the likelihood of merchant-customer conflict at their own peril, because when conflicts arise, envisioned outcomes suddenly become far less rewarding than had been planned.

With this in mind, it is my hope that this book will contribute to a better understanding of the social and economic impact that ethnic businesses have in impoverished communities, so that more people can reap the benefits and fewer can suffer from the associated losses.

ACKNOWLEDGMENTS

I express my gratitude to the Institute of Public Policy and Social Research at Michigan State University and Ann Marie Schneider for providing two Michigan Applied Public Policy Research Grants that supported this study. Iris Taylor, Mille Rojas, Mary Millar, and Tammy Spangler assisted with administrative matters and helped me obtain books and other resources. Jay Newbury, Chuck Petrin, Rosa E. Morales, and Kristiné M. Hansen provided research assistance. Jan Bokemeier helped me obtain a sabbatical during fall semester 2007 to work on the book. Chuck Spurlock and Temple Smith shared interviews and their knowledge about Detroit communities with me. Caroline Darany and Ashley Bair scanned photographs and prepared tables, and Danielle Kaltz and Elizabeth Clemens provided me with access to photographs.

I thank Nancy Foner for encouraging me to write the article upon which this book was based. She along with George Frederickson provided valuable direction and feedback. The Social Science Research Council supported two conferences that brought together scholars interested in related topics that informed much of the work. Jennifer Hochschild, John Lie, Joe Trotter, Louise Jezierski, Sharon Zukin, Frank Bean, Mario Small, Elijah Anderson, Roger Waldinger, Doug Massey, Gerald Jaynes, Kami Pothukuchi, Scott Newman, Mara Leichtman, Sudhir Venkatesh, and Carl Taylor provided valuable suggestions and data sources.

Ivan Light, Pyong Gap Min, Mary Waters, and Xuefei Ren read chapters and extended constructive comments. Joe Darden was an excellent collaborator on chapter 8 and provided valuable insights and feedback that helped me envision the entire book. Two anonymous reviewers gave suggestions and references for the manuscript's revision. Bibliographer Michael Unsworth of the Michigan State University library helped me identify sources.

Alex Masulis and Sarah Stanton of Rowman & Littlefield offered encouragement and information useful to preparing the manuscript for publication. Several entrepreneurs, business development professionals, city and county officials, and agency staff in Detroit, Wayne Country, and Lansing, Michigan, generously shared their knowledge about small business development in Detroit, Michigan.

Finally, Lisa Gold read, reflected on, and copyedited the entire manuscript. Her support and that of our children, William and Betty, kept me motivated throughout the project.

❶

INTRODUCTION

VIGNETTES

During the late 1800s, Sicilians who came to work the Louisiana sugar harvest quickly moved out of farm labor to become the proprietors of saloons and small grocery stores that were generally directed toward black consumers. The Italians' rapid economic progress was resented by local whites who took revenge by lynching them. Despite the protests of the Italian consulate, the perpetrators were generally not brought to justice because mobs acted with the complicity of police and government officials.[1] Stereotypes concerning Italians' "inherent criminality" were used to justify the brutality.

On a warm June day in 1943, violence broke out among black and white workers in Detroit, many of whom had only recently arrived from the South to take jobs in the Motor City's burgeoning defense plants. Having heard rumors that three blacks had been killed by whites in the city's Belle Isle Park, blacks looted stores owned by Jews and other ethnic merchants in the city's Paradise Valley ghetto while leaving black-owned businesses untouched. They also raided a streetcar filled with white factory workers. In reaction, close to one hundred thousand whites congregated near downtown and proceeded to attack black neighborhoods, breaking windows and mobbing stores. Assembled police failed to protect African Americans and, in some cases, joined in. Thirty-four persons were killed during the disturbance, of which twenty-five were black.[2]

In April 1992, six days of burning and looting took place in South Central Los Angeles following the acquittal of several police officers who had been videotaped beating black motorist Rodney King. While the verdict touched off the violence, businesses owned by Korean entrepreneurs, who had experienced years of tense relations with local residents, suffered the greatest financial losses. Yet, the largest number of businesses destroyed were owned by Latinos. In the course of regaining control over riot-torn neighborhoods, police and the National Guard deported hundreds of undocumented immigrants, in direct violation of local policy.[3]

In 1999, a Detroit gas station owned by a Lebanese immigrant was closed by nightly protests. Community members, led by Malik Shabazz, a Muslim minister and head of the New Marcus Garvey Movement, demanded justice for Kalvin Porter, a local man who had been beaten by two Yemeni gas station employees, following an altercation precipitated by a vulgar comment made by one of the workers to the daughter of Porter's fiancée. Although police had been called and the nearest precinct was only a block away, by the time they arrived—almost an hour later—Porter had died. Supporters in the Yemeni community hired two prominent black attorneys to represent the defendants.[4]

The incidents described above occurred over the course of more than a century, in very different settings, and involve several distinct ethnic groups. However, they also reveal some striking parallels. Most significantly, each documents a case of violent conflict between small businesses owned by immigrant or minority groups and their customers and competitors. Institutions associated with the mainstream society, such as the police and government, are implicated in setting these conflicts into motion. Yet, in each case, minority groups bore the greatest losses and the brunt of violence.

ETHNIC BUSINESS AS A PROBLEM

A historical analysis of entrepreneurship in the United States suggests that, when impoverished immigrant and minority groups do business in urban ghettos and isolated rural regions, conflicts between merchants and customers are common. In such locations—where money and jobs are scarce; where there is an absence of the well-stocked and efficiently run chain stores that provide a wide range of low-cost consumer options; and where public services like police and fire protection, trash collection, and code enforcement are in short supply—mundane financial transactions often occur within a climate of tension and hostility that can yield humiliation and provoke violence.

When local businesses are owned by persons who do not look like most residents, customers may feel deprived of basic opportunities. Despite such communities' need for retail outlets, entrepreneurs are often seen as exploiters rather than suppliers of needed goods and services. Fearful of customers' wrath, merchants harden their shops and remain vigilant against potential thefts, seeking to maximize profits before the financial and human costs of doing business force them to leave.

Conflicts between ethnic merchants and their customers are associated with several social problems. These include an overabundance of expensive and socially destructive goods (alcohol, tobacco, drug paraphernalia, lottery tickets, and so forth), coupled with a scarcity of basic foodstuffs and household necessities, the empowerment of demagogic activists who demonize opponents with racial slurs, and police brutality. The most extreme incidents, like urban uprisings or race riots described above, have resulted in the destruction of sizeable communities, the loss of human life and property, the obliteration of local institutions, and the deportation or incarceration of both merchant groups and local residents. When publicized by the mass media, activists, and politicians, such events reinforce racial and ethnic stereotypes and do lasting harm to neighborhoods and even entire cities.

While the historical record is rich with incidents of conflict, the larger society often forgets such confrontations. Immigrant and ethnic groups with few options to earn a living elsewhere are willing to open firms in inner-city locales, including those that have been recently vacated by prior owners. Cognizant of the ethnic origins of the merchants in their communities, residents express frustration about the lack of businesses owned by their group as well as their inability to access the quality, value, and service that is available in shops beyond their neighborhoods. Coethnics and local activists contrast their own long and difficult effort to develop small businesses with the speed and apparent ease with which recent arrivals establish shops, amass local dollars, and achieve a middle-class way of life beyond the ghetto.

Immigrants and natives alike who open small businesses in these locations complain about the many challenges they face. These include the scarcity of capital, myriad business regulations, risk of crime, poor city services, and the fact that business assistance programs run by the government and nonprofit agencies are commonly directed toward established and successful companies. Confronted with such obstacles, yet compelled by the need to survive, a fraction of urban businesses function in the informal economy. While this strategy allows merchants to avoid constraints, it also makes them into criminals, deprives municipalities of tax monies, denies customers of consumer protection, and promotes an increasingly cynical attitude toward government.

ETHNIC BUSINESS AS A SOLUTION

Based on these experiences, ghetto residents often regard immigrant businesses as a problem. However, members of the larger society often see them as a solution. American society glorifies entrepreneurship and increasingly sees the free market as an appropriate answer to the social ills plaguing disadvantaged groups and derelict locations. Especially in recent years, as large employers have faltered and government has become less willing and able to provide jobs to those in need of them, scholars, journalists, foundation staff members, and policy makers have publicized the successful endeavors that support their owners, create jobs, provide goods and services, and revitalize declining areas.[5] Requiring little support from public coffers or private largess, ethnic entrepreneurship is compatible with neoliberal economic strategies that favor the competitive market as the key to social problems. Indeed, entrepreneurship is increasingly emphasized as an optimal solution to a wide range of economic ills, including inequality, job loss, and community decline.

The emphasis on small business ownership as a means of advancement for impoverished individuals and groups is highly compatible with American traditions of rugged individualism and self-reliance. According to its proponents, by relying on shared skills and resources, trust-based networks, family labor, and import-export links, ethnic groups can acquire the capital, labor, business skill, and merchandise required to establish and successfully run businesses and provide employment—finding growth potential in environments that have been abandoned by mainstream economic actors.[6]

Community-based entrepreneurship's appeal extends far beyond those who typically endorse conservative policy agendas. In fact, the study and practice of ethnic self-employment as an effective basis for community development was invented by African American scholars and activists, including Booker T. Washington, W. E. B. Du Bois, and Abram Harris, as a means of escaping the privations of a racist society.[7] This tradition remains as strong as ever. Few activists who decry the presence of immigrant entrepreneurs in their communities are opposed to small businesses per se: they object to who owns local enterprises, not petty capitalism per se. In fact, survey research consistently reveals that, despite the challenges that African Americans have historically faced in establishing small businesses, they have a more positive view of proprietorship than other racial or ethnic groups in American society.[8] In part, this is because, in addition to their financial benefits, ethnic economies often embody shared values, address crucial needs, and provide those involved with economic and political skills that can be applied in other areas of life.

However, given the practical realities of economic life, many of the groups who are most in need of economic advancement—African Americans, impoverished immigrants, and poor whites—are lacking in the resources of skill, education, investment capital, business know-how, and links to influential friends required for successful entrepreneurship. Despite the desire of members of such groups to achieve upward mobility via self-employment, the many social disadvantages that they bear means that their likelihood for doing so is small. The heartening opportunities for advancement and validation offered in homilies about the "ownership society" are beyond their grasp.

Referring to the way that significant fractions of the American public now interpret political matters according to the "public morality of the marketplace," critic Amy Elizabeth Ansel asserts, "The disproportionate failure of people of color to achieve social mobility speaks nothing of the justice of present social arrangements . . . but rather reflects the lack of merit or ability of people of color themselves."[9] It seems they must suffer not only the material privations of poverty but the injuries of public condemnation as well.

Accordingly, when scholars, activists, and policy makers celebrate the free market as the solution for economic problems, they fail to offer a viable answer for those who lack the skills, resources, and fortuitous circumstances required to establish successful enterprises. Yet, by definition, the market produces failures as well as successes. When businesses large and small fail, those who relied upon them for economic support still require food, clothing, and shelter. As suggested by the slogan "No Justice, No Peace" that was shouted at protests and painted on burned-out structures during the Los Angeles Uprising in 1992, people who are not satisfied with the economic status quo sometimes make their discontent known in a manner that imposes significant costs upon the larger society. In impoverished communities, the only symbols of wealth and the sole representatives of the economic life of the larger society are ethnic businesses. Hence, such businesses often bear the brunt of residents' frustration, even if they hold relatively little responsibility for its creation.

This book explores conflicts between immigrant and ethnic merchants and their customers over the last one hundred years in American society. It provides an overview of several such conflicts that have involved a variety of groups, locations, contexts, and historical periods. In so doing, it summarizes the conditions that lead up to them and considers their broader implications. A survey of these conflicts reminds us that the establishment of small businesses does not always facilitate the renaissance of impoverished communities and the advancement of residents and merchants. Rather, in such environments, merchant-customer conflict can worsen relations between groups and destroy fragile social institutions. When politicians and pundits posit ethnic economies as a cure-all for the social and economic problems that plague impoverished communities, they generally ignore the record of conflict associated with such activities. In so doing, the larger society often sets up fertile ground for their repetition in the manner described at the start of this chapter. This book is not an argument against the potential benefits of entrepreneurship as a mobility strategy for immigrant and minority groups. Rather, it is an examination of merchant-customer conflicts that seeks to understand how American society deals with group differences associated with social and economic inequality.

PERSPECTIVES ON MERCHANT-CUSTOMER CONFLICTS

This is not the first discussion of conflicts between ethnic merchants and their customers in U.S. society. Because such conflicts are often destructive of human lives, property, and public order, they have been the subject of periodic investigation by politicians, journalists, and social scientists. The resulting body of literature is voluminous but narrow, focusing on the most violent incidents (referred to as either race riots or urban uprisings depending on the writer's interpretation) in big cities and limited almost exclusively to the interactions of three ethnic groups—Jews, Koreans, and African Americans—during specific historical periods (the 1930s through the 1960s for Jews and blacks; the 1980s and 1990s for Koreans and blacks). As a consequence of focusing on these incidents, most studies concentrate on cultural incongruities between opposing communities, such as linguistic and religious differences, conflicting norms regarding interpersonal conduct, and racial and ethnic prejudice as the primary causes of conflicts. In so doing, existing literature tends to look for answers in face-to-face interactions and on ghetto streets.[10]

Based on the assumption that merchant-customer conflicts can be best understood via multiple levels of analysis, this book examines a broader array and chronology of conflicts between ethnic merchants and their customers. These include the macrolevel, involving society's political and economic patterns, built environment, and system of racial-ethnic stratification; the midrange of group members' collective interpretations of their rightful position in the social order vis-à-vis others; and the microlevel arena of contextual factors—the effect of specific events, cultural practices, and face-to-face relationships between merchants and customers. By simultaneously considering a wide variety of merchant-customer conflicts together with a broad array of causes, we hope to construct a more comprehensive understanding than would be availed by limiting our gaze to a narrower selection of incidents, as is the case in much literature on the topic.

DEFINITIONS

Most of the business owners discussed in this book are members of minority groups defined in terms of race, ethnicity, religion, nationality, or language. Many have a history of business ownership prior to their arrival in the United States. Accordingly, their cultural legacy may include skills and social patterns that facilitate running small businesses. Moreover, as immigrants, they may have international connections that can provide business-related resources such as investment capital and imported goods. Finally, as social outsiders, they are less affected by social norms that mandate levels of consumption and that discourage locals from trading in certain goods or services and associating with certain customer groups or engaging in particular economic practices. These entrepreneurs are often described as middleman minority groups. While the term middleman minority is controversial and gendered, it nevertheless offers the most convenient available label for groups involved in small businesses that are directed at impoverished and minority customers.[11] Throughout the text, I use the terms middlemen merchants, immigrant business people, entrepreneurial ethnic groups, and ethnic entrepreneurs interchangeably.

While I define the topic of this book as merchant-customer conflict, I do so because that is the simplest terminology I could come up with to describe the complex relationships that are actually involved. It is important to emphasize that many incidents of conflict involve a far wider range of participants than just ethnic merchants and customers. First, even if they are members of the same ethnic or racial groups as the merchants and customers so described, many of the key actors in these case studies are neither merchants nor customers. Rather, in many cases, activists, politicians, journalists, artists, social workers, members of the media, and clergy define issues and represent groups involved in such conflicts and shape the nature of intergroup interactions.

In addition, politicians, police, educators, foundation staff members, nonprofit organization workers, union officials, and government personnel members play very large roles in defining the context, built environment, opportunity structure, and political outlooks that shape the milieu in which such conflicts take place. As sociologist Charles Tilly asserts, since governments are major forces in allocating resources, controlling action, and determining relations between groups, most intergroup conflict involves making claims on government. "Collective violence almost always involves governments as monitors, claimants, objects of claims, or third parties to claims."[12] Powerful figures outside of government—corporate CEOs, bankers, union officials, and foundation officers—whose actions shape social and economic conditions in the larger society, also have considerable influence over the nature of merchant-customer conflicts.

The customer groups involved in most of the conflicts examined in this book are of relatively low social standing—lower class, working class, or lower middle class. In many cases, they are ethnic, racial, or religious minorities and recent immigrants. During the early twentieth century, the customers of immigrant and ethnic merchants were often European immigrants and their children, including Irish, Poles, Germans, and Slavs. Other groups included rural whites and African Americans. More recently, customers of ethnic merchants include immigrants from Asia, Latin America, Africa, and the Caribbean.

Following Stephen Cornell and Douglas Hartmann,[13] I draw on Richard Schermerhorn's definition of ethnicity, which asserts that an ethnic group "is a collectivity within a larger society having real or putative common ancestry, memories of a shared historical past, and a cultural focus on one or more symbolic elements defined as the epitome of their peoplehood."[14] Among the shared emblems of peoplehood, Schermerhorn includes kinship patterns, geographical concentration, religious affiliation, language, and physical differences.

I define race as "a human group defined by itself or others as distinct by virtue of perceived common physical characteristics that are held to be inherent."[15] "Racial categories are not natural categories that human beings discover; on the contrary, they are 'created, inhabited, transformed and destroyed' by human action, and are therefore preeminently social products."[16] They change over time and, according to the setting, as a consequence of social action. Depending on context, a group can be regarded as racial, ethnic, or both.

Using Louis Coser's scholarship, I define conflict as "a struggle over values and claims to scarce status, power and resources in which the aims of the opponents are to neutralize, injure or eliminate their rivals."[17] This definition emphasizes access to financial resources as well as status. Merchants seek docility, cooperation, and a lack of hostility from their customers. For their part, customers desire good treatment, low prices, and high-quality goods and services from merchants. Customer groups may seek the elimination or reduction of outgroup merchants in their neighborhoods, so that members of their own group might own local businesses. Conflicts often involve members of the dominant social group as well—including police, politicians, business leaders, and media who may take sides, impose regulations, and seek to resolve social problems.

Many scholars have studied forms of ethnic conflict in the United States. However, relatively little research has been devoted to the specific case of merchant-customer conflict.[18] As noted by Coser, Susan Olzak,[19] and many others, most occurrences of ethnic conflict involve groups who share relatively similar social status and hence compete for the same scarce resources—jobs, political power, or control over turf. Because both parties seek the same resource, they repeatedly confront one another in workplaces, in political contests, or along neighborhood boundaries. Because they are pursuing the same goals, resolving conflicts and establishing mutually beneficial relations is often difficult.

In contrast, ethnic merchant groups and their customers occupy distinct social positions, with relatively higher-status merchants making a living in their own shops while customer groups generally seek paid jobs in the larger economy. Further, as observed by sociologist Jennifer Lee,[20] in an inversion of typical social relations, it is the middle-class entrepreneurial group that provides service to lower-status customers. In this manner, while equal-status groups have frequent contact, merchant and customer groups have little acquaintance outside of commercial transactions.

Noting that merchants and customers pursue distinct goals, some scholars suggest that their conflicts are both less common and milder than is the case among groups characterized by the same status.[21] In fact, there is significant potential for symbiotic relations, with merchants providing customers with needed goods in exchange for income. Moreover, while costly, entrepreneurs' loans allow customers to survive during hard times. (This is why merchants enter business and locate shops in particular neighborhoods—because they hope to find an underserved consumer market.) In many cases, customers and merchants do maintain civil and even friendly relations.[22] Long-term interactions between both parties result in a high degree of familiarity and intimacy across group lines. When conflicts occur among those who know each other well, they are often especially disturbing to those involved.

Finally, besides their differences in status and occupation, merchant and customer groups are also quite distinct in terms of population characteristics. Customer groups tend to be quite large and acquire a degree of power through size. In contrast, merchant groups are often too small to rely on numbers alone as a base of power. Because the features of merchant-customer conflict are unlike those surrounding other forms of ethnic conflict, general theories of ethnic conflict derived from studies of equal-group conflict frequently do not apply.[23]

SELECTION OF CASE STUDIES

The instances of conflict and competition between merchants and customers considered in this book take many forms. The most sensational and violent cases involving deadly violence, looting, and burning have received the most extensive documentation in existing literature.[24] However, cases of less intense conflict and ongoing tension also occur frequently. Sometimes conflict is organized and politicized through boycotts and social movements undertaken by community groups, journalists, community activists, or politicians. In other cases, while acknowledged as part of daily life, its presence receives little attention.

As a means of pursuing desired ends, ethnic business owners frequently create organizations and offer donations to encourage law enforcement, zoning boards, local politicians, police, and the public to take their side when disputes arise. As a case in point, since the late 1800s, merchants who have owned businesses in freestanding structures have used political power to ban competitors who own rent-free pushcarts. Similarly, from the late nineteenth century to the present, business owners have lobbied for the implementation of laws prohibiting the use of tools—like fishing equipment, farm implements, and means of transport—favored by competitors but not themselves. Much later, the anti–affirmative action movement sought to ban government assistance for groups underrepresented in self-employment.[25] Such activities can be considered instances of merchant-customer or merchant-merchant conflict (see chapter 6).

Given the complex origins and trajectories of urban conflict and violence, this study avoids assuming that all cases in which shops are destroyed are the consequence of protracted conflicts between merchants and customers. For example, in a number of cases, residents' hostility has been directed toward law enforcement or other ethnic groups, not business owners. As a case in point, recent incidents of urban violence—including those in Crown Heights in 1991 and Cincinnati in 2007—featured few attacks on shops.

Further, in some cases, merchants are attacked because of their ethnicity or nationality, not because of their business activities. For example, ethnic businesses have been destroyed in the course of labor conflicts, in disputes over miscegenation, and in clashes associated with neighborhood boundaries. In some cases, ethnic businesses have been targeted as a consequence of international political rivalries. When Mussolini's Italy invaded Ethiopia in 1934, African Americans protested against and attacked Italian-owned stores in New York and New Jersey. Following the Japanese attack on Pearl Harbor in 1941, Japanese Americans were placed in internment camps. In the period following September 11, 2001, businesses owned by Arabs and Muslims (as well as persons who were confused with them) were assaulted out of misguided attempts for revenge, not because of the way the businesses had been run.[26]

Popular conceptions of intergroup conflict often emphasize the image of politically focused intergroup hostility.[27] However, research suggests that the case of a broadly mobilized and ideologically focused group directing its hostility toward outgroup merchants is the exception rather than the rule. Post-riot interviews regularly find looters to be opportunists in search of merchandise and thrills who may be as likely to assail coethnic shops as those of outsiders.[28] For example, the widespread looting of shops throughout New York City in July 1977 was a consequence of a power failure, and not any clearly articulated dispute. A similar pattern occurred in Chicago following the Bulls' NBA championship in 1992.[29] In most cases, only a minority of residents support actions against merchants, and in almost every incident of hostility toward local shops, some number of local citizens put themselves in harm's way to protect merchants and their property.

While customer groups are often described as collectives lacking legitimate sources of power who must mount protests, boycotts, or collective action to pursue advantage, it is important to note that every U.S. president since Richard Nixon has supported some policies that have sought to expand business ownership among African Americans and other minority groups. Such policies have also been created at the local and state level, especially in cities with black mayors.[30] In reaction, a national anti–affirmative action movement has used proposition initiatives, legislative politics, and court cases to prevent government from extending forms of assistance to ethnic and racial groups and women underrepresented in self-employment.

Finally, given that a significant body of literature suggests that immigrant and minority group members are actively involved as entrepreneurs in the informal economy, patterns of cooperation and conflict between formal and informal businesses associated with various groups are also considered a form of merchant-customer conflict in this book.[31]

As these examples suggest, conflicts between merchants and customers are often quite complex. While explanations for these events are provided by popular stereotypes, media reports, and political leaders, real cases are often less amenable to easy generalizations. Instead, events often reflect the attempts of people with limited resources to cope with difficult circumstances.

METHODS

Data for this study were drawn from a number of sources. They include reviews of academic writing, journalistic accounts, and the analysis of official statistics and available survey data. In addition, the book relies on interviews and fieldwork conducted by the author and associates with a variety of immigrant and ethnic groups including American Jews, Soviet Jews, Israelis, Vietnamese, Arabs, Chinese Vietnamese, Chaldeans, and African Americans as well as a variety of other informants in Los Angeles, Orange County, the San Francisco Bay Area, and Metro Detroit between 1982 and 2007.

Since the purpose of this book is to broaden our understanding of merchant-customer conflicts, I intentionally sought to include examples of conflict involving groups and locations not widely reported in the literature on the topic. These include incidents of conflict between native whites and recent immigrants, rivalries among immigrant groups, the internment of Japanese Americans, the impact of urban renewal programs, and efforts by groups not customarily regarded as merchants—including African Americans and undocumented immigrants—to enhance their economic viability via self-employment.

PROPENSITY TOWARD BUSINESS OWNERSHIP

In order to examine relations between immigrant and ethnic entrepreneurs and their customers, one needs to account for the differential propensity of ethnically defined groups to become self-employed.[32] While the theoretical and descriptive literature on this question is massive, basic findings adapted from studies by Ivan Light and myself are summarized in table 1.1.[33]

Self-employment has long been glorified in American culture, and the Horatio Alger myth has been remarkably durable. Nevertheless, a sociological analysis of self-employment finds that in many cases it is a reaction to disadvantage rather than the action of unconstrained individuals seeking the most desirable conditions of work. Among other factors, Max Weber traced the invention of modern capitalism to the Protestants' need to support themselves, since they could not obtain jobs in the civil service or

Table 1.1. Motives and Resources for Self-Employment

	Comparison Groups			
	Middleman Minorities*	Foreign Born	Native Blacks	Native Whites
Coethnic business resources (capital, labor, advice, goods)	x			
Business experience	x			
Unpaid family labor	x	x		
Wage differentials (versus U.S.)	x	x		
Labor force disadvantage	x	x	x	
Ineligible for public welfare	x	x		
Language barrier	x	x		
Special consumer demand	x	x	some	
Political resources (yield influence, jobs)			x	x
State-imposed discrimination	some	some	high levels prior to 1970s	

* Refers to first generation.

Source: Adapted from Ivan Light, "Immigrant and Ethnic Enterprise in North America," *Ethnic and Racial Studies* 17, no. 2 (1984): 195–216, 210, tab. 1.

armed forces. "National or religious minorities . . . are likely through their voluntary or involuntary position of exclusion from positions of political influence, to be driven with peculiar force into economic activity."[34]

Disadvantage provides a group with the motive for self-employment. However, running a successful business requires resources, such as investment capital and management skill. Because severely disadvantaged groups often lack these, disadvantage alone is an inadequate explanation for a group's involvement in self-employment. Ethnic groups characterized by a combination of disadvantages and resources are those with the highest rates of self-employment.

Sources of Disadvantage

Economic disadvantages that may encourage a group's entry into proprietorship include being foreign born, lacking English-language proficiency, lacking knowledge of and connections to the larger society, being without U.S. citizenship, having low levels of education (or a credential or degree from an unrecognized, foreign institution), being a member of a low-status ethnic or racial group (and, consequently, being seen as an undesirable employee or as meriting only low wages), being subjected to discrimination, and being ineligible for welfare benefits. Certain disadvantages are religious in origin, including requirements to forgo work on the Sabbath, abstaining from the use of modern technology, bans on the provision of impure products and services, and prohibitions against associating with nonbelievers. Such disadvantages generally apply to native-born minorities, including African Americans and Latinos, as well as the foreign born. Few, if any, apply to the mass of native-born, middle-class whites.

Resources for Entrepreneurship

While members of immigrant and minority groups are often characterized by economic disadvantages, at the same time, their ethnic culture, their experience in the country of origin (for migrants), and their affiliation with a strong coethnic community or overseas social ties sometimes provide resources that can be beneficial in creating or running businesses. Of course, like native-born whites, immigrant and minority group members can also deploy class resources, such as education and money, toward self-employment.

Middleman minorities—ethnic groups whose propensity toward self-employment was often established prior to their presence in the United States, but sometimes developed upon arrival—are noted to be especially well endowed with entrepreneurial resources.[35] Their assets include coethnic sources of capital, labor, salable merchandise, business advice, and customers; business experience, education, marketable skills, and access to low-cost family labor; and the increased level of U.S. earnings in comparison to those in the country of origin. In addition, some ethnic groups maintain norms of family or communal cooperation and money sharing—including rotating credit and savings associations—that facilitate self-employment.[36]

Groups characterized by a combination of both disadvantages and resources are especially well suited for self-employment. Between the 1970s and the 1990s, Korean immigrants epitomized this status. As a group, they were highly educated but, due to their difficulty with English and their foreign degrees, had trouble obtaining professional jobs in the United States. Having sold their homes prior to migration, many arrived with substantial financial resources. Their establishment in business was further facilitated by access to coethnic sources of advice, loans, business service, employees, and salable goods. Korean family norms mandated the labor of wives and children in a business enterprise. Wage differentials between the United States and Korea that provided greater rewards in relation to effort than those available in the country of origin also motivated self-employment.[37] Finally, Koreans, like many groups with high rates of self-employment, maintain a variety of community organizations for social, religious, philanthropic, and educational purposes. These facilitate business-related cooperation, provide a pathway for coethnics to become self-employed, and help to resolve conflicts with competitors, suppliers, customers, and landlords.[38]

In contrast, native-born whites who lack disadvantages in the labor market generally have rates of self-employment close to or sometimes below the U.S. average. The same is true for immigrant groups who have high levels of American-style education and speak English. This applies to Nigerians, Filipinos, and Indians.[39]

Finally, groups characterized by disadvantages but lacking entrepreneurial resources, such as African Americans, Puerto Ricans, Mexicans, Salvadorans, and Laotians, have low rates of self-employment, at least as reported in official statistics. Such groups tend to be active in the informal economy, but this type of self-employment receives little official acknowledgment.[40] (See chapter 7).

The disadvantages plus resources model offers a broad and general explanation for rates of ethnic self-employment, which varies considerably according to historical period, location, and other contextual factors. As a case in point, Cuban Americans in South Florida have high rates of self-employment associated with their well-studied ethnic enclave.[41] However, Cuban Americans residing in other regions of the United States have lower than average rates of self-employment.

PLAN OF THE BOOK

The chapters in this book focus on particular cases of merchant-customer conflict that occurred in different historical periods and geographical locations from the early twentieth to the early twenty-first century. To do so, each chapter examines conventional interpretations of these conflicts and then offers a reworked view. Readers familiar with the broader literature on merchant-customer conflict will not find these interpretations to be wholly original, but it is my hope that these chapters will provide an analysis that is inventive as well as more inclusive than that which is available in existing works.

Following the introductory material in chapter 1, this book is organized chronologically as it considers merchant-customer conflict from the dawn of the twentieth century to the present. Chapter 2 concerns African

Americans as entrepreneurs and middlemen. Chapter 3 describes relations between immigrant entrepreneurs and customers prior to the Great Depression. Chapter 4 reviews activist challenges to immigrant and ethnic businesses during the Depression Era and World War II. Chapter 5 focuses on the post–World War II era, from the late 1940s through the 1970s. Chapter 6 focuses on the contemporary scene: from 1970 to 2005. Chapter 7 looks at the informal economy as a site of competition between disadvantaged populations and ethnic merchants. Chapter 8, coauthored with Joe Darden, focuses on contemporary Detroit, the largest black majority city in the United States, wherein politicians and activists have used their political and demographic dominance to support coethnic businesses in the face of competition from other ethnic groups. Finally, chapter 9 draws conclusions about the nature of conflicts between immigrant entrepreneurs and customers and what can be learned from patterns of intergroup relations and the policies invoked to address them.

②

BLACK ENTREPRENEURSHIP
FROM 1900 UNTIL 1935

African Americans are often derided for their low rates of self-employment by critics both internal and external to their group.[1] Reflecting the most current data on this long-standing differential, as of 2006, while 11.1 percent of white workers were self-employed business owners, only 5.1 percent of black workers were similarly engaged.[2] Nathan Glazer and Daniel Patrick Moynihan remark on "the almost complete absence of a [black] business class. . . . The small shopkeeper, small manufacturer, or small entrepreneur . . . has played such an important role in the rise of immigrant groups in America that its absence from the Negro community warrants . . . discussion."[3] Later, the authors attribute this to blacks' "incapacity for business."[4]

While it is true that African Americans have generally low rates of self-employment, the discussion that follows demonstrates that African Americans did (and do) have an important tradition of self-employment and that black scholars and activists have contributed greatly to our understanding of ethnic entrepreneurship. Toward that end, this chapter summarizes the experience of black entrepreneurs in the early twentieth century and reveals that, despite the massive obstacles of poverty and discrimination that they confronted, the group nevertheless created numerous businesses that provided important economic and social benefits for the black community.

Moreover, regardless of the reasons cited for African Americans' low rates of self-employment, lack of awareness of the problem is not among them. At least since the late nineteenth century, African American journalists, intellectuals, community leaders, and business owners have understood the importance of self-employment and trading with coethnic consumers as a means of group survival in environments characterized by racial hostility and economic exclusion. As sociologist John Sibley Butler notes, "Almost every theoretical idea which appears" in focal works on the sociology of entrepreneurship of the 1970s and 1980s was discussed in earlier writings by blacks.[5] Key studies include W. E. B. Du Bois's *The Negro in Businesses* (1898) and *Economic Co-operation among Negro Americans* (1907); Joseph A. Pierce's *Negro Business and Business Education* (1947); and Abram Harris's *The Negro as Capitalist* (1936).[6] The importance of self-employment to black advancement was clearly articulated prior to the twentieth century at the Fourth Atlanta University Conference on Business in 1898 and was put into action via the establishment of the National Negro Business League.[7]

DU BOIS, WASHINGTON, AND BLACK ENTERPRISE

Before 1915, the leading black economic nationalists were W. E. B. Du Bois (1868–1963) and Booker T. Washington (1856–1915). Historian Juliette Walker writes that, "while their philosophies differed on education, civil rights and black political participation, both were resolute in their insistence that business was crucial for the survival of the race."[8] Du Bois, who sought full equality for American blacks, asserted, "We must cooperate or we are lost. Ten million people who join in intelligent self-help can never be long ignored or mistreated."[9] In contrast, Washington downplayed civil rights in favor of economic development. Asserting that "agitation of questions of social equality is the extremist folly," his less-threatening approach allowed him to command a considerable following among both blacks and whites, including white elites, who provided financial support for black education and business development.[10]

As the following quote suggests, Washington believed that racial obstacles could be transcended through entrepreneurship:

> The Negro was also fortunate enough to find that, while his abilities in certain directions were opposed by the white South, in business he was not only undisturbed but even favored and encouraged. I have been repeatedly informed by Negro merchants in the South that they have as many white patrons as black, and the cordial business relations which are almost universal between the races in the South proved . . . there is little race prejudice in the American dollar. . . . A merchant, unlike a physician, for example, is not patronized because he is white or because he is black; but because he has known how to put brains into his work, to make his store clean and inviting . . . and to foresee and provide the commodities which his patrons are likely

Booker T. Washington, 1856–1915, educator, author, and founder of the Tuskegee Institute, 1911. He advocated business ownership by African Americans starting in the late 19th Century. While Washington rejected challenging the racial status quo, he saw in a segregated African American community the potential for business development and, with it, black economic autonomy. Of Washington, sociologist John Sibley Butler wrote, "he laid the foundation for economic nationalism . . . there is hardly any idea within the ethnic enclave theory that is not nested within the writings of Washington." (1991:65).

Source: Photographs and Prints Division, Schomburg Center for Research in Black Culture, The New York Public Library, Astor, Lenox and Tilden Foundations

to desire. I am convinced that in business a man's mettle is tried as it is not, perhaps in any other profession.[11]

Further evidence of African Americans' concern with developing an ethnic economy can be found in the black press. A 1916 column in the *New York Age* chided its readers for patronizing white businesses.[12] Citing a survey of Harlem businesses, the article noted that, while nonblack businesses (whose proprietors were Italians, Greeks, Jews, Germans, French, Chinese, and Russians) were fewer in number than those owned by blacks, they grasped seventy-five cents of every dollar spent by African Americans, employed only a handful of blacks, and because nearly all lived outside of Harlem, were divorced from local concerns.

From the late nineteenth century until the present, a variety of social movements and political campaigns sought to increase the number of black-owned businesses, to provide employment opportunities for black workers in ghetto stores, to enhance the quality and value of available goods and services, and to improve the treatment of minority customers. Accordingly, the underrepresentation of merchants of color in African American neighborhoods was (and continues to be) regarded as an affront to black notions of justice and fairness.[13]

The degree of success achieved by black entrepreneurs has varied according to broader social, economic, political, and demographic conditions in American society. Identifying changes in their environment, black intellectuals, activists, and business leaders have proposed and established a variety of projects intended to build black businesses. They also sought to profit from new opportunities and minimize the impact of reversals including economic recessions, worsening racial regimes, and outgroup competition. While pursuing economic opportunities in the larger society when possible, African American merchants have emphasized maintaining a mutually beneficial relationship with the black community. Despite the immense obstacles they have encountered, over the years, their community-building efforts have contributed much to the economic, educational, political, religious, and cultural lives of black Americans and to the larger society as well.

CRITIQUES OF BLACK ENTREPRENEURSHIP

So focused on the idea of the ethnic economy were black intellectuals and activists in the early twentieth century that, in addition to describing its benefits, they also cataloged its liabilities. As a case in point, Nobel laureate Ralph Bunche argued that black entrepreneurship offered little promise for the advancement of the race. "Negro business looms as a parasitical growth on the Negro society," he contended. "It demands for itself special privilege and parades under the chauvinistic protection of 'race loyalty,' thus further exploiting a downtrodden group."[14] Unionists proclaimed that blacks would benefit more by securing jobs throughout society than by trying to control small businesses in ghetto neighborhoods, while those concerned with class inequalities claimed that the financial exploitation of poor blacks was no better when undertaken by members of their own race than by members of other groups.[15]

The most influential antagonist of African American entrepreneurship was E. Franklin Frazier. His *Black Bourgeoisie* condemned black business as a myth and argued that the black middle class was small, economically inconsequential, and more concerned with maintaining the trappings of social elitism than with financial advancement.[16]

During the 1960s and 1970s, activists and intellectuals influenced by Marxism and postcolonial socialist movements criticized black capitalism as impossible, socially oppressive, or both.[17] However, by the 1980s, a series of events including the decline of the welfare state, the loss of well-paid factory jobs, an increasing emphasis on issues of community control by activists like Nation of Islam minister Louis Farrakhan, the expansion of government support for minority business programs, and the visible success of immigrant economies in American society led to a renewed interest in black capitalism.[18] As a consequence, Washington, who was sometimes derided as an Uncle Tom during the 1960s and 1970s, was redeemed as a visionary of black self-determination.[19]

BLACKS AS MIDDLEMEN

Reflecting both their understanding of the importance of self-employment to communal survival and their dedication to this endeavor, from the antebellum era until the Great Depression, African Americans created a small yet accomplished business class that ran an array of enterprises.[20] In fact, this tradition can be traced back to the creation of African-slave secret burial societies in the 1600s and free-African mutual aid societies of the 1700s.[21] "The total value of all free black-owned establishments and personal wealth in the US in 1860 was at least $50 million dollars—half of which was based in the slave south."[22]

Prior to the full implementation of Jim Crow laws and the arrival of immigrants from Europe and Asia at the dawn of the twentieth century, many black enterprises provided goods and services to white as well as black consumers.[23] This was especially the case in the North, where the small black population generated little demand. Because many of these enterprises catered to white consumers, Butler describes them as middleman entrepreneurs.[24] The existence of these businesses prior to the twentieth century suggests that discrimination, hostile legislation, and competition rather than a purported lack of aptitude have been among the fundamental causes of blacks' low rates of self-employment since that time.[25]

Early realms of black economic specialization often involved skills that African Americans had acquired during slavery. These included livery stables, drayage, construction, and various domestic occupations such as catering, sewing, and clothes washing. Some enterprises remained in black hands for years after Jim Crow restrictions made doing business outside ghettos extremely difficult. For example, in 1942, blacks still owned thirty hauling companies in Louisville despite growing competition from whites.[26]

As of 1885, there were two hundred black businesses representing twenty-seven fields of enterprise in Chicago. Thirty year later—just prior to the mass migration of southern blacks—the number had grown to five hundred. Many such businesses were small in size. However, individual entrepreneurs achieved success in more prestigious and lucrative fields, including lumberyards, furniture manufacturing, the professions, and the ownership of first-rate restaurants, like Thomas Downing's eating house near Wall Street "which catered to the leading members of New York's professional and commercial classes."[27]

In *The Philadelphia Negro*, DuBois noted that blacks owned the city's leading catering firms and sail makers.[28] In Cleveland, as in many northern cities, the pattern of black middlemen providing goods and services to white customers lasted until almost 1920. "On the eve of the Great Migration, a small group of Negro tailors, caterers, barbers, and merchants continued to serve a predominantly white clientele." Black professionals often had white as well as black customers. As late as 1915, Cleveland's black lawyers served more white than African American clients, and many of the city's doctors of color had integrated practices as well.[29]

While competition from immigrant-owned firms would deprive many black entrepreneurs of their Caucasian customers after the start of the twentieth century, European immigrants and native whites continued to patronize black doctors and dentists in northeastern, midwestern, and West Coast cities. Historian Carter G. Woodson surveyed black doctors in these regions and found that over half had white patients.[30] Similarly, in upland areas of the South where racial prejudice was less virulent—West Virginia, Virginia, Tennessee, and North Carolina—black doctors had sizeable white practices. Using the color line to provide anonymity, some whites patronized black physicians when they required medical services—such as vene-real disease care or an abortion—which they sought to conceal from the white community.

BLACK FINANCIAL INSTITUTIONS

Difficulties in obtaining business loans have been a long-standing obstacle for black entrepreneurs. To address this problem, blacks created banks and other sources of capital from the Reconstruction years until the Great Depression and after. The Freedmen's Bank was created by an act of Congress in 1865 to safeguard the unclaimed savings of black soldiers and laborers in the wake of the Civil War and to serve the financial interests of emancipated blacks. It had branches in thirty-four cities and, as of 1871, held twenty million dollars in deposits. Incorporated by the federal government, blacks assumed that the deposits were guaranteed and rushed to place their small savings in the bank. However, deposits were not guaranteed, and its staff featured only a token number of black managers and directors. Instead, members of the white business elite ran it in an incompetent and self-serving fashion, often giving themselves low-interest loans that they never repaid.[31]

After nine years, the Freedmen's Bank collapsed. Its failure soured some members of the African American population on using banks but stimulated others to create replacements that were better run and truly controlled by members of the black community. The first of these was the True Reformers Bank, opened in 1889 by a fraternal order bearing the same name. Before failing in 1910, it owned and developed a variety of enterprises and properties in the South and Midwest. Like the Freedmen's Bank, the True Reformers failed because of its irresponsible management, who used its assets to support the fraternal order's activities rather than to ensure the bank's stability. Despite its collapse, it provided a source of inspiration to the supporters of black economic cooperation.[32] Reflecting this legacy, four black banks founded at the turn of the century were still in existence in 1996.

In addition to establishing banks, African Americans created insurance companies and building funds in the early years of the twentieth century. Such enterprises were sorely needed, as white-owned firms either refused to serve blacks or charged a premium to do so. "Black banks, insurance companies, and real estate loan associations were not only symbols of the increased financial holdings of blacks but also an expression of defiance to white attempts to impose a separate and subordinate status on America's citizens of African descent."[33]

BLACK SELF-EMPLOYMENT IN 1910

Margaret Levenstein's analysis of the 1910 U.S. Census—the first U.S. Census to include data about both business ownership and race—offers a useful benchmark of black business early in the twentieth century and prior to the Great Migration of African Americans to northern cities but following the initial formation of a "buy black" movement (see chapter 4) and the creation of the National Negro Business League.[34]

In 1910, African Americans were more likely than whites to be employers and almost as likely to be self-employed (blacks' rate of self-employment was 26 percent; whites', 29 percent). By the twentieth century's end, blacks were only one-third as likely as whites to be self-employed.[35] In 1910, a significant proportion of both self-employed blacks and whites were in the field of agriculture (73 percent of blacks and 59 percent of whites). Moreover, black women were more likely to be self-employed than white women in 1910 and were heavily concentrated (74 percent) in personal services. Black women also made up twice the fraction of the black labor force (40 percent) than did white women of the white labor force (19 percent).[36] The fact that blacks and whites had nearly identical rates of self-employment in 1910 (and that black women had higher rates of business ownership than white women) would suggest that cultural explanations for today's comparatively low rates of black entrepreneurship—what Glazer and Moynihan described as "problems of incapacity for business . . . among Negroes"—are not valid.[37] Rather, as previously argued, situational factors like discrimination, urbanization, and the social and economic conditions of the larger society provide a better account for differences in self-employment rates among racial groups.

Evidence of blacks' economic prowess is found in a review of several successful agricultural enterprises of the late nineteenth and early twentieth centuries. Such was the case of Junius G. Groves. Born as a slave in Kentucky, Groves joined the black exodus to Kansas, where he came to own 500 acres of land (valued at five hundred dollars each), 1,800 peach trees, 700 pear trees, 250 cherry trees, as well as apricot orchards and grape vineyards. Producing over seven hundred thousand bushels of potatoes in a single year, Groves was known as the Negro Potato King. His worth was estimated as being in the range of forty to eighty thousand dollars. Groves was also a broker, buying and shipping potatoes purchased from other growers. He owned a private railroad trace that connected his shipping station to the main line of the Union Pacific Railroad.[38]

Another former slave, Reverend W. W. Key began farming in 1879 in Davidson County, Tennessee. By 1900 he owned 360 acres valued at twenty-five thousand dollars and worked by seven tenant-farming families. Other black farmers, including Deal Jackson of Albany, Georgia, and Reverend I. M. Powers of North Carolina, had similarly vast holdings and worked as brokers for black and white farmers in crops such as berries and cotton. Powers served as an agent for several northern commission houses, providing southern produce for the northern market.[39]

In addition to documenting African American involvement in agriculture, the 1910 Census also enumerated 5,000 black male employers in construction, 2,500 running eating and drinking establishments, 2,000 running barber shops, 1,500 running repair businesses, and 1,000 presiding over grocery stores.[40] Given that a relatively large fraction of self-employed blacks were involved in agriculture in 1910, it would appear that a significant amount of their economic output was consumed by whites. However, Levenstein notes that black entrepreneurs were more likely to be located in counties with a higher black population, revealing the importance of co-ethnic cooperation to the development of an ethnic economy even prior to formation of major black ghettos in the urban North.

SEGREGATION, IMMIGRATION, AND THE LOSS OF WHITE CUSTOMERS

Despite the efforts of black entrepreneurs to serve consumers throughout society, shortly before the turn of the twentieth century, a confluence of factors had the effect of reducing their access to white customers. With President Rutherford B. Hayes's rollback of Reconstruction policy and the Supreme Court decisions of *Hall v. De Cuvis* (1877) and *Plessy v. Ferguson* (1896), the separate but equal doctrine became the law of the land. "Segregation laws restricted blacks from competing against any other entrepreneur in an open market" by restricting the location of black-owned businesses to black neighborhoods. "On the other hand, Chinese, Mexican, Jewish and Native Americans could operate a business in the open market, drink at public fountains, eat in restaurants and sleep in hotels."[41] (See table 2.1.)

Established black businesses also lost their white clientele due to an enhanced expression of social distinctions based on race, neighborhood, status, and class.[42] The growing suburbanization of American society located affluent white areas ever further from black businesses. Since black entrepreneurs specialized in domestic services—restaurants, catering, laundry, and haircutting—additional distance made access to customers more difficult and costly. Blacks' restricted access to capital, training, technology, and travel greatly hindered their ability to participate in the economic expansion of the early twentieth century. Frazier emphasized whites' refusal to hire blacks, thus depriving them of firsthand business experience, as a key factor in hindering the development of a black business class.[43]

And while Jim Crow laws and extended patterns of social exclusion were restricting black-owned businesses to ghettos, European immigrants began to compete with African Americans as both job seekers and entrepreneurs. "During the first decade of the 20th century, the United States received annually an average of 879,539 immigrants . . . a migration unprecedented in world history."[44] As a result, "opportunity for blacks remained limited during the last quarter of the nineteenth century, at the same time that the United States provided more of it for newcomers."[45]

While they were subject to some forms of discrimination and social exclusion, immigrants were not segregated by law, as were blacks. Moreover, through effort, migrants had the potential to break the bonds of class, whereas throughout the South and in much of the North as well, blacks remained restricted by race. Competition with white immigrants in the early decades of the twentieth century rolled back much of the economic progress African Americans had achieved since the end of the Civil War. After emancipation, blacks had occupied skilled and semiskilled jobs. However, whites were favored by employers, and European immigrants whose numbers swelled early in the twentieth century quickly took over jobs held by blacks. "Black headwaiters, barber shop owners, and skilled artisans faced increasing competition from whites, especially immigrants."[46]

In 1870, the New Orleans City Directory listed 3,460 blacks in skilled positions including carpenters, cigar makers, painters, clerks, shoemakers, cooper tailors, bakers, blacksmiths, and foundry hands. By 1904, however, the number of African Americans holding such positions had shrunk to one-tenth of the earlier figure, even though the local black population had increased by half. A similar pattern was evident in the North. In 1870, a third of black males in Cleveland were employed in skilled trades. In 1910, only 11 percent were so employed.[47]

The competition from European immigrants had the same impact on self-employed blacks as it did on those working for existing firms. Accordingly, there was a "gradual disappearance of black businesses that catered to a predominantly white clientele" in all northern cities during the late nineteenth and early twentieth century.[48] This "large immigrant work force . . . was responsible for driving blacks out of barbering" and other entrepreneurial niches that they had previously occupied.[49] In 1870, 43 percent of Cleveland's barbers were blacks; in 1890, this figure slipped to 18 percent. In 1910, less than one in ten was black, and it is likely that those remaining were serving coethnics rather than the more lucrative white clientele.[50]

Table 2.1. Gainful Workers Ten Years Old and Over by Occupations in Which
Negroes Predominated in the United States: 1930

Occupation	Total all Classes	Total	Male	Female	Percent of All Classes
Bootblacks	18,784	9,499	9,481	18	50.6
Cooks, other than in hotels, restaurants, and boarding houses	321,722	220,538	17,478	203,060	68.5
Laborers, cigar and tobacco factories	20,581	12,254	8,863	3,391	59.5
Laborers, fertilizer factories	18,243	15,347	15,268	79	84.1
Laborers, turpentine farms and distilleries	37,620	30,849	30,577	272	82.0
Launderers and laundresses (not in laundry)	361,033	271,083	1,985	269,098	75.1
Midwives	3,566	1,787	. . .	1,787	50.1
Operatives, fertilizer factories	1,538	1,039	1,000	39	67.6
Operatives, turpentine farms and distilleries	1,368	726	721	5	53.1
Porters, except in stores	127,488	93,744	93,714	30	73.5

Source: Charles E. Hall, *Negroes in the United States, 1920–1932* (New York: Arno Press and *New York Times*, 1969 [1935]), 289, tab. 6.

Italian immigrants were noted for their involvement in the previously black occupation of cutting white people's hair. Blacks' loss of this niche was so widespread that Washington referred to it while speaking at Fisk University. He observed that, twenty years earlier, barbershops all over the country were run by blacks, but by 1895, he could no longer find a single large or first-class barbershop run by African Americans.[51]

Gunnar Myrdal noted blacks' loss of another niche that they had previously controlled, the laundry business:

> There are more Negro workers in this field than in any other occupation outside of agriculture and domestic service. But it was the whites and the Chinese who started commercial laundries, which have taken hundreds of thousands of job opportunities away from the Negro home laundresses. There were only a few hundred Negro owners of commercial laundries in 1930, representing about 2 percent of the total. Not only his experience as a worker but also his self-interest should have provided an inducement for the Negro to go into this kind of business as an independent entrepreneur. Yet he failed to do so.[52]

Following the Civil War, there was a considerable number of skilled black construction workers in the South as well as growing demand for factories and apartment houses to be built there. However, whites who sought to wrest this trade from blacks refused to work for black contractors.

"Under such circumstances it was impossible to make any headway. In 1910 there were . . . 2,900 Negro contractors constituting 1.8 percent of the total. In 1930 the number was down to 2,400 or 1.6 percent."[53]

Blacks lost significant fractions of trade in catering and restaurants as well. Du Bois observed that prejudice and norms of social exclusion prevented established black caterers from being invited to participate in the expansion from small- to large-scale businesses.

> If the Negro caterers of Philadelphia had been white, some of them would have been put in charge of a large hotel or would have become co-partners in some large restaurant business, for which capitalists furnished funds. . . . Moreover, they now came into sharp competition with a class of small white caterers, who, if they were worse cooks were better trained in the tricks of the trade.[54]

Myrdal also noted African Americans' exclusion from food preparation enterprises. "There have been, of course, social and political pressures, as well as economic ones against Negro caterers. . . . The few remaining [that] serve whites mainly . . . [have] the character of a novelty rather than of a regularly accepted business."[55] Blacks' loss of business niches was not limited to the eastern United States. In turn-of-the-century Los Angeles, the relatively small black population had specialized in trash collection. By 1908, Armenians had taken control of this enterprise.[56]

BLACK OBJECTIONS TO IMMIGRATION

As European immigrants entered the United States during the early twentieth century, black activists protested their competition for jobs. In an 1895 speech to the Cotton States Exposition, Washington admonished the white leaders in attendance "not to look to the incoming of those of foreign birth and strange tongue and habits for the prosperity of the South. . . . I would repeat what I say to my own race, 'Cast down your bucket where you are.' Cast it down among the eight million Negroes . . . who have without strikes and labor wars tilled your fields, cleared your forests, builded your railroads and cities."[57] "The general attitude, as put by one writer in the *Washington Colored American* in 1902 was that 'Negro labor is native labor and should be preferred to that of the offscourings of Europe and Asia. Let America take care of its own.'"[58] The black press warned against the admission of entrepreneurial groups, including Greeks, Italians, and especially Mexicans and Asians, who were said to be both unsympathetic to American institutions and inassimilable.

Black leaders noted that employers and unions favored immigrants over native blacks. Accordingly, they were generally supportive of anti-immigrant legislation including the deportation of Mexicans during the Great Depression.[59] Despite these expressions of anti-immigrant sentiment during the first half of the twentieth century, and the long-standing competition between African Americans and the recently arrived for unskilled jobs, as a group blacks have historically expressed far less opposition to immigrants than have whites.[60]

ANTIBLACK VIOLENCE

Competition from immigrants and Jim Crow policies were not the only obstacles faced by early-twentieth-century African American entrepreneurs. In addition, they found themselves to be the targets of violent attacks by whites. In 1906, a mob of drunken white youths attacked areas of African American residential and business concentration, murdered residents, and looted black-oriented businesses owned by both blacks and European immigrants in Atlanta.[61] (See chapter 3.) In the course of the riot, two barbers were murdered and their shop destroyed while numerous other black businesses were sacked. In the riot's aftermath, authorities imposed serious restrictions on black businesses. As a result, "every Negro barber shop and restaurant in the city was closed." In addition, "twenty two licenses for Negro restaurants and dives were revoked by the city council and thirty nine more were set aside for investigation." Such enterprises were considered by whites to be "gathering and hatching place[s] of criminal Negroes."[62]

In a like manner, the prosperous "Black Wall Street" of Greenwood in Tulsa, Oklahoma, was the victim of a pogrom by jealous whites in 1921. With support from police and the National Guard, the incident resulted in the death of almost four hundred persons and the destruction of 1,400 homes and businesses.[63] Similar attacks on black business communities occurred in Springfield, Illinois, in 1908, in St. Louis in 1917, and in Chicago in 1919.[64]

THE GREAT MIGRATION AND THE EXPANSION OF BLACK BUSINESS

Reduced in their ability to trade with white customers, blacks in both northern and southern cities developed a variety of enterprises to service the growing population of newly arrived rural southern migrants. As St. Clair

Table 2.2.   Cities Having a Negro Population of Ten Thousand or More in 1930, With Comparative Figures for 1920 and 1910

City	1930	1920	1910
New York, N.Y.	327,706	152,467	91,709
Chicago, Ill.	233,903	109,458	44,103
Philadelphia, Pa.	219,599	134,229	84,459
Baltimore, Md.	142,106	108,322	84,749
Washington, D.C.	132,068	109,966	94,446
New Orleans, La.	129,632	100,930	89,262
Detroit, Mich.	120,066	40,838	5,741
Birmingham, Ala.	99,077	70,230	52,305
Memphis, Tenn.	96,550	61,181	52,441
St. Louis, Mo.	93,580	69,854	43,960
Atlanta, Ga.	90,075	62,796	51,902
Cleveland, Ohio	71,899	34,451	8,448
Houston, Tex.	63,337	33,960	23,929
Pittsburgh, Pa.	54,983	37,725	25,623
Richmond, Va.	52,988	54,041	46,733
Jacksonville, Fla.	48,196	41,520	29,293
Cincinnati, Ohio	47,818	30,079	19,639
Louisville, Ky.	47,354	40,087	40,522
Indianapolis, Ind.	43,967	34,678	21,816
Norfolk, Va.	43,942	43,392	25,039

Source: Charles E. Hall, *Negroes in the United States, 1920–1932* (New York: Arno Press and *New York Times*, 1969 [1935]), 55, tab. 10.

Drake and Horace Cayton wrote in *Black Metropolis*, "The Great Migration created the 'Negro market.'"[65] Paradoxically, the deterioration in race relations at the end of the nineteenth century, as evidenced by residential discrimination and concentration, and the refusal of white insurance and banking companies to service blacks, made this possible. From 1910 until the late 1920s, the northern black population increased by some two million persons. This massive social and demographic transformation, so vital to the growth of black self-employment, was the outcome of both push and pull factors. (See table 2.2.)

During the early twentieth century, urban centers of the northeastern United States were growing at a rapid rate, fed by a demand for unskilled laborers in construction, manufacturing, food processing, and other endeavors. Prior to World War I, much needed labor was supplied by European immigrants. Some 1.2 million arrived in 1914, the year World War I began in Europe. However, wartime disruptions, including attacks on transatlantic passenger ships, resulted in a significant reduction. By 1918, European migration shrank to 110,000—one-tenth of the number that had disembarked only four years earlier. At the same time, World War I increased demand for industrial output. Accordingly, northern factories that had previously excluded black workers suddenly found them desirable and sent recruiters south to enlist more.[66]

Northern black newspapers, notably the *Chicago Defender*, advertised economic opportunities and communicated the social advantages of the northern environment over that of the South. One headline read "More Positions Open than Men for Them."[67] A northern journalist visiting the South in 1917 reported, "Trains were backed in to several Southern cities and hundreds of Negroes were gathered up in a day, loaded into cars and whirled away to the North." A black worker told him, "The best wages I could make [in Georgia] was $1.25 or $1.50 a day. I went to work at a dye house at Newark, N.J. at $2.75 a day, with a rent free room to live in. . . . The company paid my fare North."[68] Besides the promise of a lucrative job, the North also offered a less oppressive racial atmosphere and the amenities of a dynamic urban environment.

In addition to the pull provided by the promise of economic advancement and reduced discrimination in the North, southern blacks were also pushed North by the enduring poverty and continued oppression of Dixie. Following emancipation, many southern blacks found themselves mired in the debt peonage of sharecropping and restricted by Jim Crow segregation. "More intolerable than segregation was racial violence. 'For every lynching that takes place,' noted Booker T. Washington in 1903 . . . 'a score of colored people leave for the city.'"[69]

Despite the promise of a better life, conditions in northern cities were far from ideal. The huge number of black arrivals heightened patterns of racial segregation and yielded many forms of reprisal from landlords, unions, neighborhood associations, employers, and European immigrant groups. Some employers would only hire black workers as strike breakers. Given the prevailing climate of racial tension, racial violence between blacks and whites occurred with frequency. When it did, white police generally ignored blacks' complaints.

In response, blacks worked to achieve social and economic autonomy from white society during what Drake and Cayton refer to as the "Fat Years," prior to the Great Depression.

> Negroes were making money in the steel mills, stockyards, and garment factories, in the hotels and kitchens, on the railroads, and in a hundred other spots. "Why," the leaders asked, "should these dollars be spent with white men or wasted in riotous living? If white men are so determined that Negroes must live separate and apart, why not beat them at their own game?" . . . Why beg whites' stores and offices to rescue educated colored girls from

service in the white folks' kitchens and factories? Negroes were learning to
support their own businesses, and some day colored entrepreneurs would
own all the stores and offices in the Black Belt; cash registers . . . would click
merrily under black fingers.[70]

Accordingly, the Great Migration fed the growth of black business in
many northern cities, as well as southern ones, like Durham, North Carolina. For African American entrepreneurs, the period from 1900 to 1930
was the golden age. It saw the emergence of black capitalists who achieved
millionaire status and established sizeable enterprises. "Their wealth reflected their success within a black economy, which developed in response
to the nation's rise of two worlds of race."[71] "The rapid growth of the Negro
community between 1915 and 1929 was accompanied by expansion in all
types of Negro-owned business."[72]

In 1912, Chicago's black population was 46,480 and the city was home
to 526 black-owned businesses. Twenty-five years later, in 1937, the black
population had increased to 237,105, while the number of black businesses
had grown almost fivefold to 2,464. The imposition of Jim Crow laws prevented black merchants from serving white customers. As a consequence,
they focused on the African American market. Butler calls this "the economic detour."[73]

Following the leadership of Du Bois and Washington, black entrepreneurs created associations for insurance companies, bankers, automobile
dealers, real estate brokers, journalists, undertakers, retail merchants,
tailors, dressmakers, builders, beauty culturalists, and automobile clubs.[74]
When the National Association for the Advancement of Colored People
(NAACP) was formed in 1910, Du Bois was the editor of its journal, *The
Crisis*. From this position, he called for black economic autonomy and cooperation. While not rejecting capitalism outright, he advocated solidarity
with labor and announced that he was a "Socialist of the Path."[75] In this, Du
Bois, like many proponents of black economic development, valued black
progress over individual gain and was willing to stray from strict capitalism
in order to advance the race.[76]

Whites—their actions justified by the 1896 *Plessy v. Ferguson* Supreme
Court decision that confirmed the legality of separate but equal segregation—excluded blacks from access to public venues for association,
leisure, and transport. Such restrictions not only limited blacks' entrée
to important locations and blocked them from doing business in white
neighborhoods but also restricted or altogether denied blacks' ability to
engage in leisure activities and other forms of sociability. Accordingly,

when black entrepreneurs developed transport systems, meeting halls, and apartment buildings, they were not simply reserving for blacks a measure of the profits made from selling them groceries and clothing. Rather, they were providing the foundation of a civilized life, one which would not have existed in their absence.

Blacks created hotels, theaters, and other places for civic and cultural activities. Black real estate and construction firms built homes, churches, office buildings, hotels, theaters, and auditoriums. Between the late 1800s and 1920, African Americans developed rail, bus, and trolley systems in Pine Bluff and Columbus, Arkansas; Jacksonville, Florida; and Nashville, Tennessee, as well as a steamship company in Maryland. Many of these enterprises were supported by black boycotts of segregated transport systems. Blacks developed parks and resorts in North Carolina, Arkansas, Tennessee, Maryland, Michigan, and Colorado—and the Colored Citizens Country Club outside of Cincinnati.[77] They also established black baseball teams, and in Knoxville, black investors owned the park where the Knoxville Giants played.

Some of these recreation sites were connected to areas of black residential concentration by the black-owned transportation firms mentioned above. Shortly after the introduction of the Model T, blacks began to establish taxi companies. Starting their firm in 1916, New Yorkers William H. Peters and Samuel Hamilton had, by 1930, a taxi and car rental company that represented a five hundred thousand dollar investment and featured 250 vehicles and a workforce of 750.[78]

White undertakers provided some service to blacks in Chicago prior to the Great Migration. However, as time passed, black families increasingly patronized coethnic firms, which responded to enhanced demand via expansion, additional advertising, and upgraded services. A 1947 publication estimated there were three thousand black undertakers in the United States, or 10 percent of all such firms in the country.[79] In Chicago, the number of black undertakers grew from one in 1885 to nearly seventy in 1938. Located on main thoroughfares, their establishments were often elegantly appointed and provided clients with luxurious hearses and limousines. Emphasizing its investment in top-rung vehicles, one company promised "All-Lincoln funerals."[80]

To ensure customer loyalty, undertakers spent money on maintaining good relations with the black public. They were the largest and most consistent advertisers in the black press, used the media to emphasize their standing as philanthropists and social benefactors, and even deployed wives as a charitable women's auxiliary. They also curried relations with ministers to obtain word-of-mouth referrals. Black undertakers found their greatest competition not from white-owned counterparts but rather from black-owned burial associations that offered comparable services but combined undertaking with burial insurance, thus providing prepaid funerals to impecunious southern migrants.

Another business in which blacks found success during the early twentieth century was insurance. White insurance companies generally avoided African American customers, and those offering policies charged black customers higher premiums than they did whites. Given that the African American community was poorly served, black insurers had a sizeable untapped market. By 1918, black-owned companies began to compete for the trade. Upon arrival in the North, most southern blacks were already familiar with insurance provided by lodges and black firms, so they made ready consumers.

Black-run insurance firms in Chicago supported boycotts against white insurance companies as part of an effort to compel them to hire black agents, treat black customers with courtesy, and collect premiums during the evening when it was most convenient for clients to pay. When Metropolitan Life, one of the most prominent white companies serving blacks, wrote a "tactless and discourteous reply" to a black newspaper's complaint about poor service, hundreds of blacks were angered.[81] While few black customers could afford to abandon their existing policies with white insurance companies, many chose black agencies—which actively advertised their racial origins and loyalties—for new services.

African Americans became involved in the large-scale provision of grooming and cosmetological services for black women in the early twentieth century. According to Walker, the leading figures in the black hair care and beauty industry during the early twentieth century were Annie Minerva Turnbo-Malone, Anthony Overton, Sarah Washington, and Madame C. J. Walker. While only Madame C. J. Walker remains well-known today, she and Turnbo-Malone rank among the very first self-made women millionaires, black or white, in U.S. history.[82]

These beauty entrepreneurs created products, manufacturing and advertising systems, and training and distributing programs that served consumers nationally and, ultimately, internationally. Not only did the grooming business make these individuals affluent, but in addition, it generated new opportunities for black women's employment, "not only in sales but also in the establishment of beauty shops . . . which became a prominent feature of black business districts," one that continues to be important in the present era.[83]

Madame C. J. Walker and friends. (Born Sarah Breedlove, 1867–1919.) Through the manufacture and marketing of hair care products and cosmetics for African American women, Walker became one of the first self-made women millionaires, black or white, in the United States. Walker brought together product innovation, sophisticated advertising, training programs, and sales incentives to capture an international market during a time of racial segregation. By the time of her death, Walker's company had over 500 agents and sold 75 different products. Thriving within the golden age of black business, the company she established continued to grow until the Great Depression.
Source: Photographs and Prints Division, Schomburg Center for Research in Black Culture, The New York Public Library, Astor, Lenox and Tilden Foundations.

WHITE COMPETITION FOR BLACK CUSTOMERS

In the early twentieth century, the number of black-owned businesses in black residential districts often approached or even exceeded that owned by whites. However, such firms captured only a small fraction of African American spending. For example, in 1938, Drake and Cayton determined that, while blacks owned nearly as many businesses in Chicago's Bronzeville (2,600) as did whites (2,800), black-owned businesses received less than a tenth of all the money spent in the area.[84]

The disparity was even greater in a 1928 Harlem survey, which found that blacks owned only 18.6 percent of local businesses. Moreover, over a third of all black merchants were involved with low-value personal services like barber and beauty shops, and cleaners. Only 18 percent sold goods, and most of these were restaurants. In contrast, a third of white businesses sold retail goods, including groceries, meat, baked goods, liquor, furniture, and clothing. They also ran department stores. Whites' access to capital allowed them to provide credit for costly items such as furniture, an option beyond the reach of black entrepreneurs.[85] Accordingly, white-owned firms often were larger, better capitalized, had a superior selection, and offered lower prices. White stores were often more prestigious as well and thus were favored by upwardly mobile African Americans, who were sometimes criticized by ministers and journalists for failing to "buy black." Blacks dominated only those business sectors that whites avoided.

White-owned businesses were able to compete with those owned by African Americans because they had more experience, easy relations with suppliers, and political connections. White enterprises also monopolized preferred locations due to their contacts with real estate brokers and retained premises from the time prior to when the neighborhood became black. White merchants also withheld prime locations in order to undermine black competition.[86] In contrast, a significant number of black businesses were located on remote side streets rather than near major intersections, and upstairs instead of on the ground floor. Large, black neighborhoods tended to benefit black business owners, but white merchants enjoyed a larger share of minority customers where blacks were less concentrated.

Racial ties provided advantages for black doctors, dentists, and nurses. However, black health workers were constrained by restricted access to hospitals.[87] As of the 1940s, there were very few hospitals in the United States—such as New York's Harlem Hospital—where black and white doctors worked as equals. This meant that black doctors served only the poorest patients, generally those rejected by white practitioners. By the 1930s, public health services had begun to expand, but—due to racial discrimination and requirements for forms of training that they could not acquire—black doctors were often ineligible for employment therein. Hence, despite the widespread poverty of black citizens, the implementation of social welfare benefits offered few additional opportunities for black physicians.[88] Discriminatory practices maintained by medical schools also restricted the number of university-trained black doctors. In the 1930s, about four out of five black doctors in the United States received their training in only two "Negro medical schools"—Howard in Washington, D.C., and Meharry in Nashville.

Black doctors and dentists compensated for their limited income by engaging in side businesses, including investments in real estate, drug stores, and private hospitals directed toward black patients. Enterprising dentists provided beauty-enhancing cosmetic dentistry, such as the provision of gold teeth. These income-supplementing practices were sometimes criticized as unethical means of extracting extra payments from low-income customers.[89] Other black professions, including lawyers and engineers, were constrained by limited coethnic demand for their services.[90]

BUSINESS DECLINES DURING THE GREAT DEPRESSION

While competition from white merchants limited the expansion of black entrepreneurship during the 1920s, declining economic conditions after 1929 provided an even greater obstacle. This was because the Great Depression hit African Americans especially hard. While decline in retail trade for the entire United States during the 1930s was 13 percent, loss of retail trade among black firms was more than twice as great—28 percent.[91] During the same period, employment in white-owned stores remained stable, and payrolls reduced by only 10 percent. In contrast, black-owned establishments experienced a reduction in employment of 15 percent, and their payrolls shrunk by a third.[92]

In response to job loss, unemployed blacks tried to cope by opening survival businesses. Reflecting on the increase in black business start-ups during the late 1920s and early 1930s, Drake and Cayton wrote, the Depression "stimulated an increase in the number of smaller businesses, as many people with some savings saw in the opening of a small store one means of insuring themselves against starvation."[93] "'If work was plentiful, these small places would not exist,' commented a successful entrepreneur, and he was no doubt right."[94]

Thousands of black businesses failed during the Great Depression, including many larger firms and banks. While 134 black banks had been created between 1888 and 1934, only 12 remained as of the mid 1930s. As economic times became harder, conflict with white-owned businesses increased. "The impact of the Depression combined with the fierce competition for good locations, for credit and capital, also resulted in an accentuation of racial antagonisms, including anti-Semitic manifestations."[95] One product of the times was the mobilization of boycotts against white-owned shops that refused to employ blacks (see chapter 5). The goal of these boycotts was to promote black employment in existing firms, not to sustain black entrepreneurship. Nevertheless, many black business owners supported the boycotts as a means of gaining an upper hand on white competitors.

CONCLUSIONS

A range of black and white observers have long faulted the African American community for failing to develop an ethnic economy. However, this chapter demonstrates that, prior to the twentieth century, black intellectuals, activists, and entrepreneurs established a principle that would lie close to the hearts of race leaders for years to come: "that blacks could be financially successful by relying upon the buying power of the black masses."[96] Their actions not only identified a practical goal but also established the academic study of ethnic economies. Drawing from this philosophy, black ministers, activists, and business owners from the late nineteenth century to the present have encouraged black consumers to patronize black-owned enterprises. Observing early success in this endeavor, a black resident of Cleveland's Central Avenue boasted in 1905 that the area "has developed into a regular business street and we are happy to state that many of those business houses are owned by colored people."[97]

Their best hopes notwithstanding, black entrepreneurs have confronted an array of laws and social practices that have limited their ability to build upon successes like those celebrated in 1905 Cleveland. Despite such obstacles, black entrepreneurs have been able to develop creative means of earning a living and sustaining their communities against hostility and during recession. As such, black businesses have made significant and long-lasting economic, cultural, institutional, and educational contributions to both African American life and to the larger society as well.

3

IMMIGRANT ENTREPRENEURS' RELATIONS WITH CUSTOMERS IN THE EARLY TWENTIETH CENTURY

THE FABLE OF WHITE ETHNIC HARMONY AND BLACK-WHITE OPPOSITION

The most pervasive image of civil conflict in recent American history involves immigrant business owners and African American residents. This combination characterizes the urban uprisings of the 1940s, 1960s, and more recent episodes in Miami (1980) and Los Angeles (1992) that devastated not only urban ghettos but also Americans' assessment of city life more generally. Retrospectives on the fortieth anniversary of riots in Watts, Newark, and Detroit point out that neighborhoods and even entire cities have yet to recover—economically and socially—from these events that took place almost a half a century ago. Reflecting on the 1960s uprising, a *Detroit Free Press* columnist wrote, "In the consciousness of white suburbanites, conventional wisdom is that July 1967 was the turning point in Detroit's recent history, the cause of flight to the suburbs, the breeder of bad things about their once-beloved city, the event that kicked off Detroit's transformation from the world's greatest factory town to the struggling, impoverished city of today."[1]

In the popular mind, it is racial discord that made these conflicts so explosive and destructive. White Americans commonly believe that, prior to the presence of numerous African Americans in urban neighborhoods, relations between ethnic business owners and their customers were much more harmonious than they have been since. Italian Americans interviewed by Jonathan Rieder described how animosity between African Americans and ethnic merchants ruined a Brooklyn neighborhood:

> I used to go up on Pitkin Avenue when it was all Jewish. . . . Pitkin Avenue was the best shopping street you could go to in the whole world. It was be-eee-you-ti-ful.". . . "But now you drive down Pitkin Avenue at five o'clock and there are iron shutters on the stores and the police have to walk in groups of three and four. It's terrible. I am amazed what happened to Brownsville. It's like it was bombed out. It looks like Dresden after the war.[2]

Despite its wide acceptance, the fable of white ethnic harmony and black-white opposition is inaccurate. Prior to the 1920s, conflicts between immigrant entrepreneurs and customers almost always took place among whites, many of whom were themselves immigrants, while interactions between immigrant merchants and blacks were rare. This is because, until the Great Migration of African Americans to northern cities after about 1917, immigrants mostly settled in northeastern, midwestern, and western cities, while African Americans remained concentrated in the rural Southeast. In 1900, sixty-one thousand blacks lived in New York City. During the same year, there were 1,270,080 foreign-born persons in New York City, almost all of whom were white. In 1910, there were forty-four thousand blacks and nearly eight hundred thousand foreign-born whites in Chicago and in Cleveland; blacks constituted less than 2 percent of the city's population.[3]

Accordingly, while differences in ethnicity, religion, and nationality catalyzed disputes between merchants and customers, black-white opposition was not the primary nexus of contention. In fact, because immigrant groups were themselves stratified by region, dialect, class, tenure in the United States, and other factors, discord between entrepreneurs and customers of the same national or ethnic origin was common.

An interesting correction in itself, this characterization of merchant-customer conflict is of special relevance today, as many U.S. cities and regions—such as New York and Los Angeles—now reveal conflicts among a diversity of nationality groups with far fewer disputes involving native African Americans and foreign-born merchants. (See chapter 7.)

BASES OF CONFLICT

Most of the millions of immigrants from Europe, the Americas, Asia, and the Middle East who entered the United States during the late nineteenth and early twentieth centuries found jobs as laborers, as miners, or in agriculture. While fractions of all these groups (and sizeable populations of some) eventually became self-employed, this process took time. Newcomers were regarded with hostility by those already present, including native-born whites, established immigrants, and African Americans, because of the competition they generated for jobs, housing, and other scarce resources. Those most recently arrived were generally desperate for work and unfamiliar with prevailing norms in the United States. Accordingly, they were willing to take almost any job for any wage. This raised the ire of established groups because immigrants' presence reduced wages and worsened living conditions for all.

Finally, the potential for ethnic conflict was enhanced as elites promulgated ideologies that granted scientific credibility to ethnocentric stereotypes, politicians sought support by advancing policies that restricted immigrants' rights and economic opportunities, and tabloid journalism railed against foreigners. As a consequence of these many factors, the localities where immigrants settled were often marked by strife between employers and workers; between natives and foreigners; and between and within various migrant groups.

While intergroup hostility generally reflected a struggle for existing jobs and housing rather than conflicts between merchants and customers, when a group was identified as a source of competition, its businesses made easy targets and were often destroyed in the course of collective violence. This happened to black businesses and white-owned businesses serving blacks in Atlanta in 1906 and Chicago in 1919 (see chapter 2); to Italian businesses in Louisiana between 1890 and 1910; to Greek businesses in Roanoke, Virginia, in 1907, and in South Omaha in 1909; to Chinese businesses in western states from the 1850s onward; to Japanese businesses in California between 1900 and 1941; and to Jewish businesses in New York, Detroit, and elsewhere from the 1880s until the 1930s.

Few immigrant entrepreneurs suffered forms of informal and legal discrimination as harsh and all-encompassing as those encountered by African Americans. Immigrants did, however, confront significant obstacles. Disputes frequently took on a racial, national, ethnic, or religious character, with combatants justifying their attacks upon opponents in terms of popular stereotypes about targets' negative attributes. Antimiscegenation has had a profound role in the history of U.S. racism, and during the late nineteenth and early twentieth centuries, ethnic businesses were often destroyed by whites who sought to punish immigrant and minority men who appeared interested in white women.[4]

Two sets of group characteristics made immigrant entrepreneurs especially vulnerable to harassment and violence. The first involved a group's social distance from Anglo-American cultural norms and practices—those of white, middle-class, native-born, English-speaking Protestants. The second was a lack of educational, social, economic, and political resources, which prevented them from establishing advantageous positions in the U.S. economy.

Accordingly, nonwhite, non-English-speaking, unskilled, non-Protestant groups unfamiliar with the U.S. environment were especially prone to victimization. While African Americans confronted the most extensive geographic restrictions, immigrants were hounded about their inassimilable status.[5] In 1882, Senator Eli M. Saulsbury of Delaware summed up many whites' view of immigrants as he described the Chinese: "They are of a different race and possess an entirely different civilization, and in my opinion are incapable of being brought into assimilation in habits, customs and manners with people of this country." Foreign-born Asians were ineligible for citizenship and prohibited from owning land, running certain kinds of businesses, and ultimately, entering the country at all. Writing of the era, Stanford Lyman asserts, "Chinese immigration to California from 1848 to 1882 occasioned a great national and cultural debate. The doctrines of white supremacy and Anglo-conformity, which had already dispensed with full citizenship for the Negro and the Indian and suffered European immigration only with considerable distrust took on an even sharper racial and cultural edge."[6]

European groups that were significantly distinct from Anglo Americans in culture, religion, and language—including Russian Jews, Italians, and Greeks—were held in low regard because of their religious nonconformity, exotic appearance, and in some cases, their willingness to live near and do business with African Americans. Foreigners' loyalty to the United States was always in question. Due to the rise of Mussolini, Italians were depicted as fascists. Together with Jews, they were portrayed as radical anarchists and godless communists.[7] Beyond these political allegations, Jews were held to be avaricious and financially corrupt, while the pervasive myth of Italians' "inherent criminality" has justified attacks on them since before the twentieth century.[8]

Because of their unfamiliar ways, their willingness to enter untested geographies, and the economic competition they presented to locals, immigrant peddlers and merchants were subject to harassment, frequent attack, and even murder. At least one Jew and several Italian entrepreneurs were lynched by southern whites during the late nineteenth and early twentieth centuries. Politicians and police were often unresponsive to merchants' and peddlers' calls for help. In many cases, they were allied with native constituencies or with Irish Americans and, so, were more likely to side with those committing attacks than with the victims. For example, in 1902, a rabbi's Lower East Side funeral procession was attacked by Irish bystanders who were hostile to the burgeoning Jewish population that was overtaking their neighborhood. The police responded by vigorously beating, arresting, and fining the funeral marchers. Allegedly, their commander ordered his men to "club their brains out."[9]

While the widely accepted pseudoscience of eugenics held that Southern and Eastern Europeans were racially distinct from and inferior to Northern European Protestants, the sources of white ethnics' difference with the majority proved to be less permanent and more amenable to assimilation than the phenotypical characteristics of Asians and blacks. Accordingly, upon arrival and, especially as time passed, Southern and Eastern Europeans and their descendants elevated their status by learning English, wearing American-style clothing, maintaining prevailing styles of consumption, and adopting local business practices.[10]

In order to elude laws that blocked business ownership for noncitizens, immigrant entrepreneurs who were eligible became naturalized. To preclude accusations of unfair competition from merchants who operated out of store buildings, entrepreneurs' associations urged coethnic members to abandon peddling and pushcarts in favor of permanent locations. Such moves became compulsory to the owners of Chicago lunch carts when, in 1927, the Chicago city council passed an ordinance forbidding the sale of food on the city streets.[11]

Ethnic groups formed business associations to uphold standards of behavior among their members and to represent their interests to politicians, police, journalists, and the American public. By implementing these practices and distancing themselves from African Americans, European immigrants and their children were able to claim whiteness or, in other words, secure their membership in the racially dominant group of American society.

Scholars of contemporary migration often contend that actions made by the country of origin on behalf of citizens abroad are a recent phenomenon. However, there is a century-long record of certain nationalities relying on their homelands' intervention. Greek, Italian, and Japanese entrepreneurs were able to call upon representatives of their countries of origin to demand proper treatment from U.S. authorities. This option was unavailable to Irish, Russian Jews, and blacks.[12] For example, in 1907, after a series of attacks against Greek merchants in Roanoke, Virginia, C. C. Maximos, the acting general consul of Greece in New York, wired U.S. Secretary of State Elihu Root about their mistreatment. Two years later, following the killing of a South Omaha policeman by a Greek man, a riot ensued that destroyed

Greeks' property and drove 1,400 from the city. In response, Lambros Coromilas, the Greek minister to the United States, demanded that the U.S. State Department protect the community against mass punishment for the wrongdoing of a single criminal. In addition, the Panhellenic Union, a Greek American organization with fifty thousand members throughout the United States, took up the cause and protested to President Roosevelt. Finally, during World War I, when a nationalistic climate and popular resentment about Greek immigrants' exemption from serving in the U.S. military resulted in endemic hostility against Greek-owned enterprises in the United States, the Greek government and its minister of foreign affairs instructed its diplomatic and consular officials in the United States to demonstrate that Greece enthusiastically supported the allied cause and encouraged Greek citizens in the United States to volunteer for service in the American military.[13]

In a like manner, when Italians accused of crimes were lynched in Louisiana in the 1890s, Italy's ambassador Saverio Fava complained about the lack of protection, the mistreatment that the Italians received while in custody, and complicity between police and lynch mobs. The Italian government also supervised the recruitment of its citizens for employment in Louisiana. Following a 1905 visit, the Italian ambassador to the United States, Edmondo des Planches, concluded that, while owning a farm or business was an appropriate occupation for his countrymen, agricultural labor was not and told Louisiana officials as much. In 1908, when "an entire Italian community" resisted a Louisiana sheriff's posse that sought to arrest two men who had injured whites in a fight that broke out during a baseball game, Italian vice consul Gerolimo Moroni visited the Louisiana parish where the incident took place and defended the Italians, claiming that because of the climate of hostility against them in the region, the community believed that the posse threatened all of them.[14]

Japanese consular officials worked with the Japanese American community as early as 1900 to confront white hostility, and in 1908, President Theodore Roosevelt acted to ban the enforcement of a San Francisco law segregating Japanese students from whites in the public schools but did so in return for Japan's acceptance of the gentlemen's agreement that voluntarily restricted the arrival of additional immigrants.[15]

In contrast, Chinese immigrants were notably without allies. Lyman asserts, "Chinese had very few friends or sympathizers in the American West. Neither radicals nor reactionaries, liberals or conservatives, were interested in defending—much less understanding them." Their sole support came from Protestant missionaries and a few officials and attorneys.[16]

Despite diplomats' efforts to protect their countrymen running businesses in the United States, American politicians were not very responsive.
Instead, they defended their actions and generally refused to change their
behavior. For example, when a Greek official complained about the destruction of Greek stores by an angry mob in Roanoke, Virginia, in 1907,
the mayor replied,

> The city is made up of largely of working men and members of labor organiza-
> tions, and they are not especially friendly to the foreigners living in the city.
> Very few of these Greeks can speak English, and if a customer gets a fifteen
> cent lunch, and there is a misunderstanding as to the price, there is hardly a
> Greek in the place that will not upon the least provocation, grab a butcher
> knife or some other weapon and make for the complaining customer. This ac-
> tion on their part causes our people to be incensed, and it is with difficulty that
> we can prevent the smashing of their place of business. . . . If they continue
> to multiply here as they have during the past year, and do not change their
> methods of collecting bills and settling disputes you will find dead Greeks in
> Roanoke before another year rolls around.[17]

While actions by foreign governments on behalf of immigrants generally
had limited effect, Italian workers in Louisiana did receive some advantages
because local planters needed workers for the sugar and rice harvest and
did not want to further antagonize this important source of labor. In turn,
Italian immigrants' preferential treatment did not escape the African American community. Following demands by Italian consular offices for U.S.
government compensation to the families of countrymen killed by Louisiana lynch mobs, the National Association for the Advancement of Colored People (NAACP) newspaper *The Crisis* observed that such benefits
remained unavailable to U.S. citizens. "Relatives of foreigners subjected to
lynch mob justice received indemnities from the Federal Government, but
since native Afro-Americans enjoyed the 'privilege' of American citizenship
they were granted 'the inalienable right of every free American citizen to
be lynched,' without recourse to redress."[18]

While Russian Jews and Irish Catholics in the United States lacked coun-
try-of-origin representation, established coethnics did provide advocacy and
assistance. Scholars credit the activities of American coreligionists in helping immigrant Jews establish an impressive number of businesses shortly
after their arrival in the United States. In addition, Jewish philanthropists
developed a variety of assimilation-fostering and social service activities to
alleviate nativists' concerns about the potential for social disorganization
and criminality among immigrant Jews. They did this both out of concern

for their Jewish brethren and because they worried that the presence of these impecunious coreligionists—exotic in their dress, Orthodox in their religion, socialistic in their politics, and Yiddish speaking—might arouse anti-Semitism. Ultimately, the fears of established Jews were borne out. After the 1920s, when the impact of millions of Eastern European immigrants was fully felt, Jewish attendance at elite schools, universities, and vacation resorts, as well as their employment in major corporations and law firms, was either limited by quotas or altogether banned. Even the elite of established Jews were impacted as sons were barred admittance to social clubs that their fathers had helped to found.[19]

Similarly, Irish involved in political machines defended coethnics and helped Hibernian entrepreneurs to acquire lucrative government contracts. Historian Ronald Takaki writes, "In New York, Boston, Chicago and San Francisco, Irish political machines functioned like 'Robin Hoods,' taking taxes from the Yankee middle class and giving revenues to the Irish through public payrolls." Links between Irish American politicians and coethnic construction companies secured public works contracts to build roads, bridges, tunnels, subways, and public buildings. Irish employers and workers "shared job opportunities only with their sons and compatriots." As a result, by 1870, Irish builders constituted a fifth of all contractors in the country.[20]

REGION AND CLASS: CONFLICTS WITHIN A SINGLE GROUP

Ingroup conflicts were relatively common within immigrant groups during the early twentieth century. Migrants often had close ties with relatives and compatriots hailing from the same village, region, or dialect group that fostered collaboration. In contrast, rivalry and competition developed among coethnics bonded by weaker ties. Italian migrants identified with their village of origin or region, regarding themselves as Lombards, Sicilians, or Neapolitans. It was only due to the efforts of U.S. activists like Bank of America founder A. P. Giannini, who weaned immigrants away from locally based identities and mutual aid societies so they would save in his "progressive" Italian American bank, that such migrants began to conceive of themselves as Italians.[21]

In some instances, closeness did not eliminate the potential for hostility because unscrupulous entrepreneurs relied on homeland ties to lure unsuspecting countrymen into sponsored migration agreements that verged on indentured servitude. A muckraking Greek American journalist criticized his countrymen for this practice, complaining that "Greeks were ready to fight the Turks and Bulgars for enslaving and degrading their countrymen. . . . Still they had no scruples about enslaving their own youth in the shoeshine parlors of the United States."[22]

Ethnic gangs and mafias, which existed in several nationality groups, were criminal entrepreneurs. Most commonly, they directed their protection rackets, shakedowns, and other activities against merchants of their own ethnic groups. In addition to their violent and criminal actions, they also maintained a strong sense of loyalty to local neighborhoods, providing philanthropy, jobs, security, and protection from other ethnic gangs. "There is the understanding, then, among the community that the gang is a resource that can be counted on, particularly in situations where some form of force is necessary."[23]

Chinatowns of the late nineteenth and early twentieth centuries featured secret societies called Tongs that were involved in the provision of illegal services like gambling, drugs, and prostitution. Such organizations sometimes helped prevent intragroup conflict by limiting the number of competing businesses that could be located in a given area. At the same time, however, rival crews also engaged in indiscriminate violence and gunfights as they sought to wrest control of criminal enterprises from each other.[24] Lyman emphasized the intragroup nature of such disputes: "Conflict in Chinatown was intramural, and it made no sense unless carried out within the ghetto community. Chinese clan feuds were directed against one another and not against American families or Irish clans."[25]

Contemporary authors generally frame conflicts between merchants and customers in light of opponents' ethnic or national origins. Historical evidence suggests that class was also a crucial determinant. For example, working-class Polish Catholics often preferred Jewish merchants over coethnic shop owners. In order to secure coethnic patronage, Polish business owners appealed to customers' national pride and issued anti-Semitic canards. Masked by references to nationality, the issue was not tribal loyalty but rather which petit bourgeoisie would pocket the Polish workers' expenditures.[26]

The *Jewish Daily Forward* described a 1902 incident in which working-class Jews who were immersed in a culture of radical labor activism boycotted coethnic merchants and wholesalers who they felt were seeking excessive profits. Outraged by a 50 percent increase in meat prices, Jewish women in New York's Lower East Side, Harlem, and Brooklyn besieged coethnic meat vendors' shops and poured kerosene, oil, and carbolic acid on their merchandise. "Those who persisted in buying meat were pursued through the neighborhood and forced to return their purchases." Some protestors even invaded private homes, where they tossed meat onto the street and trampled it. The women enlisted the support of local rabbis to their cause, asked male synagogue congregants to discourage their wives from patronizing the offending merchants, and cited religious passages that permitted the consumption of nonkosher meat during dire emergencies.

Since the boycott involved members of a single ethnic group, it clearly hinged on class rather than religion, nationality, or ethnicity as the basis of opposition. "When arrested and brought in front of a judge, one woman defended herself by pointing to the indissoluble bonds between individuals and community. She argued that those who ignored the meat ban were abandoning the community."[27] Even though the meat boycott was not a labor issue per se, its organizers' revealed their class identification as they referred to themselves as "strikers and soldiers" and vilified violators of the boycott as "scabs."

In fact, the kosher butchers, who were of the same Russian origins as the boycotters, were trapped between their customers and established German-Jewish meat wholesalers. The butchers had communicated their customers' anger about rising prices to the wholesalers but to no avail, thus precipitating the strike. Activists emphasized their class loyalties by asserting that "millionaires" had bribed supervising rabbis to disregard the impact of inflated meat prices on the Jewish masses.

Jewish workers engaged in similar conflicts with coethnic landlords. Rent wars took place in 1894, 1905–1906, and 1907–1908 when tenants objected to increases in their rents beyond affordable levels. Demands for reasonable rents were accompanied by calls to the community to boycott landlords who evicted tenants. Defiant strikers hung red flags from their windows and fire escapes. "Boycotts against shops, theaters, music halls, and landlords were widely broadcast, and reviling and denouncing publicly those who offended against communal norms were much-used strategies."[28]

Intraethnic conflicts also occurred among Italian, Chinese, and Greek merchants, workers, and customers. For example, in January 1929, Chinese laundrymen in San Francisco went on strike against coethnic employers for higher wages and shorter hours. The owners tried to hire black women— members of another minority group extensively involved in clothes washing—as scabs but found few willing to break the strike. Black labor activists praised the event as a stirring example of class solidarity among black and Asian workers.[29] Finally, merchants who did business from rented storefronts frequently complained about unfair competition from pushcart operators and peddlers who sold the same merchandise but with little overhead. Often, these competitors were members of the same ethnic group.

Class-based conflicts between entrepreneurs, customers, and workers who share common origins persist to this day. They are extensively documented among an array of ethnic and nationality groups including Chinese, Koreans, Israelis, Cubans, African Americans, Vietnamese, Russians, Cambodians, Mexicans, Indians, and others.

COETHNIC AND OUTGROUP MARKETS AND PATTERNS OF CONFLICT

All immigrant and ethnic groups maintain a set of grocery stores, restaurants, taverns, and coffee shops to satisfy coethnic demand for traditional goods and services.[30] Generally remaining within ethnic neighborhoods, these businesses enjoyed a degree of security from conflicts with outgroup members. They were subject to disputes during large-scale "race riots," shakedowns from organized crime and corrupt police, as well as disagreements with suppliers, landlords, and competitors (such as chain stores). However, difficult relations with outgroup members were the exception rather than the rule.[31]

However, ethnic groups that commonly traded with outgroups, including native whites, other immigrant populations, and African Americans, needed to deal with potential conflicts on a regular basis. Historical evidence gives us some insight into which nationalities were most involved in serving outgroup demand, the types of goods they provided, and the nature of their relations with customers.

According to the 1911 Dillingham Commission, which collected social and economic data from immigrant groups in several U.S. cities, the foreign-born groups that had the highest rates of male self-employment were as follows: Greeks, 32.6 percent; Hebrew Russians, 33.6 percent; Hebrew Other, 35.2 percent; and Syrians, 55.4 percent. (In New York City, a phenomenal 75.1 percent of Syrian men were self-employed.) North Italians' self-employment rate was 7.8 percent, and South Italians' was 12.8 percent.

Of U.S.-born men, Hebrews had the greatest proportion employed in trade, 42 percent. They were followed by the Swedish, 26.1 percent; Slovak, 22.2 percent; South Italian, 16.6 percent; German, 16.8 percent; Bohemian and Moravian, 12.1 percent; Irish, 14 percent; white, 14.6 percent; and Negro, 10.6 percent.

Women's rates of self-employment, which were generally much lower, mirrored the rankings of men. Of the foreign born, only Syrian women's rate of self-employment, 28.1 percent, exceeded 10 percent. (Like Syrian

men, these women commonly worked as peddlers.) Hebrew Russians and
Hebrew Other followed at 7.0 percent and 5.7 percent, respectively. Of
native-born women, Hebrews had the highest rate of involvement in trade,
36.2 percent, followed by Swedish, 25 percent; and German, 10.1 percent.
Other groups had rates of self-employment below 10 percent.[32]

Groups with the highest rates of self-employment were involved in trade
with members of the larger society, often as peddlers and pushcart owners,
since such occupations required the smallest investments. For example,
"Of the roughly 5000 pushcart peddlers in Manhattan at the turn of the
century, approximately 60 percent were Jews. In turn, peddlers bought
their merchandise from Jewish wholesalers and retailers, providing jobs
for many other Jews." Pushcarts, especially those selling fruit, vegetables,
and prepared foods, were run by Greeks and Italians. This pattern was not
limited to New York but is documented in many other cities as well.[33]

Further verifying the tendency of entrepreneurial groups to be oriented toward non-coethnic customers, Robert Boyd notes that, in 1900,
Russian, Italian, and Polish men and, in some cases, Austro-Hungarian
men (most Russians and many Poles and Austro-Hungarians were Jewish)
had "astonishingly high rates of peddling and merchandising" in several
midwestern cities where these groups' numbers were relatively small.[34]
This demonstrates that these groups were extensively involved in sales to
outgroup consumers.

In California, Japanese were known for their provision of goods and
services to outgroup members as they "moved briskly towards exploitable
sources of money" in agricultural entrepreneurship. "A common Los Angeles ethnic stereotype before World War II was the Japanese vegetable
man: polite, a bit peculiar in his English, and able to sell unusually attractive produce." Japanese generally started small plots on marginal land but,
through the use of careful planning, imported technologies like irrigation,
and coethnic cooperation, were able to produce "superlative fruits and vegetables" that yielded significant profits. Eventually, they integrated several
segments of the industry, including wholesalers, suppliers, retailers, and
labor contractors, to form an ethnic niche that competed directly and effectively with whites. Accounting for a tiny fraction of California's population,
the Japanese developed a near monopoly in many agricultural commodities.
Japanese prosperity "did not go unnoticed by jealous whites" who railed
against "the Japanese menace" in labor organizations, political speeches,
and newspaper headlines.[35] (See chapter 4.)

Paradoxically, efforts to exclude Japanese from rural occupations and
deny them jobs in existing firms ultimately forced them into urban self-
employment, which increased their competition with native whites.

Urban self-employment absorbed the energies of Japanese men who faced discriminatory barriers in agriculture and in the urban labor market. By 1919, for example, 47 percent of hotels and 25 percent of grocery stores in Seattle were Japanese owned. . . . Although a culturally derived preference for self-employment clearly supported this development, the Japanese interest in commercial self-employment was also a plain response to a discriminatory opportunity structure which precluded wage or salary employment at non-menial levels.[36]

Soon after the start of the twentieth century, by working cooperatively and recruiting teenaged boys directly from the homeland as laborers, Greeks came to dominate the shoeshine industry, which had previously been the province of African Americans and Italians. Following the example set at that time by big businesses like oil, banking, and railroads, Greek immigrants organized the shoeshine industry into a trust. They established chains of ornate shops in high-rent areas, each of which included rough dormitory and dining quarters to house and feed their adolescent workforce. A single Greek named Smerlis operated over one hundred establishments in New Jersey. Greeks also cornered the market in other service industries. They owned 925 candy stores and confectionaries in Chicago in 1906, and ran more than 4,000 Chicago restaurants in 1917 (about a third of all restaurants in the entire city) as well as 564 eating places in San Francisco in 1923.[37] As recently as 1950, men of Greek ancestry were twenty-nine times as likely to work in the restaurant business as the average white male.[38]

While Greek, Jewish, Chinese, Japanese, and Syrian businesses were consistently directed toward outgroup customers, Italians' involvement reflected their regional origins. As suggested by the Dillingham Commission data above, southern Italians, notably Sicilians, often sold goods and services to members of the larger society in environments ranging from New York to rural Louisiana. In contrast, northern Italians were less involved in retail trade and, if they had businesses, tended to direct them toward coethnics. In his study of St. Louis's "Hill" Italian neighborhood, which was dominated by Lombards, Gary Ross Mormino found that almost all businesses served conationals. While generally less educated than northerners, many southern Italians—like the extended family of Sicilian fishermen who ran a chain of grocery stores in Cleveland—were able to draw on premigration work experiences and family ties to become entrepreneurs in the United States.[39]

Over time, many Italian businesses, including macaroni factories, fruit sellers, bakeries, soft drink bottlers, and saloons, began to market their products and services to the larger society. Italians' premigration skills in making and selling beer and whiskey brought throngs of outgroup consumers to Hill saloons during prohibition. However, this market collapsed when alcohol again became legal. At least in St Louis' Hill neighborhood, however, co-ethnics were the major customers for Italian entrepreneurs until the 1970s, when non-Italians came to patronize newly opened Italian restaurants, created specifically to serve white consumers.[40]

The propensity of certain groups to engage in trade with non-coethnics can be explained by several factors. First is access. As noted in chapter 2, after the full implementation of Jim Crow, black entrepreneurs were unable to trade with white customers because their businesses were restricted to black neighborhoods. The propensity of Jews, Syrians, and Chinese to sell to members of the larger society can be explained by the fact that, as middleman entrepreneurs, they were party to a tradition of selling to non-coethnics prior to their arrival in the United States. Limited alternatives for employment in existing firms is another explanation. For example, Japanese and Chinese were systematically excluded from most jobs in existing firms and were offered only the least desirable positions during times of greatest need. If hired at all, they received low pay and sporadic work.[41] Russian Jews' links to established and highly entrepreneurial German Jews facilitated their self-employment. In addition, Jews' levels of urban experience, literacy, occupational skill, and education, which were significantly higher than those of other major migrant populations of the late nineteenth and early twentieth centuries, also contributed to their high rates of self-employment.[42]

Entrepreneurial groups' propensity to sell to others is sometimes accounted for in cultural terms. A coterie of scholars contend that these groups believe that self-employment is both a psychologically and economically rewarding activity and have a strong tradition of independence, resourcefulness, and hard work.[43] Such explanations are unsatisfactory because, without unique evidence, it is difficult to demonstrate that one group more greatly values independence or has a larger capacity for hard work than another. More convincing is research demonstrating that certain groups maintain identifiable practices like rotating savings and credit associations (ROSCAs) for the acquisition and sharing of investment capital that facilitates business ownership. A final factor that must be considered is context. The case of the Japanese Hawaiians—who had low rates of self-employment in contrast to the high rates of entrepreneurship maintained by their cousins on the mainland—demonstrates that group culture alone cannot explain rates of self-employment. Rather, even those groups with specific entrepreneurial resources must settle in contexts where entrepreneurship is a viable economic strategy.[44]

The habit of directing businesses to outgroup members offered many advantages to immigrant entrepreneurs. By doing so, they gained access to a much larger group of consumers who were generally more affluent than impecunious coethnics. In many cases, they also faced less competition. Finally, since they lacked close relations with customers, they were generally exempt from coethnic obligations to do favors, provide free merchandise, extend loans, or offer generous wages. At the same time, however, by trading with outgroup members, immigrant merchants were more likely to encounter conflicts with customers.

In some cases, immigrant merchants retained economic relationships with outgroup customers that had been established prior to migration. This was often the case for Polish Jewish merchants and Polish Catholic customers. "Even towards the end of the nineteenth century [in Poland], when Christians began to provide many of the same [economic] services, the [Polish] peasants preferred to trade with Jews. Their manner and place in the community were understood whereas the role of the new entrepreneurs was often misunderstood."[45] In *The Ghetto*, Louis Wirth notes that Poles in Chicago retained the uneasy but familiar patterns of trade with Jewish merchants that they had developed in Eastern Europe.

> These two groups detest each other thoroughly, but live side by side. . . . A study of numerous cases shows that not only do many Jews open their businesses on Milwaukee Avenue and Division Street because they know that the Poles are the predominant population in these neighborhoods, but the Poles come from all over the city to trade on Maxwell Street because they know that there they can find the familiar street-stands owned by Jews. These two immigrant groups, having lived side by side in Poland and Galicia, are used to each other's business methods.[46]

With the growth of a Polish American entrepreneurial class, the Polish-language press encouraged ingroup loyalty. For example, the *Dziennik Zwiazkowy* (a Chicago newspaper) featured anti-Jewish diatribes and emphasized ethnic and religious solidarity in advertisements that discouraged Poles in the United States from patronizing Jewish merchants. Advertisements for a clothing store referred to the firm as Polish owned and used the saying "Swoj do Swojego" ("Patronize Your Own"). "This was a reminder not to buy in non-Polish, that is, Jewish, shops." The broadsheet advertised an entrepreneurs' association called the Commercial Club, which was guaranteed to have no Jewish members and published an article about a Jew in South Chicago taking advantage of a Pole. Jews expressed their animosity by ridiculing Poles in a vaudeville sketch at a Chicago theater. In response, the Polish press called the sketch "slanderous, insulting and unbecoming to members of a race who are continually complaining about race baiting."[47]

As this indicates, common European origins and shared immigrant status did not preclude hostile, tense, and violent business relations among white immigrant groups. The Jewish Peddlers Union was formed in Detroit in 1900 as a self-defense organization to resist sometimes-fatal attacks by Polish and Irish ruffians. Suggesting the importance of economic conditions in provoking conflict between merchants and customers, hostility was magnified during the depression of 1893–1894, when unemployment, the Eastern European Jews' high visibility, and age-old stereotypes of Jews as exploiters and Shylocks led to their being targeted. Peddlers encountered similar troubles in New York, Chicago, Rochester, Philadelphia, and Milwaukee. As early as 1892, Baltimore Jews organized to protect themselves against German and black gangs that attacked them on the streets.[48]

During a 1909 riot in South Omaha, Nebraska, Greek workers, strikebreakers, and entrepreneurs were attacked by a crowd including immigrants, native whites, and blacks. Some thirty-six Greek-owned enterprises were destroyed. John Bukowczyk notes that, during a series of strike-related riots in 1915 and 1916, the largely Polish workforce sacked Bayonne, New Jersey, businesses owned by Jews and Irishmen. Similar incidents befell Chinese on the West Coast, especially during economic recessions when white workers sought jobs.[49] "Sparked by the agitation of labor leaders and politicians, the urban anti-Chinese movement entered a violent phase" in the late 1800s in California. In reaction to the 1871 deaths of two policemen and a bystander during a Tong war in Los Angeles' Chinatown, a white mob attacked the Chinese quarter, killed nineteen persons, including women and children, burned several buildings, and looted shops.

Anti-Chinese riots occurred with some frequency between 1880 and 1907 in San Francisco, Truckee, and Martinez, California; Denver, Colorado; Rock Springs, Wyoming; Seattle and Tacoma, Washington; Gold Hill and Virginia City, Nevada; and Vancouver, Canada. In each case, businesses were attacked and buildings destroyed. Chinese agricultural endeavors were ruined by riots after the 1870s.[50] A Chinese old-timer who ran a laundry near a mining camp describes the constant threat of violence:

Every Saturday night, we never knew whether we would live to see the light of day. . . . Saturday was the night for the miners to get drunk. They would force their way into our shop, wrest the clean white bundles from the shelves and trample the shirts. One night . . . a mob . . . ransacked our shop, robbed us of the $360 that was our combined savings and set fire to the laundry. We were lucky to escape with our lives.[51]

Reflecting popular sentiments, an article was added to the California State Constitution in 1879 that forbade the employment of Chinese in any corporation formed in the state, and on any state, municipal, or county public works, and provided for legislation whereby a city or town might expel its Chinese inhabitants.

A variety of laws in California, Nevada, and Montana specifically sought to limit Chinese involvement in a range of businesses including farming, laundry, and fishing as well as restricting the hours that Chinese could work and the tools they could use. Regulations taxed Chinese fishermen and charged extra fees for laundrymen who traveled from house to house without horses. (Since Chinese were the only laundrymen who did not use steeds in their work, the goal of this regulation was clear.) Similar laws banned the use of Chinese carrying poles for peddling vegetables and sought to prohibit ironing clothes at night. Many but not all of these anti-Chinese laws were rejected by the State Supreme Court.[52]

A series of California laws also made it illegal for nonnaturalizable aliens (of which Chinese were the only nationality prior to the 1880s) to own land and fish. Chinese were also denied the right to testify against whites in courts and were segregated in California's public schools. In response to attacks and discrimination, Chinese concentrated in businesses directed toward coethnics and those that would not compete with white enterprises—noodle parlors, curio stores, tailor shops, and rooming houses. Some occupations, such as cooking and washing clothes, were considered "women's work." During the first decades of the twentieth century, about 25 percent of all Chinese in the United States—a heavily male population—were laundry workers.[53]

John Higham's 1957 article "Anti-Semitism in the Gilded Age" offers extensive documentation of conflicts between Jewish merchants and both native and European groups. During the late nineteenth century, upper-class Americans resented the economic success of German Jews who entered the United States after 1848. In addition to being foreigners and non-Christians, Jews were also seen by elites as the harbingers of modern capitalism and, as such, responsible for "replacing the refinement of the old aristocracy with materialism and a commercial, bourgeois society." In 1893, Henry Adams reflected this sentiment as he wrote, "In a society of Jews and brokers, I have no place." His abhorrence of the ways of modern life, supposedly ushered in by Jews, was so great that he claimed to look forward to the initiation of open warfare between Jews and established whites, stating, "Then perhaps, men of our kind might have some chance of being honorably killed in battle."[54]

Immigrant whites of more humble means and limited tenure in the United States, including the immigrant working class and their American children, often shared with the well born a dislike of Jews. "The teeming Jewish districts that sprang up in the slums of big cities were surrounded by other immigrant enclaves where anti-Semitic attitudes could thrive." Migrants gobbled up yellow press coverage that implicated Jews in all sorts of conspiracies to warp Americans' opinions, steal their money, damage their health, and topple their government.[55]

European immigrant authors spread continental notions of Jew hatred to the American populace during the 1880s. One such author was Mme. Zanaide Alexeievna Ragozin, a Russian immigrant who sympathetically explained why Russians of that time period were persecuting Jews in Eastern Europe. Telemachus Timayenis, a language teacher from Greece who viewed European history as a struggle between noble Aryans and plotting Jews, introduced to American readers an ideology akin to that which would be central to Nazism.

According to Higham, old-world anti-Semitism was more than an intellectual curiosity for some immigrant communities. Rather, it was a call to action. "In the urban slums of the late nineteenth century 'Jew-bating' became a daily occurrence." Jewish peddlers who plied their trade in the poorer districts of large cities were continually taunted, stoned, and otherwise manhandled by street gangs. Later, during the 1920s and 1930s, anti-Jewish organizations like the Bund and the Christian Front recruited their membership from immigrant enclaves.[56] (See chapter 4.)

Greeks, who like Jews ran small businesses in majority neighborhoods, were also targets of abuse by native whites and other immigrants. During hard times, rivals vandalized their shops and complained that they monopolized good jobs. Customers would sometimes order meals at Greek restaurants but would refuse to pay, complaining about poor service or rotten food. Because proprietors knew little English, they had nowhere to turn when confronted with customers' dishonesty and intimidation. Many were harshly beaten when they sought to resolve conflicts on their own. Reflecting general hostility toward immigrant entrepreneurs, during the 1920s, competing restaurants would sometimes post signs saying "Operated by an American" or "Pure American. No Rats, No Greeks."[57]

In 1909, the Rhode Island legislature considered a bill that would have banned noncitizens from fishing for lobsters. It was aimed at Greeks by locals who felt Greeks were crowding natives out of a profitable trade and gaining too much control over the industry. In 1911, a Greek immigrant who hauled the trash of conational restaurateurs was warned by Irish competitors to "get out of the garbage business or we will kill all of you Greeks."

In 1916, chain stores (including five-and-ten-cent stores and druggists) who wanted to drive Greek entrepreneurs out of the candy and ice cream business in Chicago sought to enact a municipal ordinance that would have required candy stores to close on Sundays. While the ordinance was not passed, competition from larger firms, as well as the impact of the Depression, did reduce the number of Greek American candy stores in Chicago from near 1,000 in the teens to 350 by the late 1940s. In 1916, a Phoenix labor journal accused Greek and Chinese businesses of imperiling the future of local merchants, informing readers, "They are a menace to YOU."[58]

Greek-American ice cream store. Greek immigrants have long gravitated toward food-related business. By 1917, Greeks in Chicago owned some 925 candy stores and confectionaries and 4000 restaurants. Locals expressed their resentment against these entrepreneurial immigrants by condemning their unwillingness to enlist for service in WWI. The original caption of this photograph (which was taken 24 years after the Armistice) seeks to refute the ubiquitous allegation. "Southington, Connecticut. May 1942. Dimitrios Giorgios, who came from Greece, runs a soda fountain. He wasn't here long before the country entered World War I. He joined up and today is a member of the American Legion (shown making banana splits)."

Source: Photograph by Jacob Fenno. Credit: Library of Congress, Prints and Photographs Division, FSA-OWI Collection LC-USW3-042106-E.

In contrast to Jews, who as refugees from Russia and Poland had minimal rates of remigration, Greek immigrants initially viewed their stay in the United States as a temporary one. Accordingly, they had low rates of naturalization. Given the environment of hypernationalism that prevailed during World War I as well as the fact that Greek nationals were exempt from military service, Greek entrepreneurs were accused of benefiting from the U.S. economy without contributing to the war effort. In reaction, Greek business associations encouraged their members to follow U.S. regulation and treat customers well, and the broader coethnic community to support the U.S. war effort in numerous ways, including by buying war bonds (Greek Americans bought thirty million dollars' worth) and volunteering for service in the U.S. army.[59]

Despite these many incidents, relations among immigrant entrepreneurs and white customers were not always troubled. For example, Syrian and Lebanese peddlers are noted for their generally good relations with native whites. Despite their middleman role, German Jewish cattle merchants in upstate New York enjoyed better relations with Gentile customers—for whom they provided a vital service—than with local Russian Jews who didn't own cattle. Native whites and German Americans happily patronized Italian taverns in St. Louis. Finally, Lyman asserts that Chinese entrepreneurs' relations with whites on the West Coast were never difficult until the discovery of gold. Once the precious metal was found, however, native and foreign-born whites sought to exclude Chinese from obtaining it and began to treat anything associated with the Chinese population, businesses included, with hostility.[60]

IMMIGRANT ENTREPRENEURS AND AFRICAN AMERICANS IN THE SOUTHERN UNITED STATES

Immigrant business owners of the late nineteenth and early twentieth centuries initially catered to foreign and native-born white consumers. This is because the African American population in many northern cities, where most immigrants settled, was minuscule prior to the Great Migration. Given that relatively few immigrants and blacks resided in the same regions of the United States, it was in the racially segregated and economically backward regions of the agricultural South, not the industrial centers of the Northeast and Midwest, where Italian, Jewish, Greek, and Chinese immigrant entrepreneurs first began to service black consumers.

Self-employment offered the only viable avenue for upward mobility to the small number of European and Asian migrants of the late nineteenth and early twentieth centuries who settled in the South. In contrast to the northern environment, the South offered fewer industrial positions, and discrimination, unions, seasonal unemployment, and low wages discouraged migrants from taking existing jobs.

In Louisiana, for example, immigrants were recruited to work the sugar harvest when African Americans became increasingly reluctant to do so. Sicilian laborers who initially did the same work as blacks and made no effort to separate themselves from people of color were derided by local whites as "Negroes with White skin."[61] As time passed, they felt compelled to enhance their status, but the local economy offered few alternative jobs. By becoming self-employed as farmers, saloon keepers, and shop owners, increasing their levels of consumption, and adopting prevailing white attitudes about race, the Italians became more acceptable. Selling to blacks offered a route not only to economic survival but to approbation by native whites as well.

Noting Sicilians' embrace of self-employment, sugar planters who had recruited them as farm laborers complained that it was difficult to retain them in this capacity for more than two seasons, since "by [that] time they have laid by a little money and are ready to start a fruit shop or a grocery store at some cross-roads town. Those who do not establish themselves thus strap packs and peddle blue jeans, overalls and red handkerchiefs to the Negroes."

"One observer in Iberville Parish noted in 1890, 'Our town is flooded with melons but strange to say none have been raised about here. They are imported by the dago fruit vendors, who find ready sale for them among the darkies.'" Charles Cangelosi, a Baton Rouge businessman who earned his living in the fruit-grocery trade, maintained that, since African Americans offered the best market for cheap goods, it was easier for a beginner to establish an outlet of this type. While they had to endure epithets and even suffered lynchings along the way, by 1912, "the transition from agricultural proletarian to entrepreneur seemed complete" for Italian immigrants in Louisiana.[62]

After the 1870s, Chinese men who could no longer find work on western railroads traveled by train to the Southeast. In Mississippi, they established grocery businesses that catered to black consumers. Expected by their families back home to remit earnings, the Chinese found that the southern sharecropping system was incapable of generating adequate revenue. Like the Louisiana Italians described above, they saved and borrowed funds from coethnics and relatives to start small shops—as little as one hundred dollars was needed in the early decades and only four hundred dollars as late as the 1940s. To conserve money, they used the store building as a residence as well as a place of business. Until the advent of supermarkets in the post–World War II era, Chinese had a near monopoly over the grocery business in the Mississippi Delta, especially among those serving black shoppers. Indeed, almost 97 percent of Chinese in the region were employed in this single occupation.[63]

Chinese men in the South also entered the laundry business. However, "the strength of black washerwomen as a collective force impeded the further development of Chinese laundries." In the 1870s in Galveston, Texas, and thirty years later in Richmond, Virginia, black women demanded that Chinese laundries in the city close and initiated a series of raids against them. Hannah Monroe, president of the washerwomen's union of Richmond, criticized Chinese men for doing women's work and depriving poorly paid colored women of their already limited means of support.[64]

Jews also ran numerous businesses in small southern towns. In fact, because the South was so concerned with race, religious differences—including those between Christian and Jew—received less emphasis. Accordingly, the Ku Klux Klan notwithstanding, "in the South Jewish merchants established themselves with little difficulty." One study has even asserted that "probably in no other region of the United States have they been so integrated with the general population or subject to less discrimination."[65]

In *Caste and Class in a Southern Town*, John Dollard describes how, during the 1930s, Jewish store owners held a virtual monopoly over the retail sale of dry goods, running shops frequented by both black and white consumers. It was said, "If there is a Jewish holiday, you cannot buy a pair of socks in the whole country." The Jews were especially successful in selling to African Americans. "The Jews have treated the Negroes with courtesy or at least without discourtesy in strictly business relations."[66]

Immigrant entrepreneurs found little competition for this captive market. Native whites were castigated for trading with blacks and found the level of frugality required to turn a profit to be unacceptable. For example, in the case of saloons that attracted African Americans, the Italians took over from native whites. A "colored" service establishment would be of little prestige, however profitable, in a segregated society, so Italians might have been granted this inroad in a noblesse oblige fashion.[67] Competition from black merchants was limited because African Americans were largely excluded from business ownership due to poverty, lack of experience, Jim Crow laws, and discrimination from banks, wholesalers, and distributors.[68]

During the late nineteenth and early twentieth centuries, southern whites' hostility to blacks often spilled over to the immigrant entrepreneurs who catered to them. Accordingly, riots occurred with some frequency that involved assaults on both entrepreneurs and customers. The Atlanta riot of 1906 involved a sizeable and organized attack by a mob of "rough, half drunken young men and boys" who were incited to violence by a soap box speaker reproving claimed assaults by black men on white women. The violence, which was concentrated in the black commercial district of Atlanta and a black suburban area called Brownville, went on for several days. Before it was over, more than ten blacks and two white policemen had lost their lives and many more persons had been injured. Order was only restored through the long-term presence of police and militia.[69]

While blacks were most heavily victimized, an article in *Harper's Weekly* made it clear that immigrant merchants, including Greeks and Jews who served black customers, were also targeted by rioters and by city officials afterward. During the riot, the district's saloons and hardware stores (many of which were owned by immigrants) were smashed and looted. Following the cessation of open violence, serious restrictions were imposed on businesses owned by or serving African Americans. Every saloon in the city was closed indefinitely. In addition, "twenty two licenses for Negro restaurants and dives were revoked by the city council and thirty nine more were set aside for investigation."

Reflecting the racial prerogatives of the time, white merchants, "mostly foreigners, Russian Jews and Greeks—[who] run many of the saloons, pawn-shops, and restaurants, which cater to a Negro trade"—were harshly condemned and described as racially inferior:

> As to white foreigners who cater to Negro trade and Negro vice in this locality, it is left to the judgment of the reader which is of the higher grade in the social scale, the proprietors or their customers. That this plague spot is responsible for much crime is unquestionably the case. The very lowest classes of blacks gather there and their minds are inflamed by cocaine, the miserable stuff called whiskey, bad pictures and gross talk.[70]

As the Atlanta riot suggests, immigrant business owners in the South were in the difficult position of filling a gap between the white elite and black customers. As middlemen entrepreneurs, they experienced strained relations with both groups, yet depended on a system of racial segregation that limited their own social standing in order to earn a livelihood.

The frailty of their status was brought home during the 1960s. Fearing they would lose white customers, southern Jewish entrepreneurs resisted calls for the desegregation of stores that both black customers and northern coreligionists demanded during the Civil Rights Movement.[71] Similarly, Chinese grocers in Mississippi who faced violence and boycotts during the 1960s ultimately left the area. A Chinese American college student reflected on his group's marginal position: "Sometimes I feel as if my skin is just a shade darker than white, and sometimes that it's just a shade lighter than Negro."[72]

IMMIGRANT ENTREPRENEURS AND AFRICAN AMERICANS IN THE NORTH

While immigrant entrepreneurs in the South had directed their businesses toward black consumers since the late nineteenth century, it was only after they had established economic relations with native-born whites and immigrants that many in the North began to sell to African Americans, who were moving there as part of the Great Migration. Indeed, despite the fact that Jews and blacks had coexisted in Harlem for decades, they lived parallel rather than integrated lives and were largely ignorant of one another before the 1920s. In 1912, for example, a reporter for an African American newspaper observed that crammed Yiddish theaters reflected favorably on Jews' self-patronage and suggested that blacks should follow their example by creating their own Harlem venues rather than patronizing white-owned theaters.[73] This is a far cry from commentaries about Jews' dominance of Harlem's retail sector that would absorb the black press after 1930.

One of the earliest accounts of Jews selling to African Americans in New York appeared under the headline "The New Ghetto" in *Harper's Weekly* in 1897. The article describes how Polish Jews had moved from Baxter Street in the Jewish enclave of the Lower East Side to Manhattan's West Side, ultimately outnumbering black residents.[74] Here, Jews had opened some fifty shops, selling secondhand clothing, shoes, and hats to African American customers. The article notes that both Jews and blacks paid exorbitant rents for poor accommodations.

Making ample use of stereotypes, the author claimed that the Jews disliked their black neighbors but ignored racial norms and remained in the district because of the financial rewards available. In a parodied Yiddish accent, readers hear a shop owner's philosophy: "Pizzness is pizzness. Eef colored peoples come in mine shtore, I make him vellcome, and sell him goods, eef he pays." The article concluded, "Still, notwithstanding the adage that Negroes are poor customers, the former denizens of Baxter Street could scarcely have chosen a better locality wherein to dispose of their cast-off wares."[75]

Immigrant merchants and African American customers began to interact in Chicago when black migrants from the South entered the same Chicago neighborhoods—on the south and west sides—where European

Illustration from an article entitled "The New Ghetto" in Harper's Weekly. *It is one of the earliest accounts of immigrant Jewish merchants directing goods and services to African American customers in a northern city (New York), 1897.*
Source: Harper's Weekly

immigrants settled. As in the South, Jewish, Greek, and Italian shop owners remained either ignorant of or willing to ignore predominant racial codes. Wirth, one of the founders of the Chicago School of urban sociology, wrote, "Unlike the white landlords and residents in other parts of the city, the Jews have offered no appreciable resistance to the invasion by the Negroes. . . . The prevailing opinion of the merchants on the near West Side is that the Negro spends his money freely, and usually has some to spend, and thereby is a desirable neighbor."[76]

Immigrant entrepreneurs found relatively little competition from native whites in selling to blacks within black neighborhoods. Outside of ghettos prior to the 1940s, however, white store owners in the South as well as in northern cities including New York, Cleveland, and Chicago offered limited service or refused to sell to blacks altogether in order to maintain patterns of racial segregation. (Such patterns remained in place until the lunch counter sit-ins of the early 1960s.)

Department stores would not allow blacks to try on clothes and would not hire black salespeople, even when they were located in black neighborhoods and had mostly black patrons. Movie theaters, transit companies, and hospitals limited blacks' access or banned them outright. Among the infrequent instances when African Americans were served by white merchants or rented apartments by native white landlords, they were overcharged.[77] Given this racial and economic climate, some blacks valued the presence of immigrant shop owners in their neighborhoods, if they treated blacks well.[78]

Because immigrants' shops were often better capitalized than those run by blacks, the former were often seen as more prestigious, less expensive, and offering better merchandise than African American shops.[79] At the same time, immigrant entrepreneurs often found more opportunity and acceptance among black than white consumers. Hence, at least in some cases, immigrant entrepreneurs and customers enjoyed a symbiotic rather than conflict-ridden relationship. A degree of shared interest brought the two groups together.

African Americans were not the only minority population whose department stores were run by ethnic groups. A study of St. Louis's Italian American enclave points out that, even though members of this group were both insular and highly entrepreneurial, the community's largest businesses, furniture and department stores were run by Jews. Present in the United States longer than many other immigrant groups and having greater access to capital, Jews have been noted as the proprietors of larger businesses in many minority neighborhoods from the 1930s to the present.[80]

CONCLUSIONS

Conventional wisdom maintains that the most volatile conflicts in American cities have invariably involved African American consumers and immigrant merchants, while relations between immigrant entrepreneurs and white customers have been relatively harmonious. Such disputes are seen as precipitated by the unethical business practices of business owners and vengeance seeking by customers and are not attributed to the actions of power holders. The real case is much more complex.

Prior to the 1930s, conflicts between immigrant entrepreneurs and customers in the North involved native white and European immigrant customers because few blacks were present. In fact, many such conflicts occurred within single ethnic groups. Rather than occurring as a consequence of entrepreneurs' greed and customers' vengeance, conflicts were often a by-product of disputes over access to jobs and housing, strike breaking, and control over white women. Socially marginal institutions like labor movements and tabloid journalism encouraged such conflicts. However, so did representatives of respectable society like intellectuals, police, and elected officials. Finally, the earliest contacts between ethnic merchants and blacks occurred in the rural South and only developed in northern and western cities after African Americans moved to these locations in search of work and a better life. Race has indeed played a significant part in conflicts between immigrants and their customers. However, it has not always been the central feature of such interactions.

In recent years, the arrival of numerous immigrants from Asia, Latin America, and elsewhere has transformed many American cities, making neighborhoods long associated with a single racial or ethnic population now newly diverse. At the same time, a whole variety of groups now work as merchants in such settings. In these localities, the racial and ethnic dynamics of merchant-customer conflict have become much more complex and less focused on the black-nonblack color line than had been the case for decades. Accordingly, the nature of merchant-customer conflict in some American cities now bears greater similarities to that of the pre-1920 era than it does with the period between the 1940s and the early 1970s when most disputes involved immigrants and native-born blacks.[81] (See chapter 7.)

4

THE FATE OF MINORITY MERCHANTS DURING DEPRESSION AND WAR

The 1930s and early 1940s were hard times in the United States, marked by economic depression, xenophobia, and a growing awareness of the coming war. Even during the prosperity of the previous decade, resentment against immigrants and minorities had risen. The educated classes subscribed to ethnocentric theories that proclaimed the biological inferiority of those whose origins were not in Northern Europe. Concurrently, many of the less privileged supported movements that opposed immigrants, blacks, Catholics, Jews, and Communists. Such sentiments contributed to the passage of the Johnson-Reed Immigration Act of 1924 that imposed strict quotas on the entry of Southern and Eastern Europeans and excluded Asians altogether.

Once the Great Depression began in 1929, hostility against immigrants and racial minorities increased as millions who lost their jobs angrily sought scapegoats. It was during this time that two very different movements directed hostility against minority entrepreneurs in separate parts of the United States. In cities of the East and Midwest, merchants with origins in Southern and Eastern Europe (including Jews, Italians, and Greeks) who ran businesses in black ghettos were challenged by African Americans who sought more control over their communities. On the West Coast, the highly entrepreneurial Japanese American community was subject to increasing restrictions that, during a climate of wartime hysteria, ultimately resulted in their internment in concentration camps.

The experience of these merchants was marked by several commonalities. As outsiders, both Japanese and Jews could be berated without challenging the racial-ethnic status quo. Both groups were excluded from residential neighborhoods, access to education, and employment opportunities. Finally, in the eyes of many Americans, both were intellectually gifted but untrustworthy because of their supposed adherence to "un-American" religions, political beliefs, and national loyalties.

Despite these parallels, it is important to acknowledge the differences that distinguish these entrepreneurial groups and their contexts. The most significant is race. As nonwhites, Japanese were exposed to levels of both informal and legally sanctioned restriction that surpassed those encountered by any other migrant group in American history. Japanese entered the United States after Chinese laborers were banned by the Exclusion Act of 1882. Accordingly, they were not regarded as potential citizens but rather as temporary laborers whose presence was dependent upon the needs of whites. Their exclusion from social membership was made clear by an ever-expanding set of laws that prohibited their acquisition of citizenship, ownership of land, and marriage to a Caucasian. Lacking political rights and powerful allies, the Japanese had no basis upon which to demand fair treatment in American society.

In contrast, Southern and Eastern Europeans, including Jews, were white, more numerous, and settled throughout the country. They could own land, become citizens, and vote. While many were recent arrivals, some fraction of these groups had been residents since before the American Revolution, held high office, and played important economic and social roles in American society. Finally, the group with whom they had the most extensive conflicts during the 1930s and 1940s—African Americans—were poorer, less educated, confined to ghettos, and had fewer rights than they did.

Their minority status notwithstanding, both African Americans and Jews had access to political participation that provided a means to express their concerns and work toward the acquisition of additional rights and resources. Moreover, their political influence increased during the 1930s, when both the Democratic Roosevelt administration as well as Republican politicians like New York mayor Fiorello Henry La Guardia and Chicago congressman Oscar DePriest pursued ethnic and minority voters. In fact, from the mid 1930s onward, African Americans and European immigrants established patterns of political activism both separately and together that would shape American life for years to come.[1] In dramatic contrast, the Roosevelt administration provided no such support for Japanese Americans. On the contrary, its actions greased the skids for their rapid incarceration after the attack on Pearl Harbor.[2] This chapter explores movements against

European and Japanese merchants during the Depression and World War II. In so doing, it reveals how issues of race and politics resulted in distinct outcomes for entrepreneurial minority groups.

SEGREGATION AND SELF-DETERMINATION IN DEPRESSION-ERA GHETTOS

Difficult conditions in the recently expanded ghettos of northern and midwestern cities during the Depression motivated residents to seek social change. As noted in chapter 3, following the arrival of hundreds of thousands of southern blacks in search of employment and social equality, racial segregation expanded. Accordingly, people of color found themselves excluded from a wide variety of jobs, sources of housing, schools, and other social settings to which they formerly had some access.[3] The few unions that had organized blacks became more racially exclusive. During World War I, Cleveland's Amalgamated Association of Iron and Steel Workers actively recruited black workers. As a result, Cleveland was among the few locations where blacks actively supported the Great Steel Strike of 1919. However, after 1920, the "general conservatism and racism" of the labor movement prevailed, fueled by the "feelings of antagonism and dislike" with which immigrant steelworkers regarded blacks.[4] In the 1930s, 95 percent of unions nationwide excluded African Americans and took actions including picketing to keep them away when white employers offered jobs.[5]

Even blacks with college degrees were limited to the lowliest positions of porter, laborer, and janitor in firms and government organizations. Black doctors and nurses were not permitted to practice in hospitals, and black policemen and firemen were restricted in both number and level of advancement.[6] Black women were especially disadvantaged. Limited family income compelled them to find paid work far more often than whites. Lacking other alternatives, a substantial portion were forced to toil as domestics in the homes of whites, an occupation that exposed many to degrading forms of servility reminiscent of the era prior to emancipation.

The onset of the Depression made life even more difficult for blacks. Being "last hired and first fired," they lost many of the jobs obtained during the 1920s. With money tight in black ghettos, a significant number of black-owned businesses let go of their employees and many ultimately folded. As a consequence, black-owned banks and cooperative ventures like the Colored Merchants' Association also failed. Unable to pay rents and mortgages, blacks' properties reverted to the ownership of the whites from whom they had been purchased. White employers often laid off black employees to provide jobs for unemployed whites. Hard-pressed Caucasian families fired their African American domestic help, eliminating yet another source of income. Finally, relief organizations provided proportionally fewer jobs to black applicants than they did to whites.[7]

While money was scarce, hopes for a brighter future were not. Thus, recently established and sizeable urban communities of color fostered a sense of shared fate and solidarity that had not existed before. Illustrating this trend, an article published in the *New York Times* shortly before the Depression announced the emergence of Harlem as the Race Capital and pointed out that its 175,000 black residents exceeded the entire population of major cities like Dallas, Texas, and Worcester, Massachusetts.[8]

During the 1920s, the idea of black unity and self-sufficiency had been popularized by a social movement called the Universal Negro Improvement Association (UNIA) lead by a Jamaican immigrant named Marcus Garvey. Garvey's association celebrated African culture, proposed that blacks create their own institutions, sought the global unification of African-origin people, and called for a return to Africa via the movement's own Black Star steamship line. While short lived, the UNIA honored black pride and racial solidarity, emphasized the development of black businesses, and discouraged cooperation with whites. Through their participation, a cohort of young men who would become leaders in other movements for black self-determination acquired valuable experience.

Because Garvey himself lacked an extensive education and had been denigrated for having dark skin in his native Jamaica—where mulattos were seen as superior—his movement encouraged blacks from humble origins to voice their own concerns and pursue positions of leadership. Prior to the existence of the Garvey movement—and to a good extent after it— African American leaders were disproportionately from the well-educated and often light-skinned middle class.[9] For these reasons, Garvey's activities shaped the way African Americans thought about merchant-customer relations and set the stage for Black Power movements that would become especially influential after the 1950s.

ORGANIZATIONAL GROWTH DURING THE DEPRESSION

The combined influence of large and segregated African American communities, calls for black self-determination, and the grinding poverty of the Great Depression reinforced African Americans' race consciousness and provided fertile ground for the establishment of mutual assistance organizations. Describing the era, historian Kenneth Kusmer wrote, "The idea of racial unity, which black businessmen, politicians, and self-help advocates had been trying to inculcate for years, now grew much more rapidly because it was constantly reinforced in everyday life in the black community."[10] Building on these outlooks, African Americans created a variety of religious, fraternal, philanthropic, and political organizations, unions, and various social movements to address collective concerns.[11] Many groups that were established to provide the community with material assistance during the early years of the Depression went on to became politically active and sought to influence laws and policies in ways that would be beneficial to their members.

With the election of reform politicians, including President Franklin Roosevelt in 1932, Mayor La Guardia in New York City in 1934, and various like-minded officeholders in other cities and states, the potential for minority groups to secure desired action from government was enhanced. "The New Deal also politicized the black community. It freed black organizations from the immediate task of providing food and shelter while acknowledging that government had a role to play in ameliorating hardship."[12] Finally, the poor economic conditions of the Depression only increased blacks' resentment toward white-owned businesses in ghetto neighborhoods. If such businesses were to continue to play a major role in the ghetto economy, at least they should provide fair and honest service as well as employment to blacks—whose hard-earned dollars supported them. Accordingly, such enterprises—which were among the only representatives of white society present in black communities—were a magnet for community members' anger at the unjust circumstances they faced.

Hostility against Immigrants and Jews

While the Depression had an especially severe impact on blacks, it also affected the white immigrant groups who owned ghetto businesses. From the 1920s onward, entrepreneurial immigrants—due to economic competition and social preference—were increasingly limited in their ability to attend universities, find jobs in existing firms, or run businesses in white communities. During the first half of the twentieth century, "help wanted" ads throughout the United States often specified "Christian Only" or "No Jews," thus directing Jews into the ethnic economy.[13] Such factors caused ethnic merchants to seek out underserved markets like those in black neighborhoods, where they could run businesses with little competition.

Because of their demographic and occupational profiles (urban residence, relatively high levels of literacy and education, involvement in the recession-resistant discount goods niche, access to loans from Jewish communal organizations, and low rates of factory employment), Jews were less adversely impacted by the Depression than many other groups.[14] Their relative prosperity was resented by Gentiles who "voiced the opinion that Jews took care of their own and in the process everyone else suffered, reflecting the common belief in Jewish clannishness and self-centeredness."[15]

The era was further characterized by significant hostility toward Jewish Americans, including the rise of Nazism in Europe and the prominence of anti-Semitic movements in the United States. The most popular of these was led by Father Charles Coughlin of Detroit who ranted weekly to an estimated thirty million radio listeners about Jewish domination of American society. Other anti-Jewish groups included the Black Hand, German-American Bund, Ku Klux Klan, and Christian Front (a largely Irish group that included numerous New York policemen).[16] The Christian Mobilizers engaged in anti-Jewish boycotts and violence intended to reduce Jewish influence in American society.[17] In newly invented public opinion polls conducted in the 1930s and 1940s, Americans admitted to believing that Jews benefitted from the suffering of Christians: 67 percent felt that Jews had too much power in America, and almost 50 percent said they had a low opinion of Jews.[18] So hostile was the climate of the early 1930s that the American Jewish Congress discouraged Jews from responding to public displays of anti-Semitism in order to deprive their authors of publicity.[19] Observing the general level of hostility directed toward Jews by the larger society, it is not at all surprising that African Americans focused on members of this group as a target for their expressions of antagonism toward the larger society. As E. Franklin Frazier wrote, "In expressing their hostility towards Jews, they are attempting at the same time to identify with the white American majority."[20]

Within this climate, conflicts developed between African American activists and white merchants who catered to black consumer demand. Popular and scholarly literature describes Jews as the predominant entrepreneurs in black neighborhoods from the 1930s until the 1970s.[21] However, credible sources indicate that other ethnic populations and nonethnic whites also directed enterprises toward black consumers and, as such, also encountered conflict. In *Negro Business and Business Education*, African American scholar Joseph A. Pierce described "numerous businesses operated by Jews, Greeks, Italians and other whites which cater to Negro patronage."[22] Italians owned 75 percent of the saloons and cabarets in Harlem during the 1930s.[23] Additional evidence of Italian American involvement in ghetto entrepreneurship is revealed in numerous accounts of blacks expressing anger at and boycotting Italian American restaurants, saloons, pushcarts, and ice vendors following Mussolini's invasion of Ethiopia.[24] St. Clair Drake and Horace Cayton assert that, "in New Orleans, where Italian merchants owned numerous businesses, 'Dagoes' were the target of attack" by community activists.[25]

A 1934 jobs campaign by Harlem activists enumerated 151 Greek businesses on 125th Street that refused to hire blacks.[26] Harlem journalist Roi Ottley noted a significant number of Chinese stores on Harlem's Lenox Avenue during the 1940s.[27] Charles Choy Wong and Scott Kurashige describe friction between Chinese and Japanese merchants and African Americans in Los Angeles during the first half of the twentieth century.[28] Finally, because many of the most significant conflicts between white-owned stores and black activists involved chains like Woolworth, Kress, and A&P, which hired few non-WASPS, nonethnic whites were also active in running ghetto firms.[29] Hence, while disputes between African Americans and Jews are well documented from the 1930s through the 1960s, other groups were also involved in merchant-customer conflict.

Jewish Merchants in Black Communities

Regardless of the presence of businesses owned by other groups in black ghettos, Jews were identified as the group most heavily involved. Summarizing the period, historian Cheryl Greenberg asserted, "Issues between owners and clients, between whites and blacks, seemed to many in this decade to become black-Jewish fights."[30] As described in chapter 3, in many ghettos, blacks and whites owned approximately the same number of enterprises. However, because blacks lacked the capital needed to acquire a costly inventory, they specialized in service-oriented businesses and therefore received only 10 to 20 percent of all local expenditures.[31] Whites, especially Jews, owned many of the largest businesses in ghettos, including department stores, hardware stores, and furniture stores.

Paradoxically, a major reason for pervasive conflicts between Jewish merchants and black customers was Jews' willingness to associate with blacks. Indeed, Kelly Miller, founder of Howard University's sociology department, wrote, "The Jew makes the most acceptable merchant among Negroes because he knows how to reduce race prejudice to a minimum."[32] Unlike Poles, Slavs, Hungarians, and Italians, Jews seldom used violence to exclude blacks from their neighborhoods.[33] Accordingly, in almost every city in the United States—from Harlem and the South Bronx to Boston's Roxbury, to Cleveland's Glenville, to Detroit's Hastings Street and Paradise Valley, to Chicago's Maxwell Street, and to San Francisco's Fillmore— blacks moved into formerly Jewish neighborhoods. When Jewish residents left, entrepreneurs retained their real estate holdings and small businesses and as such found themselves in the role of outgroup entrepreneurs and absentee landlords.

In other cases, Jewish entrepreneurs sought out black customers. One of the most extensive developments of this type was the South Center shopping district on Chicago's West 47th Street. Opened in 1927 and 1928 by developers Harry M. Englestein and Louis Englestein, it featured the Regal Theater, Savoy Ballroom, South Center Department Store, and several other businesses. Unlike many white-owned businesses in black districts during the era, these businesses employed numerous African Americans in a wide variety of positions. For example, according to the *Chicago Defender*, in 1928, more than 125 of the South Center Department Store's approximately 150 regular employees were African American.[34]

In addition to their roles as merchants and landlords, Jews were immersed in an array of other relationships with African Americans, generally in positions of power and control. Jews often employed African Americans outside of ghettos, in small business, in factories, and in other capacities. Jewish housewives engaged black women as domestic servants. The context within which African American women were hired and then supervised in Jewish homes was especially humiliating. At least in New York, this practice came to be known as the "Bronx Slave Market." After public complaints, the La Guardia administration created employment offices to provide black domestic workers with an additional measure of security and dignity.[35] "Whatever the personal qualities of shopkeepers and landlords, Negroes are thus often in contact with Jews who are making a living from them."[36]

Jews were active in the entertainment business and owned a significant fraction of the nightclubs where blacks performed, including Harlem's Apollo and Chicago's Regal. They also worked as managers, music publishers, and record company owners in the field of race music. While unions generally excluded African Americans, those that organized blacks, like the International Ladies Garment Workers Union (ILGWU) were often directed by Jews. Even crime syndicates in black neighborhoods were often Jewish. In 1931, the Jewish gangster "Dutch" Schultz took over the numbers game in Harlem, cutting out African American runners. This deprived blacks of yet another source of employment in a field that relied upon black patronage.[37]

Because Jews were largely excluded from white-collar jobs in private firms, they flocked to government employment.[38] Accordingly, the social workers, teachers, and other public officials that African Americans encountered were often Jewish. And because educated African Americans were also dependent on public sector jobs, their supervisors were likely to be Jews. Finally, many communal organizations and philanthropic programs that provided advocacy for blacks, including the National Association for the Advancement of Colored People (NAACP) and National Urban League, were founded with the assistance of Jewish activists and relied on Jewish financial support and professional expertise. For all of these reasons, a disproportionate number of the whites that African Americans interacted with were Jews.

Reports about the extent of black hostility toward Jewish entrepreneurs vary according to locality and author. Of Harlem during the Second World War, Ottley avowed, "Negroes have never been associated with any overt forms of anti-Semitism, such as the 'Buy from Christians' movement, though attempts have been made to enlist their support."[39] In contrast, in the classic study of Depression-era Chicago, Drake and Cayton reported, "As the most highly visible and most immediately available white persons in the community, Jewish merchants tend to become the symbol of the Negroes' verbal attack on all white businessmen, and anti-Semitic waves sometimes sweep through Bronzeville."[40]

Several studies contend that the cost of goods and services in inner cities was higher and their quality lower regardless of who sold them. Reasons for this included the high rates of shoplifting and robbery, higher rents, higher costs of insurance, and greater difficulty in getting goods delivered. Other works found that "the poor (and black) pay more" and hence implicate merchants for overcharging.[41] The relative difficulty African American customers had in finding alternative sources of goods and services made them captive to the caprices of local merchants. In an article about ghetto enterprises, Sturdivant points out "One of the cruelest ironies of our economic system is that the disadvantaged are generally served by the least efficient segments of the business community."[42] Moreover, because Jewish businesses such as department stores, furniture stores, and clothing stores more often offered credit than those owned by other groups, customers were especially likely to develop long-term and unpleasant debtor relationships with Jewish entrepreneurs.

Being well organized, Jewish communal associations took note when Jewish merchants were accused of inappropriate behavior. When African American journalists or activists complained about the exploitative behavior of ghetto merchants, Jewish spokesmen often resisted accepting responsibility and instead labeled accusers as anti-Semites for referring to the merchants' religion. Contending that Jewish merchants treated blacks no worse than other whites did, they objected to being singled out. However, revealing Jews' lack of interest in addressing their own patterns of discrimination is a 1943 report jointly written by the American Jewish Committee and Anti-Defamation League. It admitted that "few Jewish organizations have developed policies and activities for combating general prejudice and discrimination against Negroes."[43] Even when they sought to do so, Jewish organizations found that policing Jewish shop owners' mistreatment of African American customers was a challenge because they often had little connection to or influence over inner-city merchants who happened to be Jewish.[44]

From the African American perspective, Jews taking offense at being identified as such appeared to be hypocritical, since they were so quick to condemn discrimination directed toward themselves.[45] In his classic essay "Negroes Are Anti-Semitic Because They're Anti-White," James Baldwin explains, "It is galling to be told by a Jew who you know to be exploiting you that he cannot possibly be doing what you know he is doing because he is a Jew."[46]

Partly because of this dilemma, there has been a long and complex discussion regarding the nature of both connection and antipathy between blacks and Jews in American society. Journalists, scholars, religious leaders, and communal activists have sought to explain the relationship in light of religious symbolism, class conflict, cultural orientation, and political expediency. Moreover, members of both groups have sought to classify the relationship between Jews and African Americans as mutually beneficial, exploitative, or a combination of both tendencies depending upon the time, place, and occupation of those involved.[47]

Regardless of the causes of conflicts between African Americans and Jews during the 1930s and 1940s, both groups could be counted on to at least react to each others' accusations. This was during a time when large fractions of the majority population along with major American institutions—including the military, higher education, corporations, and the government—maintained policies that openly discriminated against blacks and Jews. Their many differences notwithstanding, both African Americans and Jews had vested interests in condemning bigotry, lest they appear hypocritical as they demanded equitable treatment.[48]

THE "DON'T SHOP WHERE YOU CAN'T WORK" CAMPAIGN

It was in this climate of economic depression, with hostility directed toward minority groups generally and specific instances of tension between ghetto merchants and residents, that the "Don't Shop Where You Can't Work" campaign (also called the Jobs for Negroes movement) developed.[49] Despite high unemployment rates, white-owned businesses in ghettos, ranging from small mom-and-pop stores to large department stores and especially

chain grocers—which derived nearly all of their business from black customers—hired few blacks.[50] Those who were employed were generally in
bottom-rung positions like janitors and porters. Illustrating the prevailing
attitude of white merchants, when requested to hire African Americans,
the white manager of one Cleveland grocery responded he would "rather
die and go to hell before I employ a Negro in my store." (Following a boycott, the store owner sold his store and left town. Its new owner agreed to
employ African Americans.[51]) The same refusal to hire black workers was
maintained among many nonretail businesses—ranging from dairies to bus
companies and public utilities—which derived a large part of their income
from sales to black consumers.

During the late 1920s, a Chicago street activist who called himself Bishop
Conshankin, chief minister of the Ahamidab Church, developed a new approach to boycotts that was particularly suited to exerting pressure on white
stores. Rather than engaging in the extensive legwork required to compel
the community to bypass a targeted shop, he mobilized a group of followers
to undertake direct-action picketing. "Since few black people were willing
to cross a picket line in public display against a race effort," the strategy
worked like a charm.[52] Inspired by this example, other groups followed
suit, and by the summer of 1930, "literally thousands of people in one way
or another participated" with loudspeaker trucks, newspapers, and street
speakers exhorting shoppers and passersby to support the campaign.[53]

When the city of Chicago sent "lily white" work crews to repair South
Side streets, public sector jobs were brought into play as unemployed
African Americans ran workers off and staged a sit-in at construction
sites. After a tense interim, the city agreed to integrate work crews in
Bronzeville. Shortly thereafter, employers, including Woolworth, agreed
to replace departing workers with blacks until 25 percent of the company's South Side labor force was African American. By the end of 1930,
some 6,800 jobs had opened up for blacks. Several hundred additional
positions were secured in 1931.[54]

News of the successful jobs campaign spread, and activists in New York,
Cleveland, Detroit, Washington, D.C., Baltimore, Toledo, Pittsburgh, Philadelphia, and Newark initiated their own boycotts.[55] Bishop Conshankin,
who played a central role in developing the direct-action approach in Chicago, moved to Harlem in 1932, where, renaming himself Sufi Hamid, he
spearheaded the jobs movement there as well.

National in scope, the local nature of the campaign reflected the conditions, personalities, and interest groups of the city in which it was located.
These campaigns elicited diverse reactions from the black populace. The
primary goal was to obtain jobs for black workers in ghetto shops, not

ownership per se. Accordingly, boycotts and protests were just as often directed at chain outlets like Woolworth, A&P, or Kress as they were at stores owned by ethnic entrepreneurs. In fact, since large firms had more employees than small mom-and-pop businesses, greater numbers of jobs could be obtained by actions directed at them.

Despite their popularity, boycotts associated with the "Don't Shop Where You Can't Work" campaigns remained a source of controversy in the African American community. Progressives and nationalists supported them as did store owners, who saw in them a means of reducing competition from white rivals. The members of several Detroit women's organizations opposed boycotts, fearing that large stores—in league with the Better Business Bureau—would fire their black employees to punish pickets.[56] Communists objected to making racial distinctions among workers, while unionists saw the campaigns as counterproductive since many more jobs could be obtained if all workplaces—not just those located in ghettos— were opened to African Americans.

Some working-class blacks resented the movement as a means by which middle-class business owners could gain more patronage for their shops and jobs for their educated, light-skinned children, while darker-toned youths remained unemployed on the picket line.[57] Finally, while fledgling black newspapers supported the movement as a means of connecting with the public, major publications like New York's *Amsterdam News* were less enthusiastic because their largest advertisers were white-owned businesses.[58]

Factionalism divided even those who endorsed the movement. Many of those who developed the direct-action protest were street activists who had strong connections with the unemployed and rank and file. They were energetic, if unrefined, in their approach and wouldn't hesitate to use rough language, physical intimidation, ethnic slurs, or an occasional rock tossed through a store window to make their message clear. While the achievements of their mobilization impressed more reserved members of the African American community, their tactics did not.

In addition, the growing popularity of street-based leaders like Hamid was threatening to young members of the African American middle class, who regarded themselves as "New Negroes," destined to lead the race in its next chapter of advancement. Accordingly, multiple groups with different styles and agendas directed boycotts in major cities. Cognizant of their disparate tactics, they informally collaborated or at least stayed out of each others' way as they exerted pressure on employers.

Statements against Jews and whites were a major source of contention not only between pickets and merchants but among activist factions as well. Hamid frequently and pejoratively mentioned the ethnicity of Harlem's white merchants. He and his followers became notorious for their anti-Jewish proclamations.[59] Jews, however, were not the only targets of ethnic slurs. Hamid derided Italian entrepreneurs as "spaghetti slingers" and "wops," Greeks as "swine herds," and middle-class blacks as "uppity niggers." While a fraction of Harlemites responded positively to the chorus of epithets, others, like members of the Harlem Housewives Association, were offended by Hamid's "Hitleresque charge against the Jewish community."[60] In response, they contacted Harlem's ministers to organize a more respectable alternative to Hamid's campaign.[61]

Opponents fought back. A group called the Anti-Nazi Minute Men kept tabs of Hamid's street protests and brought legal charges against him for making inflammatory and anti-Semitic statements. A barrage of newspaper and magazine articles condemned Hamid as an anti-Semite, Communist, and fascist. Black organizations and newspapers that resented Hamid's tactics as well as his growing influence joined the chorus, referring to him as a Black Nazi, while the Marxist *Liberator* deemed him a "Chauvinist Black Fascist." Still other boycott leaders echoed Hamid's anti-Jewish diatribes that "reached the point where anti-Semitic handbills bearing bogus union labels, were openly distributed to the community."[62]

Store owners initiated legal action against the boycotts—successfully challenging a law that protected a workers' right to picket on the grounds that race was not a valid basis for union organizing. While the legal decision was handed down in November 1934, business owners cynically waited until January to lay off their black employees so that they could take full advantage of the Christmas shopping season before angering customers and provoking another boycott. The resulting layoffs left only 13 of 2,791 jobs on Harlem's 125th Street in the hands of African Americans.[63]

Bitterness and frustration among community members erupted into violence in the Harlem Riot of 1935. Touched off by rumors that employees of a Kress store had beaten a Puerto Rican teenager who had stolen a pocket knife, the uprising resulted in two million dollars' worth of damage, thirty people requiring hospitalization, and 120 arrests for looting, disorderly conduct, and weapons charges. A black nineteen-year-old named James Thompson was shot and killed by a police detective who claimed he had been looting an A&P store.[64]

According to several sources, white and Jewish-owned stores that refused to hire blacks were the most heavily vandalized.[65] However, demonstrating that white and Jewish-owned businesses were not indiscriminately targeted and emphasizing the goals of the jobs campaign is the fact that Koch's and Blumstein's—two Jewish-owned stores that did employ black workers— were left untouched.[66] Following the riot, Mayor La Guardia's Commission on Conditions in Harlem conducted a yearlong investigation. It concluded that the revolt resulted from the "deep seeded sense of wrongs and denials and the resentments of people of Harlem against racial discrimination and poverty in the midst of plenty."[67]

While the aggressive actions of openly anti-Semitic and antiwhite activists like Hamid and his cohorts were sources of embarrassment to many members of the African American community, in the context of the 1935 Harlem riot, they put pressure on merchants to provide customers with better treatment. While the white Harlem Chamber of Commerce denied that anger over economic conditions caused the riot—saying, "Does anyone seriously believe that those gangsters are concerned over Harlem's economic problems?"—they called for harsher police control and threatened to close their shops. At the same time, white merchants also urged their fellows to "lean over backwards" to obey price ceilings, hire blacks, and avoid raising rents in order to deter further violence.[68]

Skillful and charismatic leaders like Harlem's Dr. Adam Clayton Powell Jr. and Cleveland's John Holly were able to marshal extensive community backing and overcome factional disputes, making boycotts a powerful tool. Of one demonstration on 125th Street, Ottley wrote, "Harlem supported the drive, loudly and wholeheartedly. Everyone in the community, it seemed, participated in the boycott, even giving social affairs to raise funds. Business dropped to the vanishing point."[69]

In perhaps the most visible protest of the era, Powell organized a rally beyond Harlem—in front of the Empire State Building offices of the upcoming 1939 World's Fair—to demand the hiring of blacks. (Grover Whalen, president of the World's Fair, which had the theme of "Building the World of Tomorrow," initially stated, "I do not see why the world of today or tomorrow of necessity has to have colored people playing an important role."[70]) Pickets, who were entertained by Bill "Bojangles" Robinson and chorus girls from Ethel Waters's latest show, ensured the hiring of several hundred African Americans. Having acquired employment for blacks in ghetto stores, the movement went on to open up positions in utilities, transit companies, hospitals, dairies, government agencies, and other enterprises dependent upon black patronage.

In retrospect, the "Don't Shop Where You Can't Work" campaign had many important impacts. It gave blacks a degree of control over employment in their neighborhoods and contributed to black access to jobs in public utilities, transport companies, and a wide array of public and private firms, often in higher positions than had been previously available. In her study of black women, work, and the family, Jacqueline Jones claims that neighborhood "Housewives Leagues" in Chicago, Baltimore, Washington,

Detroit, Harlem, and Cleveland "captured an estimated 75,000 new jobs for blacks during the depression decade . . . an economic impact comparable to that of the CIO in its organizing efforts."[71] Gary Hunter concluded, "outside the federal government, no other organization during the depression was responsible for bringing more employment to the black community than job campaigning."[72]

In contrast to Jones's and Hunter's rosy appraisals, Frazier's response was circumspect: "Negroes succeeded in breaking the color-line in some white stores. But on the whole, this movement did not affect greatly either the extent of Negro employment or the character of Negro business enterprises."[73] While the jobs movement failed to transform racial and economic patterns for African Americans, it did offer a moral victory and an enhanced sense of community control during a time when blacks were experiencing few triumphs in their struggle for expanded opportunities.

IMPROVED RELATIONS AFTER THE LATE 1930s

As a consequence of the Depression and merchant-customer conflicts, by the late 1930s relations among Jews and blacks were poor. Jewish organizations refused to support the 1934 Costigan-Wagner antilynching bill in Congress. Frequent street protests by African American activists mixed legitimate anger with a tendency to blame the Jewish religion for unethical behavior and thus denigrate all Jews. In turn, Jewish merchants and landlords justified their practices as socially acceptable and economically necessary while claiming that any objections to them were anti-Semitic.[74]

In an attempt to redirect this pattern, certain black and Jewish organizations began to work together. Jews' concerns were often international in scope—focusing on the Nazi menace. In contrast, blacks were most interested in policies that had an impact in the United States, such as passing a law prohibiting lynching and reducing patterns of segregation that excluded them from education, jobs, and other social rights. Nevertheless, African Americans embraced the anti-Nazi crusade because it could serve as a means of generating support for their own goal of black equality in the United States.

Local chapters of black and Jewish organizations worked jointly to improve race relations and pass civil rights laws, while the groups' publications, including the *Chicago Defender, Negro Quarterly, Amsterdam News, Jewish Forum,* and *Jewish Frontier,* engaged in interracial discourse and encouraged readers to support a shared agenda. In 1943, a major Jewish women's organization announced "a program to study Negro problems and a concerted effort to bring about social action which will help to solve them."[75] African Americans, Jews, Catholics, and other ethno-religious groups collaborated under the leadership of African American unionist A. Phillip Randolph to compel President Roosevelt to pass Executive Order 8802, which prohibited discrimination by companies with federal contracts. Writing of these partnerships in the early 1940s, Ottley optimistically asserted, "So today, relations between Jews and Negroes have entered a totally new phase [of] racial rapprochement."[76]

Illustrative of 1930s coalition formation was attorney Samuel L. Liebowitz's presentation to the 1939 annual meeting of the African American fraternal organization, the Improved Benevolent Protective Order of Elks (IBPOE). Liebowitz, who had been made a lifetime member of the IBPOE for his defense of the Scottsboro Boys (nine African American youths sentenced to death after they were falsely accused of raping two white girls in 1930s Alabama), claimed that good relations among blacks and Jews must be preserved so that the two groups could continue their mutual battle against discrimination. Addressing conflicts between Jewish merchants and black customers, Liebowitz called for a "truce" between the groups. Accepting the legitimacy of African Americans' complaints of being victimized by Harlem landlords, Liebowitz stated, "We Jews denounce exploiters. If you register your complaints where Jews are involved" with one of several Jewish organizations "I am sure something can be worked out." Liebowitz went on to discourage blacks from supporting radio priest Father Coughlin's anti-Jewish movement because "Coughlinism is synonymous with Ku Klux Klanism"—a menace that threatens blacks and Jews alike.[77]

Taking a similar position, L. D. Reddick, African American curator of the Schomburg library collection and a lecturer at New York's City College, made a case for the two groups to address their differences in a climate of mutual respect. "Jewish leaders must use community pressure against unfair Jewish businessmen, and black leaders must remind their communities that an exploiter 'who happens to be a Jew . . . should be fought, not as a 'dirty Jew' but as a callous landlord or dishonest merchant.'"[78]

MERCHANT-CUSTOMER CONFLICT DURING WORLD WAR II

The start of World War II brought prosperity, mobility, and rising expectations but also new challenges to American society. The growing need for wartime labor, coupled with the draft, increased the demand for workers. Executive Order 8802 that banned discrimination by companies receiving government contracts expanded opportunities to minority group members and women after 1941.[79] However, the full range of wages and jobs available to white men remained out of reach for nonwhites and women. For example, almost no wartime contracts were extended to African American businesses.[80] In addition, black servicemen returning from a war widely publicized as being against fascist and racist enemies bristled as they confronted the enduring reality of Jim Crow. Thousands of white and black workers relocated in order to take defense jobs, thus increasing demand for housing in already cramped districts. Finding housing was especially challenging for blacks, whose residential options were limited by segregation and restrictive covenants.

While merchants and customers continued to be at odds, black and Jewish organizations with broader constituencies worked to cooperate, stressing shared interests. For example, sensing the tense racial climate in Detroit prior to the 1943 riot, a report on Negro-Jewish relationships in Detroit was sponsored by the Jewish Community Council of Detroit, the Detroit Branch of the NAACP, and the graduate school of Wayne University to study "the causes of the conflict" between blacks and Jews. The report downplayed the racial origins of discord. Replacing the volatile language of public confrontations with the more neutral terminology of social science, it suggested that racial conflicts were determined by culture and class. One section concluded that "Jewish exploitation as shown by prices charged is highly exaggerated." Another emphasized that since *both* black and Jewish merchants were least satisfied with customers in the Hastings area, "The type of customer rather than his race determines dissatisfaction."[81]

Despite such efforts to address tension, during 1943, significant riots occurred in Detroit and Harlem, resulting in arrests, injuries, deaths, and the destruction of ethnic businesses. In Detroit, the riot was an outcome of racial conflicts that developed as thousands of black and white rural migrants sought jobs, housing, and social space in the overcrowded and segregated neighborhoods of the Motor City. Building from a series of racial skirmishes in Belle Isle Park, the riot quickly spread to residential and commercial districts. Having heard a rumor that three African Americans had been killed, a black crowd attacked a streetcar conveying white factory workers and "began taking their spite and resentment out on some 400 'white' stores and properties," especially those "of a decidedly exploitative character," in the city's Paradise Valley ghetto. Black-owned shops were left untouched.[82] As time passed, a group of close to one hundred thousand whites congregated near downtown and proceeded to storm black neighborhoods, attacking residents, breaking windows, and looting stores. The police provided blacks with little protection and, in several instances, assaulted them. Thirty-four persons were killed, twenty-five of them black.[83]

Ethnic merchants, many of them Jews, occupied an uneasy location between combatants in the Motor City. Whites blamed Jews—who had been involved in interracial dialogue—as instigators and supporters of black activism, while Jewish merchants, as the only white presence in the poorest black neighborhoods, were visible targets for the community's resentment toward an unjust system.[84] Because the Detroit Riot of 1943 involved groups of whites, abetted by police, attacking black residential areas, it was consistent with race riots of the late nineteenth and early twentieth centuries. In fact, it may have been the last large-scale riot of this type.[85]

Later in 1943, Harlem exploded when a uniformed black serviceman was shot by a policeman for interfering with an arrest.[86]

In contrast to the Detroit riot, the Harlem Riot of 1943 (like that of 1935) involved blacks directing violence toward symbols of the establishment—police and shops—within ghetto neighborhoods. This pattern, which featured little mass black-white confrontation, characterized the urban uprisings that would take place in black neighborhoods for the remainder of the twentieth century. Observers attributed the Harlem riot to the fact that blacks' opportunities and living conditions showed few signs of improvement, despite the

Looters, Harlem Riot, 1943. The riot broke out when a New York policeman shot a uniformed African American soldier who attempted to interfere with an arrest.
Source: Corbis, originally published in *Life Magazine.*

booming wartime economy. As a consequence of the riots of 1943, many ethnic entrepreneurs abandoned their businesses in both Harlem and Detroit's ghetto neighborhoods.

Over the course of the war years, tensions between ghetto merchants and residents persisted as antagonists became more sophisticated. This is exemplified in a sociological study of conflicting ghetto business organizations in Chicago, one all black in membership and another biracial. To compensate for whites' greater economic resources, the black group adopted "the self-assumed role of race protector" and emphasized black solidarity as the means to achieve success. Its members depicted white competitors as Jews who sought to silence critics by labeling them as anti-Semites while doing "nothing themselves to restrain the greed of Jewish merchants, realtors and money lenders" operating in black neighborhoods.[87] In contrast, the biracial group included a small but highly visible number of black merchants that allowed the largely white organization to avoid being seen as "patronizing" in an environment of racialized competition. In this, we see the evolution of patterns of conflict, as black and white merchants sought to maintain advantageous relations with both African American customers and the majority community, while simultaneously depicting their opponents as self-serving and discriminatory.

The combination of cooperation and antagonism that characterized black and Jewish relations after the 1930s became a ubiquitous feature of American life. The two groups are noted as the most loyal supporters of the Democratic Party, have been extensively involved in the American left, and have worked together on many social and political agendas. As sociologist Louis Coser suggests in *The Functions of Social Conflict*, groups that are originally brought together through disputes sometimes learn to work together in a mutually beneficial manner.[88] That said, subgroups of both communities have also been antagonistic, asserting that their ongoing relationship has been unrewarding to their side while providing benefits for the other party and thus calling for its abandonment.

While the rocky relationship between African Americans and Jews during the 1930s and early 1940s can be seen as yielding benefits to both parties, another conflict occurring at the same time—involving Japanese and whites on the West Coast—had a far more one-sided outcome.

THE FAILURE OF JAPANESE AMERICAN ACCOMMODATION

Although the actual internment of Japanese Americans did not take place until 1942, in many ways, it was the culmination of trends in U.S. race relations that began in the 1800s. During the late nineteenth and early twentieth centuries, the West Coast of the United States required labor for agriculture, extractive industries, and the building of infrastructure. Faced with a small population and separated from sources of European and native white employees by long distances, employers relied on Asian workers. At the same time, however, members of the European American population sought to prohibit the arrival and settlement of nonwhites. In his study of white supremacy in California, sociologist Tomás Almaguer asserts that "European Americans at every class level sought to create, maintain, or extend their privileged access to racial entitlements in California." They "railed against racialized groups in an attempt to arrogate for themselves a set of material interests that they ultimately defined as being their due as a 'white population.'"[89] Members of labor movements were especially hostile to Asians, whom they feared as competitors for jobs.

When such sentiments resulted in the exclusion of Chinese in 1882, agriculture and other industries continued to require workers. Accordingly, increasing numbers of Japanese began to arrive. While the Japanese were considered racially inferior, at the same time they were seen to be hard working, organized, and so skillful as entrepreneurs that whites could not compete with them. In business, "Japanese were not merely as good as white Americans, they were better."[90] Whites also believed that the Japanese had both the ability and the desire to invade and ultimately overtake California. Such trepidation gained credibility following the Japanese victory over Russia—a European nation—in the Russo-Japanese War of 1904–1905.

While the Japanese initially worked as agricultural laborers, their population was highly organized and quickly advanced from being field hands to owners. By the early twentieth century, they achieved dominance in several occupations, overwhelming whites in direct competition.

Realizing the low regard with which the majority population viewed them, the Japanese followed a collective strategy to avoid antagonizing whites. This was achieved within an ordered and hierarchical community featuring churches, occupational guilds, Japanese-language newspapers, the Japanese Association (a body devoted to both group defense and internal supervision), and an array of prefectural confederations or *kenjinkai*. Organization was further enhanced by the strong and influential position of notables in the community. Finally, Japanese American leaders enjoyed the support of the Japanese consulate as well as a "prestigious group of white Japanophiles: churchmen, educators and international businessmen."[91]

In his study of Japanese Americans in Southern California, John Modell called this management of relations with whites *accommodation*. It involved suppressing undesirable aspects of Japanese American behavior,

Japanese store owner Hanwamon Natsumeda stands at his grocery store at 5021 South Broadway, Los Angeles, 1923. Japanese immigrants were heavily involved in the cultivation and sale of produce. Source: Photograph courtesy of Shades of L.A. Archive, Los Angeles Public Library.

emphasizing "Americanism," and avoiding illegal and otherwise problematic conduct—even to the point of sanctioning and seeking the deportation of conationals who engaged in gambling, joined unions, or otherwise threatened the status quo. Japanese Americans chose not to protest their discriminatory treatment from whites and were reluctant to move into neighborhoods where residents made it known that they were unwanted. As a consequence, despite their relative prosperity, they lived in some of the poorest quality housing in Los Angeles.[92] Epitomizing accommodation were comments made by the secretary of the Los Angeles Japanese Association in 1925, "I advise the Japanese not to demand their rights . . . or to expect to be treated on fifty-fifty basis with white men. . . . The Japanese question is very quiet now, though public spirit is easily aroused against us. As long as we keep quiet and make no move the public forgets us."[93]

The sole area in which Japanese Americans displayed aggressive behavior was in the economic realm, where they labored tirelessly on small farms and in businesses. While their economic competence was threatening, it also created wealth for white partners. Other minority groups—notably African Americans—have been blocked from developing successful businesses through the denial of credit. In contrast, the Japanese reputation for business became so well established that their credit rating was equal to that of whites. Because their communal approach to work allowed them to commit to future deliveries, Japanese fishermen were preferred over Italian and Slavic competitors by white-owned canneries in the Los Angeles harbor. White agriculturalists even supported Japanese farmers during a strike by leftist farm workers during the 1930s.

Despite the exemplary behavior of the Japanese and the fact that their hard work provided profits for white landowners, bankers, agricultural interests, and consumers, most whites endorsed restrictions. The continuing immigration of Japanese laborers to the United States was terminated by the Gentlemen's Agreement of 1908. The Alien Land Law, passed in 1913, prevented property ownership by noncitizens. To sidestep such limitations, Japanese-born farmers made their American-citizen children the owners of their land or developed cooperative arrangements with whites. Then, in 1920, even harsher laws—advertised with the slogan "Keep California White" by senatorial candidate James Phelan—were passed that further excluded Japanese access to farmland.[94] While Phelan was defeated, the law restricting Japanese farming passed easily. Three years later, additional limitations were approved.[95]

Having excluded the Japanese from all but a few occupations, whites sought to remove remaining options. Paradoxically, by limiting the range of economic opportunities available to the Japanese, these laws furthered the group's economic dominance over the handful of enterprises—small grocery stores, restaurants and hotels, and truck farming—that were available.[96] Constituting less than 2 percent of the state's population in 1923, Japanese Americans grew 85 percent or more of California's celery, berries, onions, mixed vegetables, and lettuce; 65 percent or more of the state's asparagus, cantaloupes, tomatoes, and deciduous fruits; and a sizeable fraction of other commodities.[97]

While Japanese Americans played an important role in the California economy, racism rather than economic competition was the underlying motive for many anti-Japanese sentiments and actions. Analysis of voting patterns for the 1920 Alien Land Law Proposition reveals that the highest rates of approval were in lower-middle-class suburbs of Los Angeles, where the Japanese were not economically active. In contrast, more affluent semirural regions where many Japanese businesses were located maintained consistently less support for the anti-immigrant measure.[98]

Ambitious politicians, including future Los Angeles mayor Sam Yorty, emphasized the threat posed by local Japanese in order to garner visibility and political support. In one popular fabrication, alarmists warned that the Japanese American fishing fleet was not only efficient at harvesting seafood but, moreover, constituted an alien military force, which was known to fly Japanese flags when at sea and engage in espionage and, when the time was right, could lay mines and fire torpedoes at American ships. From the middle 1930s until the early 1940s, several bills were proposed in the U.S. Congress to deal with the "Japanese Fishing Menace."[99]

In addition to being subject to official discrimination, Japanese Americans were also the target of social movements, media campaigns, and informal racism. Public and private employers refused to hire workers of Japanese descent, newspapers published defaming articles that provoked street violence, groups like Swat the Jap and the Anti-Jap Laundry League antagonized persons of Japanese origins, and labor activists assaulted Japanese restaurants and their customers. Despite the numerous ideological and cultural differences that divided voters in the large and diverse state of California, San Franciscans and Angelenos were unified in their antipathy to the Japanese.

Admitting that they were polite and took excellent care of their homes, whites nevertheless organized to keep Japanese Americans out of their neighborhoods and schools. In one part of Los Angeles, a white neighbors association actively campaigned to exclude a Presbyterian church that a Japanese American congregation had hoped to build.

As hostility between Japan and the United States heated up in the months prior to World War II, the Japanese American community made extra efforts to demonstrate their loyalty. Japanese American defense organizations mobilized, not to challenge mistreatment by whites, but rather to impose further discipline on the community and demonstrate their good will. The population even collaborated with John Lechner, a "professional patrioteer" who helped organize a mass meeting at the Hollywood Legion Stadium to exhibit Japanese American patriotism. Endorsed by the American Legion, the "I Am an American" Foundation, and the California Women of the Golden West, the event featured a pledge of allegiance and a ceremonial renunciation of Japanese citizenship. While Lechner declared the event to be a huge success, Japanese Americans were disappointed that there were few Caucasian Americans in attendance.

Given this level of hostility, when calls for the mass incarceration of Japanese were heard at the start of the Second World War, there was little opposition, and white agricultural groups actively supported the cause. In early 1942, the anti-Japanese chorus included voices from farming interests such as the Grower-Shipper Vegetable Association, the Western Growers Protective Association, and the California Farm Bureau Federation. "'We've been charged with wanting to get rid of the Japs for selfish reasons,'" the Grower-Shipper Vegetable Association stated in the *Saturday Evening*

Post. "We might as well be honest. We do. It's a question of whether the white man lives on the Pacific Coast or the brown man. They came into this valley to work, and they stayed to take over. . . . If all the Japs were removed tomorrow, we'd never miss them in two weeks, because the white farmers can take over and produce everything the Jap grows."[100]

While the New Deal is credited with outreach to immigrant and minority groups in other parts of the United States, including the Jews and African Americans described earlier in this chapter, the Roosevelt administration failed to protect the Japanese American community. In fact, President Roosevelt had already begun to devise a plan for the incarceration of Japanese aliens and citizens without due process of law five years before the war began. Ignoring the advice of Attorney General Francis Biddle and FBI Director J. Edgar Hoover, both of whom argued that "mass evacuation of the Japanese could not be justified for security reasons," Roosevelt provided General John L. DeWitt—the head of Western Defense Command—"a blank check" to evacuate the Japanese and place them in internment camps.[101]

Following the attack on Pearl Harbor, the Japanese were transported away from coastal regions and into detention camps for the duration of the war. Given little time to prepare for their evacuation, their property and businesses were sold for pennies on the dollar, while crops went unharvested. Although there was little public outcry about the treatment of the Japanese Americans, some pundits expressed concern regarding America's ability to feed itself without the commodities they produced.

In 1942, the entire population of almost 120,000 Japanese Americans living on the mainland United States was locked up. Paradoxically, however, fewer than 1,500 Japanese Americans were taken into custody in Hawaii, where the population of over 140,000 had few businesses but made up a major part of the local labor force. When internment for all Japanese Hawaiians was encouraged by Navy Secretary Frank Knox and other officials in Washington, General Delos Emmons, military governor of Hawaii, backed by most of Hawaii's leading businessmen and *kamaaina hoales* (old-timer whites), successfully resisted.[102]

The fact that Japanese Hawaiians were not seen as meriting internment while conationals on the mainland did suggests that the mainlanders' involvement in businesses—an issue about which whites had long complained—was a major reason for their removal. Reflecting on the internment, Modell wrote, "If the wish to reduce economic competition from independent Japanese American farmers and businessmen motivated some of the proponents of the evacuation, it is clear that their objective was satisfied."[103] Following their release from the internment camps, many Japanese Americans returned to their entrepreneurial occupations. However, hav-

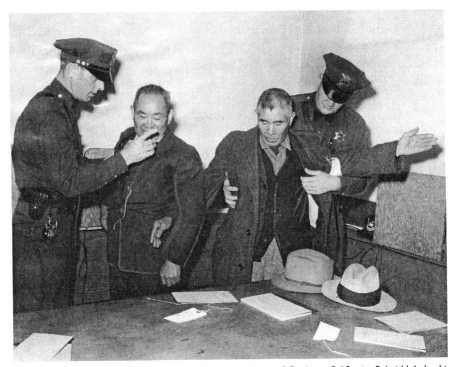

Japanese store owners incarcerated. Two Japanese residents of Gardena, California, Sohei Hakehashi, 55, a storekeeper, and Koichi Oriba, 58, a farmer, are shown being searched by deputy sheriffs after they were taken into custody on March 13, 1942, in a giant roundup staged by federal agents and other officers to intern persons of Japanese ancestry.
Source: Photograph courtesy of *Herald Examiner Collection*, Los Angeles Public Library.

ing lost their businesses, many had to enter domestic service occupations, including contract gardener and maid in the homes of whites. Such jobs offered little competition to the white agriculturalists who had objected to the Japanese presence before the war.

CONCLUSIONS

The 1930s and 1940s were marked by hostility toward minorities generally, and loathing toward entrepreneurs in particular. The most visibly targeted merchant groups were Jews in northern cities and Japanese Americans on the West Coast. Both were subject to popular derision and singled out for exclusion in recently passed immigration laws. However, a confluence of racial, demographic, and political factors shielded Jewish entrepreneurs from the unhappy fate of the Japanese Americans.

In addition to being more numerous, white, and eligible for citizenship, Jewish and other European-origin entrepreneurs were protected by the fact that their most vociferous opponents were African Americans, a group that was less endowed with political rights and more subject to discrimination than they were. In an attempt to gain strategic advantage, African American activists often depicted all entrepreneurs in ghettos as Jews—an unpopular minority group—as they demanded employment and protested unjust treatment. While many white Gentiles disliked Jews, few appeared ready to join forces with blacks to sanction them. Paradoxically, the stigmatized status in the larger society—to which both Jews and blacks were subject—offered a basis for collaboration as well as enmity. In addition, as a consequence of the New Deal, both groups had a growing political voice that enabled them to make demands upon government and public institutions and to defend themselves.[104] Such efforts failed to transform the fundamental racial and ethnic inequalities that characterized American society during the 1930s and early 1940s. Nevertheless, with the passage of time, most Jews and many African Americans experienced greater opportunities than they had during the Depression and war.

In contrast, the Japanese Americans lacked political representation. They had been permitted to enter the United States, not as potential citizens, but rather as a provisional workforce, brought in only because Chinese workers had been excluded. Regarded as unassimilable outsiders, they had few allies or supporters. Accordingly, they were unable to access the degree of organizational, communal, and political influence that blacks and Jews used to assert their rights and defend their positions. Ultimately, after the attack on Pearl Harbor, the same governmental entities that provided Jews and blacks with their basis of political and economic support facilitated the Japanese incarceration. In this, we see that the outcome of conflicts between ethnic merchants and customers are not determined solely by those involved. Rather, the context of the dispute and the actions of the larger society play a powerful role as well.

5

GOVERNMENT POLICY, GHETTOS, AND MERCHANT-CUSTOMER CONFLICT AFTER WORLD WAR II

GOVERNMENT POLICY AND MINORITY ENTREPRENEURSHIP

In the period between World War II and the present, the most notorious conflicts between ethnic merchants and their customers were associated with the urban uprisings (often called "race riots") that occurred during the middle 1960s. While residents' clamor against police brutality sparked many riots, nearly all involved the looting and destruction of businesses owned by ethnic merchants, suggesting the centrality of merchant-customer conflicts among these events. In addition, many of the persons to die during riots were victims of inexperienced, frightened, or hostile law enforcement officials who were attempting to subdue looters.[1]

A considerable amount of scholarly research, as well as political and journalistic writing reflecting nearly every ideological and economic outlook imaginable, has addressed the social disorders of the 1960s and has proposed an array of potential solutions. However, despite the extensive concern that these events have received from scholars, pundits, and activists, relatively little attention has been devoted to the role of government in creating the social and economic contexts within which they occurred. Instead, most analysis has fixed upon intergroup tension and rioters' motivations as the cause of collective violence. It has only been since the 1980s and 1990s that scholars have identified the extent to which government programs shaped the environments in which African Americans and other racialized groups reside.[2]

In the wake the civil disorders of the 1960s, government policies were put into motion to address the patterns of inequality that contributed to the outbreak of the riots. Among these were programs that sought to enhance rates of self-employment among economically disadvantaged groups. Such programs, however, were controversial because they challenged the individualistic ethos of American economic life and allocated resources to groups long deprived thereof. In reaction, a powerful anti–affirmative action movement sprang up. It used the courts, legislation, and ballot initiatives to restrict or eliminate programs that sought to assist groups that were identified as suffering historical disadvantage on the basis of race, ethnicity, or gender.[3]

This chapter explores the crucial but largely neglected role of government policy in shaping the environments in which post–World War II merchant-customer conflicts took place. Its goal is not to reject the importance of particular cultural or contextual factors in causing conflicts. Rather, it considers how government actions resulted in the formation of a series of contradictory policies that first established environments inhospitable to business, then sought to foster entrepreneurship among residents, and finally demanded the elimination of such programs as unfair.

THE GROWTH OF SEGREGATION DURING THE CIVIL RIGHTS ERA

Emphasizing milestones like the Supreme Court's *Brown versus Board of Education* decision, the initiation of racial integration in public schools and the military, and the entry of African American individuals into positions of visibility and leadership in popular culture, sport, and politics, history textbooks and popular memory often characterize the post–World War II era as one of significant improvement in the life chances for black Americans.[4] While important achievements did occur, it was also during this era that policies concerning home finance, public housing, and urban renewal led to the creation of large, segregated, impoverished, and poorly serviced black ghettos in American cities.[5]

EXPANDING THE GHETTO: URBAN POLICY AFTER WORLD WAR II

Following the achievements of the New Deal and World War II, many politicians, academics, and civic leaders had come to see ambitious and imaginative government policies as viable means of solving the problems faced by American society. It was with this mindset that the Federal Housing Administration (FHA) loan program, first established in 1934, was enlarged.[6] By providing low-cost, government-supported home financing, its framers intended to correct long-standing housing shortages, while reviving stagnant construction, home furnishing, and related industries. Planners hoped that these actions would create millions of jobs, foster economic growth, increase rates of home ownership, and improve the standard of living for many Americans. However, these programs also assumed that loaning money to racial minorities involved excessive risk. As a consequence, government policies both subsidized and hastened the movement of the white population away from urban centers, while confining racial minorities in economically declining central cities.

In addition to home financing, other policies including urban renewal, highway construction, and large-scale public housing also contributed to the decimation of black and integrated urban shopping districts, the destruction of viable housing stock, and the creation of unprecedented levels of residential segregation and concentrated poverty. Indeed, the ambition with which these policies were carried out meant that the resulting problems for African American citizens, the merchants who served them, and ultimately, the society at large were massive.

As the U.S. economy returned to full strength after the Depression and war, major northern "employers once again turned to black migrants from the rural South to fill the demand for labor in manufacturing, heavy industry and low-wage services."[7] Prior to the Depression, whites generally sought to avoid African Americans by reinforcing racial boundaries between adjacent neighborhoods.[8] After the war, the growth of "lily white" suburbs allowed Caucasians an alternative means of avoiding blacks.

Middle-class whites' rapid departure opened up a sizeable stock of previously off-limits housing for impoverished, low-status newcomers, including "Negroes, Puerto Ricans, Appalachian Whites and Mexicans."[9] "The combination of rapid white suburbanization and extensive black immigration led to an unprecedented increase in the physical size of the ghetto during the 1950s and 1960s."[10] Accordingly, the percentage of black residents doubled in many large northern cities between 1940 and 1960 and quadrupled in many by 1980. (See table 5.1.)

Credit standards that had been used by private banks and real estate firms since the 1920s were adopted by government entities like the Home Owners Loan Corporation, the FHA, and the Veterans Administration. These considered a neighborhood's racial makeup as well as the quality of its housing stock in assessing creditworthiness. Consequently, neighborhoods that included (or

Table 5.1.   Percentage of City Population That Is Black, Twenty Largest U.S. Cities, 1940–1980

City*	1940	1960	1980	City*	1940	1960	1980
New York	6	14	25	Washington, D.C.	28	54	70
Chicago	8	23	40	San Francisco	<1	10	13
Philadelphia	13	26	38	Milwaukee	2	9	23
Detroit	9	29	63	Buffalo	3	13	27
Los Angeles	4	14	17	New Orleans	30	37	55
Cleveland	10	29	44	Minneapolis	1	2	8
Baltimore	19	35	55	Cincinnati	12	21	34
St. Louis	13	29	45	Newark	21	34	58
Boston	3	9	22	Kansas City	5	17	27
Pittsburgh	9	17	24	Indianapolis	3	21	22

*Cities are listed by rank of total population in 1940.

Source: Gerald D. Jaynes and Robin M. Williams Jr., *A Common Destiny: Blacks and American Society* (Washington, D.C.: National Academies Press, 1989), 62.

were adjacent to) only a few blacks, Jews, or other ethnic or working-class persons were defined as mediocre or even poor credit risks. Relying upon residential security maps, "even those neighborhoods with small proportions of black inhabitants were usually rated Fourth Grade or 'hazardous,'" and hence declared unworthy of funding.[11]

By establishing minimum standards for lot size, setbacks, and separation from existing structures, FHA loans made it difficult to rebuild or remodel an existing urban residence. Such regulations were also biased in favor of suburban land use patterns that were inimical to urban housing forms, like row houses and attached dwellings. Restrictions were so rigid that entire cities were sometimes deemed ineligible for FHA funding. Such was the case for Patterson and Camden, New Jersey, in 1966, two declining industrial cities with growing minority populations.[12] During the 1940s, a Detroit real estate developer was compelled to construct a concrete wall six feet tall and a half mile in length to demonstrate to federal officials that the dwellings he planned would be inaccessible to blacks, and hence creditworthy.[13]

When the FHA refused to grant loans in certain districts, private lending institutions generally accepted government judgments of creditworthiness and also avoided making loans within the affected areas. This made it all but impossible for "owners to sell their homes, leading to steep declines in property values and a self-perpetuating cycle of disrepair, deterioration, vacancy, and abandonment."[14]

In many cases, the net effect of government loan policy made it less expensive for an urban resident to purchase a suburban home than to rent an apartment or to renovate an existing property in the city. However, because

Wall separating whites from blacks. This wall, 6 feet tall and a half a mile in length, was constructed during the 1940s in northwest Detroit near the intersection of Wyoming and 8 Mile by a real estate developer to ensure that blacks would not have access to his planned community, thus ensuring its creditworthiness as required by federal loan standards. Such policies subsidized segregation and white flight while restricting blacks to inner city locations.

of the tolerance or even encouragement of racial segregation in suburban housing, this option was available only to whites. Between 1940 and 1950, seven million persons entered the suburbs, with millions more following in the years after.[15] While only one-third of U.S. metropolitan residents were suburban dwellers in 1940, by 1970, suburbanites constituted a majority of metropolitan America.[16] Yet, during "the suburb-shaping years between 1930 and 1960 . . . fewer than one percent of all mortgages in the nation were issued to African Americans," even though blacks constituted about 10 percent of the U.S. population at the time.[17]

In addition, legal decisions, urban renewal programs, highway building, the creation of public housing, and the actions of discriminatory real estate brokers and neighborhood associations also led to the concentration of African Americans in impoverished ghettos. The Supreme Court's outlawing of restrictive housing covenants (which prevented homes from being sold to African Americans, Asian Americans, Latinos, Jews, and other minority groups in affluent white areas), in *Shelley v. Kraemer* (1948), would be assumed to have had a positive impact on minorities' ability to obtain housing.

Paradoxically, however, by increasing whites' feelings of insecurity, the decision actually hastened their exit from many urban communities. Along with the large-scale clearance of older housing via urban renewal, the end result was to disperse the black population over a much wider area, making African Americans majorities or near majorities in many major cities.[18]

While patterns of increased racial segregation were concentrating the African American population, other seemingly progressive measures, such as urban renewal and desegregation, also weakened the foundation of stable black neighborhoods and forms of entrepreneurship rooted in them. Despite the expansion of poor and racially segregated areas in many large cities, most retained districts that were important to middle- and upper-class whites. Elite institutions like universities, hospitals, libraries, foundations, businesses, stadiums, music halls, houses of worship, and museums were tied to urban locations by large capital investments, a significant infrastructure, and long-standing traditions.

Faced with a steady decline in the safety, prosperity, and upkeep of the local area and the continual encroachment of the black ghetto, these institutions and their patrons turned to the federal government for relief. The resulting legislation—the Housing Acts of 1949 and 1954—provided funds for local authorities to acquire slum properties and clear them for redevelopment. The laws required that an adequate supply of affordable replacement housing should be made available for displaced residents. The construction of large, high-density public housing projects was undertaken to satisfy this stipulation. While "liberal planners often tried to locate the projects away from ghettos," and discouraged high-rise structures, mobilization by white politicians and citizens groups carried the day.[19] Many of the projects were huge and built in black districts. While protecting the interests of white elites, this pattern ensured several negative outcomes for African Americans, including racial segregation, high density (since projects had to house both current residents as well as those evicted from areas that had been cleared for urban renewal), and the destruction of viable black neighborhoods, businesses, and communal institutions.

One of the most famous of these is the now-demolished Robert Taylor Homes. Completed in 1962, it was the largest public housing project in the United States at the time and included twenty-eight identical sixteen-story buildings stretching for nearly two miles in Chicago's traditional black belt, adjacent to Stateway Gardens, another giant high-rise complex and directly across the Dan Ryan Expressway and rail lines from white neighborhoods. The project included 4,300 apartments. During its peak years of occupancy, it was home to twenty-seven thousand residents; nearly all of them impoverished black women and their minor children. Only three years after the

Stateway Gardens, Chicago. This massive housing project, which included a series of eight 16 story apartment buildings, was built from 1955 to 1958 in an exclusively black neighborhood on Chicago's South Side. It was adjacent to another even larger project, the Robert Taylor Homes, that included 28 buildings. The creation of such housing projects reveals how government policy produced patterns of racial segregation and concentrated poverty that have predominated in the United States since WWII. Poorly maintained and plagued by crime, both projects were fully demolished by 2007.
Source: Steven Gold.

project's opening, the *Chicago Daily News* ran a six-part series describing how residents "faced a daily nightmare of broken elevators, erratic heat, excessive vandalism, and unsettling violence."[20]

Such neighborhoods were unprecedented in not only their size but also the degree of their racial segregation. Social scientists, journalists, and policy makers often compare black ghettos with ethnic neighborhoods occupied by Italians, Jews, Mexicans, Poles, or Chinese, assuming their similarity.[21] In so doing, they also contrast the dynamic enclave economies of immigrant and ethnic groups with the relative dearth of businesses located in black ghettos.

However, these comparisons are poorly conceived because there is a substantial difference in the extent of ethnic and class homogeneity and continued existence of black ghettos on the one hand and that of ethnic neighborhoods on the other.[22] Douglas Massey and Nancy Denton's analysis reveals that, while the most concentrated ethnic neighborhoods were only about 50 percent populated by a particular group, black areas are much more highly segregated. "The myth of the immigrant ghetto was perpetuated by Ernest Burgess, a founder of the Chicago school of urban sociology. In 1933, he published what would become a well-known

map showing the spatial locations of Chicago's various immigrant groups."
However, a reanalysis of the data revealed that these immigrant ghettos
were more fictional than real, as diverse groups resided there. Of the
many nationality-based ghettos that Burgess originally explored—German, Irish, Italian, Russian, Polish, Swedish, and Czech—only Poles
made up a bare majority of the population (54 percent) of their neighborhood. In contrast, in the areas that Burgess identified as being part of the
black ghetto, blacks comprised 82 percent of the local population.[23]

Further, most members of European ethnic groups did not live in immigrant ghettos. Only 3 percent of Chicago's Irish resided in the neighborhood Burgess identified as the city's Irish ghetto, and only 50 percent
of Italians (a group noted for its concentration in "urban villages" in the
United States) lived in Little Italy.[24] Among European groups, Poles were
the sole nationality of which a majority resided in coethnic enclaves. Sixty
one percent of Chicago Poles lived in neighborhoods identified as Polish.
In contrast, 93 percent of Chicago blacks lived in black ghettos.[25] Finally,
while residence in immigrant neighborhoods was to a large extent voluntarily, blacks were compelled to live in ghettos by law and social practice.[26]

Ethnic segregation was not only far less intense for white immigrants
than blacks but also much shorter lived. The peak year for immigrant segregation was 1910. After that, the American-born children of immigrants increasingly moved away from ethnically concentrated localities. In contrast,
as whites departed urban settings, blacks remained. Black ghettos became
more concentrated, such that members of the black middle and upper class
increasingly complained of being forced to live in crowded and run-down
neighborhoods, often with people below their social and economic standing. (See table 5.2.)

This had the effect of transforming the diverse, socially stratified and
largely autonomous black neighborhoods of the pre–World War II era
into the impoverished ghettos of more recent times.[27] Formal policies and
informal practices by police, the real estate industry, white neighborhood
organizations, and the courts further hardened neighborhood boundaries.
Blacks who tried to move outside the confines of the ghetto were often
subjected to violence.

Paradoxically, while southern blacks had moved North in search of a
less restrictive racial order, northern cities featured patterns of racial segregation that often outstripped those prevalent in the South. In the South,
where an established black middle class had an impressive record of home
ownership, African American middle-class districts were relatively durable.
They helped pass on traditions of black self-determination, including entrepreneurship, to children raised within them. "In the South, living in

Table 5.2.   Indices of Black Isolation within Neighborhoods of Cities, 1930 and 1970

Northern	Cities		Northern	Cities	
City	1930	1970	City	1930	1970
Boston	19.2	66.1	Los Angeles	25.6	73.9
Buffalo, New York	24.2	75.2	Milwaukee	16.4	74.5
Chicago	70.4	89.2	New York	41.8	60.2
Cincinnati	44.6	63.9	Newark, New Jersey	22.8	78.3
Cleveland	51.0	86.6	Philadelphia	27.3	75.6
Columbus, Ohio	—	65.2	Pittsburgh	26.8	70.8
Detroit	31.2	77.1	St. Louis	46.6	85.1
Gary, Indiana	—	83.2	San Francisco	1.7	56.1
Indianapolis	26.1	65.5	Average	31.7	73.5
Kansas City	31.6	75.6			

Source: Douglas S. Massey, "Origins of Economic Disparities: The Historical Role of Housing Segregation," in *Segregation: The Rising Costs for America*, ed. James H. Carr and Nandinee K. Kutty, 39–80 (New York: Routledge, 2008).

excellent housing has never been problematic because of Afro-American suburbia. . . . Descendents of this group are more likely to instill in their offspring a respect for and the need to participate in historically black institutions."[28] Conditions in northern cities meant that even middle-class blacks were unable to preserve neighborhood stability.[29] The shakiness of black neighborhoods meant that African Americans were often deprived of home equity, a vital source of capital for businesses and other investments.

POSTWAR GHETTOS AS POOR ENVIRONMENTS FOR BUSINESSES

Along with their much higher levels of racial concentration, black ghettos tended to be much poorer than the neighborhoods associated with other ethnic populations, yielding concentrated poverty, a snowballing effect of abandoned housing, and other forms of disinvestment. Black areas became increasingly incapable of supporting small businesses. As a case in point, sociologist William J. Wilson determined that these factors caused neighborhoods in Chicago's West Side ghetto to lose 75 percent of their businesses between 1960 and 1970.[30]

In addition to making black ghettos economically unfavorable for the creation of new businesses, urban renewal programs often destroyed existing black-owned enterprises by leveling neighborhoods and failing to provide the resources necessary to reopen in a new location.[31] Joe Darden and colleagues cite the case of Detroit's Elmwood Park Phase I program of the

1960s. While a few larger businesses with a citywide clientele survived and even benefited from relocation, about half of all those in the area folded.

> The effect on most businesses, however, was devastating; 69 percent of the 64 businesses in Elmwood Park Phase I were small, neighborhood convenience stores, mainly operated by owners who depended on surrounding residents for customers. Half of the businesses were owned by blacks, and all but two black businesses were local convenience stores. Fifty seven percent of the businesses owned by blacks did not survive relocation. The small, black-owned barbershops, grocery stores, and pool halls, which were so unlikely to survive relocation, were also important community institutions. The majority performed non-economic functions that greatly helped neighborhood cohesion: They extended credit, supervised juveniles, and served as centers of communication and contact. Many of these businesses simply could not survive as neighborhood establishments once their neighborhoods were destroyed. Some former proprietors remained bitter years after their relocation. Urban renewal had killed a large pocket of viable minority enterprises.[32]

During the same era, freeways, which were constructed with federal funds but with little input from local residents, displaced minority communities and businesses, while providing easy access to residents who wished to live and shop in the suburbs. "Freeways in major cities connected white suburbs to central business districts, but they were often built through core areas of black settlement. Many urban black areas lost their neighborhood shopping districts and successful small businesses as a result."[33] Among those active in the civil rights movement of the 1960s, the construction of "the Interstates was derided as building 'white men's roads through black men's homes.'"[34] While urban renewal and interstate highway programs generally included some funding to compensate persons forced to relocate, only property owners were eligible. Accordingly, slumlords received payments, but residents and merchants who rented their residences and store buildings did not.

Massey concludes, "After two decades of urban renewal, public housing projects in most large cities had become black reservations by 1970, highly segregated from the rest of society and characterized by extreme social isolation . . . this new segregation of blacks—economically as well as socially—was the direct result of an unprecedented collaboration between local and national government."[35] According to the author of a major study on the creation of postwar ghettos, "The lasting damage done by the national government was that it put its seal of approval on ethnic and racial discrimination and developed policies which had the result of the practical abandonment of large sections of older, industrial cities."[36]

Paradoxically, while large urban areas were becoming more segregated, other environments, including some middle-class districts, educational institutions, the military, politics, and both public and private sector workplaces were becoming more racially integrated. Postwar racial integration offered numerous benefits. However, it also had adverse impacts on certain black economic activities. For example, black-owned shops, restaurants, and hotels lost patronage as they were leveled by urban renewal and as African American customers were given the option of patronizing better stocked, and more affordable, white-run businesses.[37]

Integration also reduced the number of jobs available in black communal institutions like schools, colleges, newspapers, and nightclubs, while diverting talented and well-educated young blacks into government and corporations rather than ethnically bounded settings.[38] Accordingly, the number of blacks who were directed into self-employment or who obtained business skills and training via employment in a relative's business was further reduced.[39]

As racial tensions increased during the 1960s and 1970s, new patterns of interracial interaction took place in either racially neutral areas, such as downtowns, or predominantly white environments like college campuses. Because of both black self-assertion and white fear, few whites ventured into African American neighborhoods after the late 1960s, thus limiting the customer base that had sustained one of the last segments of black enterprise to rely on white customers. For example, as recently as the early 1960s, hundreds of thousands of white patrons annually—some coming from as far away as France—frequented black-owned nightclubs in Harlem and other black neighborhoods.[40] This kind of patronage would have been difficult to imagine a decade later.

Reflecting on these conditions, Massey and Denton wrote, "Segregation plays a key role in depriving poor black families of access to goods and services because it interacts with poverty to create neighborhood conditions that make it nearly impossible to sustain a viable retail sector . . . poor blacks live in neighborhoods that typically contain only the barest rudiments of retail trade. They are left without goods and services that are routinely available to the poor of other groups."[41] Such locations are characterized by additional business liabilities as well, including high rates of shoplifting and theft, costly insurance, high taxes, and poor quality public services.[42]

Low-income neighborhoods associated with other ethnic populations—such as those of recently arrived Latinos or Asians—are noted to have more extensive entrepreneurial activity than those of African Americans. This is because such neighborhoods are less ethnically concentrated and less impoverished than those of poor blacks.[43] As Mary Fischer, Douglas Massey, Mario Small, and Monica McDermott note, neighborhoods that feature a high concentration of impoverished African Americans have fewer small businesses than other neighborhoods. "A high rate of metropolitan poverty sharply lowers the odds that a group's members will be self-employed."[44] While the initial creation of concentrated black neighborhoods in northern cities during the teens and 1920s (a consequence of the Great Migration of southern blacks into northern cities after World War I) led to the golden era of black entrepreneurship, there is little evidence that far greater levels of black residential concentration after the 1960s had a similar benefit.[45] As Fischer and Massey assert, "Whereas some degree of geographic concentration is probably beneficial for certain types of ethnic entrepreneurship (businesses catering to the tastes of a particular racial or ethnic group, for example), higher levels of residential segregation are likely to be detrimental to entrepreneurial endeavors because of the tendency for segregation to concentrate poverty. . . . Our results reveal that beyond moderate levels, residential segregation actually works to lower the odds of entrepreneurship . . . creating . . . supremely unfavorable economic environments."[46]

The impoverished conditions of inner-city communities meant that chances for business success were especially low for African Americans. According to a 1970 study of urban businesses in Boston, Chicago, and Washington, D.C., between 1966 and 1968 that included ninety-two African American respondents, black entrepreneurs felt especially prone to losing their businesses during civil disorders because of their lack of capital, low profit margins, inability to obtain insurance, and need to maintain positive relations with customers via giveaways.[47] Jennifer Lee's study of black, Jewish, and Korean merchants in New York and Philadelphia during the 1990s offers similar findings about African Americans' difficulties in making a profit while dealing with requests for preferential treatment from coethnic customers.[48] (See chapter 8.)

Because of these several disadvantages encountered by black entrepreneurs, even in cities where there is a relatively small foreign-born population—in places like Cleveland, Detroit, and Flint—middleman groups, who are well endowed with business skills and have access to investment capital from extended families but few options for well-paid work in the larger society, dominate the retail sector in black neighborhoods.[49]

THE RIOTS

Large, poorly served, and impoverished black neighborhoods of the type expanded by government policies were rocked by ghetto revolts between 1964 and 1969. A national advisory commission tabulated 164 such riots during the first nine months of 1967, and 1,893 between 1964 and 1969.[50] The single largest event of the era occurred in Detroit and resulted in the death of thirty-three persons, the looting of 2,700 businesses, and destruction of fifty million dollars' worth of property, leaving some five thousand persons homeless, most of them black.[51] A notable feature of these 1960s riots was attacks on white-owned businesses. According to Ivan Light, "Although the various riots differed in intensity and duration, wherever they occurred, they usually involved attacks by local blacks on white-owned stores in their neighborhoods. Looting and burning of retail stores was the basic scenario of nearly every riot, disturbance and uprising."[52]

While the events took a variety of forms, the fact that sociologist Morris Janowitz labeled them "commodity riots" to distinguish them from the intergroup confrontations he called "communal riots" that predominated prior to the 1940s suggests the prevalence of attacks on businesses in these events.[53] One estimate asserts that, during the uprisings of the 1960s, more than ten thousand stores were looted.[54]

Not all events, however, took place in major cities such as Newark, Detroit, or Los Angeles. Small towns like York, Pennsylvania (1970 population at fifty thousand), were also rocked by racial violence.[55] James Loewen describes how long-established Chinese and white-owned grocery stores in small Mississippi Delta towns were also targeted both by violence and boycotts during the late 1960s.[56]

Coverage at the time of the riots often focused on the anger and hostility of rioters.[57] Retrospective research, however, suggests that a considerable amount of the violence and lives lost could be attributed to the actions of ill-trained National Guardsmen, vengeance-seeking police, and trigger-happy business owners.[58] For example, civilians in Detroit and Newark were killed by police and National Guard troops who sought to detain looters and eradicate "snipers" (who probably did not exist).[59] The Newark riot included what came to be known as the infamous "soul brother" shootings, whereby, in an act of vengeance, white police fired hundreds of rounds of ammunition at black-owned businesses whose proprietors had written "soul brother" on the front of their shops in order to discourage fellow blacks from looting them.[60] In Detroit, white business owner Richard P. Shugar was given a life sentence by an all-white jury for the shotgun murder of Nathaniel Edmonds, an African American auto worker who was killed in his own backyard following an argument that ensued when Shugar, who drove past the victim's residence, accused him of breaking into his store.[61]

A voluminous and often contradictory literature addresses the 1960s uprisings and identifies a wide range of contributing factors. They include African American members of the baby boom generation entering their

Richard P. Shugar, a white store owner who was given a life sentence by an all-white jury for the shotgun murder of Nathaniel Edmonds, an African American auto worker who was killed in his own backyard following an argument that ensued when Shugar, who drove past the victim's residence, accused Edmonds of breaking into his store during the civil disorder in Detroit in the summer of 1967.
Source: Walter P. Reuther Library, Wayne State University.

teens and early twenties; blacks' feelings of frustration at their difficulty in achieving middle-class status and equality (especially in contrast to the images of affluence displayed on increasingly available television); the impact of various social movements of the 1960s—civil rights, antiwar, black power, and anticolonialism—that catalyzed demands for community control; the public condemnation of police brutality; the apparent willingness of the Kennedy and Johnson administrations to respond to black demands; and, later, the race-baiting law and order agendas of Nixon and Agnew, George Wallace, and the like.[62]

Significant debates also exist about the motivations of those who attacked businesses. Some authors contend that their actions were political and that rioters were striking back at an oppressive social order with looters targeting the most exploitative merchants.[63] Others assert that rioters were disaffected and marginal youth or criminals whose actions received minimal support from most local residents.[64] Still another body of scholarship contends that looting was opportunistic. Given that "riots" occurred in so many cities during the middle 1960s, as well as the difficulty of assessing the social characteristics and motives of those involved, it is challenging to provide an inclusive and satisfactory explanation for the many forms of merchant-customer conflict that transpired during the urban uprisings of the 1960s and since.[65]

While evidence of rioters' seeking out specific groups of ethnically defined merchants does exist, a considerable body of data suggests that stores were selected for burning and looting by opportunism rather than intentional targeting. For example, in their comprehensive analysis of newspaper reports of "race riots" in 204 U.S. cities between 1954 and 1992, Susan Olzak and Suzanne Shanahan found that only 17 percent of events involved grievances against one particular ethnic group as a reason for rioting. In contrast, several reports suggest that looting and burning of shops was based on the type of merchandise they carried as opposed to the ethnicity of their owners.[66] Food, liquor, and merchandise were favored, while restaurants were generally left alone.[67]

Surveys of arrestees also find opportunism rather than intergroup hostility as an explanation for looting. Suggesting this pattern, the persons who sacked Grinnell's Music Shop in Detroit in 1967 removed electric guitars and jazz albums but left classical records untouched.[68] Additional evidence indicates that burning and looting was initiated for reasons beyond customers' anger at merchants. Owners sometimes ignited stores during the time of chaos in order to collect insurance. According to "the head of the Detroit branch of the Anti-Defamation league . . . organized crime had taken advantage of the riot to burn dry cleaning establishments and bowling alleys that they had been unable to take control of."[69]

Challenging the centrality of racial conflict in the selection of stores for looting is the fact that black stores were frequently targeted. For example, while African Americans owned 38 percent of the stores in the city during the time of the Detroit Riot of 1967, 27 percent of the looted stores were black owned, including long-established and widely respected communal institutions like the city's finest African American restaurant, a black-owned pharmacy, and a successful clothing store.[70] Considering that Detroit stores owned by nonblacks, notably Jews and Chaldeans, were larger than those in the hands of blacks and carried more desirable merchandise, the fraction of black-owned stores that were looted appears to be quite large.

A fifteen-city study of ghetto merchants and civil disorders determined that other factors were "far more important" than race in determining which businesses would be vandalized. Ghetto residents often saw white and black merchants as "very much alike in the way they treat[ed] customers."[71] According to Howard Aldrich and Albert Reiss's 1966–1968 study of 466 businesses in urban areas, black shop owners were more likely to have purchased a gun for store protection than whites. The authors concluded, "The situation for non-whites [merchants] is much the same, if not worse" as it is for whites.[72] Accordingly, many observers assert that attacks on stores have been motivated as much by class as racial antagonism. As sociologist Jeffrey Page argued, "Apparently class position as defined purely by economic position is the major determinant of rioting."[73]

A trend toward opportunistic rather than targeted looting is well documented in post-1960s uprisings as well. While there was extensive discussion of tension between African Americans and Koreans both before and after the Los Angeles Uprising of 1992, 40 percent of destroyed businesses were owned by Latinos—a group seldom mentioned as parasitic entrepreneurs prior to the event. Further, the one business owner killed during the melee was Thanh Lam, the twenty-five-year-old Chinese Vietnamese proprietor of a Compton shop.[74] Analyses of looting and damage associated with the 1992 Chicago Bulls riot and the 1980 riot in Miami also determined that a wide variety of ethnic merchants were looted and that opportunism rather than nationality played an important role in target selection.[75]

Finally, even if some of those who targeted stores were motivated by their anger at the ethnic merchants who owned them, studies suggest that relatively small fractions of ghetto residents actually supported rioters' actions. Generally, less than 5 percent of local residents actually participated in any form of rioting, and the approval of the actions of rioters includes only a minority. Support was highest among young males, but only about 30 percent of all African American residents of Detroit (in 1967) and 30 percent of residents in Watts (in 1965) "reported that they sympathized with the rioters." In contrast, a review of ghetto uprisings reveals that some fraction of local residents typically engage in antiriot actions, sometimes at risk to their own safety.[76]

Rather than attributing the destruction of businesses to ethnic antagonism, several studies suggest that civil disorders are associated with forms of economic and social oppression that are products of persons being compelled to reside in impoverished ghettos. These include police brutality and competition for scarce resources like housing and jobs, especially during periods of population growth.[77] Such conditions are consistent with the patterns of increasing poverty and racial segregation associated with post–World War II urban America. Moreover, while the specific events that ignited civil disorders in one city are likely to be distinct from those in another, nearly all of the environments where uprisings have occurred since the 1960s share factors of concentrated poverty, racial segregation, police brutality, and high rates of unemployment, especially among young males.[78] Accordingly, violent conflicts between merchants and their customers often appear to be a product of the larger context.

MERCHANTS DEPART FROM THE GHETTO

A significant consequence of the 1960s riots was the large-scale exit of businesses—be they owned by corporations or individual entrepreneurs—from inner cities. A 1969 survey of three hundred merchants in Boston's black ghettos found that 25 percent had liquidated their operations and another 50 percent intended to do so.[79] Businesses left because of fear of crime, inability to obtain insurance, lack of profitability, and other factors. Another study claimed that "some businesses move without finding a buyer, leaving vacant and boarded-up stores behind as they head for the suburbs. This trend shows no signs of abating."[80]

The civil disorders of the 1960s were but one of the factors making conditions economically difficult in urban neighborhoods. Additional sources of decline had global origins. These included the two oil price shocks of the 1970s and the rise in international economic competition. Their result was to reduce demand for U.S.-made products, thus yielding massive layoffs as major employers began to leave inner-city locations for the suburbs, the sunbelt, and ultimately, offshore production. Among the industries most directly affected were the unionized manufacturing concerns that provided a large fraction of the best jobs to inner-city residents.[81] Between 1970 and 1984, New York City lost almost 500,000 jobs requiring less than a high school education, while Philadelphia lost over 150,000 such positions. From 1978 to 1989, South Central Los Angeles lost nearly 200,000 jobs, and between 1967 and 1985, Detroit lost 195,000 jobs.[82]

Moreover, urban redevelopment policies since the 1970s have generally been directed toward downtowns and suburbs, leaving the settings where African Americans live in dire conditions.[83] Such schemes created many jobs. However, they generally fell into two categories—highly skilled and service related—both of which were generally beyond the reach of ghetto residents. The former required high levels of education that ghetto residents lacked. The latter were directed, according with employers' preferences, to recent immigrants through the use of ethnic hiring networks.[84]

With jobs scarce, formerly crowded ghettos began to lose their population, thus reducing consumer demand. This led to the closing of numerous
shops.[85] As a consequence, not long after their construction, it became all
too apparent that many of the giant, segregated housing projects created
between the 1950s and the 1970s were an abysmal failure. Filthy, isolated,
dangerous, and plagued by crime, many were demolished only a few decades after they had been built.[86]

SPONSORED DEPARTURE

Jews were the largest group of ethnic merchants in black ghettos between
the 1930s and the late 1960s.[87] During the 1930s and 1940s, Jewish communal organizations defended Jewish merchants against black customers'
and activists' complaints about poor treatment or unfair competition. (See
chapter 4.) However, by the 1960s, the American Jewish population had
become much more educated and upwardly mobile, and less dependent
on small business as a major base of income.[88] As such, Jewish organizations increasingly regarded conflicts between Jewish merchants and African
Americans as politically repugnant and detrimental to Jews' reputation in
American society.

While the decision to close ghetto shops was ultimately made by the
business owner, the coethnic community encouraged niche abandonment
through programs that would foster the sale of inner-city shops to African
Americans. In 1966, articles appeared in *National Review* and *Conservative
Judaism* suggesting that the larger Jewish community should both assist and
compel Jewish inner-city merchants and slumlords to sell their holdings to
blacks in order to advance black self-sufficiency and diffuse a major source
of black-Jewish tension.[89] Toward the same end, in 1969 and 1970, the
American Jewish Congress and the Interracial Council for Business Opportunities sponsored "Project Transfer" to encourage the purchase by blacks
of profit-making, white-owned businesses in the ghetto, with several of the
sellers being Jews nearing retirement age. By the 1970s, Jews had largely
abandoned their ownership of small businesses in inner-city locations and
had reduced their involvement in retail enterprise more generally.[90]

Of course, not all Jews and other white ethnics endorsed campaigns encouraging ghetto merchants to sell their firms. Some, including those who
lost stores during riots, remained committed to the communities where their
businesses had been located.[91] Others supported law and order agendas that
challenged liberal approaches to urban problems and went on to become active in the Republican Party and other conservative organizations.[92]

Activists and local residents hoped that the exit of white entrepreneurs would expand black entrepreneurship. However, low rates of black business ownership continued in most locations. Aldrich and Reiss's study of 466 inner-city businesses in Chicago, Washington, D.C., and Boston from 1966 to 1968 found that, following the disorders, only three enterprises had changed hands from black to white.[93] By the mid-1970s and 1980s, a growing number of shops in inner-city neighborhoods were in the hands of recent immigrant groups, including Koreans, Arabs, Vietnamese, and Cubans who purchased them from Jewish and other white entrepreneurs.[94] As newcomers who often lacked knowledge of U.S. history and culture, they were generally without institutional ties through which they might resolve tensions with customers. In addition, they were themselves subject to racism and xenophobia. In many cases, disputes between new immigrant entrepreneurs and ghetto residents were as bad as or worse than those that previously embroiled European-origin merchants and black customers.[95]

BUSINESS DEVELOPMENT PROGRAMS

The peak period of ghetto uprisings or riots was quite brief, with numerous events taking place only between 1964 and 1969. However, their occurrence provoked a significant policy transformation, one that at least acknowledged the terrible conditions under which numerous blacks were forced to live and specifically sought to increase available opportunities to remedy them.[96] Among these, a variety of government programs were established to expand the ability of ethnic minorities, women, and other disadvantaged groups to participate in the mainstream economy. Some programs sought to increase the number and viability of businesses owned by targeted groups. Others expanded opportunities for education and for jobs in existing firms. While not focused specifically on self-employment, the latter often contributed to the growth of ethnic economies by allowing group members to develop the skills needed to run a business, to qualify for credit, and to amass the personal savings, experience, and connections that facilitate self-employment.[97]

During the 1960s and early 1970s, proponents of black self-determination, notably black Muslims, addressed the importance of coethnic businesses and emphasized views of black independence that had been advocated by W. E. B. Du Bois, Marcus Garvey, and Booker T. Washington.[98] At the same time, however, many black and white progressives embraced Marxism.[99] Convinced of the flaws of capitalism, they often concurred with E. Franklin Frazier's critique and held that businesses had little to offer the mass of blacks.[100] Epitomizing this sentiment, Manning Marable suggests that small business owners—regardless of race—are often proponents of right-wing political agendas that will ultimately harm black people. "The black entrepreneur's quest for profits could become part of the political drive to discipline the entire black working class."[101] In addition, because of the strong association of African American business with black nationalism, "support of Afro-American business constitutes . . . a threat to the overall goal of integration," which was a major objective of the civil rights movement.[102]

Accordingly, many activists rejected entrepreneurial solutions for the economic problems faced by black Americans. In the following quote from a 2006 interview, the director of a minority business development organization in Detroit referred to this.

> When Coleman Young became [Detroit's first African American] mayor in the '70s, a lot of opportunities opened up. You did see a shift in the power. But we were not ready to take advantage. I think that we weren't trying to be entrepreneurs. We had manufacturing jobs. We could make big money [in the auto industry] and not have to worry about becoming the head of some business, being some [kind of] entrepreneur.

Since the late 1970s, however, minority activists and their allies have reassessed the value of business ownership to their community's well-being. Drawing on traditions of black collectivism, some defined black self-employment as a means of communal empowerment rather than simply as a path to individual enrichment.[103] Indeed, black entrepreneurship generates popular enthusiasm among those directly involved as well as those who simply believe that the creation of ethnic minority enterprise is a good thing.

Government programs that encourage the growth of ethnic economies can be traced to the late 1960s. His campaign promises to discipline black youth notwithstanding, shortly after taking office, President Richard M. Nixon emphasized the importance of minority business ownership as part of his urban and race relations policy.[104]

> To foster the economic status and the pride of members of our minority groups we must seek to involve them more fully in our private enterprise system . . . both in the areas where they now live and in the larger commercial community—and not only as workers, but also as managers and owners . . . not only to share the economic benefits of the free enterprise system more broadly, but also to encourage pride, dignity, and a sense of independence. In order to do this, we need to remove commercial obstacles which have too

often stood in the way of minority group members—obstacles such as the unavailability of credit, insurance, and technical assistance.[105]

Even prior to Nixon's election, in 1967, an amendment was made to the Economic Opportunity Act (EOA) that directed the Small Business Administration (SBA) to emphasize the growth of small businesses owned by low-income persons or those located in areas of high unemployment. The SBA set about fulfilling this requirement in two ways: by providing increased access to investment capital and by directing government agencies to purchase goods and services from minority enterprises. According to several sources, the latter program was far more successful than the former.[106]

Michael Woodard described three government loan programs as underfunded and poorly managed, hence largely unsuccessful, at least with regard to black clients.[107] Despite this negative evaluation, other reflections of their impact are mixed. Some entrepreneurs praise these programs. For example, Light and Edna Bonacich found that Korean entrepreneurs in Los Angeles preferred SBA loans even to those available from Korean banks because they offered preferable interest rates.[108] According to Timothy Bates, Chicago's Southshore Bank experienced mixed results in efforts to revitalize a red-lined region of Chicago with some SBA support. Retail firms met with little success. However, remodeling and real estate development companies were quite profitable.[109]

The second means of supporting ethnic economies—providing access to government procurement—has accomplished more than loan programs. Starting in 1969, the SBA 8(a) "set aside" program awarded 8.9 million dollars in contracts to disadvantaged businesses, a figure that grew to 4.3 billion dollars by 1985, with considerable support from the Carter administration.[110] As a result of this captive market, "many small and black-owned businesses stabilized and grew."[111] The 1977 Public Works Employment Act had a similar impact, requiring all large general contractors bidding for public works projects to allocate at least 10 percent of their contracts to ethnic minority subcontractors, without regard to the size or disadvantaged status of the enterprise.

Following this governmental initiative, large corporations also established set-aside programs. In 1982, through the National Minority Supplier Development Council, companies purchased 5.3 billion dollars in goods and services from minority-owned businesses. A decade later, this figure had doubled to ten billion dollars.[112] According to Minority Business Development Agency figures, in 1992, 5 percent of black-owned businesses derived more than one-half of their revenue from state and local government, while 17 percent derived more than one-half of their revenue from the federal government.[113]

Programs that direct a proportion of public spending to minority- and women-owned businesses exist at federal, state, and city levels. Their approaches are various and subject to frequent revisions as a consequence of legal challenges, changing officeholders, executive orders, and alterations in enabling legislation. This makes a holistic assessment of women and minority business development programs extremely difficult.[114]

Sociologist Roger Waldinger's New York–based fieldwork with African American contractors gives insight into the real experience of minority entrepreneurs seeking to take advantages of set-aside programs.[115] Doing construction work for government clients is an activity that would appear to fit well the needs and resources of African American entrepreneurs. Construction has relatively small requirements for capital, pays well, and involves a system of subcontracting that is able to link fledgling businesses with major projects. Moreover, because municipal construction projects are generally close to areas where minority groups live, they are largely immune to problems of spatial mismatch associated with jobs in ex-urban communities.[116]

Despite these advantages, Waldinger found that success in the construction business remains elusive for many African American contractors. This is because the construction industry is highly dependent on durable social networks both within one's own ethnic group and among the larger community of construction entrepreneurs. African Americans, who are subject to discrimination and often lack extensive connections with established players in the industry, face significant obstacles for entry. As newcomers to the trade, U.S.-born blacks had a hard time acquiring skills that white contractors had learned from family members already in the field and immigrants acquired prior to arrival in the United States. In addition, blacks described being excluded from the social networks that white owners rely on to get to know one another and exchange referrals, information, and resources.

Public sector work provides a degree of protection from arbitrary discrimination as well as offering incentives for employing black and women contractors, but it also imposes liabilities. For example, government agencies are notoriously slow to pay, which yields significant cash flow problems for small firms that lack access to lines of credit.[117] Moreover, government jobs often demand that contractors employ costly and highly regulated unionized workers. This reduces flexibility and precludes the use of personal or coethnic networks to select familiar employees. Other groups of start-up contractors, such as Korean immigrants, also mentioned the difficulty of dealing with government jobs. However, because they had access to employment from affluent coethnic customers, they were able to avoid the limitations associated with government contracts, and thus could more fully maximize benefits linked to their ethnic networks.

Finally, because they are not immigrants, African Americans lack some of the social resources immigrants use to achieve entrepreneurial success. These include access to high levels of family and communal cooperation, the aforementioned skills obtained outside of the United States, and close ties to recently arrived coethnics willing to accept poorly paid, entry-level positions like janitor, laborer, and the like (see chapter 1). Immigrant groups' links to such workers underlies their control over occupational and entrepreneurial niches that the U.S. born avoid. Accordingly, while subject to similar types of racism as African Americans, Caribbeans and other immigrants of color have access to certain forms of cooperation, experience, and solidarity that native blacks lack. As such, they fare somewhat better in the construction business. Finally, once naturalized, like African Americans, they are also eligible for affirmative action programs.[118]

Because of these several factors, African Americans in New York and elsewhere tend to focus on public sector employment rather than contracting.[119] Finally, Waldinger notes that immigrant status alone does not mean that a group will be successful in self-employment. Koreans, Chinese, and South Asians in New York—all groups characterized by relatively high levels of education—have made impressive accomplishments in self-employment. In contrast, Dominicans, Puerto Ricans, and Mexicans have been less competitive in recent years.

Several government agencies have worked to address the challenges encountered by minority firms, especially those involving their relatively small size.[120] As a case in point, the city of Chicago appointed Montel Gayles as chief procurement officer to help achieve Mayor Richard Daley's goal of providing 25 percent of all city contracts to minorities and 5 percent to women.[121] "Instead of awarding the project to large-sized general contractors (a type of firm that includes few minorities), who would then hire subcontractors, Gayles learned to break public projects into manageable pieces, focusing on specific task areas like masonry and steel. This allowed the city to hire minorities as prime contractors for each."[122] Not only did this make it easier for African Americans to bid on public contracts, but it also allowed their firms to show that they had functioned as prime contractors, thus proving their competence to future clients. Despite these innovations, the cost of bond insurance continues to be excessive for small, black-owned businesses, thus limiting their ability to obtain government contracts.

The State of Maryland assists women and minority contractors through the Maryland Small Business Development Finance Authority for working capital assistance. This organization provides certified minority business entrepreneurs (MBEs) that have contracts with government or regulated public utilities with funding to complete their procurement activities if they are unable to obtain it from commercial banks.[123] In Michigan, the Minority Supplier Development Council (MMSDC), a privately funded, nonprofit corporate services organization, brings together major corporations with MBEs. It enables corporations to direct a fraction of their contracting to minority-run firms and, in so doing, access minority consumers. It also provides minority enterprises with a setting where they can approach well-established corporate clients. While the organization is a nonprofit (and thus is unaffected by the state's anti–affirmative action Proposal 2), it maintains good relations with government entities that share the goal of fostering minority business growth.[124]

ENTERPRISE ZONES

Since the 1980s, enterprise zone and empowerment zone (EZ) policies have sought to contribute to the development of ethnic economies in economically depressed communities. Toward this end, EZs provided tax and other incentives to businesses willing to locate in designated areas, provide jobs to residents, and work together with local residents and community organizations. "Emphasizing neighborhood-based change and community involvement and recognition that economic development required the participation of a wider range of stakeholders, the legislation represented an attempt to promote collaborative efforts to invest in the community and build social capital that would contribute to the lasting revitalization of neighborhoods."[125]

During the Clinton administration, EZs were established in seven major cities (Chicago, Camden, Detroit, New York, Philadelphia, Atlanta, and Baltimore). A 2005 report on their economic and social impact indicates that they had generally positive, if weak, impacts. The strong economy during the evaluation period (1995–2000) made it difficult to determine if positive economic outcomes were due to the EZ program or to broader economic conditions. Nevertheless, evaluation research indicates that job growth in four of the seven EZs outpaced that in predetermined comparison regions and contiguous areas. Additional positive outcomes included a substantial increase in the employment of EZ residents. An increase in the number of minority-owned businesses was observed in six of the seven locations.[126]

Resident participation and community-based partnerships fostered cooperative decision making about zone priorities. However, such arrangements were generally short lived and associated with participants' access to payments. Once funds were no longer available, cooperative activities between employers and community members subsided.[127] In addition to federal EZs, several states have developed their own enterprise zone policies.

Based on their findings that black employers are much more likely than whites to hire black workers, Bates and colleagues have criticized EZ programs as a means of creating jobs for blacks. "Available evidence suggests that the predominant beneficiaries of such (EZ) policies are unlikely to be the residents of inner-city minority communities."[128] Instead, these authors favor increasing the number of black-owned businesses regardless of their location as the best means of enhancing the employment of African Americans and other minority groups.

CLASS AND MINORITY BUSINESS DEVELOPMENT

According to several authors, the impact of programs seeking to improve economic standing and entrepreneurship among disadvantaged groups vary according to social class. Middle-class persons in possession of skills, education, and personal savings encounter growing opportunities in existing firms, the public sector, and entrepreneurship.[129] They are also much better credit risks. However, far fewer possibilities are available for minorities and women lacking class resources. They create businesses because of few alternative options for work, yet their lack of skill and capital limits their earnings and chances for success.

Traditional forms of black-owned business, like food stores and restaurants directed at black clients (generally run by proprietors without a college degree) declined by 33 percent between 1971 and 1997. In their analysis of the 1986 Urban Poverty and Family Life Survey, Cedric Herring and colleagues determined that, among blacks and Mexican Americans in Chicago's high poverty areas, self-employment "is associated with lower rather than higher incomes."[130] In contrast, the number of black-owned business services firms, generally serving a racially diverse or nonminority clientele, increased from fewer than 11,000 to almost 105,000 (by 867.5 percent) during the same period. By 1997, such firms employed 156,974 workers.[131] On a positive note, the number of persons of color with the educational credentials required to engage in these forms of entrepreneurship is substantial. In 2001, more than ten thousand African Americans were in possession of an MBA degree.[132]

As a consequence, it is often the most successful and privileged members of minority groups who are judged as most worthy of loans, assistance, and targeted hiring. In contrast, the neediest and most truly disadvantaged members of these groups have a much harder time receiving business assistance and achieving success. This paradox is especially vexing with regard to businesses in ghetto communities.

Despite the poignant absence of black enterprises in ghetto neighborhoods, the principles of good business management mean that relatively few African Americans who are well qualified to run businesses will pursue retail ventures in impoverished communities. Instead, they are likely to become involved in activities with good potential for profit but little visibility. Making successful minority businesses even less detectable, research suggests that suburban rather than inner-city locations and sunbelt cities with relatively small black populations are the most hospitable and economically rewarding locations for black entrepreneurs. Consequently, the recent success of minority entrepreneurs remains largely invisible in the communities where African Americans reside.[133]

In sum, since the 1960s, a broad range of activities and policies undertaken by federal, state, and city government, by the private sector, and by members of minority communities have sought to enhance the self-employment activities of women and minority groups. While many programs have been at least somewhat successful, they have done more for those already in possession of some advantages—educated middle-class persons—than members of the working class. Not surprisingly, such programs have been largely unable to resolve issues of economic inequality in American society. As we see in the section that follows, they have, however, energized opponents.

ANTI–AFFIRMATIVE ACTION PROGRAMS

The implementation of controversial policy initiatives often creates reactive movements. As we have seen, urban policies that fostered the expansion of ghettos contributed to urban uprisings during the 1960s and afterward. In turn, these events led to legislation that assisted members of minority groups to obtain education, jobs, and better chances for self-employment. However, backlash against these programs precipitated powerful anti–affirmative action movements that sought to eliminate government assistance to groups disadvantaged as a result of their race, ethnicity, or gender. Starting with the Supreme Court's *Bakke* decision (1978) that ruled that fixed quotas for admissions of minorities into universities (in this case, University of California, Davis Medical School) were unconstitutional, the movement developed a multilevel campaign of opposition in lawmaking bodies (at the city, state, and federal level) and in the courts.

The most widely discussed impact of affirmative action has been with regard to women's and minority groups' access to education and jobs. For example, in order to desegregate public schools in accordance with *Brown v. Board of Education*, and reinforced by *Green v. County School Board* (1968), the Supreme Court ruled that school districts that operated segregated schools had an "affirmative duty to take what[ever] steps were needed to end racial discrimination."[134] This led to bussing programs that transported white children to largely black schools and vice versa. Bussing was effective at reducing black students' concentration in predominantly minority schools. However, this measure was divisive and encountered a series of legal challenges. In 1974, in *Milliken v. Bradley*, the Supreme Court ruled that students could not be bussed across district lines to achieve integration, and by the 1990s, the courts ended court-ordered bussing. As the authors of a review article on affirmative action write, "Desegregation efforts have now all but disappeared and school segregation has returned to its pre-AA levels."[135]

Among colleges and universities, affirmative action efforts were undertaken without legal compulsion. Since such policies were implemented, the number of students of color at highly selective universities has increased substantially. However, because affirmative action programs in public universities can be banned by legal actions or policy decisions made by the state government, they are at considerable risk of curtailment. Indeed, following the passage of California's anti–affirmative action Proposition 209 in 1996, the number of African American students entering the University of California, Berkeley, Law School dropped by 81 percent.[136]

Anti–affirmative action movements have also had significant impacts on programs assisting women- and minority-owned businesses, both through the removal of set-asides and due to the elimination of business assistance programs and loan funds. In the 1989 decision *City of Richmond v. J. A. Croson Company*, the U.S. Supreme Court ruled against programs that reserve a certain amount of public purchasing for designated groups and asserted that affirmative action could only be used in public contracting when actual discrimination or underrepresentation of specific groups was documented. The Court further asserted that narrowly tailored race-conscious measures could only be used to address discrimination when race-neutral means were not sufficient.[137] Following this decision, at least thirty-three states abandoned their set-aside programs. "The *Croson* decision, to a large extent, legitimated the idea of reverse discrimination in government procurement."[138]

During the 1990s, "a variety of challenges to the set-aside requirements of government programs began to emerge."[139] In reaction, some government entities developed strategies that sought equal opportunity and diversity without focusing on gender, race, or ethnic origins.[140] While private sector programs took important measures to support minority enterprise, the economic downturns that occurred after 2000, together with "escalating pressure on government to dismantle set-asides," created a climate that "would confound even the largest and most prolific businesses" let alone struggling minority start-ups. Accordingly, governmental and private sector support for minority entrepreneurship became scarce, and the profitability of businesses owned by underrepresented groups flattened.[141]

During the 1990s, activists established a legislative program to ban affirmative action through state-level elections. The first of these was Proposition 209, passed in California in 1996. Similar proposals were approved in Washington (Initiative 200) in 1998, Michigan in 2006 (Proposal 2), and Nebraska (Initiative 424) in 2008. Having successfully promoted anti–affirmative action propositions in these states, the American Civil Rights Institute, led by California businessman and former University of California Board of Regents member Ward Connerly, made plans to expand the program to several more states.[142]

The anti–affirmative action movement enjoys little support from major political actors, large corporations, and other influential organizations, which regard such attacks on minorities as destructive in an increasingly diverse society. For example, in Washington, Eddie Bauer, Microsoft, and Starbucks funded opposition to the campaign for Initiative 200.[143] The coalition opposing Michigan's Proposal 2 received significant funding from Ford Motor Company, the Dow Chemical Company, and Detroit's Greektown Casino and was endorsed by the League of Women Voters, the United Auto Workers, and the Arab-American Institute.[144] Moreover, Proposal 2 was opposed by both Democratic and Republican gubernatorial candidates who were seeking office in the same election. However, the anti–affirmative action movement has significant appeal to white male voters, which is why Connerly's organization promotes the anti–affirmative action cause through state initiatives rather than legislatures that might alter outcomes. "Indeed, as evidenced in the public opinion polls, whites overwhelmingly object to government assistance targeted at blacks. . . . Whereas eight of every ten African Americans believe that the government is not spending enough to assist black people, only slightly more than three of every ten white Americans feel this way."[145]

Michigan's anti–affirmative action proposition is relatively recent. Accordingly, there is little data on the impact of the law on women- and minority-owned businesses. However, the California law has been on the books for over ten years, so some data on its effects are now becoming available.

A study evaluating the impact of a California Department of Transportation (Caltrans) program that directed purchasing to women- and minority-owned businesses determined that only a third of the state's certified MBEs were still in existence ten years after the law went into effect. In addition, MBEs received only half of the awards and contracts from Caltrans that they had received prior to the law; African American- and women-owned contractors suffered the most adverse impacts after Proposition 209; and many of the MBE contractors still in existence "could not have initially succeeded or maintained their success" without incentives that helped them gain equal access to bids.[146] Analysis by the Insight Center for Community Economic Development found that women- and minority-owned businesses were less likely to expand in the years immediately after passage of the anti–affirmative action propositions in California and Washington than were women business entrepreneurs (WBEs) and MBEs in Oregon and Maryland, states that did not change their affirmative procurement policies between 1996 and 2001.[147]

The authors of a recent review of the impact of affirmative action contend that governmental programs are increasingly challenged by activists and the courts. However, major institutions including universities and corporations remain committed to the goal of increasing access to underrepresented groups in schools and the workplace, even if the broad, government-based mandate for it has been weakened.[148] Further, despite the mobilization against affirmative action purchasing programs, the number of states with inclusive business programs actually increased. Between 2003 and 2006, seven states curtailed inclusive business programs. However, during the same period, fourteen states either initiated or enhanced such programs.[149]

CONCLUSIONS

Conflicts between ethnic merchants and minority customers are often explained in terms of the cultural attributes of the groups involved and in light of specific incidents that were thought to have brought on the conflicts. While such factors did contribute to looting of shops, little attention has been devoted to the importance of policies that create the environments in which such merchant-customer interactions take place. This chapter contends that the creation of large and impoverished African American ghettos in many cities yielded extremely inhospitable locations for businesses. Among the only viable institutions in these neighborhoods, such stores were available targets during the civil disorders of the 1960s as well as in more recent events, such as those in Miami in 1980 and Los Angeles in 1992.

Literature suggests that looters' motives were more likely to be opportunistic—a chance to obtain something of value—than due to antipathy against business owners selected on the basis of their ethnicity. Rather, conditions of crowding and joblessness have been consistently correlated with outbreaks of urban violence. In an attempt to remedy the barren environments of urban ghettos following the uprisings of the 1960s, policy makers created several programs to increase minority education, job access, and business ownership. Such programs had mixed results but were ultimately unable to resolve the many disadvantages that native-born minorities confront in trying to establish businesses and otherwise improve their lives. As the memories of the 1960s riots faded, political commitment to rebuilding ghettos declined. Ambitious and costly plans for addressing urban problems were abandoned in favor of other goals.

In reviewing the social and economic conditions that prevail in ghettos, sociologist Dalton Conley considers the costs associated with the exclusion of blacks from owning businesses, homes, and other assets in American society.[150] High among these is the existence of violent conflict between merchants and customers. Conley questions whether the burning and looting of businesses and apartments would have taken place if integration had succeeded or if a majority of businesses in ghettos during the 1960s and since were black owned.

> How likely would riots have been if the African American community had been dispersed evenly among whites and other races. . . . Even without residential integration, if the majority of African Americans had owned the homes in which they resided, how likely would a riot have been . . . ? The answer to all of these questions is that if owning businesses and homes were a part of African American life, the risk of civil unrest would be dramatically lowered. The counterpoint to this conclusion is that as long as African Americans face major institutional obstacles to property ownership, the risk of such conflict remains.[151]

Since World War II, federal, state, and local government has issued an array of contradictory policies that have increased segregation, degraded infrastructure, and concentrated poverty in urban locations where minority groups often reside, while at the same time attempting to enhance economic opportunities via self-employment. This record yielded neither satisfactory results nor a political consensus on how to assist groups and communities that have long been denied many of the basic resources required for advancement. Meanwhile, proponents and detractors of affirmative action continue to debate. Rather than working to resolve these issues, policy makers and other observers often blame ghetto residents for failing to maintain civil behavior within the inhospitable circumstances that their own ambitious, if short-sighted, agendas created.

6

DEMOGRAPHIC CHANGE
AND URBAN TRANSFORMATION:
INTERACTIONS BETWEEN
IMMIGRANT BUSINESS OWNERS
AND CUSTOMERS, 1970 TO 2005

The period from the late 1960s until 1979 featured relatively few conflicts between immigrant merchants and customers. However, the last two decades of the twentieth century witnessed a substantial increase in these events, the largest of which was the Los Angeles Uprising of 1992. Brought on by the exoneration of four police officers whose brutal beating of African American motorist Rodney King was captured on a widely shown video, the riot involved six days of disorder and violence among a variety of ethnic and racial groups. It resulted in the death of fifty persons, 2,300 injuries, the destruction of 2,314 businesses, the loss of one billion dollars in property (including some 1,100 buildings), sixteen thousand arrests, and the deportation of close to five hundred undocumented immigrants.[1] As had been the case in major uprisings during the 1930s, 1940s, and 1960s, while police brutality touched off the rioting, ethnic merchants in ghetto neighborhoods bore the brunt of the destruction.

The Los Angeles Riot or Uprising, however, was only the most visible of numerous incidents that occurred from coast to coast during the period. Nearly every major city in the United States experienced violent conflicts between immigrant merchants and native minority customers during the 1980s and 1990s with disputes leading to deaths, boycotts, and social disorder. In addition to the actual clashes between immigrant entrepreneurs and customers, popular awareness of tension between groups was elevated through frequent reports provided by expanding media outlets and by social activists. During this period, political spokespersons and academic

Destruction of ethnic businesses, Koreatown, Los Angeles, May 1992
Source: Steven Gold

researchers reminded the public about such events, dramatized their impact, interpreted their meaning, and proposed responses.

In fact, the issue of conflict between immigrant merchants and their customers transcended news venues to animate the story lines of popular entertainment, including films like *My Beautiful Launderette* (1985), *Do the Right Thing* (1989), *Boys in the Hood* (1991), and *Menace II Society* (1993), and hit songs ranging from Ice Cube's "Black Korea" (1991) to "Mr. Patel's Rap."

By the end of the 1980s, conflicts involving ethnic merchants had moved beyond the traditional location of the urban ghetto. While journalism and academic discourse emphasized merchants' conflicts with African Americans, new immigrant entrepreneurs tussled with a wide range of social groups including suburban whites, established ethnic populations, various immigrant communities, government, and subgroups of their own population.[2]

As a case in point, the expansion of non-English signage on local stores incensed middle-class whites from Queens to Chicago and Los Angeles, who formed neighborhood associations in opposition.[3] In a pattern reminiscent of the era of Asian exclusion, they petitioned politicians to ban foreign-language signs, restrict business ownership by immigrants, and prohibit migrants' business practices. During the late 1980s, a bumper sticker with the slogan "Will the Last American to Leave Monterey Park Please Bring the American Flag" was widely displayed in the Los Angeles community that became known as America's first suburban Chinatown.[4]

A CELEBRATION OF ETHNIC BUSINESS

The reaction to new arrivals and their businesses was not, however, universally negative. A unique feature surrounding recent immigration to the United States has been that pundits, business leaders, and politicians have hailed newcomers' achievements as broadly beneficial. Their ability to find jobs, start businesses, and obtain an education—in the same settings that natives claimed were bereft of opportunities—was praised in popular books such as Joel Kotkin's *Tribes*, Philippe Legrain's *Immigrants: Your Country Needs Them*, numerous academic studies, and newsmagazine articles, such as *Time*'s 1985 cover story, "The Changing Face of America." A Chicago professor quoted in the issue explained, "Their work ethic serves them well and serves us well. In a sense they are refurbishing our work ethic."[5]

While rap artists' verses derided immigrant merchants, not all voices among the native minority populations were hostile. For example, in 1985, the *Amsterdam News* hailed the arrival of a Korean-run barbecue shop on Harlem's 125th Street, noting that its ribs and chicken were delicious, that the restaurant's employees included blacks and Latinos, and that its owner's children admired Martin Luther King.[6]

Meanwhile, social scientists' discoveries that Cuban, Korean, and Vietnamese immigrants were opening numerous businesses, creating jobs, and transforming neighborhoods gave Americans reasons to embrace the newcomers.[7] Such revelations converged with the ethnic revival of the 1970s to convince academics, policy makers, and members of the wider public that immigrants' habits, traits, and social forms—including cooperation, hard work, and ability to defer gratification—had a major role in their success.[8] In this way, the accomplishments of immigrant business owners made many discard the Americanizing approach that had shaped immigrant integration policies for the last hundred years. Instead, many came to believe that multiculturalism and the retention of traditional practices could yield benefits for both immigrants and the larger society.[9] As a consequence of these discussions, by the late 1980s, Americans had been exposed to arguments that both celebrated and condemned the place of immigrant entrepreneurship in U.S. society.

A new political environment also evolved. Previous periods of conflict between immigrant merchants and customers—the 1930s and 1940s, and the 1960s—were associated with the New Deal and Great Society—the most ambitious and well-financed efforts at social reform in U.S. history (see chapters 4 and 5).[10] In contrast, the 1980s were a time of Reaganomics, reductions in public spending, opposition to unions, near record interest rates, and deindustrialization. Describing the context surrounding the 1980 Miami riot, Bruce Porter and Marvin Dunn assert, "The War on Poverty had virtually been called off. Public enthusiasm for improving conditions in the ghetto was muted."[11] As such, since the 1970s, immigrant merchants and their customers faced the challenge of resolving their social and economic difficulties with little government backing.

ENTREPRENEURIAL AND POLITICAL RESOURCES

Entrepreneurial immigrant groups often had significant intellectual, financial, and collective resources that allowed them to be successful in running businesses.[12] With the exception of Cubans in Miami, however, most were poorly endowed with political assets. Small in number, recently arrived, and limited in English, they generally lacked the skills and contacts required to effectively communicate their version of events to the larger society or to acquire the assistance they needed to face down opponents.[13]

At the same time, native minorities' complaints about the adverse impact of immigrant merchants in their communities generally went unheard in the larger society, which increasingly rejected minority assistance programs as a wasteful indulgence for an undeserving underclass.[14] The lack of support from the larger society notwithstanding, due to the civil rights movement, white flight, the action of community organizations, minorities' growing access to media outlets, and shared resentment against immigrant merchants in communities of color, African American activists were able to marshal a degree of coethnic backing for their agenda.[15]

Accordingly, the last decades of the twentieth century revealed both established and unprecedented patterns of conflict between immigrant entrepreneurs and customers. Important trends included economic decline followed by resurgence (in some cities), the arrival of a new cohort of mostly nonwhite migrant groups as residents and entrepreneurs, and the political mobilization of both merchants and customer groups.

At the time, political, journalistic, and media interpretations of these events emphasized the cultural and racial dimensions of opposition between native customers and immigrant merchants as the primary cause of friction. Accounts asserted that African Americans and immigrant merchants differed with regard to eye contact, smiling, friendliness, and expectations about customer service and often viewed each other through malevolent stereotypes.[16]

Since that time, however, a growing body of scholarship has attributed such conflict to the broader structures of society that created a context in which racialized populations with limited resources struggle for survival under circumstances that they neither created nor can control.[17] This chapter examines the nature of conflicts between merchants and customers that have occurred in the United States from the 1970s until the present in light of the period's major social, economic, and demographic patterns.

CHANGING DEMOGRAPHICS AND ECONOMICS IN AMERICAN CITIES

Since the late 1960s, two major trends—economic and demographic—have shaped relations between merchants and customers in U.S. society. After the 1960s, urban areas experienced considerable economic decline. This pattern accelerated as global competition and rising energy prices yielded economic restructuring that significantly reduced the number of well-paid industrial jobs for less-educated workers.[18] Losing jobs, political power, population, and taxable income, cities suffered financially and had a hard time maintaining basic services.

While these trends affected the entire United States, their greatest economic impact and longest duration was in older industrial cities of the Midwest and South. In contrast, by the 1990s, certain localities began to experience economic growth and skyrocketing real estate values.[19] As of 2005, sizeable sections of the rustbelt continued to suffer from economic stagnation. In coastal and sunbelt locations, however, urban merchants and customers found themselves increasingly priced out of their dwellings and shops by real estate developers, home buyers, and retail chains that saw former ghettos as pockets of affordable real estate ripe for redevelopment.[20]

The second major trend that transformed U.S. cities by the 1970s was demographic. In 1965, Congress passed the Hart-Cellar Bill, also known as the Immigration and Nationality Act of 1965. Adopted in the same atmosphere of tolerance and reform that surrounded the implementation of the Voting Rights Act, the Immigration and Nationality Act of 1965 removed most national quotas on the entry of immigrants to the United States and ultimately resulted in the influx of millions of nonwhite immigrants. Immigration laws passed in 1986 and 1990 provided additional opportunities for those seeking to enter the United States. Added to the number of foreign born in the United States were more than a million refugees.[21] Finally, a significant cluster of undocumented persons—estimated at about eleven million as of 2008—have joined the U.S. population.[22]

While these immigrants would ultimately transform regions throughout America, their impact was most immediately felt in the major cities where most came to live, including greater New York, Miami, San Francisco, Los Angeles, and Chicago. Voluntary immigrants often followed the advice of friends and relatives in choosing points of settlement. In contrast, refugees' initial destinations were determined for them by resettlement agencies.[23] (See tables 6.1 and 6.2.)

Despite the difficult economic climate that prevailed in many locations, recent immigrants and refugees often domiciled in inner-city neighborhoods where housing was inexpensive, coethnic communities already established, and public transportation available. In cities like New York,

Table 6.1. Consolidated Metropolitan Areas with the Largest Immigrant Populations, 2000 (in Thousands)

CSMA	No. of Immigrants	Percent Immigrant	1990s Immigrants	Total CSMA Population Growth 1990–2000
Los Angeles	4,707	29.6	1,471	1,688
New York	4,688	22.9	1,767	737
San Francisco	2,007	28.2	773	642
Miami	1,647	42.7	678	558
Chicago	1,070	12.3	421	693
Washington-Baltimore	857	12	348	701

Source: Steven A. Camarota, "Immigrants in the United States—2000: A Snapshot of America's Foreign-Born Population," Center for Immigration Studies, December 2000, table 18.

Table 6.2. U.S. Metro Areas with the Most Immigrants, 2007

Metro Area*	Total Population	Foreign-born Population
1. New York, NY-NJ-PA	18,815,988	5,328,891
2. Los Angeles, CA	12,875,587	4,488,563
3. Miami, FL	5,413,212	2,005,178
4. Chicago, IL	9,522,879	1,679,074
5. San Francisco, CA	4,203,898	1,245,007
6. Houston, TX	5,629,127	1,204,817
7. Dallas, TX	6,144,489	1,092,361
8. Washington, DC-VA-MD-WV	5,306,125	1,088,949
9. Riverside, CA	4,081,371	911,982
10. Phoenix, AZ	4,179,427	736,068

*Ranked by size of foreign-born population.

Source: Audrey Singer, "The New Geography of United States Immigration," Brookings Immigration Series 3 (Brookings Institution, Washington, D.C., July 2009), at www.brookings.edu/papers/2009/07_immigration_geography_singer.aspx (accessed April 11, 2010), 6.

Miami, and Los Angeles, immigrants' arrival was contemporaneous with and contributed to the exit of middle- and working-class African Americans, thus diluting blacks' political power. In Houston, Orange County, Greater Washington, D.C., Detroit, Long Island, and other localities, migrants congregated in older suburbs.

While thousands of well-paid, unionized, industrial jobs for less-skilled workers had left urban areas, other positions with lower wages, fewer benefits, and less security continued to exist.[24] These were in fields like garments, electronics, food processing, light manufacturing, and packaging where employers generally preferred immigrants to native-born minorities and whites.[25]

In points of immigrant settlement, competition over turf, political power, and jobs often yielded antagonism among natives and immigrants. In addition to their participation in manufacturing, immigrants also became extensively involved in the expanding service sector in fields like health care, restaurants, janitorial work, landscaping, delivery, business services, child care, and entertainment. After they obtained citizenship, they sought government jobs.[26]

Immigrants also became proprietors, often purchasing shops from owners retiring or moving to the suburbs to escape crime and cater to more affluent customers.[27] They created a host of services, lines of merchandise, and ways of doing business. Some enterprises involved the sale of tasty and inexpensive ethnic cuisines—Japanese, Thai, Lebanese, Indian, Ethiopian, and Mexican—that, prior to the latest immigrant wave, had not been part of the American diet. Others sold conventional fast food. For example, during the 1990s, Cambodians, who had only recently fled starvation and violence in Pol Pot's Killing Fields, came to run doughnut shops throughout Southern California. The low cost of entry, relative simplicity of the work, and limited need for English matched with the migrants' willingness to labor for long hours in seedy environments. As a consequence, this enterprise employed a considerable fraction of the Cambodian population—at least until after 2000, when national doughnut chains like Dunkin' Donuts and Krispy Kreme would challenge their near monopoly.[28]

Immigrant entrepreneurs perfected ways of delivering fashion merchandise and personal grooming assistance in an inexpensive and accessible manner. In so doing, they made these goods and services available to consumer segments that had previously been unable to afford them. The merchants' timing was spot on, since expanding employment in sales and services had recently increased employees' need for good grooming.[29] Among these innovative enterprises were dry cleaners, nail salons, beauty parlors, beauty supply companies, wig shops, and clothing swap meets.[30] In many cases, the products sold in ethnic merchants' shops were provided through coethnic links to off-shore producers.[31]

Vietnamese maintained a virtual monopoly over the manicure trade in Southern California, which catered to not only coethnic consumers but also women of all ethnic groups and class levels. One hundred and sixty three such operations, ranging in location from tony Beverly Hills to impoverished South Central were listed in the 1991 *Vietnamese Consumers' Guidebook of Southern California*. In greater Los Angeles, the group was estimated to own and operate 80 percent of nail salons, as well as an array of affiliated firms that delivered supplies and trained workers—with tuition often covered by refugee benefits. As of the late 1990s, Vietnamese ran about 30 percent of the twenty-two thousand nail shops nationwide.[32] Like doughnut shops, such enterprises appealed to recent immigrants because they required little investment capital, could utilize low-cost family labor, and found a ready demand for their services.

THE CLASS ORIGINS OF NEW IMMIGRANT ENTREPRENEURS

A large fraction of contemporary immigrants lack the education, skill, and capital required to become self-employed upon arrival (see chapter 7). However, others, hailing from the middle or upper classes of their countries of origin, are skilled and educated. Through the premigration sale of property and coethnic financial networks, many had access to financial resources.[33]

The arrival of so many educated immigrants after 1970 can be partly attributed to the displacement of former elites in revolutionary countries like China, Cuba, Vietnam, Iran, and the Soviet Bloc; the desire of foreign students to remain in the United States upon completion of their education; and immigration laws that granted priority to highly skilled persons, as well as to those investing in the U.S. economy.[34]

Despite their impressive backgrounds, as recently arrived immigrants with limited English, with unrecognized credentials, and subject to discrimination, a portion of these could not find jobs in the fields for which they had been trained. Accordingly, they entered self-employment because it provided better wages and working conditions than the alternative—entry-level positions in existing firms.[35]

During a 1989 interview, a representative of the Vietnamese Chamber of Commerce in Orange County told me how self-employment permitted Vietnamese engineers to avoid the "glass ceiling" that restricts corporate promotions: "Well, I don't want to say discrimination, but I attended a top American university, and I feel there isn't room past a certain level for a

Vietnamese. Like right now, most of the Vietnamese engineers can't wait to get out of the corporate rat race and open their own company. They can't get into the upper level of established corporations."

Discrimination and outgroup status notwithstanding, high levels of education helped immigrant entrepreneurs to master language skills, learn about new technologies, and appreciate emerging markets. Finally, educational credentials yield prestige that can favorably impress community members, loan officers, fellow entrepreneurs, and others who can provide assistance. These skills and contacts allow entrepreneurs to acquire the resources to expand their businesses. For example, as Alejandro Portes demonstrates, character loans extended to well-respected but impoverished Cuban refugees by coethnic bankers were important to the rapid development of the Cuban ethnic economy in South Florida during the 1960s and 1970s.[36]

Because of education, business skill, and access to goods and capital from abroad, some recent immigrant groups have been able to establish sizeable business districts.[37] These enclaves provide immigrants with access to housing, services, consumers, and other basic resources that facilitate business start-ups and permit their entrepreneurial involvement in costly environments that are beyond the financial reach of less well-connected immigrants as well as natives who lack access to significant amounts of capital.[38] Finally, high levels of education and skill underlie patterns of intergenerational mobility among entrepreneurial immigrants' children that allow them to leave their parents' adaptive occupations to join the professional middle class.[39]

CONFLICTS WITH NATIVE MINORITIES

Following the riots of the 1960s, many ethnic entrepreneurs and chain stores vacated their ghetto shops. Whether they sold out to African Americans or to recent immigrants, or simply closed down, by the late 1970s and early 1980s, new immigrant entrepreneurs, including Arabs, Chaldeans, Koreans, Cubans, Chinese, Armenians, Iranians, Russian Jews, Israelis, Palestinians, Lebanese, and South Asians had taken their place to become major business owners in many cities.[40]

While a 1968 survey found that blacks owned almost 60 percent of businesses in central Harlem, within a few years, new immigrant groups dominated local trade.[41] By the early 1990s, Koreans owned nine thousand businesses in New York City, including five thousand in the Bronx and Brooklyn.[42] As of the early 1990s, Koreans owned one thousand shops on Chicago's South Side. In 1997, they held over seven thousand businesses—including some 1,800 dry cleaners—in metropolitan Chicago.[43] During the same period, Korean Americans owned 80 percent of the businesses in South Central Los Angeles. Their dominance over the retail sector was facilitated by vertical integration, as Koreans also owned import firms, distributors, food wholesalers, and garment manufacturers that supplied goods to coethnic retail businesses.[44]

Sociologist Gary David estimates that, during the late 1990s, Chaldeans owned 80 to 90 percent of the businesses in Detroit and noted that Detroit's grocers' and gas station owners' associations were largely Chaldean in membership.[45] Despite the fact that Chaldean businesses were hard hit by looting during the Detroit Riot of 1967, sociologist Mary Sengstock reported that they remained committed to inner-city entrepreneurship as the number of groceries that the group owned increased from 120 in 1962 to 278 a decade later.[46] In Miami, Cubans and other Latinos increased their ownership of gas stations from 12 percent in 1960 to 48 percent in 1979. Between 1972 and 1977, the number of Latino businesses in Dade County grew by 70 percent. Average earnings were eighty-four thousand dollars annually—twice that of black-owned businesses.[47]

Ownership varies in its rewards. Paul Ong and colleagues cite figures from the 1990 U.S. Census on the income distribution of self-employed Koreans in Los Angeles. While a third made less than twelve thousand dollars, a fifth earned at least forty-eight thousand dollars.[48] Some found that the niche could be very lucrative. According to In Chul Choi, despite the risks involved in running a shop on the Southside of Chicago, among Korean entrepreneurs, the district "first and foremost stood for wealth."[49] Sociologist In Jin Yoon heard the following description of what it was like to do business during the 1970s from the owner of a Southside wig store: "I made money as if I grabbed leaves scattered on the ground. Because business was so good, I did not have time to count my takings at the site. I dumped money into a laundry bag and spent the night by counting all the money I had earned during the day."[50]

Racial Change among Merchants

Between the 1940s and the early 1970s, most immigrant merchants in inner-city areas were Caucasian. However, after 1980, the owners were increasingly nonwhite.[51] This made relations between migrants and customers more complex than they had been before. On one hand, shared minority status opened up the possibility for potential coalitions with native-born minority groups. In his study of Korean entrepreneurship, Yoon asserts, "When Koreans first entered black areas, they were not subject to the same level of antipathy and rejection as Jewish and Italian business owners had been." In fact, Koreans located their businesses in black neighborhoods partly because "in these areas [there] was [a] . . . lower level of discrimination and hostility compared to that in white areas. Blacks were perceived by Koreans as easy to please, whereas whites were seen as condescending."[52] Moreover, in her research on inner-city businesses, Jennifer Lee observed that blacks generally receive worse treatment in stores outside of their own neighborhoods than those within.[53]

Despite the potential for empathy based on their shared minority status, conflicts between nonwhite entrepreneurs and customers also took on ethnic, religious, and racial dimensions. Recently arrived immigrants often adopted racial prejudices that were held in the larger society, only to find themselves subject to discrimination as well. In a 1992 survey, Pyong Gap Min found that a majority of Korean merchants embraced negative stereotypes of African Americans.[54] For their part, nonwhite customers sometimes sought to enhance their own standing by reminding immigrant entrepreneurs of their low rank within America's racial, ethnic, and religious hierarchy.

What is more, journalists, academics, politicians, and the public at large often took sides in disputes between immigrant merchants and native minority customers by contrasting the apparent success of "model minority immigrants" with the record of failure associated with native minorities. In her analysis of TV news reports about an African American boycott of Korean stores in New York City, Claire Jean Kim observed the disputes were "depicted [as] the bad minority persecuting the good minority . . . show[ing] hardworking immigrants trying to achieve the American Dream and angry blacks trying to prevent them from doing so."[55]

Immigrant Merchants Confront Community Control

Merchants and customers generally sought to maintain civil relations in routine interactions.[56] Despite this, tension and conflict were pervasive. Local residents often regarded the presence of immigrant merchants as a humiliating reminder of newcomers being able to enjoy the opportunities that blacks have unsuccessfully sought for themselves. Min's 1992 survey of black New Yorkers found that between one-third and one-half agreed that Korean merchants had a negative impact on them.[57]

Conflicts were enhanced as newly established merchants often lacked the hard-earned skills, contacts, and practices required to maintain a modicum of civility in their relations with customers. These included long-term relations with individual customers, familiarity with their outlooks and forms of sociability, a record of generosity, and a willingness to provide jobs. Indeed, residents of the Philadelphia ghetto where Elijah Anderson did fieldwork accepted the presence of long-established Jewish business owners, whose willingness to extend credit had allowed many to survive hard times. In contrast, residents regarded newly arrived Asian merchants as a threat to their economic well-being. As a consequence, they treated them with hostility.[58]

The reality of merchant-customer conflict was brought home in riots in Miami (1980), Chicago (1992), and Los Angeles (1992); boycotts in New York (1991), Los Angeles, Detroit, and Chicago; and in a pattern of violent store robberies throughout the United States. At the same time, some merchants' behavior toward local residents and customers—characterized by suspicion, hostility, lewd comments to women and girls, a lack of employment opportunities for local residents, and a "shoot first, ask questions later" approach to self-defense—demonstrated that violence was a threat to customers as well as merchants.[59]

African American Reactions

African American spokespersons have long regarded political and economic obstacles—including the lack of black-owned businesses and the presence of immigrant entrepreneurs in ghettos—as symptomatic of "the larger economic/political system which perpetuated a climate that suppressed the self-determination of black people."[60] Since the late nineteenth century, leaders and activists have worked to create an ethnic economy and to confront the array of barriers to this goal, ranging from Jim Crow laws and lack of education to difficulty in securing loans.[61]

African American leaders have described their objections to immigrant merchants in different ways, reflecting the various outlooks, political constituencies, and styles of self-presentation that exist in this sizeable and diverse population. Reactions have included spontaneous street actions, protests, boycotts, lawsuits, and government policies formulated by elected officials. Nevertheless, African Americans have learned—through years of effort—to advance collective and solidarity-based solutions to communal problems. Manning Marable describes this "as a black political project . . . grounded in grassroots struggles around practical questions of daily life. Such struggles bring into the public arena diverse and sometimes ideological and social forces."[62]

In a manner reminiscent of Sufi Hamid, the 1930s street speaker from Harlem and Bronzeville who helped catalyze the "Don't Shop Where You Can't Work" movement of the Depression Era, some spokespersons used ethnocentric and racist language to rebuke their opponents (see chapter 4). For example, when a Korean clothing store opened in a South Chicago neighborhood where black entrepreneurs were already being challenged by heavy competition from Korean and Jewish shops, the 47th Street Black Merchants' Association organized a boycott against Jewish- and Korean-owned businesses, during which Koreans were called "Korean Jews."[63]

Similarly, in an article in the *Amsterdam News*, Wilbert A. Tatum reflected on Louis Farrakhan's ability to connect with a fraction of the African American community by accusing Jews of exploiting blacks. "Anyone preaching a doctrine of hope and survival based upon the truth of our (African Americans') condition," wrote Tatum, "is going to be listened to. And the tragedy here is that Farrakhan developed a scapegoat that he could blame for our condition while virtually ignoring the sins and hypocrisy of the much larger and more powerful racist white society as it pertains to the shoddy treatment of . . . us."[64]

Not all black activists, however, describe their outlook in such coarse terms. Others articulate African Americans' opposition to what they regard as exploitative merchants without epithets or threats of violence.[65] Such activists refute charges that blacks who object to the nefarious impacts of non-black entrepreneurs are guilty of racial prejudice. As evidence, they point out that African Americans condemn the actions of merchants of color as often as they vilify nonblack business owners.[66] (See chapter 8.)

Such arguments, however, are seldom advanced without being countered. This is because significant portions of the media, many politicians, and members of the larger society condemn African Americans' efforts to control the inner-city economy as an illegitimate endeavor. Opponents assert that such actions are undemocratic and liken them to communism, mob rule, vengeance, and street crime.[67] In so doing, they draw upon racial stereotypes about blacks' inherently violent nature that date back to the Reconstruction era, if not before.[68]

A common strategy used by those who would discredit black activism is to claim that violence directed against merchants is broadly endorsed by local residents and encouraged by misguided liberals. For example, in an article decrying the victimization of ghetto merchants during the 1960s, historian Jonathan Bean argues, "African American activists, the heirs of Stokely Charmichael, organized boycotts that said 'GET OUT OF OUR COMMUNITY!' . . . Liberals . . . argued that African Americans and Hispanics were protesting their exclusion from the mainstream economy."[69]

While common, claims of the larger black population's endorsement of violence against immigrant merchants are supported by neither common sense nor social scientific data. African Americans—not immigrant merchants—are the most frequent victims of urban violence and suffer the largest number of fatalities during both riots and routine periods. What is more, in

ghetto neighborhoods, African Americans are the ethnic group most likely
to be left jobless, homeless, and without access to shopping venues following an urban uprising.[70]

Rather than universally endorsing violence, ghetto residents regularly defend merchants who have treated them well—often at considerable risk of
personal injury.[71] Finally, post-riot surveys suggest that a considerable fraction of those living in riot neighborhoods condemn looting and violence and
that community members are much more upset with police brutality than the
actions of immigrant merchants.[72] In fact, large-scale looting has been mostly
absent from several of the most significant recent uprisings. For example,
despite the hostility and violence that occurred among African Americans,
Caribbeans, and Hassidic Jews during the 1991 conflict in Brooklyn's Crown
Heights, only a handful of businesses were looted.[73] Similarly, episodes of
civil unrest in New York's Washington Heights in 1992 and Cincinnati in
2001 featured little looting or other forms of damage to ethnic businesses.[74]

To convince the public that significant fractions of the African American
community are ethnocentric and threatening, opponents gather the most
outrageous statements they can find (many of which have been condemned
by black leaders), take them out of context, and circulate them widely in
publications, mass mailings, news programs, and websites.[75]

As indicated in the following quote, African Americans' explanations
of their desire to develop community control in a manner that condemns
scapegoating specific groups are frequently circulated in the black press
and articulated by African American intellectuals. "These neighborhood
struggles . . . greatly enrich our understanding of the possibilities for change
within the entire society and we should support them and learn from them.
At the same time, we must consciously oppose the racial essentialism and
antidemocratic trends . . . inherent in many community-based formations
and struggles."[76]

Statements by black activists that condemn racism while also seeking
community control are rarely presented in mainstream publications and are
infrequently available in scholarly venues. Even academics who study relations between black communities and immigrant merchants often describe
the strategy as reflecting black nationalism, commonly described as a hostile, threatening, and extremist social movement associated with dogmatic
leaders and mob rule.[77] Such accusations are destructive of African Americans' political capital because they depict blacks as "a powerful, persecuting
majority" while ignoring their "own bitter experience of racial oppression"
as well as their general commitment to antiracist action.[78]

In striking contrast, the sizeable popular and academic literature re-
counting activities used by entrepreneurial immigrant groups to pursue

collective self-interest portrays such actions as positive, rational forms of solidarity and cooperation.[79] This literature does not refer to immigrants' collective quest of advantage as a form of Lebanese, Cuban, Greek, or Chinese nationalism. Similarly, studies of the extreme actions taken by native whites to maintain privileges seldom identify the agents of these actions as white nationalists.

Despite the larger society's opposition to the forms of communal activism used by African Americans to address the economic hegemony of immigrant merchants, it is likely that blacks will continue to rely on this approach because they lack alternative means of achieving their goals. Indeed, African American activists have challenged ethnic business owners in inner-city settings through local elections, boycotts, and zoning regulations as well as environmental impact reviews, the withholding of liquor licenses, lawsuits, and demands for the punishment of shop owners who have injured customers.[80]

During the 1980s, Al Sharpton established the National Action Network, which was involved in a nationwide campaign to improve the treatment of black customers in inner-city stores.[81] Following the Los Angeles Uprising of 1992, Danny Blakewell's Brotherhood Crusade sought to ensure that African Americans received a share of the funding and jobs distributed by government and often staged protests against white contractors, Latino workers, and Asian merchants in South Central Los Angeles.[82] Malik Shabazz organized a movement against what he regarded as abusive immigrant merchants in Detroit during the 1990s.[83] Significant boycotts were mounted in New York, Detroit, Chicago, and elsewhere. As Min notes, while not violent, the impact of a boycott is longer lasting than a single incident of violence and hence a greater financial threat.[84]

NONBLACKS ALSO OBJECT TO IMMIGRANT MERCHANTS

During the 1980s and 1990s, journalistic and academic accounts depicted African Americans as immigrant merchants' greatest opponents. A broader review, however, reveals that immigrant merchants have also been embroiled in disputes with numerous social groups, including middle-class whites, established business owners, government agencies, real estate interests, wholesalers and suppliers, unions, other immigrant groups, and subgroups of merchants' own ethnic communities.[85] By examining the broader array of conflicts encountered by immigrant merchants, we can develop greater insight into the social transformations associated with the presence of immigrant merchants in American society and recognize the fact that African Americans are not the only group in U.S. society that is challenged by it.

Studies of ethnic merchants document their being swindled and physically and verbally abused by more powerful social groups, including native-born whites.[86] For example, in the first book-length study on Korean entrepreneurs in the United States, Illsoo Kim described how Korean greengrocers suffered from discrimination in pricing, blocked access to parking, racist slurs, and physical intimidation from Jewish and Italian dealers in a wholesale produce market in the Bronx. Since that time, immigrant merchants have had numerous other conflicts with competitors, customers, suppliers, landlords, unions, and others.[87]

On the upper Texas coast, Vietnamese fishers and shrimpers were attacked by native-born whites who asserted they used illegal fishing practices and received government grants to buy boats. During 1981, "in the coastal town of Seabrook, 18 miles from Houston, two Vietnamese fishing boats were burned, and the Ku Klux Klan held an anti-Vietnamese rally and vowed to return control of coastal fishing to whites."[88]

In 1980, two hundred white residents upset by the burgeoning growth of Vietnamese businesses in Westminster, California (home to Little Saigon, the largest Vietnamese enclave outside of the country of origin), filed a petition asking the city business licensing office to deny licenses to Indochinese refugees, claiming that such enterprises burdened public coffers, increased unemployment, expanded the crime rate, and resulted in crowding and traffic congestion.[89] A few miles to the northeast, in Monterey Park, organized residents—including whites and U.S.-born persons of Mexican, Chinese, and Japanese ancestry—voted out Asian and Latino city council members in favor of an "all Anglo" slate. Their organization also proposed laws to prohibit the proliferation of Chinese-language signs, sought to make English the official language of the United States, and demanded restrictions on immigration.

Deriding the proliferation of Chinese stores in the town, an elderly Anglo resident complained, "We can't walk downtown to get anything . . . it's all Oriental groceries stores . . . stacks of rice in the window. . . . We're not against them but they want to buy our city, take our city."[90] Residents of Queens and Chicago raised similar objections to the number of foreign-language signs and the growing presence of Taiwanese, Korean, and South Asian businesses in their communities.[91]

Following the attacks of 9/11, Arab and Muslim business owners (as well as Sikhs, who were incorrectly assumed to be Arabs or Muslims) were attacked throughout the United States.[92] Between the late 1990s and 2002, members of various New York unions reported Korean greengrocers for labor law violations and picketed stores.[93] The City of Detroit and the Michigan Department of Agriculture developed special programs, including a 1-800 phone number, to simplify the reporting of merchants (nearly all of whom are of Middle Eastern origins) who were suspected of violating the city's food safety laws.[94] Finally, as described in chapter 5, from the 1980s onward, opponents of immigrant-, minority-, and women-owned businesses mounted a battle against business assistance programs in the courts, in lawmaking bodies, and through anti–affirmative action initiatives.[95]

CONFLICT BETWEEN IMMIGRANT ENTREPRENEURS AND IMMIGRANT CUSTOMERS

Conflicts between native customers and immigrant entrepreneurs are well documented. However, given the diverse nature of contemporary American society, immigrant merchants also do business with other immigrant groups. As noted in chapter 3, such interactions were commonplace prior to the 1920s. While tension does occur when immigrant merchants deal with immigrant customers, observers have noted that, when both parties to such interactions are foreign born, conflict is often less severe than when customers are U.S. born.

As a case in point, in their study of the Los Angeles Uprising, Edward Chang and Jeannette Diaz-Veizades cite the experience of Brenda Hughes, a seventeen-year-old daughter of Salvadorian immigrants who was shot and killed in a car in the Highland Park neighborhood of Los Angeles by Jo Won Kim, a Korean store owner, who suspected her companions of shoplifting.[96] While tragic, the Hughes event did not appear to have a major impact on Latino-Korean relations. In contrast, the case of Soon Ja Du—a Korean shop owner who shot and killed Latasha Harlins, an African American teenager accused of stealing, and received no jail time—was widely reported. It greatly increased tension between blacks and Koreans in Los Angeles and is seen as a major antecedent of the 1992 Los Angeles Riot.

Several explanations account for the relatively benign relations between immigrant entrepreneurs and foreign-born customers. Lucie Cheng and Yen Le Espiritu hypothesize that these groups see each other as fair competitors rather than hostile exploiters. Immigrant customers have fewer feelings of ownership or "rights" in U.S. society.[97] Accordingly, they are less concerned with and perhaps less cognizant of their relative social standing than are African Americans and also have less political power and savvy, so they are less likely to express their discontent through political and legal channels.[98] Because neither proprietors nor customers feel a strong sense

Sign seeking sewing machine operators in the Los Angeles garment district, 1992. After the mid-1960s, millions of immigrants and refugees entered the United States. They often had better relations with immigrant entrepreneurs than did native-born populations, at least partly because business owners sought to employ them. Errors in written Spanish suggest that someone not themselves fluent in Spanish was intentionally seeking Latino workers.
Source: Steven Gold

of agency and ownership within the host society, they conduct commercial interactions in a generally businesslike manner. This contrasts to the significant discomfort that the native born feel as they confront limited community control and low rates of business ownership.[99] Another reason for the relatively easy relations between immigrant entrepreneurs and immigrant customers is that migrant entrepreneurs commonly prefer immigrants to native-born whites or blacks as employees. Hence, for migrants, prospects for employment in ethnic shops are relatively good.[100]

Although they are marked by social, economic, linguistic, and legal disadvantages, even impoverished, undocumented, and recently arrived migrant groups—including Haitians, Central Americans, Dominicans, Mexicans, and Senegalese—appear to maintain higher levels of entrepreneurship (albeit, sometimes via very small-scale, informal businesses) than do U.S.-born blacks and Latinos.[101] While these immigrant entrepreneurs face many problems, including raids by police and shakedowns by coethnic gangs, their businesses do offer goods and services, provide training, yield earnings, and help groups develop a feeling of connection to and control over their local environments.[102]

Finally, while both native blacks and low-income, nonwhite migrants often reside in segregated neighborhoods, rates of isolation from whites are considerably lower for most Latinos and Asians than for blacks, and intermarriage with whites is much more frequent. A considerable body of evidence suggests that the Asian and Latino migrants' pattern of concentration is to a large extent voluntary and hence is not regarded simply as a form of ill treatment at the hands of the host society, as is commonly the case among native- and foreign-born blacks.[103] Accordingly, local business owners—regardless of their ethnicity—are less likely to be seen as the most visible representatives of an unjust and oppressive society.

It remains to be seen if these migrant populations will continue to maintain relatively benign relations with merchants or if, over time, their conflicts will begin to resemble those between native-born populations and ethnic entrepreneurs.

INTRAGROUP CONFLICTS

Emphasizing cultural conflict, observers often posit that the most severe merchant-customer conflicts are likely to occur among distinct ethnic, racial, and nationality groups, with better relations being maintained among those sharing religious, linguistic, racial, and cultural commonalities.[104] While this is often true, a significant amount of tension often exists within a single ethnic or nationality group. As suggested in chapter 3, intragroup conflicts were common among immigrants during the early twentieth century. Given the large number of immigrants and refugees arriving in the United States, since the 1970s, similar patterns have flared up as populations have imported disputes from the country of origin or otherwise fought with those with whom they share a common nationality or ethnicity.

José Cobas and Jorge Duany concede that the degree of antagonism meted out to Cubans in Puerto Rico is minor in comparison to the conditions encountered by Jewish or Korean entrepreneurs in U.S. ghettos. Nevertheless, the authors demonstrate that entrepreneurial Cubans are seen as "opportunistic and ungrateful parasites, who are arrogant and difficult to deal with as business owners and employers" despite the fact that both populations are Latino and share many cultural commonalities including religion and language. As a result of these sentiments, the Senate and House of Representatives of Puerto Rico called for the investigation of the Cubans' "discriminatory hiring practices" and the negative impacts of Cuban immigration on the well-being and happiness of Puerto Ricans.[105]

A related pattern exists among Chinese workers and owners in New York's garment industry. After the early 1970s, women who operated sewing machines in coethnic factories enjoyed stable wages and health benefits as a consequence of their union membership. However, since the late 1990s, this cooperative arrangement has fallen apart, with business owners relocating their shops beyond Manhattan in an attempt to find lower rents and avoid unions.[106] During the 1990s, Mexican street sellers competed with other Latinos in New York City, while in Miami, African Americans and Haitians competed over jobs and customers.[107] In New York, Miami, and other locations, African American leaders have attempted to recruit black immigrants to their efforts to sanction ethnic merchants. Due to different expectations, outlooks, and cultural practices, they have had a mixed record of success.[108]

In Detroit, Middle Easterners, who own most of the city's gas stations, liquor stores, and mini markets, maintain complex and multifaceted patterns of both cooperation and conflict. They reveal diversity in terms of nationality, religion, tenure in the United States, and location of residence as well as in their relations with each other and established white and black populations.[109] However, running businesses in a highly competitive environment can lead to volatile relations. During 2007, a price war between Syrian and Lebanese owners of nearby gas stations on the city's West Side become violent as the proprietors and their employees agued in Arabic. Before the fracas was over, one of the owners had been shot dead.[110]

At least during the 1980s and early 1990s, the most commonly discussed merchant-customer conflicts within the Vietnamese populations in several locations, including Northern and Southern California and Seattle, did not involve blacks, whites, or Latinos but rather fellow Southeast Asian refugees. Drawing on their premigration history, ethnic Vietnamese often complained about the economic power of the Chinese-Vietnamese population who they felt had unjustly controlled commerce in both Vietnam and the United States.[111]

MRS. DOAN: In Vietnam, the Chinese, they kept to themselves. They don't trust, they don't like to mingle a lot. They don't marry out either. They're real old-fashioned.

When we (ethnic Vietnamese) were back home, I still remember, when we talk about the Chinese (even though some of my distant relatives are from China), we talk like we don't respect them. We said they are just there to do some business and promotion; they don't try to have an education. They are mostly in business. Sell, buy, and trade. We Vietnamese go to school and get good grades, so we don't look at them as our equal.

The Chinese can get rich anywhere. My husband kind of jokes around; he says, "Open the mouth of an alligator and you can find the Chinese there doing business."

The Chinese is real good at selling and saving. We don't save. The more we get, the more we spend. They don't. If we go out to have fun, we GO OUT TO HAVE FUN! Even if we don't have money, we want to show it off. But not the Chinese—they really stingy, frugal. They don't care much for showing off and everything. That's how they get rich.

Another Vietnamese business owner complained, "They should to call this place Little Cholon [after Saigon's Chinatown] rather than Little Saigon" because of the economic power that the Chinese-Vietnamese maintained in the community. In fact, the community's major real estate developer and nearly all of its largest stores, supermarkets, factories, and restaurants were known to be owned by persons of Chinese origins—either from Vietnam or other national origins—such as Hong Kong or the Philippines.[112]

While the ethnic Chinese did have considerable influence over businesses in Vietnamese enclaves, at least during the 1980s and 1990s, the ethnic Vietnamese—especially the first wave who entered the United States between 1975 and 1977—were much better educated and more numerous, and as such, dominated professional occupations, leadership, and activist positions. Members of these two subethnic populations rub shoulders in business and communal activities and often reside near one another but also regard each other with resentment, mistrust, and suspicion.

As a response, some Chinese-Vietnamese increasingly identified solely as Chinese, lived in Chinese American neighborhoods, and failed to mention their links to Vietnam in the census, thus reducing the size and political influence of the Vietnamese American population.[113] This is reflected in the following excerpt from an interview conducted with a Chinese Vietnamese entrepreneur in Los Angeles's Chinatown in 1991.

> MR. HOA: The Chinese, we have 5,000 years of tradition. We stay together, work together, in our own business. My wife and I, we work hard six days a week, ten hours a day. I make sure my children study hard and learn English. I give them money, buy them a car so they can study. After they study, they work.
>
> Some Vietnamese are so good, but not so many. Many of the young man, girl go to the coffee shops, sit down, drinking, smoking. The parents don't take care for the children, the family. They don't work hard or stay together. They lose their business, closed.
>
> The Chinese, we help together. Say I am Chinese, I come from Vietnam. Example, you are Chinese and you come from Taiwan or maybe Singapore, or maybe Hong Kong. I need money—I need you to help support my business. How come you help me? I like to tell you. Because I, I have good experience and I have good credit. You have the money, but you don't know how to do that. So you check on my credit and ask the other people. I want to buy this restaurant. You help me; maybe you become my partner, because you believe in me. Maybe you are partner, or maybe I give you interest after six months. It works because we are all Chinese. The Vietnamese cannot do that.

While Vietnamese and Chinese-Vietnamese refugees who grew up in Vietnam maintain a suspicious view of each other, their American-raised children are often less focused on traditional antipathies. Instead, they frequently expressed a feeling of connection toward other persons of Vietnamese or Asian descent.[114] This interpretation is suggested as two refugees who came to the United States as adults discussed the shrinking tension between Vietnamese and Chinese-Vietnamese youth in the United States:

> INVESTIGATOR: So do you think as time goes on the Chinese-Vietnamese will go in one direction and the Vietnamese in another or do you think they will get together?
>
> MRS. DOAN: I don't think any kind of race can survive on their own. Vietnamese should know better. Back there, we had to struggle for survival. But here, the younger generation doesn't care if a person is Chinese or Vietnamese. They can't even speak Chinese or Vietnamese. They could care less if you're Vietnamese or Chinese.
>
> MR. HOA: Vietnamese, Vietnamese-Chinese, both escape from there. Now they are the same in the United States. They must accept the U.S. education. Everything from the past must be forgotten. In Vietnam, maybe they had

conflict. It's different at home. Today they are in the U.S.A. The young, they study, they like the United States. Some community leaders say Vietnamese are no good or that Chinese no good. No, I don't like to say that. Here, everybody needs to be together.

CRISIS, EXIT, AND ORGANIZATION

Immigrant entrepreneurs are aware of the vulnerable position they face in U.S. society in terms of their conflicts with customers, competitors, community activists, bureaucrats, and criminals. Accordingly, many created coethnic organizations and sought to curry favor from government officials and public servants, including politicians and law enforcement officials, via donations of money and goods. However, because they were recent immigrants, who spoke little English, spent many hours in their stores, and were largely unfamiliar with the functioning of American society, they were unable to develop the kinds of resources and relationships that could provide assistance when conflicts erupted. (An exception, the large and well-organized Cuban community in Miami, is discussed below.) As Angie Chung argues in her study of Korean American activism, "Donations could not compensate for lack of political voice and representation in local politics."[115]

During crises, the weakness of merchants' political connections became evident. For example, in the Los Angeles Uprising of 1992, "The police were egregiously absent in the lower-income neighborhoods of South Central and Koreatown, where many Korean business owners worked. It was reported that Los Angeles chief of police Daryl Gates failed to make adequate preparations for defending these areas despite strong advice to that effect from other officials. Once the riots broke out, officers were to protect the higher-income areas until order had been fully restored."[116]

Departure from the Inner City

Migrant entrepreneurs engaged in various strategies to deal with these crises. One strategy was to leave the inner city. Following the 1992 Los Angeles Uprising, a fraction of Korean entrepreneurs chose not to rebuild their businesses in South Central Los Angeles, and some even left the United States.[117] Similarly, according to David, over time, numbers of Chaldean business owners left Detroit and opened shops in suburban locations or took up white-collar work. "The growing entry of Chaldean youth into college shows the emphasis now being placed on professional occupations as opposed to store ownership."[118] Another option is to leave conflict-prone retail businesses for less volatile service enterprises. Min notes that, as time has passed, increasing numbers of Koreans have opted to run dry cleaners rather than greengrocers or clothing shops in black and Latino neighborhoods.[119]

Organization Efforts

Not all inner-city merchants flee conflict. Instead, some work to improve organizational capacity and political skills to defend their interests. They establish fund-raising campaigns, support political candidates, and initiate dialogue with other groups. For example, Korean Americans have increasingly relied upon American-educated and English-speaking group members to expand their power base in the United States.[120]

Initially, the most influential members of the Korean American community were affluent, first-generation, male entrepreneurs. They maintained dominance through respect accorded to their age, via their connections with home-country elites, and because of their business-based income, but they had little experience with or knowledge about the host society.[121] However, following conflicts with African American customers and activists as well as white suppliers, landlords, unions, politicians, police, and the media, the political limitations of the merchant elite became apparent.

For example, while Korean Americans suffered the greatest financial losses during the Los Angeles Riot, Rebuild Los Angeles (RLA), a nonprofit, multiethnic agency formed to deal with the riot's aftermath through investment in the inner city, didn't even include a Korean American board member. Instead, Koreans, who were defined as a part of the larger "Asian American faction," were to have their interests represented by a Chinese American. Not surprisingly, RLA failed to elicit the compensation that Koreans sought to cover their losses.[122]

The broader Korean community recognized that effective leaders were needed to function in the United States. A new generation with extensive knowledge of the American system accepted this task. Instead of blaming looters for the destruction of their stores, they focused on American institutions, such as the media, police, and government—for inciting tensions, reinforcing economic and political inequalities, and indirectly instigating urban violence. For the first time, Korean Americans presented themselves as "victims of white racism."[123] They organized a long-term demonstration of riot victims outside of Los Angeles City Hall "to demand attention and services from the mainstream institutions that had abandoned them during the rioting."[124] In this way, "the civil unrest became the first opportunity for younger people to develop a greater sense of political awareness from their personal experiences, which had been largely absent."[125]

In addition to providing sophisticated and effective leaders for the community, this transformation also challenged the entrepreneurial elite by opening positions of influence to women, unionists, leftists, and advocates of multiethnic coalitions. These activists were less concerned with maintaining entrepreneurial advantages and more interested in developing improved relations and coalitions with various actors—including those antagonistic to the interests of business leaders.[126] In this way, Korean American politics were transformed as representatives became involved in a variety of groups and issues beyond those of direct concern to the merchant class.

Other entrepreneurial immigrant groups have also developed multifaceted strategies in order to deal with the larger society. For example, following violent conflicts between merchants and customers in Detroit, the Harmony Project and Crisis Intervention Task Force were created to allow blacks and Arab Americans to discuss their concerns and reduce tension without calling the police.[127]

Because of their numerical size, political and economic power, and international concerns, Miami's highly entrepreneurial Cubans initially expressed little interest in developing multiethnic collations, even as they encountered conflicts with native blacks and whites. According to Portes and Alex Stepick, "For many, the native minority's rallies and riots were simply a nuisance."[128]

However, with time in the United States, like other merchant groups, Cuban organizations moved away from a singular focus on businesses and began to develop political coalitions. They established a "more balanced understanding that blacks were a permanent part of Miami and that there was no shying away from their problems." Moreover, realizing that whites and Jews sometimes sought to recruit black voters to support "an anti-Cuban platform" and confronting racial discrimination that frustrated their attempts to obtain high-level positions in local institutions, Cuban Americans came to appreciate the need for outreach to African Americans.

During the late 1980s, Cuban leaders began to emphasize their community's racial tolerance. Pointing out that Cuba was largely a black nation, they claimed Cuban racism to be more mild than that typical in the United States, while also asserting that they had contributed more to black progress in Miami than had whites. Despite such overtures, Miami's African Americans continued to be suspicious. For their part, most members of the Cuban community remained more oriented toward conationals than multiracial coalitions. While the possibility of improved relations had opened up, Cuban–African American relations remained in flux.

REGIONAL VARIATION IN
MERCHANT-CUSTOMER CONFLICT

After the 1990s, groups represented as residents and business owners in inner-city settings became increasingly diverse. Areas long considered to be African American ghettos, including South Central Los Angeles, the Bronx, and Hunters Point in San Francisco, became immigrant communities, with patterns of merchant-customer relations distinct from those prevalent in the 1980s and 1990s.

As a result, the polarization of specific groups of customers and merchants lost the degree of intensity that existed when fewer groups were present. Explaining why merchant-customer conflicts had reduced after the early 1990s, Min wrote,

> Indian, Pakistani, Middle Eastern, and African immigrants have moved into Harlem for commercial activities since around 1995. . . . A positive aspect of the change is that the ethnicity among business owners is now so diverse that Korean merchants . . . are no longer perceived unfavorably. Neither Koreans nor any other group in Harlem are perceived as middleman merchants, although they still do serve that function.[129]

Moreover, gentrification meant that many ghettos ceased to be centers of concentrated poverty. Instead, after the mid 1980s, urban pioneers began to prize homes in New York's Harlem and Bedford Stuyvesant, Detroit's Corktown, Los Angeles' West Adams, and New Orleans' French Quarter, causing the urban poor to compete with professionals for housing and ethnic entrepreneurs to vie with chains like Starbucks, Wal-Mart, and the Body Shop for customers and business locations.[130]

In her research on gentrification in New York City, sociologist Sharon Zukin describes a process of "boutiquing" wherein ethnic mom-and-pop stores are replaced by more upscale shops appealing to the middle class. "Harlem for the past few years has experienced a startling rise in property values and an equally dramatic—although less pervasive—increase in big chain stores as well as in elegant restaurants, shops, and cafés."[131]

If available, minority customers increasingly favored malls and super-stores over ethnic retail shops, thus reducing trade and tension between local residents and immigrant entrepreneurs.[132]

While some corporate and franchise businesses provided jobs, good service, and competitive prices to inner-city consumers, the corporate return to the inner city was not without its downside. Chains of pawn shops, loan companies, rent-to-own furniture stores, and other enterprises that were

New Museum, Lower Manhattan. With gentrification, low income communities like New York's Lower East Side have become much more affluent. When cultural institutions like the museum (which cost an estimated $64 million for the building and its endowment and requires a $12 fee for entry), together with boutiques, nightclubs, and affluent people move in, low income residents and the shops that serve them are often forced out.

Source: Steven Gold

Check cashing company, Southern California, 2005. Because their neighborhoods lack banks, the residents of impoverished urban areas must satisfy their financial needs in other institutions, such as check cashing stores. These companies offer few loans or other services conducive to the creation of small businesses.
Source; Steven Gold

subsidiaries of NationsBank, Transamerica Corporation, American Express, and other firms traded on Wall Street, opened in inner-city neighborhoods, where conventional banks and stores remain rare.

While cleaner and more presentable than ethnic shops of days gone by, these companies use misleading advertising to lure customers and charge exorbitant interest rates to those with few alternatives. Several have been the target of government investigations and class-action lawsuits for their exploitative practices.[133] Moreover, the firms' extensive resources mean that neither African American nor immigrant-owned businesses have much of a chance to compete. According to Marable, corporate interest in black customers has a largely negative effect.

Historically, rapid black business growth occurred *only during the period of rigid racial segregation*, when relatively few white corporations made any attempt to attract black consumers. The Civil Rights Movement and desegregation permitted the white private sector to develop a variety of advertising strategies to extract billions in profits from black consumers, all in the name of "equality." The net result was the increased marginalization of the black entrepreneur, the manipulation of black culture and social habits by white corporations, and a new kind of economic underdevelopment for all blacks at all income levels.[134]

However, not all American cities are the destinations of diverse and growing migrant populations, nor are they witnessing the return of corporate businesses. Instead, such cities—often in the Midwest and South—are characterized by economic stagnation and population loss. They generally maintain long-established patterns of conflict between a limited number of entrepreneurial groups and native-born, minority customers. Local residents in these communities continue to struggle to fulfill basic needs in ethnic shops.[135] (See chapter 8.)

Finally, regardless of local economic conditions, immigrant merchant groups tend to focus on inner-city entrepreneurship for only a relatively brief period of time. As business owners become more financially secure or tire of running businesses in ghetto environments, they move out and their American-educated children show little propensity to take over their parents' livelihoods.[136] In a process Min calls serial middleman entrepreneurship, new nationalities occupy the small business niche, altering the nationality of those involved in merchant-customer relations even as the patterns of interaction surrounding them remain largely unchanged.[137]

CONCLUSIONS

The last two decades of the twentieth century were marked by political, demographic, and economic transformations of America's major cities that made merchant-customer conflict an issue of popular concern. Economic restructuring, marked by job loss, population decline, and reduced public spending, yielded tough times in most locations. Moreover, the ascendancy of antiwelfare ideology curtailed the possibility of government intervention.

The period also marked the arrival of numerous, nonwhite migrants who would both live and do business in urban locations. As they took over the niche of inner-city entrepreneurship, conflicts erupted with local residents who complained of mistreatment and resented newcomers' rapid advancement that appeared to block their own entry into the middle class. In response, residents engaged in both spontaneous and organized activities to limit the influence of immigrant merchants in their communities. Despite the image maintained in much journalism and scholarship, African Americans were not immigrant merchants' sole opponents. Rather, suburban whites, established business owners, real estate interests, unions, local government, and other immigrant groups also engaged in disputes with immigrant entrepreneurs.

Not all natives resented the newcomers. The popular celebration of cultural pluralism and free market capitalism since the 1970s meant that a group of intellectuals, politicians, and journalists regarded immigrant merchants as good examples for locals and harbingers of diversity, vitality, and economic revival.

As they encountered conflicts, immigrant merchants who lacked the numbers, political refinement, and media savvy to curry favor with groups and institutions of the larger society suffered significant losses from restrictive policies, riots, boycotts, and robberies. They responded by establishing more sophisticated forms of organization such as incorporating the skills of Americanized group members, establishing outreach activities, making demands of politicians, participating in multiethnic coalitions, and employing local workers. Ultimately, however, many merchant groups reduced their involvement in ghetto entrepreneurship as their American-educated children found desirable jobs in the larger economy. In their ability to exit inner-city locations, new immigrants reveal a capacity for economic mobility that exceeds that of working-class African Americans, Latinos, and other disadvantaged groups.

As a consequence of the demographic and economic changes of recent decades, merchant-customer conflict has become much more complex. The presence of immigrants reduced the political and demographic power of native-born groups. Newcomers now take on both merchant and customer roles in inner cities. Their conflicts are generally less volatile than those between immigrant merchants and natives. Finally, the return of chain stores in some environments provides local residents with shopping and employment options while permitting them to eschew interactions with immigrant merchants.

Alliances and loyalties become more varied as the system of ethnic stratification becomes more diverse. Members of the same nationality are fragmented by rivalries retained from the country of origin; immigrants regard ethnic merchants not as oppressors but rather as potential employers; and populations with similar racial and cultural identities find that some situations encourage cooperation, while others foster competition. Migrant groups with high levels of education and access to capital and goods from overseas drive less-endowed competitors out of business.

Finally, there are regional differences in patterns of merchant-customer conflict. In coastal cities, new residents dilute hardened patterns of intergroup conflict, while gentrification displaces both customers and entrepreneurs. In contrast, in rustbelt cities—like Detroit, Gary, and

Cleveland—worsening poverty, population loss, and negligible rates of immigration have kept the situation in a holding pattern, such that the dynamics of merchant-customer relations are not appreciably different from those of years gone by.

In sum, native- and foreign-born groups continue to engage in conflicts over community control and scarce and valued resources. Such disputes are generally a product of the larger society's structure of opportunity, not racial, cultural, or ethnic factors per se. As noted by Marable, "Petty differences drawn from language, cultural traditions and mores and codes of public conduct and courtesy can be misinterpreted in antagonistic ways, dividing communities who share in most respects common material and political interests."[138]

The popular myth of racial antipathy and cultural conflict among immigrant merchants and minority customers provides a convenient model through which members of the larger society can frame opposition without implicating themselves. Ultimately, however, the larger economic and political structure underlies many of their struggles.

7

THE INFORMAL ECONOMY AS A SITE OF COMPETITION BETWEEN DISADVANTAGED POPULATIONS AND ETHNIC MERCHANTS

A sizeable body of research and writing on ethnic mobility separates populations into groups that maintain high rates of self-employment and groups that do not. Such classifications are generally invidious, describing those with extensive self-employment as bearing positive attributes, including a strong work ethic, self-control, and salutary patterns of familial and communal cooperation. In contrast, groups identified as lacking significant rates of self-employment are often portrayed as deficient in the qualities required for success.[1]

Drawing these distinctions, authors go on to suggest that entrepreneurial capabilities predict a positive future for groups who possess them. The descendants of entrepreneurial populations are described as likely to become well educated, upwardly mobile, and over time, represent the best of their host society. Conversely, less entrepreneurial groups are seen as undersupplied with many of the fundamental traits and resources required for achievement. As such, their future prospects are deemed to be poor and likely to involve intergenerational poverty.[2]

For example, Dinesh D'Souza and Tony Brown, journalists who contrast the cultural attributes of immigrants with those of native minorities, assert, "Blacks have done very poorly in small business, a vital source of American jobs and upward mobility."[3] While addressing class, structural, political, and historical issues, in addition to the cultural factors that concern D'Souza and Brown, sociologists Alejandro Portes and Robert Bach also note considerable differences in patterns of success revealed by more and less entrepreneurial groups. In their analysis of Mexican and Cuban migrants with six years of residence in the United States, they note that 5.5 percent of Mexican men and 0 percent of their wives were self-employed. In contrast, after the same time in the United States, 21.2 percent of Cuban men and 5.0 percent of their wives in the United States were self-employed. These divergent rates of entrepreneurship were found to be consistent with other forms of accomplishment, most notably, the allocation of employment and assistance to coethnics.[4] In her analysis of media depictions of conflicts between Korean merchants and black customers in New York City, Claire Jean Kim finds a similar rubric, concluding, "By this view, Asian immigrants have something that blacks do not—namely the right cultural stuff. They are modern day Horatio Algers."[5]

To dramatize purported differences in worldview and achievement motivation between more and less entrepreneurial groups, writers often describe their contrasting behaviors in the inner-city settings that they share. Despite the barren surroundings, merchants find ways to build enterprises that support their families and ensure the mobility of their children. Nonentrepreneurs are overwhelmed by their circumstances and remain mired in poverty.[6]

While recognizing their lack of progress, nonentrepreneurial groups fail to learn from their industrious neighbors' example. Rather than starting enterprises of their own, they become envious and react by intimidating merchants, boycotting stores, and criticizing owners' greed. Such accounts emphasize the nihilism and self-destructiveness of residents' conflicts with ghetto merchants, asserting that attacks are done out of vindictiveness, ultimately making circumstances worse by damaging the fragile social and economic conditions of neighborhoods already in decline.[7]

Such characterizations of impoverished immigrant and minority populations as nonentrepreneurial are relatively common. However, they are also largely inaccurate. Nearly every ethnographic study of economic life in impoverished, minority, and immigrant neighborhoods conducted since the late nineteenth century describes these settings as beehives of economic activity, entrepreneurship, and small business. Accounts of life in African American neighborhoods during the 1930s and 1940s mention pushcarts, food stands, and other small businesses run by local residents.[8] Reporting on Depression-Era Harlem, journalist Roi Ottley details the ubiquity of informal enterprises: "Elongated wooden boxes stood upright at the entrance to basements, marking the location of fuel sellers, who dispensed bundles of wood and bagfuls of coke. Lean-tos—squat unpainted shacks of wood and tin built against larger structures housed hopeful little enterprises—fish frys, moving-van concerns, news-stands, and shoe-shine parlors." Similarly, Jacqueline Jones describes how black women who supported themselves "as healers, religious leader, and entrepreneurs . . . still offered their services to friends and neighbors," even as they had to adjust their fees or barter for food or clothing as a consequence of the realities of Depression life.[9]

Urban ethnographies from the 1960s and 1970s, including *All Our Kin* and *Tally's Corner*, elaborate on the many activities that poor African Americans used to make ends meet.[10] Betty Lou Valentine's *Hustling and Other Hard Work* describes economic strategies used by residents of Blackston, an impoverished ghetto neighborhood in a large northern city during the 1960s and 1970s. "Hustling involves a wide variety of unconventional, sometimes extralegal or illegal activities, often frowned upon by the wider community but widely accepted and practiced in the slums and ghettos of large cities. . . . Everyone beyond early childhood has knowledge of and at least indirect contact with these operations." Valentine describes how Blackston's residents engage in a variety of informal enterprises, including child care, food preparation and sales, home remodeling, and pay-to-enter house parties. Persons who have access to apartments or cars rent them out or barter goods for their short-term use. Those employed in construction and remodeling often arranged with their bosses to develop properties of their own during off hours and then rented them out in order to increase their income.[11]

More recent studies document informal economic practices ranging from sidewalk merchandising to child care and garment assembly, and to home renovation. These allow immigrants and native minorities to cope with the economic scarcity produced by welfare reform, deindustrialization, undocumented status, and rising prices.[12] Drawing on long-term fieldwork in a South Chicago neighborhood he calls Maquis Park, sociologist Sudhir Venkatesh found that, as economic conditions and the availability of services declined in the area and middle-class residents left, "the underground economy was fast becoming a primary economy for black ghetto dwellers."

If one were to canvass the entrepreneurs in Maquis Park, a rich and busy portrait would emerge, contradicting the area's stark physical decimation. Beneath the closed storefronts, burned-out buildings, potholed boulevards, and empty lots, there is an intricate fertile web of exchange, tied together by people with tremendous human capital and craftsmanship[:] Electricians, mechanics, glassmakers and welders, accountants and lenders, carpenters and painters, sculptors, clothing designers, hairstylists and barbers, cooks, musicians and entertainers.[13]

While few of these service providers are advertised in the yellow pages, lo-cal residents know where they can be found. They are the foundation of the community, and their actions create an alternative public sphere.

Sociologists Marta Tienda and Rebeca Raijman discovered similar prac-tices a few miles away in Chicago's Little Village.[14] Here another popula-tion noted for its low rates of self-employment—undocumented Mexican men and especially women—are shown to be extensively entrepreneurial. Describing these patterns of work as "quasi-employment," these scholars observed that Little Village residents combined multiple forms of entre-preneurship (such as child care, food preparation, street corner sales, and home repair) with regular and informal employment; they also bartered exchange of domestic services (like sharing food and taking in boarders) and, occasionally, collected government benefits. These manifold forms of income generation enhance earnings and levels of consumption, help group members cope with a slack economy, allow customers to acquire basic ser-vices at a low price, and assist budding entrepreneurs in amassing both the skills and the investment capital required to transform informal businesses into formal ones. As these case studies reveal, rather than being nonentre-preneurs, marginal populations including native minorities and immigrants are often highly entrepreneurial. Accordingly, their many informal enter-prises are "the most visible signs that urban poor communities do contain a heady spirit of work and entrepreneurship."[15]

What distinguishes the entrepreneurship of poor blacks, immigrants, and refugees from that of classic middleman populations such as Koreans, Chal-deans, Lebanese, Iranians, Cubans, Greeks, and Jews is not the propensity to run businesses per se. Rather, it is the enumeration practices of the U.S. Census that tabulate legitimate businesses while ignoring informal ones. As Ivan Light explains in *Cities in World Perspective*, the economic success of immigrant entrepreneurs like Cubans in Miami raises the question of why other marginal groups have been unable to accomplish as much. "Unfortu-nately, these people cannot be statistically enumerated, but if they were it would be evident that . . . urban blacks in general are not underrepresented in informal sector self-employment. Their underrepresentation occurs only in small business enterprise—not in marginal self-employment."[16] Making a comparable argument, Tienda and Raijman assert, "Studies based on cen-sus data cannot take into consideration multiple job holding and informal activity."[17] If they did, they would generate a very different image of the groups involved in ethnic entrepreneurship.

It is well established, then, that several ethnic and racial groups who are characterized as having low rates of self-employment are often quite en-trepreneurial and rely on multiple business activities in order to survive in circumstances where earnings are hard to come by. Moreover, the reason such groups are described as being uninvolved in entrepreneurship is due to enumeration, not actual behavior.[18] When we consider the fact that many impoverished groups who are defined as lacking entrepreneurial propensity are in reality extensively involved with self-employment, our understanding of life in minority settings generally, and of conflict and competition between customer groups and immigrant entrepreneurs, in particular, is transformed.

Traditionally, the hostile actions taken by customer groups in impoverished urban neighborhoods against local merchants have been seen as motivated by jealousy or as part of an agenda of political intimidation that seeks to secure kickbacks from business owners or entitlements from the government.[19] By acknowledging residents' extensive involvement in self-employment, such actions can be understood as pursuit of free market advantage, or in other words, as efforts to build their own business niches.

CONFLICT WITH MERCHANTS AS REALISTIC CONFLICT

In his classic study of social conflict, Louis Coser makes a distinction between realistic and unrealistic conflict.[20] When group A expresses hostility toward group B because group B is preventing group A from achieving a desired goal, then this conflict is realistic. However, when group A expresses hostility against group B even though group B is not preventing group A from reaching a desired goal, then this is unrealistic conflict. Group B is simply a target for group A's hostility and frustration. In common terminology, group B is serving as group A's scapegoat.

Drawing on Coser's distinction, we see that, when scholars and pundits ignore the existence of self-employment among groups like ghetto residents and undocumented immigrants, they assume that their opposition to ethnic merchants is unrealistic conflict. Merchants are presumed to be targeted due to frustration, jealously, and ethnocentrism. However, by acknowledging the significant levels of entrepreneurship maintained by disadvantaged populations, we realize that their opposition to immigrant merchants can be a form of realistic conflict. They are engaging in market-based economic competition. Rather than taking it for granted that disadvantaged groups lack the capability for success in American society, we recognize their entrepreneurial spirit. Such groups *do* have the cultural "right stuff" required for achievement and mobility, after all.

Marginal groups' conflicts with outgroup entrepreneurs can be understood as efforts to compete against legally sanctioned businesses whose owners have greater access to capital and more extensive experience and skill in entrepreneurship, as well as political connections, ties to law enforcement, degrees and certificates, and other resources. As Juliette Walker, Regina Austin, and other scholars note, established entrepreneurs often use government connections to obtain support for their enterprises and for the suppression of competitors. "In America, government support, both direct and indirect, is critically important for business success. . . . There is a propensity in American culture to view the social and economic condition of blacks as one of failure, as opposed to acknowledging that the government has failed [to assist] blacks."[21] As sociologist Donald Light notes, groups with ample access to money and power exert their influence over politicians to "move the goal posts" or, in other words, to have the law changed, "as major industries do so that they can openly enjoy today what were illicit means yesterday."[22]

Along with not being counted, a lack of formal business organizations is another feature that distinguishes informal businesses from their legitimate counterparts. Lacking the advantages that formal, well-financed, and well-connected businesses enjoy, immigrants, minority group members, and others who operate informal enterprises rely on communal resources that allow them to run successful enterprises on their own terms. In many cases, they seek to enhance available advantages in order to make their operations more competitive with formal enterprises.

Such conflicts can be destructive. However, in many instances, the worst-case scenario of violent discord between formal and informal enterprises is not realized. Because of their distinct resources, disparate goals, and contrasting relations with the institutions of the larger society, informal and formal businesses often maintain complementary relations, such that each benefits—at least partly—from the existence of the other.[23] Many forms of collaboration are spontaneous and don't involve an actual agreement between formal and informal entrepreneurs. In some cases, however, informal entrepreneurs and legitimate merchants do develop cooperative and mutually beneficial arrangements.

CURRENT PERSPECTIVES ON INFORMAL ENTERPRISE

Prior to the 1970s, social theorists noted the existence of the informal economy but linked it to underdevelopment.[24] They assumed that, with the passage of time and with economic modernization, small, community-based enterprises including informal operations would become obsolete because government planners and major enterprises had enough skill in managing economic growth and extending its benefits throughout society, and that such marginal activities would be neither needed nor profitable.[25] After the economic shocks of the 1970s—which combined growing unemployment with escalating inflation and fiscal austerity—this view began to change. Scholars acknowledged that informal economic strategies based upon kinship and community were not limited to preindustrial settings but were viable in postindustrial settings as well.[26] We now recognize the prevalence and importance of informal economies in locations epitomizing economic development, including New York, Los Angeles, Paris, and Amsterdam.

Saskia Sassen sees the informal economy as vital to satisfying needs associated with groups at opposite ends of the urban economic hierarchy. On one hand, it delivers goods to immigrant and minority groups who cannot afford to fill their needs through established businesses. On the other hand, the informal economy also caters to the specific and just-in-time production demands of cutting-edge firms and efficiently allocates luxury consumables prized by the high-income populations that work for them.[27]

Economists and policy makers sometimes object to informal enterprises on moral grounds, viewing them as deviant, socially destructive, and of limited economic impact. In recent years, however, many pragmatic scholars and bureaucrats have abandoned such judgments and instead evaluated their social benefits and costs on an empirical basis.[28] Reflecting this perspective, a growing body of theorizing and research acknowledges the importance of informal entrepreneurship in the global economy. While earlier analyses assumed that the informal economy consisted of inconsequential enterprises like baby sitting, selling matches, or collecting scrap metal, theorists now realize that the informal economy plays essential roles in allowing large-scale and cutting-edge industries to function. Further, patterns of work associated with the informal economy, including its low cost, creativity, and openness to nonorthodox ways of doing business, make it vital to many forms of innovation that benefit large-scale firms and stimulate economic growth.[29]

For example, subcontractors, who are often members of immigrant or ethnic groups, permit major firms to rapidly and inexpensively manufacture products within global cities. The existence of such manufacturing schemes allows firms to combine the low cost and labor discipline of third world settings with the proximity and control of local production.[30] Informal businesses also provide a wide array of services such as cooking, cleaning, child care, delivery, moving, security, transport, remodeling, dog walking, plant care, sex work, clerical services, and health care. They also staff hotels, restaurants, airports, industrial parks, and other locations that are essential to cutting-edge corporate and governing processes.

Defining the Informal Economy

A major challenge confronting scholars and policy makers who are interested in examining the impact of informal entrepreneurship is definitional. How can one distinguish between benign forms of unregulated commerce, on one hand, and socially destructive criminal enterprises, on the other? While there are a variety of schemes for categorizing the informal economy, Manuel Castells and Alejandro Portes provide a simple distinction between formal, informal, and illegal businesses.[31] The formal economy includes enterprises that deliver goods and services in conformity with laws and regulations. The informal economy consists of unregulated and unrecorded economic activity that occurs off the books and pays no taxes.[32] Finally, the illegal economy encompasses the production and distribution of legally prohibited goods and services, such as drugs, prostitution, and illegal gambling.

Because of the stigma associated with the illegal economy, most analysts who emphasize the positive impact of informal entrepreneurship exclude such activities from their analyses.[33] Nevertheless, research by economist Robert Fairlie demonstrates that entrepreneurial skills (and investment funds) acquired in the illegal economy are applicable to the running of legitimate enterprises.[34] Of course, there is significant overlap in these three subcategories. Finally, sociologists realize that categories such as normal, deviant, criminal, and illegal are socially defined and subject to change.[35]

Measuring Informal Entrepreneurship

Measuring the size of the informal economy is difficult because its participants seek to conceal the income it creates. However, researchers who have developed various techniques for estimating its size generally conclude it to be considerable and to have important economic and social impacts. A census-based estimate found that informal employment and entrepreneurship accounted for 9.4 percent of the U.S. economy in 1980 and 8.1 percent in 2000.[36] A study by the U.S. Internal Revenue Service found that 47 percent of workers classified as independent contractors did not report any of their income for tax purposes. Hence, almost half of independent contractors can be considered informal entrepreneurs.[37] Another measure of the size of informal entrepreneurship involves the concealment of unemployment. Several economists have concluded that about 20 percent of those officially listed as unemployed in the United States are actually active as workers or entrepreneurs in the informal economy.[38]

An estimate of involvement in the U.S. informal economy, based upon data collected by the Survey Research Center of the University of Michigan, found that over seventy-two billion dollars was spent on informal purchases in 1985, an amount representing almost 15 percent of all expenditures that year. The same source found that 83 percent of all households made use of at least one informal supplier. Home repairs and improvements, food, child care, other personal and domestic services, and auto repairs were the leading areas of informal spending.[39] The U.S. Bureau of Labor Statistics estimated that some 260,000 workers seek employment on street corners throughout the country.[40]

With respect to specific localities, the value of untaxed street corner sales in Los Angeles County was estimated to be 250 million dollars in 2002.[41] A 2002 study of informal employment in Los Angeles estimated that the region had five hundred thousand more employed residents than jobs reported by employers and that, in Southern California, "self-employment has often been associated with the informal economic activity because it offers more flexibility and is typically less accountable than waged and salaried employment. In fact, a number of researchers have used self-employment as an estimate of the informal economy."[42] Finally, Abel Valenzuela counted between twenty and twenty-two thousand day laborers at ninety-five sites in Southern California in 1999.[43]

In 1993, a *New York Times* article cited an estimate from the New York City comptroller that the unreported economy was fifty-four billion dollars, or 20 percent of the city's retail sales. The same article estimated that street vending in New York—which included some ten thousand unlicensed vendors—was a three-hundred-million-dollar-a-year industry, that illegal industrial homework, involving garment work and the assembling of goods in private homes, generated one billion dollars' worth of business annually, and that there were some five thousand informally run apparel sweatshops in New York's five boroughs.[44]

Earnings of Informal Entrepreneurs

Individual earnings from informal self-employment vary considerably and are not always small. In a study of informal economic activities among twenty documented and eighteen undocumented Latinos in New Jersey, Elaine Edgcomb and Maria Armington found that earnings ranged between 27 dollars and 4,600 dollars each month, with the average revenue being just under 800 dollars a month. These thirty-eight respondents owned a total of fifty-one businesses. Sixteen respondents regarded their economic activities as necessary for economic survival rather than being the result of personal choice.[45]

Street vendor selling handbags in New York City, 2005. Revealing the size of the informal economy, a 1993 New York Times *article estimated that 10,000 unlicensed vendors earned $300 million annually in the city.*
Source: Steven Gold

A similar study of fifty-five African American men and women involved in the informal economy in Baltimore (n = 25) and Chicago (n = 30) conducted during late 2002 found that proprietors devoted considerable time to informal economic activities, averaging about thirty-eight hours a week, but ranging between eight and seventy hours weekly. Their mean earnings were 910 dollars monthly, stretching from 200 dollars monthly for a hair stylist to 2,400 dollars monthly for the proprietor of a moving business. The thirty-nine respondents who were operating their own businesses earned a great deal more than the sixteen who worked for others (1,013 dollars for self-employed; 702 dollars for workers). Women earned slightly more than men (women, 963 dollars; men, 879 dollars). Eighteen of those surveyed also obtained income from formal-sector employment. Finally, 36 percent were involved in job training or educational programs, often in an attempt to improve their economic prospects.[46]

Among Southern California day laborers, the mean yearly income was slightly above the poverty threshold for a single family in 1999. The mean hourly wage of $6.91 was about $1.75 higher than the federal minimum wage and about $1.15 higher than the California State minimum wage. At this rate, full-time, year-round employment would earn a day laborer about 14,400 dollars, almost 175 percent above the federal poverty threshold for a single person in 1999. However, because day labor is unstable, workers are likely to earn less than that amount. That being said, being a day laborer in Southern California "is certainly comparable to other types of low-skill and low-paying jobs in the formal market, and the mean yearly income is about $200 above the federal poverty threshold."[47]

The Attractions of Informal Entrepreneurship

Researchers offer several reasons ghetto residents and migrants become involved in informal self-employment. Perhaps the most commonly cited reason is that other sources of income—including work and public assistance—if available at all, are so small that they must be supplemented to ensure recipients' survival. In some localities, factory work is the only source of employment for low-income populations.[48] Since the loss of well-paid, unionized manufacturing jobs in the 1970s and 1980s, factory jobs tend to be dirty, dangerous, stressful, sporadic, and poorly paid. As such, other means of earning a living are actively sought.

Another significant motive for informal self-employment is to conceal sources of income from the government. Hidden income is desired by some workers who receive public assistance and disability benefits. Immigrants without work permits as well as those lacking the licenses, training, and economic resources required to do business legally have little option but to engage in informal economic activities.

As sociologists Daniel Bell and Robert Merton have argued, there is generally a demand for various goods and services that are illegal or excessively expensive to obtain legally.[49] Ambitious persons lacking the resources required to earn a living in the legal economy will often accept the risk involved in filling such demand. Informal enterprises provide a mobility ladder for those with high aspirations but limited ability to acquire legitimate income.

> Certain subgroups and certain ecological areas are notable for the relative absence of opportunity for achieving these (monetary and power) types of success. They constitute in short, sub-populations where the cultural emphasis

upon pecuniary success has been absorbed, but where there is *little access to conventional and legitimate* means for attaining such success . . . the result is a tendency to achieve these culturally approved objectives *through whatever means are possible.* These people are on one hand "asked to orient their conduct toward the prospect of accumulating wealth [and power] and on the other, they are largely denied effective opportunities to do so institutionally."[50]

Legal scholar Austin describes the outlook of African American street vendors via this frame: "Most black street vendors work without a license and in violation of applicable vending regulations and sales tax laws. Yet, when asked about their illegal status, the vendors maintain that vending is an 'honest living' that they should be allowed to pursue legally."[51] Due to their origins in cultural contexts different from those of the mainstream United States, members of immigrant and ethnic groups often desire goods and services, ranging from cockfights to Peking Duck (which is prepared under conditions that violate established food safety regulations), that cannot be legally sold in the United States.[52] Accordingly, if they are to acquire these commodities, they must do so via unregulated sources.

Lacking the assets needed to open businesses—including investment capital, business experience, education, familiarity with the mainstream culture, language skills, and legal status—but immersed in family and community networks, impoverished immigrants and minority group members in inner-city areas find the informal economy particularly well suited to their economic needs and resources. For these reasons, Valenzuela attributes the motives of informal business owners to both disadvantage (they lack other viable means of earning a living) and values (they enjoy greater independence and realize benefits from being self-employed that would be unavailable under other work conditions).

The Community Context of Informal Businesses

Members of marginal populations often have skills and resources that allow them to fulfill coethnic consumer needs in low-income, immigrant, and minority communities that members of other populations cannot satisfy. Social and economic relations within such communities follow distinct norms, sometimes clearly unlike those predominant in other realms of society. In many cases, resources are based upon family or communal relationships, location of residence, or other factors and are difficult for outsiders to access. In contrast, living close to customers and maintaining relatively small stocks of goods, coethnic vendors can gauge shifts in demand and adjust their inventories accordingly and thus respond to changing conditions faster than established firms.[53]

Within such environments, norms regarding cooperation that have developed to ensure mutual survival can also allow individuals to access one another's resources in ways that downplay economic individualism and encourage the distribution of money and other goods among community members.[54] For example, Elijah Anderson, Venkatesh, and Carol Stack note that urban blacks exchange and share resources as a means of survival. While honoring collective obligations may keep members from acquiring resources sufficient to permit their escape from the ghetto, the practice nevertheless permits such communities to survive in barren and impoverished environments.

As Anderson points out, monetary transactions with legitimate merchants often result in money leaving destitute communities. In contrast, funds spent in the informal sector remain in the local setting. Such norms have "the effect of increasing social capital: bonding people to one another and providing opportunities for informal contact, while putting people on notice that they must pay their debts or risk tension and conflict."[55] According to Venkatesh, the widely reported difficulty that residents of disadvantaged communities confront in obtaining credit has a partial silver lining. Because funds from banks are all but inaccessible, informal lenders become the sole source of credit. As a consequence, interest from loans that in other settings would enrich nonresident bankers is acquired by loan sharks and political bosses. Despite their nefarious reputations, these economic actors may have a greater commitment to the local community than do legitimate financiers. Finally, Venkatesh contends that because they fear the unfamiliarity and racism of the larger society, a fraction of Maquis Park entrepreneurs, who would appear to have the skills and capital needed to run successful firms in more affluent environments, continue to manage informal businesses in the familiar, if impoverished, realm of the ghetto.[56]

While minority communities are seldom affluent, they still contain significant consumer demand. Yet chain stores and even ethnic merchants have long been reluctant to fill the needs of such customers. For example, a 1950 speech by Claude A. Barnett of the Associated Negro Press complained about the poorly developed retail milieu in Chicago's Bronzeville:

> What has happened right here on the South Side on nearly every cross street? Why do we have four or five times as many restaurants or eating places in a block as necessary, most of them dirty and unsanitary? Who ought to police that sort of thing and insist on limiting the number of each type of business in a given area, so we might have one successful business instead of a lot of

half-run establishments cutting each other's and the public's throats? . . . Who does it in the white neighborhoods? . . . There is enough money in these areas to support first class stores. Why do the high class merchants run away? Why is it that on 35th Street near where I office for example, there are three liquor dives, with wine heads and half stupefied people staggering in and out all day long, all owned by low type white people in full view of and right across from a police station?[57]

Such conditions had been identified by 1950. However, since that time, a series of events, including the urban uprisings of the 1960s, patterns of disinvestment by business and government that followed the 1970s oil shocks, population loss, and a general decline in infrastructure and services have only worsened economic prospects in South Chicago and communities like it across the United States. A case in point is sociologist William Wilson's account of North Lawndale. Following the riots that swept through Chicago's West Side after the assassination of Martin Luther King Jr., the neighborhood lost 75 percent of its business establishments. In 1986, the community, with a population of almost seventy thousand, was largely without conventional services. It had only one bank and one supermarket.[58] While a handful of small shops run by Koreans, Arabs, African Americans, and whites remained, these businesses could hardly satisfy the full range of local demand. Accordingly, local residents are unable to fulfill many of their basic needs without leaving, and lacking transport, they are limited in their ability to travel. As a consequence, informal entrepreneurs in inner cities often have access to a sizeable captive market.

Anderson, who has conducted a series of ethnographic studies of U.S. ghettos, finds certain benefits in the unregulated economy that arise out of such circumstances.

> The informal economy enables poor people to obtain the same service as middle class people at rates they can afford. People have their hair done by a friend or have someone make a CD for them. People sew clothes for one another and help one another with house and car repairs . . . the exchange of service is a well-established custom among the poor. But these activities have also filled some of the gap created by the loss of government payments. The reliance on social capital among the poor means that money goes further and is more likely to stay within the community, [rather than going into the pockets of nonresident entrepreneurs].[59]

In this way, informal businesses fill some of the gaps that have resulted from capital flight and disinvestment. A final benefit of such informal businesses is that they often provide persons lacking credit and business experience with a means of acquiring both in such a way as to facilitate the establishment of legitimate enterprises.[60]

Research by Mario Small and Monica McDermott suggests that low-income black neighborhoods with shrinking populations in poor cities of the northeastern and midwestern United States reveal the smallest number of local enterprises. In contrast, densely populated, low-income immigrant neighborhoods in more affluent cities of the South and West are likely to have more small-sized businesses but relatively few large ones.[61]

Consumer Markets and the Color Line in Informal Entrepreneurship

As noted in chapter 2, since the late nineteenth century, discriminatory practices have largely prevented African American entrepreneurs from providing goods and services to white customers. In contrast, nonblack ethnic groups have had greater access to majority consumers.[62] A similar pattern is evident within the informal economy. Nonblack immigrants often direct enterprises (formal and informal alike) toward other ethnic populations and whites as well as coethnics. For example, in their study of Latino informal entrepreneurs in New Jersey, Edgcomb and Armington found that cleaning and remodeling work were most often targeted toward the mainstream market. Similarly, Pierrette Hondagneu-Sotelo and Abel Valenzuela describe Latino immigrants as providing numerous informal services to other ethnic and racial groups.[63] In contrast, as a result of the significant level of racial segregation that impacts U.S.-born blacks, African Americans' informal entrepreneurship is most extensive in areas of black residential concentration.[64]

There is some evidence that this pattern varies with the immigrant population of a locality. For example, Kathy Kaufman's research on child care finds that, in Philadelphia, African American women are active in providing this service for middle-class whites. In New York City, however, which has a much larger foreign-born population, immigrant women generally dominate this niche. Several factors may be involved in these differing patterns, including the wage levels sought by workers, customer preferences, and the means by which employers and workers contact each other.[65]

THE NATURE OF COMPETITION BETWEEN FORMAL AND INFORMAL BUSINESSES

As part of a campaign to establish community control and ethnic self-determination, residents of minority communities often oppose shops owned by outgroup members. Austin describes the legal context of such conflicts.

On one side are the vendors, their loyal customers and those who are interested in the welfare of recent immigrants or the marginally employed. On the
other side are city authorities concerned about taxes, congestion, sanitation,
aesthetics, and property values; fixed location merchants, who must compete
with vendors whose only overhead concern is the weather; producers and distributors who want to know how their wares wind up on vendors' tables; and
middle class residents who prefer streets marked by order and decorum. . . .
Naturally, the interests of these contending forces are balanced differently in
every instance, the outcome being determined according to the relative political clout of opposing parties.[66]

Direct Conflict

When legal and informal enterprises compete for customers, established firms offer freestanding premises, name-brand goods, and loans. In
contrast, informal enterprises frequently provide consumers with greater
convenience by doing business in their homes or other accessible locations.
They are generally familiar with customers' life patterns, work routines,
tastes, and language. This contrasts with outgroup entrepreneurs who may
have "very little understanding of the social context of . . . business practices,
especially the ways through which inner city merchants interact with their
environment and the role of informal, underground and illegal economies
in the lives of these businesses."[67] In black neighborhoods, informal entrepreneurs may seek patronage by appealing to African Americans' historical
desire to control the economic life of their communities. For example,
Austin notes that "vendors frequently harass shoppers who patronize stores
owned by nonblacks."[68]

Studies of Latino immigrants' involvement in the underground economy
show how entrepreneurs satisfy coethnic needs in a familiar and intimate
manner that outgroup members would be incapable of duplicating. In the
course of his fieldwork, Christian Zlolniski met Laura, an undocumented
Mexican woman who lived in an apartment complex with her husband and
daughter in a largely Latino neighborhood in Silicon Valley. When her husband was unable to find stable employment, Laura (who had been involved
in informal entrepreneurship prior to migrating) learned from a relative
how to prepare traditional Mexican food like corn on the cob and *chichar-
rones* (pork rinds) and became a street vendor.

Unfamiliar with the city, fearful that she might be caught, and initially
ashamed of what she felt was a lowly occupation, Laura nevertheless had
ambitious plans. She expanded her inventory to include a broader menu
as well as soft drinks and candy, matched her work schedule with that of
her husband Alberto, to care for their daughter, and became a success-

ful entrepreneur. She further enlarged her business by feeding single men in her home and offering customers amenities including water for hand washing and bags for their purchases. By becoming involved in the parents' association of the local elementary school, Laura became well known in the neighborhood. Consequently, she was able to sell treats to neighborhood children on credit, confident that she would be repaid by their parents with whom she was well acquainted. This increased the volume of her operation.

As Laura's business expanded, Alberto took on tasks related to both the business and housekeeping that Laura had originally done herself. What began as a short-term solution to Alberto's unstable employment became a permanent, albeit informal, income-generating strategy for the family. In terms of conflict with legitimate firms, Laura's business does probably drain customers from established restaurants and food stores. However, she also creates additional income for groceries through her purchases of meat, produce, soft drinks, and candy for resale.[69]

While informal entrepreneurship commonly involves activities such as food preparation, domestic service, and residential construction, more skilled workers and even professionals also conduct their careers in this manner. Zlolniski describes the case of an immigrant dentist from Latin America who maintains a practice among a community of undocumented workers in a garage jerry-rigged with a dentist's chair. Unable to acquire the necessary credentials to work legally in the United States, he provides dental care for those who cannot afford to buy it from the established system.

Legal enterprises use a variety of resources and techniques to reduce competition from informal businesses. Historically, legitimate business owners have demanded the passage of ordinances to ban the sales of goods and services by those without a permanent store location.[70] In addition, food safety regulations, requirements for licenses and fees, and mandates that firms withhold sales and payroll taxes are commonly used to justify the closing of informal businesses. Locations where groups of scruffy day laborers congregate often provoke complaints from neighbors, law enforcement officials, and local merchants that yield crackdowns.[71] With little access to defensible space and lacking in legal protection, street vendors find themselves subject to harassment and shakedowns from criminal gangs or corrupt police, who sometimes collaborate with shop owners to drive them out of business.

Despite such measures, informal entrepreneurs attempt to fight back by appealing to customers, by avoiding opponents, and through sheer tenacity. Most informal entrepreneurs pursue their trades because they must in order to survive. Consequently, they resist regulation. Because their premises involve minimal investment, they can be easily reestablished even if police or toughs confiscate or destroy their assets (which may consist of little more than a blanket to sit on and a basket of sandwiches).

Austin asserts that, by patronizing coethnic informal business, disadvantaged groups make a political statement about self-support and solidarity. In so doing, they refuse to cooperate with an alien legal system that has played a significant role in their oppression.

> The lesson of economic advancement through economic cooperation must be taught with words and deeds and delivered at every level. . . . There is no better place for the instruction to begin than in the streets. . . . [It] presents an opportunity and a site where ordinary, everyday black people, whether sellers or consumers, can engage in the political struggle to build a more viable black public sphere and actually experience firsthand the results of their labor.[72]

As Austin suggests, the informal economy provides a site of resistance where minority communities can reclaim forms of cultural and economic production that have been expropriated by members of the larger society. For example, mainstream media companies have a history of copyrighting and profiting from songs and musical styles—from folk, blues, jazz, and rock to hip hop—invented by racial and ethnic minority groups. Lacking legal representation, original composers were generally unable to benefit from the music that they wrote.[73] Turning this process on its head, informal entrepreneurs create a salable product by sampling or remixing music owned by others. According to the law, this form of music entrepreneurship constitutes theft. However, some regard it as just compensation for the victims of exploitation. As a case in point, Donald Light shows how computer-savvy youth have processed and repackaged digital music into a new kind of art form.[74] "Some argue that the real revolution lies beyond making copies into making music liquid: 'you can filter it, bend it, archive it, rearrange it, remix it, mess with it. . . . With digitization, music went from being a noun to a verb . . . music is becoming a commodity that is traded, cocreated and coproduced by a networked audience.'"[75] Had these innovators conformed to the intellectual property and copyright regulations of the formal economy, they would have been unable to create or profit from their invention.

Cooperation between Formal and Informal Enterprises

While informal and formal businesses in ghettos, immigrant neighborhoods, and other disadvantaged locations are involved in economic competition, these entities often engage in various forms of cooperation as well. For example, raw materials and supplies that are essential for informal economic production are sold by legal businesses. This interchange allows informal businesses to exist, while simultaneously increasing sales for formal ones. It is widely documented that African American women are extensively involved in beauty salons as both formal and informal enterprises.[76] This occupation requires a wide array of cosmetics, hair preparations, and equipment, which are often difficult to obtain in ghetto neighborhoods. However, over time, Korean American, Vietnamese, and other ethnic entrepreneurs have developed well-stocked stores specializing in beauty products sought by African American women. In this way, there exists significant cooperation between formal Asian American distributors and informally run African American beauticians. In the following interview, conducted in early 2007, African American women discuss the relationship between Asian beauty supply stores and black beauty salons in Detroit:

> INTERVIEWER: We talked about this a long time ago like with that whole beauty supply phenomenon. . . .
>
> RESPONDENT: Yeah.
>
> INTERVIEWER: Like at Seven Mile, Van Dyke area, like Eight Mile and Gratiot, Kelly, Lee, all of those; those are not black business suppliers.
>
> RESPONDENT: Detroit is a black hair capital, but we don't own [the] black hair [business.] So if you're thinking about beauty shops on every other corner, you know, we own beauty salons, but we don't own the beauty supply stores. Those are largely Asian owned, and like I said, I think it's a post Civil Rights issue. I mean, Jack Laree, they were a major black supplier of hair care products, and they recently shut down. . . .
>
> INTERVIEWER: Weird.
>
> RESPONDENT: I don't know why. They had two businesses on the East Side, and I don't know why they closed down, but they're gone, and there's one major Asian supply store that's on Yorkshire and Warren on the East Side of Detroit that is booming.

Another form of cooperation between informal entrepreneurs and formal business owners involves day laborers and the sellers of construction materials. It has become common practice for male day laborers to congregate near stores associated with labor-intensive jobs like painting, landscaping, moving, and home improvement, where they offer their services to contractors and home owners. In this way, job seekers are brought together with those in need of their skills, while store owners are able to increase sales to customers who can readily locate inexpensive workers to assist them.[77] While privately owned stores may welcome day laborers, so do sites sponsored by municipalities and nonprofit organizations. These locations generally provide amenities like shelter, bathrooms, tool rental, dispute resolution, and some regulation of wages.[78]

Not all workers who frequent these sites are uneducated, unskilled, and recently arrived single men frantically seeking employment, however. Some are skilled, educated, and have many years of residence in the United States. They exchange business cards, cell phone numbers, and e-mail addresses with employers and fellow workers to advertise their skills and access to tools and vehicles. While most are Mexican, Central Americans, whites, African Americans, and other nationalities also seek employment this way.

For example, Israeli building contractors in Los Angeles told me they acquired employment by posting business cards in Southern California tile warehouses.[79] In the following quotation, Betty, a Hebrew-speaking employee of a school that provides test preparation for the California State Building Contractor's License examination, describes patterns of cooperation between undocumented Israeli subcontractors and the Israeli-American real estate developers who employ them.

> They are mostly young guys, age 25–32. The big majority are Sephardic or Eastern [Jews whose families are from North Africa and the Middle East]. Whatever their background, they meet each other, become friends and sit together in class.
>
> They enter contracting because it is the easiest field to work in without knowing English. They don't have to deal with Americans. They get orders from [Israeli] general contractors and that's it. Working with hammers and saws and wood doesn't require any specific language skills.
>
> The weird thing is that they complain about each other but they will always work together. They like each other but will always compete. They like to cooperate because they share the same language and outlook. They all work very hard, they help each other, they work long hours. They cut some deals and cut some corners which they could not do if they worked with American general contractors. They understand each others' approach.[80]

Dan, an established Israeli-American real estate developer, describes his reliance on Israeli subcontractors. "There is no question that with Israelis, there is some kind of a connection. No question about it. A lot of my subcontractors are Israelis. I mean, you would sometimes go through one of my developments and you think you're in a Kibbutz somewhere because you hear so much Hebrew spoken."[81]

In this relationship, the subcontractors' work increases the developers' profits and control. At the same time, by working for coethnics, subcontractors earn much more than most undocumented laborers in the region.

Relations between formal and informal entrepreneurs in the construction trades are not always cooperative, however. In the following interchange, Yossi, an Israeli building contractor, describes how conationals sometimes move beyond the subcontractor role and compete directly for customers. This has caused him to stop working with them and, instead, to employ outgroup workers.

> YOSSI: Well you see, Israelis, I find most of them are like me. They took me as an example for them. They want to also become self-employed. I think it's just the nature of the Israeli.
>
>   So there was sometimes friction and they care too much about the details of how I run my company, and I don't like that. I don't want to say that they are spying, but they copy me which is perfectly okay, but only as long as it helps me.
>
> INVESTIGATOR: Yeah. They'll open their own business and then make it harder for you.
>
> YOSSI: Right. But I understand that and I accept that as long as they are not cheating on me that's fine with me. But if I need to be somewhere else for a while and a [potential] customer comes to the work site and asks for a contractor and they give their card or leave their number—that's cheating. I don't accept. So I need to be careful of Israelis and now I hire Mexican workers more.
>
>   A dishonest [Israeli] guy like that, I will eventually get rid of. I will just throw them from the job. Many times it has happened and I have been hurt. I would not hire another Israeli. I'd hire a Mexican instead. That's very unfortunate, but they can't stop me from hiring someone that needs the money.[82]

Other patterns of cooperation between formal and informal coethnic businesses include the ubiquitous displays in ethnic shops of advertisements for services ranging from child care and dance lessons to livery services and translation. In poor neighborhoods, local residents often agree to watch over parked automobiles for a fee. This provides the merchant and customer alike with assurance that the customer's car will remain safe, thus permitting the patronage of a business in an otherwise risky location.

I found patterns of informal entrepreneurship during fieldwork among recently arrived refugees from Vietnam and the former Soviet Union in California during the early 1980s.[83] Unfamiliar with the U.S. economy but with their survival skills sharpened by years of living under communism and in refugee camps, refugees were able to combine various income sources to earn a living.

Refugees who were active in the informal economy tended to speak little English and maintained minimum contact with American society. Some wanted their businesses to be inconspicuous in order to conceal income from agencies that provided Refugee Cash Assistance, Aid to Families with Dependent Children (AFDC), food stamps, unemployment insurance, or welfare. Operations were hidden because they were thought to be illegal by their proprietors. For instance, several Vietnamese refugees involved in informal credit and banking arrangements and rotating credit associations believed that such activities were akin to "pyramid schemes" and hence against the law. Others who did not understand tax or licensing laws or health codes tried to remain inconspicuous for fear of being cited for violations.[84] Accordingly, informal businesses were often located in refugees' homes or other inconspicuous locations. Members of both groups prepared foods, assembled clothing, repaired electronic equipment or automobiles, taught a variety of skills, and ran translation, photographic, and video-taping services out of their apartments. Because many Soviet Jews had backgrounds in building and engineering, several were involved in unlicensed construction businesses.[85]

A 1987 *Los Angeles Times* article confirmed refugees' involvement in this employment pattern. "The underground economy is found in Southeast Asian communities throughout the state. Officials estimate that as many as half of the state's Southeast Asian families on welfare—about 22,000 families numbering 100,000 refugees—are earning illegal income." Much of this is derived from working in sweatshops, selling at swap meets, and the like.[86]

Finally, legitimate merchants may run businesses that blur the distinction between formal and informal operations. Venkatesh observes that, when formal businesses on Chicago's South Side confront hard times, they may become active in the informal economy.

> When they patronize a loan shark or pay for cheap labor under the table, they participate in a common system of exchange that integrates state-regulated entrepreneurship and off-the-books commerce . . . irrespective of their commercial acumen, the shady economy lends them flexibility and quick access to resources, thereby enabling them to develop and sustain . . . ventures in an entrepreneurial landscape that changes quickly and unexpectedly.[87]

Similarly, formal businesses may supplement their income by selling homemade foods, individual cigarettes, or drug paraphernalia; legitimate building contractors may employ undocumented workers or provide cash-only services on evenings and weekends; and licensed cab drivers may turn off their meters and provide customers with unrecorded transportation.[88] Finally, several reports suggest that inner-city merchants sell outdated food products.[89] In these situations, both formal and informal enterprises rely on extralegal tricks to reduce business costs and increase earnings. While profits can be enhanced through these practices, they involve risks as well, including fines and legal action. Hence, while combining formal and informal activities may keep a business alive, it may also prevent it from growing. In either case, the mixing of legitimate and unregulated business practices by the same operator shows that the distinction between formal and informal entrepreneurship is not a hard and fast one.

Benefits from Informal Businesses

Theorists and policy makers have come to realize that informal businesses can provide economic benefits. They support poor people, provide employment, and fill needs that are not satisfied through formal enterprises. Such activities, which are embedded in communal relationships, group values, and specific neighborhoods, build social capital. As Valenzuela asserts, "Where street vendors, day laborers, domestic workers and food cart merchants abound . . . survivalist entrepreneurs produce goods and services that enhance . . . their community's wealth."[90]

Informal entrepreneurs often have altruistic goals and seek to assist coethnics and neighbors. For example, in her study of African American women's involvement in the beauty industry, Adia Harvey Wingfield noted that "making other black women look and feel beautiful became something that they greatly enjoyed. The genuine satisfaction they gained from doing this heavily influenced their decision to pursue full-time work in the hair industry." One such entrepreneur, Jamie, describes her motivation for working with coethnics: "I am more comfortable working with blacks in a black situation. I love to cater to us and knew I would get to do that in this job. I have a natural talent for hair, so it just makes sense to be here where I can . . . just use that talent for black people."[91]

By providing a means of earning a living, distributing goods and services, and encouraging street traffic, informal enterprises can improve neighborhood conditions. They create performance space for public discussions, spiritual communion, and the pleasure of shopping. "Street vendors lend the flavor of an African marketplace to otherwise drab stretches of empty stores and barred facades." They provide public safety for customers and legitimate merchants. Informal businesses also increase the number and influence of coethnic businesses in minority neighborhoods, thus lending community control to populations lacking a viable business class.[92]

> The growth of the day labor market in Los Angeles and Orange County is related to the recent increase in small immigrant businesses that have developed in the area. . . . Most of these businesses do not have the necessary resources to support a large employee base, but can hire cheap temporary labor when labor shortages occur or when extra workers are needed. To adjust to business cycles and an unstable workforce, small businesses use the day labor pool.[93]

In addition, informal enterprises offer local residents the goods, services, and equipment required to take jobs in the formal economy. These include clothes washing, food preparation, transport, work attire, tools, child care, and language and skill training.

Proponents of informal entrepreneurship point out that street vendors can deliver needed products and yield economic growth and neighborhood revitalization when formal-sector businesses fail to do so and public funds are too scarce to accomplish the goal. Accordingly, they have fostered the implementation of public policies to establish sidewalk vending areas, urban enterprise and empowerment zones, and abatements on taxes and regulations as well as programs that offer technical assistance and micro-loans for informal enterprises. All of these seek to encourage the growth and normalization of informal entrepreneurship.[94]

Realizing the potential value of informal enterprises, policy makers and foundations have commissioned a number of studies that seek to assist, expand, and legalize such endeavors.[95] Some pundits may object to the lack of regulation of street vendors, home remodelers, and garment assemblers in the informal economy. Paradoxically, however, by allowing disadvantaged people to support themselves, informal entrepreneurship entails a market-based solution to economic needs and allows governments to minimize welfare expenditures in a manner that is encouraged by neoliberal economics.[96] Further, it is important to point out that very large-scale enterprises, such as hedge funds—secretive, high risk, investment instruments that cater to the very rich—are also largely free from audits, taxation, and other forms of regulation. Moreover, a number of regulatory policies involving worker safety, pollution control, and homeland security—which apply to some of the largest corporations in the United States—are also voluntary.[97] If a lack of regulation is seen as an acceptable incentive for some of the largest businesses in the country, why shouldn't it also work as an inducement for small enterprises?

Informal Entrepreneurship Is Not without Drawbacks

Despite the many positive attributes of informal businesses, such firms are not free of liabilities. They deny local governments tax revenues. In addition, they exclude businesses, workers, and consumers from a host of regulations associated with the legitimate economy. These include consumer protection public health and food safety requirements. Accordingly, such firms' may exploit workers and owners who are economically desperate—yielding a Dickensian work environment. Finally, informal enterprises are often associated with illegal activities. Secondhand sales can easily function as fence operations to sell stolen goods. Unregistered business owners who seek to avoid detection are unable to call the police when robbed or harassed. Hence, they are prone to victimization.

Because proponents of informal businesses sometimes become unrealistically optimistic about the potential of market-based economic development programs, they fail to appreciate the difficulties involved in running informal businesses and assume that such enterprises can solve economic problems that lie beyond the capability of even large, established, and resource-rich formal enterprises. Finally, as Gregg Kettles points out, programs that regulate informal vendors by permitting their operation only in restricted locations tend to be both costly and ineffective.[98]

As a consequence, policy makers try to develop schemes through which the benefits of informal entrepreneurship can be realized while discouraging negative practices. Such programs can be helpful, especially when they provide informal entrepreneurs with technical assistance, loans, and recognition. However, efforts to turn informal businesses into conventional firms can also undermine the social and economic basis that allows them to be successful. In the introduction to their book on street entrepreneurs, John Cross and Alfonso Morales warn that policy makers must attend to "the features that make markets and merchants successful—the spirit of survival and flexibility that attracted scholars to this activity in the first place."[99]

CONCLUSIONS

By acknowledging the extensive amount of informal entrepreneurship that exists among marginal groups, and the unique ways that such activities function, we can better understand the nature of conflicts between them and immigrant entrepreneurs. Such conflicts may reflect more than customer groups' jealousy and desire to destroy what they don't own. In some cases, contention between customer groups and merchants can be considered *realistic* conflicts over the opportunity to earn a living. As such, they embody disadvantaged groups' desire to challenge the social, legal, and economic advantages of formal entrepreneurs in their communities so that they too can have a piece of the action.

By recognizing the entrepreneurial activity of marginal groups, creative policy makers can work to develop approaches that capture the financial and social benefits of informal entrepreneurship, rather than enforcing laws to curtail such practices. Restrictions on the informal economy make life more difficult for disadvantaged groups, who lack jobs and hence must find ways to survive. In addition, such prohibition further alienates them from mainstream norms and gives them even less of a stake in the economic and social system of the larger society.[100] Finally, increased earnings and forms of consumption generated via informal entrepreneurship have been shown to generate economic and social benefits for formal enterprises and members of the larger society.

If permitted to flourish, informal enterprises have the potential to provide members of impoverished communities with income and job skills, as well as services and environments for positive forms of social cooperation and engagement that government, nonprofit agencies, and legitimate enterprises have a hard time supplying. While hardly a cure-all, informal entrepreneurship can deliver solutions to some of the economic problems of disadvantaged communities and contribute a sense of social justice. By acknowledging that some competitive actions taken by inner-city residents in relation to ethnic merchants are not simply destructive but rather reflect their efforts to build an ethnic economy, we move toward the creation of an urban economy that is both more dynamic and more equitable than has previously been the case. In addition, rather than labeling residents of disadvantaged communities as lacking the potential to be part of the economic life of the larger society, we acknowledge that they are already demonstrating the possession of these very attributes.

8

ETHNIC MERCHANTS IN A BLACK MAJORITY CITY: THE CASE OF DETROIT

with Joe Darden, professor of geography, Michigan State University

As noted throughout this book, scholars and activists have seen self-employment as a promising means for African Americans to control their economic fate. Leaders ranging from Booker T. Washington and W. E. B. Du Bois to Louis Farrakhan have suggested that, by running their own businesses, blacks could avoid relying on whites to provide jobs. Patterns of residential segregation as well as forms of shared subjectivity created by encounters with white supremacy were seen as having the potential to link African American business owners and customers in a manner that would benefit both.

Unfortunately, a significant black ethnic economy has yet to develop in the United States. Instead, research suggests that, in nearly every center of African American population, a series of immigrant and ethnic groups have dominated small businesses activities.[1] However, much of what we know about small business in contemporary black communities has been acquired in studies of ethnically diverse gateway cities like New York, Los Angeles, Chicago, and Miami, where blacks do not account for a majority of the local population and hence have limited demographic and political power.[2] In contrast, relatively little research has been conducted in urban communities in the Midwest and South, where white flight, coupled with relatively low rates of in-migration have made African Americans the majority population. In such settings, African Americans do possess significant resources that offer potential benefits for the creation of a black ethnic economy.

For example, Frank Bean and colleagues contend that, in addition to being characterized by certain social and economic disadvantages, regions of black concentration also produce social and economic benefits that function as a "'cushion,' as it were from the competitive effects stemming from the influx of immigrants into the labor market." These include reduced economic antagonism with immigrant workers and the return of highly educated blacks to the inner city, as opposed to their continuing exodus to surrounding suburbs, which often occurs in locations that reveal intergroup competition.[3]

As the largest black majority city in the United States, Detroit is the archetypal environment where African American demographic and political dominance and extensive representation among nonprofit organizations could support the creation and sustenance of black-owned businesses. It is the origin of the modern American blue-collar middle class.[4] The vast majority of Detroit's residents (82 percent as of 2000) are African American. Moreover, they control the city's political apparatus and hold executive positions in many of the city's public institutions and nonprofit organizations.[5] Research has shown that black mayors (a product of black demographic dominance and political solidarity) were responsible for the initial opening of the government-procurement market to black-owned businesses. Further, many cities headed by black mayors aggressively sought to steer city contracts to minority- (and women-) owned businesses in the 1970s and 1980s, via set-asides, loans, training programs, and other policies.[6]

In addition to their possession of political power, African Americans are the ministers and parishioners in a majority of Detroit's churches. Newspapers, radio stations, unions, and schools are often run by blacks and serve an African American constituency. While the fortunes of many residents have declined in recent years, the city retains a sizable African American middle class who remain strongly committed to the city and its residents.[7] Census data from 1950 to 1990 showed clear evidence of the emergence of a prosperous black elite in Detroit.[8]

Due to these factors, in an environment like that of Detroit, African Americans have considerable political and institutional power. It stands to reason that, in such localities, relations with nonblack entrepreneurs would be distinct from patterns observed in communities where African Americans remain in the minority. For example, city officials, politicians, and local institutions would be less likely to discriminate against black residents and entrepreneurs in places where most voters are black. One might expect that the organizational life of such places would be structured in such a way as to appeal to popular consensus, thus transforming relations that have been common among merchants and black customers.

Mayor Dinkins and Red Apple Market. New York City Mayor David Dinkins visiting the owner of Red Apple, the Korean green grocery that was the target of a boycott for a year and a half, February 22, 1992. Black mayors of multi-ethnic cities, including David Dinkins of New York and Tom Bradley of Los Angeles, sometimes side with non-blacks in disputes between residents and ethnic merchants. This pattern may be less common in black majority cities like Detroit.
Source: Photo courtesy of Chong-Gwon Park, *Korean Central Daily News.*

This chapter explores black entrepreneurship in Detroit and considers the nature of conflicts surrounding businesses run by nonblack merchants in a municipality where African Americans are politically and demographically dominant.

CONTEXT

While Detroit's concentrated population provides African American businesses with demographic and political advantages, at the same time, local and regional economic and political conditions pose major obstacles for entrepreneurs. Ranked as the poorest large city in the United States in 2009, Detroit experiences the full catalogue of urban problems, including poverty, population loss, poor services, unemployment, and crime.[9] Moreover, Southeast Michigan is among the most highly segregated regions in the United States, and Detroit maintains a relatively poor relationship with surrounding communities.[10] The auto industry, which is the region's major economic engine, has been in terrible shape for many years, limiting employment prospects, tax coffers, and philanthropy. Making matters even worse, a scandal resulting in Detroit Mayor Kwame Kilpatrick's resignation in 2009 deprived the city of coherent leadership at the same time that its economy went from bad to worse.[11]

As a consequence of decades of economic decline, population loss, and racial polarization, retail trade is poorly developed in Detroit. Despite its having more than eight hundred thousand residents, the city's shopping options are extremely limited. There are virtually no major chain groceries, department stores, or big box retailers like Wal-Mart, Target, or Home Depot within the city limits, so basic commodities must be purchased from small- to medium-sized "mom-and-pop" grocers, mini-marts, and gas stations. Describing this, "a 2003 University of Michigan study of Detroit supermarkets showed there were only five grocery stores in Detroit with over 20,000 square feet. The report concluded that the city could support 41 supermarkets with at least 40,000 square feet of space based on its population and spending habits."[12] In theory, the lack of competition from established chains reduces competition for African American merchants. Nevertheless, blacks do not control the retail niche. Rather, a very large fraction of Detroit's stores are owned by Middle East–origin entrepreneurs, most notably Chaldeans.[13]

Reflecting on the shopping options available in Detroit, residents interviewed for this study stated in a matter-of-fact manner that, beyond casual clothing, sneakers, fast food, and grooming services, there was virtually nothing to buy within the city limits. In the words of an African American college student, "What do I buy in the city from black owners? I would say at this time, nothing really."

Finally, while other political entities with large racial minority populations, including the cities of Atlanta and Chicago, and the state of Maryland, maintain programs to encourage the growth of business ownership among African Americans, women, and other minority groups, state-supported affirmative action initiatives including minority business development activities, set-asides, training, and loan funds were banned in Michigan by an electoral proposition, Proposal 2, passed in 2006.[14] In sum, while Detroit is characterized by African American political and demographic dominance, it is also an impoverished city that exhibits a wide range of urban problems and is limited in its ability to direct economic assistance to minority group members. These obstacles restrict the creation and growth of small businesses.

In order to explore black business development in Detroit, we used two research strategies. First, to assess the extent of business development, we reviewed census data that describes the number of black-owned businesses

A protest against Proposal 2, Michigan's Anti Affirmative Action Proposition, Michigan State Capital, May 2005. The proposal became law in November 2006 and prohibited state-funded education, employment, or business assistance programs for racial and ethnic minorities and women.
Source: Steven Gold

and their economic impact in the city. Then, to understand how residents interpret the state of small business in Detroit, we review several sources of data that reflect local views on the issue.

CENSUS-BASED FINDINGS

Drawing from Small Business Administration data, we use two measures—the fraction of black-owned businesses among all businesses and the black business participation rate (BPR), which is the fraction of the local black population employed by African Americans—to evaluate the status of black-owned businesses in Detroit. Our approach to examining black self-employment in Detroit relies on a unique strategy. While nearly all studies of minority business ownership examine rates of business ownership within the metropolitan statistical areas (MSA), this study addresses entrepreneurship at the city level. We do this because, as a political unit, the city is the location wherein black demographic and political power is most strongly felt and hence most able to influence patterns of entrepreneurship.

According to the first measure, we find that a larger percentage of all businesses in Detroit are owned by blacks than in any other city in the United States.[15] Moreover, Detroit's black-owned businesses create more jobs and have higher wages per employee than is the case in other major U.S. cities. A greater fraction of black-owned businesses in Detroit have employees (14.17 percent) than in other major U.S. cities; Detroit's black businesses also exceed those of other cities in sales and receipts, fraction of all employees, and fraction of entire payroll.[16] (See table 8.1.)

One interpretation of these findings is that black solidarity in Detroit has altered relations with ethnic merchants in such a way as to protect black-owned businesses, resulting in black entrepreneurs serving a larger part of black consumer demand than in any other city in the country. Given that Detroit is the largest black majority city in the United States, this is significant. In fact, recent research finds that Detroit has the second largest number of black businesses in the United States, exceeded only by New York, which has both a much larger population and a much more dynamic economy.[17]

While Detroit reveals impressive performance in terms of the fraction of total enterprises owned by blacks, it has a less noteworthy record in terms of the black BPR, which is calculated by dividing the number of black businesses in the city by the black population. The BPR for Detroit is 25.17, which is considerably lower than other large black majority cities, including Washington, D.C. (35.53), Atlanta (33), Jackson, Mississippi (30.5), and Memphis (29.24). Moreover, while many cities reveal an elevated black

Table 8.1. Black-owned Businesses in Selected Cities, 1997 and 2002

City	# Black-owned Businesses		Black-owned/ All Businesses		Sales & Receipts/ Business ($1,000)		Paid Employees/ Business	
	1997	2002	1997	2002	1997	2002	1997	2002
United States	823,499	1,197,567	0.04	0.05	86.50	107.64	0.87	0.92
Detroit	11,262	19,530	0.43	0.56	120.40	140.61	1.07	1.04
New York	63,327	98,080	0.10	0.12	58.40	80.07	0.51	0.47
Atlanta	7,853	8,434	0.20	0.19	129.00	124.25	NA	1.19
Chicago	23,576	39,419	0.13	0.19	104.00	121.77	1.05	0.93
Los Angeles	17,593	25,954	0.05	0.07	50.30	108.53	0.26	0.75

Source: U.S. Census Bureau, "Minority- and Women-Owned Businesses," 1997 Economic Census, 2002 Economic Census, Survey of Business Owners, Company Statistics Series, August 2006.

BPR among businesses with employees, Detroit's black-owned businesses with employees have an even lower BPR representation of 10.91. When considering black-owned businesses with employees, Washington, D.C.'s black BPR increases from 35.53 to 39.4; Atlanta's, from 33 to 51.48; and Jackson, Mississippi's, from 30.5 to 34.10.

The highest fraction of blacks who find employment in black businesses are found in sunbelt cities, like Los Angeles and Miami, where the economy has been relatively strong and blacks are not in the majority.[18] The poor economic climate of Detroit has resulted in a long trend of population loss. In contrast, Washington, D.C., and Atlanta, which rank among the most economically dynamic black majority cities in the United States, have increased their black population in recent years.[19]

In sum, we see that Detroit's African American population has been able to mobilize demographic, political, and communal resources such that it controls a larger fraction of the city's businesses than in nearly any other urban environment in the United States. However, while impressive in terms of black control over local resources, the total amount thereof is quite small. As such, it is incapable of generating a significant number of jobs for Detroit's sizeable population. With its large population and relatively small number of firms, Detroit appears to have significant potential for business growth. But several measures suggest that this environment is far from economically vibrant.

PERSPECTIVES ON THE BLACK ETHNIC ECONOMY

Because Detroit is a black majority city, the dearth of black-owned businesses and the corresponding control of most retail enterprises by nonblack immigrant and ethnic entrepreneurs has long been an issue of concern for many local residents. This has been a topic of popular discussion, journalism, social movements, and academic research since the 1940s.[20] (See chapter 4.)

Academics, economists, and other professional observers have written histories of minority business formation and economic progress in American cities, including Detroit.[21] However, these scholarly accounts do not necessarily square with the lived experience of Detroit's residents, entrepreneurs, activists, and bureaucrats who may remain unconvinced by academics' interpretations of the conditions within which they live.

By exploring their diverse views on the topic, we are able to gain insight into how local stakeholders regard small businesses in the city, their views of entrepreneurs, and the actions (if any) they would endorse to transform the city's retail environment. Toward this goal, we collected several forms of data. These included newspaper articles published in the mainstream press (*Detroit Free Press*, *Detroit News*, and *New York Times*), ethnic publications (African American papers including the *Michigan Citizen* and *Michigan Chronicle* as well as the *Chaldean News*), and government sources. Finally, we conducted in-depth interviews with twenty-five individuals. Respondents included government officials, business development professionals (working for the public, nonprofit, and private sectors), and black and Chaldean entrepreneurs. To gain the perspective of African American Detroit residents, we interviewed eight college students.

Interview respondents were identified through a number of sources. Business development professionals, city officials, and black entrepreneurs were located through newspaper articles, organizational and governmental websites, and snowball sample referrals from other interviewees and informants. Contacts with Detroit residents and Chaldean entrepreneurs were established through the networks of our graduate student research assistants.

Interviews with government officials, business development professionals, and African American entrepreneurs were jointly conducted by two professors, an African American male and a white male. Detroit residents were interviewed by an African American female graduate student research assistant who grew up in Detroit. Finally, interviews with Chaldean entrepreneurs were conducted by a white male graduate research assistant involved in research with this community. Interviews were tape recorded and transcribed. All respondents are identified by pseudonyms to protect their identities.

Shared Views

Nearly every person we interviewed and every statement regarding black businesses that we read in our review of journalism emphasized the potential for cooperation among African Americans in Detroit as a resource for the development of a coethnic economy. To begin with, the value of small businesses was universally endorsed by everyone we interviewed and every article we read. No one asserted that capitalism should be rejected as a means of solving Detroit's problems. At the same time, references to small businesses as an individualistic activity were largely absent. Respondents assumed that small businesses were linked to and controlled by groups rather than individual owners. Most commonly, they linked businesses with racial or ethnic collectivities. However, businesses were also associated with social classes and with regional categories—downtown, the neighborhoods of Detroit, or the suburbs.

Institutional and Racial Blocks to Black Entrepreneurship

When asked about the small number of black-owned businesses in Detroit, all respondents referred to the legacy of racism. In addition to interpersonal discrimination, they identified government policies, such as urban renewal and highway construction, that destroyed vibrant black business districts. They also blamed corporations for their unwillingness to locate businesses in Detroit. Several respondents held banks responsible for refusing to lend money for Detroit initiatives generally and African American businesses in particular.

In the following excerpt, Darlene, an African American woman who runs a large and well-established nonretail enterprise in Detroit, described the dismal climate for black retailers.

DARLENE: You have several dynamics going on. One is clear redlining and clear, intentional blocking out of retail. Detroit kind of stands alone [among all cities] in terms of the absolute percentage of black population. And I do think that this is the issue in terms of entrepreneurship. When [black] people do try to do things [create businesses], they don't get the support. They don't get the support from the banks or the financial institutions.

We are dealing with the same issues that we were dealing with fifteen years ago—that there is not equity available. So, you have that kind of scenario. I was talking to some bankers from Morgan Stanley in New York City. They have an urban fund. But where are they going with that urban fund? They are going to New York City; they are going to California. So, when you look at it, cities like Detroit, in particular, have been written off.

INTERVIEWER: I agree with what you said, but if you think back, there was a very well-developed black business community in a small section of Detroit. I mean it was there, and it pretty much thrived for a while until integration came about and then blacks went.

DARLENE: They did in most of these [black business] communities. They put I-75 [local freeway] right through the middle of it and I-94 [another local freeway] right through the middle of those businesses and destroyed those businesses. Not only did the businesses disperse, but the population dispersed. When I look at the city of Detroit, you have to recognize that we are still dealing with residual effects of disinvestment, as well as actually purposeful destruction.

Economic Conditions

In addition to mentioning the negative impacts of discrimination by government, corporations, and banks, a wide range of respondents referred to the poor economic condition of the region and the decline of American manufacturing, more generally, as being harmful to African American businesses in Detroit. In a 2006 interview, Eric and Mary, staff members of business development agencies, referred to this harmful effect:

ERIC: The trickle-down effect from the federal government has a huge impact. We're not getting the money that we got even last year or the year before. You know, we gotta get more federal money coming in, not only to support these businesses, but just to support the programs that, for example, keep kids at camp for the summer.

MARY: A weak economy, in a nutshell, is truly affecting all we need to do to have a strong city. Don't get me wrong. We understand that there are some other cities around the country that are having the same problem that we're having. Everybody is suffering. But Detroit truly is at the top of the heap in terms of a large major city struggling based on the fact that we're a manufacturing town, and these jobs are closing up and going away.

According to an African American college student, the poor economy encourages the best and brightest young people to leave Michigan for opportunities elsewhere, thus depriving the city of the energy and intelligence it needs to move forward.

Another thing that makes Detroit a very unique case is that Michigan does not retain their professionals. People can get educated here at Wayne State, U of M, Michigan State, and then they flee. They flee. Michigan does not retain people that they educate in comparison to New York or Chicago. You can go to Northwestern, and nine times out of ten, you may stay in Chicago to work there. You get educated in New York; you may stay in that area because there are opportunities galore in those areas. But in Detroit, where there are not enough opportunities, the unemployment is just terrible. We're in a consistent year-by-year recession. Especially since Bush has been in office, it hasn't got better, so it really isn't attracting people. I just got my degree, and I want to get this job, but no one's hiring in Detroit. I've interviewed, and I haven't got a position in Detroit. Well, I'm going to flee, so I think that's another issue that we need to look at, you know, how professionals flee.

Think about the Great Migration. We left [the South] because we weren't surviving. You know, Ford was offering that hot deal, five dollars an hour. We was like, "Well, we'd go for four dollars now." It's not like that no more. The industry is messed up, the automobile industry. They're moving out of Detroit. They're moving into the suburbs now, and the Big Three isn't what it used to be years ago. It's different now.

The Impacts of Racial Integration

In addition to describing racism as harming Detroit's prospects for black business growth, a number of respondents also referred to two improvements in Detroit's racial climate that occurred during the post–World War II period as having a negative impact on black entrepreneurship. First, the reduction of racial segregation in retail sales, restaurants, and accommodations permitted black shoppers to patronize businesses beyond the ghetto and, as such, had the effect of shrinking black merchants' captive market. In addition, the opening up of industrial jobs for African Americans meant that fewer people of color needed to rely on small businesses to earn a living.

In the following interview excerpt, a college student describes how integration led to the demise of a long-established clothing store:

> This black-owned clothing store, it lasted through the '43 riots, through the '67 riots. They passed the test of time, and that is something that is very, very rare—a black business that is selling clothes. Their appeal would be to professional women. You know, middle-class women in Detroit. They had a customer base that they would just rely on. In the pre–Civil Rights [era], I might go over there and get my hookup. But hey, now we don't have to go there. We can go where we want to go now . . . [there is] that mystique about what's on the other side of the mountain. . . .
>
> We don't have to shop from our own now. Is it in vogue to support your own now? That's not in vogue any more. Pre Civil Rights, it was like, "We are all we got. We have no choice, whether it's in vogue or not, we have no choice but to support our own." Now, if you think about it, that's not a major thing—for people to support our own anymore. We have to be honest about why we're not supporting our own.

The most commonly cited reason for low rates of black self-employment described by our respondents was that African Americans became accustomed to finding well-paid jobs in the automobile industry and related manufacturing fields. These required little training or initiative to obtain, yet provided a comfortable standard of living. The availability of such jobs was a short-term prospect, however. By the late 1960s, older plants in Detroit were being closed and replaced by newer ones in suburban locations.[22]

Moreover, after the 1970s, because of the general decline of the U.S. auto industry, community members who had long relied on these jobs were left with few alternatives. Finally, laid-off workers found that the job skills they had developed during industrial employment had little applicability to other occupations. An economic development specialist working for a Detroit nonprofit organization explained:

> We had manufacturing jobs. We could make big money and not have to worry about becoming the head of some business, being some [kind of] entrepreneur.

[In contrast,] my husband, he's from Alabama, and the culture here is much different compared to that. The difference is that, in the South, you have to educate and refine yourself in order to make seventy, eighty, one hundred thousand dollars. Whereas, here, you could make seventy thousand a year with just a high school education. So I think the [that's why] we don't have a lot of [black-owned] businesses here; the manufacturing era was something that hurts us now. Your granddad worked at Ford, and he did pretty well and drove a Cadillac, and you think, "I'm not gonna work [in a small business] for five dollars an hour for fourteen hours a day."

Small Businesses and the Political Agenda

Both entrepreneurs and business development personnel told us that, until fairly recently, local politicians had been uninterested in supporting the creation of small businesses because each enterprise offered only a small number of jobs and, as such, were unimpressive.

ENTREPRENEUR: I don't think retail businesses have been a big priority for any political administration because they don't have any appeal. [Politicians are interested in] the big visible symbol. The push has always been on the number of jobs that something [a policy] creates and, you know, these big buildings. But a lot of these retail businesses may employ ten, twelve people, and I don't think [that matters much] in the political realm.

Self-blame

In explaining the small number of black businesses, Detroit residents, politicians, and business owners commonly pointed to the discriminatory actions of white society that have restricted African Americans' ability to become self-employed. At the same time, however, advocates of black entrepreneurship have long held the black community itself responsible.[23] These criticisms were frequently mentioned in our interviews with residents and often appeared in the journalistic sources that we reviewed.

A common accusation was that blacks preferred shopping at white-owned stores because they had internalized the larger society's negative view of the race. The result was that they were reluctant to patronize black-owned firms.[24] In the words of a business development program director,

I guess one of the challenges is the self-hatred category. I hear people say, "I went to that black business and got bad service. I'll never go to another black business again." You would not hear that if they went to a white-owned business. "I'll never go . . ." I hear that so much. . . .

INVESTIGATOR: Is that right? You mean we haven't got over that in the Civil Rights revolution? The Black Power movement didn't get us out of that?

RESPONDENT: No, there are seeds of self-hatred. We say that our businesses are somehow inferior. I have people say, "I won't go . . ." They make those same generalizations, and it is a shame.

In addition to mentioning that residents' avoidance of black businesses is due to racial concerns, interviewees claimed that local consumers regarded the city as a low prestige venue for shopping. Compounding the situation, since Detroit residents tend to be poor, desirable, brand-name products are rarely marketed in the city's limited retail sector. The director of a privately funded business development program describes how, in their search for reputable stores and quality merchandise, Detroit residents tend to make major purchases at suburban malls rather than in city shops:

I think that they've got this [view that there is] more panache in going to Troy [an affluent suburb] or to some other place to purchase this item as opposed to doing so within the city. People feel there's some emotional benefit, and I guess there is some kind of high-named brand clothing, high fashion type of stuff that they can say that they went to Somerset Mall and purchased as opposed to purchasing the same goods in Detroit. I don't know. I wish I could have an answer for this. I've thought about this and have had a beer or two too many discussing this issue.

And really I haven't been able to get my hands on it. I think it's part[ly] some mix of self-hatred and of poor service from businesses that are under-capitalized. I think it's a result of the mix of consumer goods and services that are offered when you have a population that is heavily on the poor side. The last thing I read is that Detroit is the poorest big city in the US.

Like many black activists before her, an entrepreneur and business development specialist refers to blacks' unwillingness to spend money in coethnic businesses as hindering the creation of a black ethnic economy.

I was just doing some research . . . four hundred billion African American dollars were spent outside of the African American community last year, resulting in the black dollar not turning even once in its own community before it left. On the contrary, the Jewish dollar turns ten times in the community before it leaves, and there are similar stats for other communities, and I think that even as a business owner myself, some of the challenges that we face are in that realm.

And if I think I could be loose in this statement, it's sort of that we're waiting for our forty acres and a mule still, you know—that belief of entitlement versus empowerment. Nothing's coming, it's not gonna happen, and we sort of have to take the reins in our communities, and we have to raise the level of service that we offer one another and invest in appreciating items as opposed to deprecating items. So I think there are some cultural issues as well, how we define ourselves. Then we need to define what our priorities are from an economic standpoint.

Several respondents faulted African Americans for their lack of commitment to each other. Seeking better deals and greater convenience, black shoppers were criticized for patronizing local shops owned by nonblacks or driving to suburbs where they could shop in malls. While respondents asserted the need for community members to do business with black-owned firms in Detroit, at the same time, several acknowledged the limited options available in the city that made it a difficult goal. Gordon Alexander explained his position with regard to groceries: "There is only one store in the city I'll pick some stuff at, but my kids jokingly call it 'the ghetto store' because everything is subpar."[25] Making the same point, a young interviewee said that, even though she would like to utilize black-owned businesses in Detroit, to do so meant that she had to expend considerable time and effort to locate and then visit stores that carried the merchandise she wanted. In contrast, visiting a suburban mall provided a "one-stop shopping" experience with the possibility of comparing items offered by several shops.

I think that sometimes it is hard to locate where the black businesses are. When I went home [from college], I would always go to this one oil change place. One day, I went there, and they were closed, and I'm like, "Well where do I go to find a black business to do my oil changes from now on? What do I do next?"

Along the same lines, a friend said, "I think there is like one black-owned bank in Detroit." Well how many people know that? How many people know it exists? How many people know where it is located? Just different things like that. I think that marketing and advertising is an issue, too. Like people need to know that you exist and where you are and where to utilize your services. Because we see a Kroger everywhere, but we may not see John-John's [black-owned] grocery store.

It was not entrepreneurs and business developers but rather college students who contended that black customers seek special deals from African American shop owners. This expectation, they assert, makes it difficult for black merchants to make a profit when serving a black clientele.[26] Cynthia describes her uncle's experience:

Cynthia: I think it's a major issue. People say, "I'm black; I should get special treatment at a black store," like well, "Hook me up, you know . . ."

I remember my uncle. He opened up a fish fry restaurant, and he gave so many free fish dinners that he really didn't have no profit at the end of the day, so he had to close up after a year. Like, he just did not make it. I'm like, "Well, Uncle, you're giving out free food to everybody in the 'hood, like you ain't gonna make no profit." So I think that we largely want a hook up on the black hand side.

They have to have checks at the end of the day. They have to make a profit, or they won't survive. They gotta pay the bills to even open, so, I mean, I know that's an issue.

Kelvin offers a similar anecdote:

It's been said jokingly, but "cut a brother a deal" is never a line that's spoken to a Korean. Well, I shouldn't say never, but it's not a lot relied upon to the Korean business owner, the white business owner, the Arab business owner, whatever; it's not relied upon. "Cut a brother a deal." That's something that's usually reserved and relied upon within the African American community. "You should give me a discount. You know my situation." You know how it is—it's not always treated as a business relationship. It's treated more as a personal relationship, even if there is no personal relationship established between the two parties involved. Based on race and cultural similarities, it's assumed that "you should understand where I'm coming from."

In addition to their criticisms of black customers, informants also disparaged black shop owners who, they complained, did a poor job of running businesses in an efficient and reliable manner. Several respondents suggested that, ironically, Asians knew much more about appealing to and serving black customers than did blacks themselves.[27] A female college student commented on Vietnamese and Koreans: "They know what's appealing to us. They have studied us and what we're interested in, I mean, they got it down to a science, like they really do."

Black women did note that black women entrepreneurs could provide a value-added and personal interaction that customers prized and, as such, went out of their way to patronize certain businesses that were run by black women.[28] This is shown in the following interview interchange among two college students:

RESPONDENT: It's so important to build that rapport. It's so important to build that committed customer base that's going to be faithful to you no matter what—if you move or relocate, no matter if your prices go up a little, no matter. If you practice sales like you should—it's important to just build that rapport.

INTERVIEWER: And they build it with you?

RESPONDENT: And they build it. Sharon's really good at. She is very person-able, very sweet; she calls you [to say], "I got some products that you may like. You should come by and check these out," or she sends some e-mails, just constantly keeping that communication going. That's important. You can't just expect people to just come to you. You have to come to them and make the products seem attractive to them, make them feel important. Sharon will really make you feel important. You could buy something as simple as a card, and she's gonna wrap it up really cute with the tissue and a little cute bag, and you feel like, "This is my little gift for me." You know, you really feel like, "I opened up my own Christmas gift again in July." It feels good, so she has those little packages she uses that makes going to her attractive. It makes it fun; it is sweet to go to her. Those things are wise business practices. That's smart. That's the customer service at the end of the day.

Several faulted African Americans for lacking the cooperative spirit that immigrant entrepreneurs relied on to acquire the resources needed to run businesses.

They [immigrants] depend on their family, you know, 'cause like where they come from, they would love to see their people, you know, do well. So they will help doing the business up and running and making money so they can continue to start other businesses. But us as African Americans really don't do that. We really don't like to help each other out. I don't know why. Maybe it goes back to slavery, whatever. But we really don't like helping each other out, so that's why we can't really own up our own businesses 'cause it is hard for us to like get the amount of money that we need to start opening them up. It is a money factor.

A final criticism that some African Americans have of their community as discouraging business success is the group's emphasis on informal entrepreneurship. Angela and Gregg, college students from Detroit, observed that, due to African Americans' lack of access to capital and training, they often run survival-type businesses rather than formal ones:

ANGELA: Black people, they don't have a building to sell stuff to people. It don't mean that they don't have a business, you know what I'm saying, 'cause some people operate inside their home with like daycares and what else . . . she had a travel agent business, she [is] doing that, you know, from inside her house.

GREGG: Most [members of the] black community of Detroit seem to know more about hustling as opposed to business in general—though hustling is a business. It is a form of a business. They seem to know how to get the perks of manipulating people as opposed to more of a legal way of doing business.

INVESTIGATOR: Say more about that, like what do you mean? Like more black people could hustle? Like doing what?

GREGG: Gambling. One thing I could say is gambling. In high school you see everyone gamble, cards, dice, you see that on the street. You see people sell weed—it's another way to hustle. Black people in Detroit seem to understand about getting money, but they can't seem to find a legal way to do it. Other cultures, well I say other people that are not black that come to Detroit, they open businesses because they know how to market stuff to us.   .

Rebuilding Entrepreneurial Traditions

When confronting the obstacles involved with running a business in Detroit, members of the community often drew inspiration from the legacy of black self-employment that existed prior to the 1960s. They felt that these achievements and the traditions that undergirded them demonstrate the potential for business development in the contemporary period. Business development personnel would describe thriving black business communities of Paradise Valley and Black Bottom as a source of motivation as they asserted that small businesses would provide a pathway to self-determination and economic security. An entrepreneur, who also worked as a staff member of a business development program, summarized this view.

We have those traditions from people whose grandparents were entrepreneurs, whose forefathers or siblings either owned their own business or did some type of professional service where they may have worked for a company, but they also used their expertise to do things on the side in their community. Entrepreneurship has always been a part of us since slavery.

I think we've always been a culture who has had to find a way to be able to provide for our families, to be self-sufficient. And at the end of the day . . . you talk about Black Bottom, when you talk about Paradise Valley in the city of Detroit—which were major African American economic hubs some time ago in the 50s and 60s, and things of that nature. But then integration happened, black folks got good jobs, and we let our businesses go. Our kids that were from families where the father may have owned their own business went away, went to school, and started working for corporate America and didn't come back to keep those businesses going. So it seems as though from my limited view of things that now is the opportunity where we are kind of getting back to our roots.

Accordingly, respondents agreed that there needs to be an enhanced emphasis on organizations that provide skills and financial resources to establish more black-owned firms.

There isn't a network of organizations that work together to build small businesses. You have a sort of a hit or miss approach, and so there isn't a full network. So I think the mindset is to teach about it. It's a long process where African Americans [have to develop] a mindset, but it's more complicated than that. You need a series of things to feed into that mindset. You need capital resources. You need minorities to support minority businesses.

I'm a little young to remember back in the 1930s or 20s, but African Americans did have something back then. They had the infrastructure. They had insurance companies. They had restaurants. They owned a whole lot.

My opinion is that, number 1, culturally, ownership and business ownership has not been as stressed as it has been in other [ethnic group] cultures and also there have been fewer opportunities for people to have the principal role models in that area. I came from a generation where parents said "go to college, get good grades, get a good job . . ." without realizing, the dynamic that a number of younger folks in African American communities realized, and I think folks in other cultures realized, that when you work for someone else, when you die, your good job goes to the grave with you. . . . As opposed to business ownership, where you can create wealth, and if successful, you can create lasting, multigenerational wealth.

CONTRASTING PERSPECTIVES ON BUSINESS DEVELOPMENT IN DETROIT

As the discussion above reveals, Detroit residents, business development personnel, and entrepreneurs shared common understandings of why there are few black-owned businesses in America's largest black majority city. At the same time, however, we discovered that proponents of business development also disagreed about the causes and possible solutions to this problem.

Drawing on traditions of black solidarity, one group emphasized race-based solutions. They define Detroit as a black city and, as such, stressed collaboration among African Americans as the best path to economic development. In this view, because whites have been blacks' major impediment in developing businesses, efforts toward resolving the problem should be strictly race based. They argued that nonblacks, including investors and corporations who might provide funds, jobs, capital improvements, and enhanced retail options to Detroit, should be excluded. Following the same rationale, they contended that ethnic entrepreneurs, who control most of Detroit's retail stores, draw patronage away from black businesses and siphon scarce and hard-earned financial resources away from Detroit into the suburban realms where they reside.

Many of the most enthusiastic proponents of the race-based perspective on black business development in Detroit were community activists and politicians. They hoped this approach would appeal to residents who were frustrated by the limited retail options, poor service, and lack of African American merchants in Detroit's neighborhoods. This, in turn, could enhance the influence of organizations and movements with which they are affiliated.

In contrast, another group concerned with business development emphasized place rather than race as Detroit's most fundamental basis of identity and, as such, sought to increase economic growth within the city's municipal boundaries. Acknowledging that Detroit is a black majority city and needs more black-owned businesses, at the same time, they welcomed beneficial participation from all comers.

As such, advocates of the place-based view don't express uniform hostility to the city's ethnic entrepreneurs or corporate chains. Not surprisingly, this position is especially attractive to nonblacks involved in Detroit's economic life, who draw upon it to assert that they have a rightful place in the community and should not be seen as interlopers or parasites. While proponents of the race-based view were often political activists, advocates of the place perspective included business development staff, entrepreneurs, and others associated with business interests.

While contrasting perspectives on business development in Detroit were held by factions that emphasized either race or place, another major source of contention with regard to business development was class. In our analyses of the city's organizational life and of newspaper articles and interviews, small-sized, neighborhood-based business owners often squared off against affluent and well-connected entrepreneurs who used their economic resources and access to politicians, corporate interests, and local philanthropists to obtain benefits.

Despite popular references to political solidarity among African Americans and Detroit residents, the fact that African Americans hold diverse perspectives toward business development is hardly surprising. At least since the early twentieth century, observers have noted the significant degree of diversity and segmentation that exists among the greater black population. Leading students of African American life, from Du Bois to St. Clair Drake and Horace Cayton, to E. Franklin Frazier, William J. Wilson, and Mary Pattillo have each contributed to our understanding of the community's diverse experiences, outlooks, philosophies, access to resources, and regional, cultural, and economic traditions and ways of life.[29] This diversity often underlies the population's disparate reactions to business development and ways of relating to outgroup entrepreneurs with whom they compete for the patronage of customers. The section below describes contrasting perspectives on business development maintained by African Americans and other groups in Detroit.

RACIAL SOLIDARITY AND THE DEVELOPMENT
OF BLACK SELF-EMPLOYMENT

Given the long and significant role of racism in limiting opportunities for Detroit's African American community, some voices within the population seek to reduce the influence and power of nonblack interests over blacks' lives as a means of alleviating their social, political, and economic problems.[30] These activists argue that, through collaboration within the African American community, a considerable measure of self-determination may be achieved and major problems solved. Indeed, as Joe Darden and colleagues assert, "One of the most remarkable stories in the constellation of potential narratives about politics in the Detroit region is the story of the growth and development of black political power."[31] Since the 1960s, as the city approached and then attained black majority status, policies directed toward the city's racial majority have stimulated the imaginations of residents, community activists, and elected officials.

During the 1980s and 1990s, as conflicts between African American communal activists and immigrant entrepreneurs received extensive exposure in the national news media, Detroit activists catalyzed collective action against nonblack merchants whose actions were resented by local residents (see chapter 6). These included protests and boycotts against ethnic entrepreneurs who injured or killed black customers, provided poor service, and sold outdated food products.[32] For example, in 1997, when Mark McCloud, a twenty-three-year-old black customer, complained about a spoiled sandwich he purchased at a Chaldean-owned market on Livernois Avenue, he was insulted and threatened with a gun. In response, he organized a protest against the store and later enlisted the New Marcus Garvey Movement and its director, Minister Malik Shabazz, to help him exert pressure on the store's owners. Following five days of protest, Minister Shabazz and the store's owner, Sam Brikho, and manager, Neil Brikho, entered into negotiations to end the protest.

Upon completion of the negotiations, both parties promised to issue public apologies. In addition, the store agreed to employ at least one black worker, compensate McCloud, sponsor four area block clubs and community activities, and work along with other local merchants to support an area elementary school. For their part, community members consented to alert business owners about theft and vandalism on the condition that store employees promised to treat them with kindness and respect. In a statement reflecting his attitude toward nonblack merchants in Detroit, Minister Shabazz considered the conflict's resolution. "All in all, I think its okay. . . . It's the next best thing to closing them down and black folks taking ownership."[33]

Minister Malik Shabazz addresses the 60 protestors that came out to march in front of the Epicurus Restaurant on Warren after an alleged assault to a 65 year old man who wanted to use the restaurant's rest room facilities, March 8, 2007. Shabazz and other activists engage in protests outside of businesses in Detroit whose owners or employees are seen as abusing or exploiting local residents.
Source: Daniel Mears/The Detroit News

In 1999, the killing of Kalvin Porter by two Yemeni employees at a
Chaldean-owned Detroit gas station resulted in long-term protests by the
victim's family and black activists groups and greatly enhanced tensions
between immigrant merchants in Detroit.[34] In 2001, a series of incidents
of abuse of African American customers in Arab- and Chaldean-owned gas
stations led to the creation of a B-gas (black gas) campaign, which encouraged African Americans to patronize black-owned stations. Describing the
program, Reverend Horace Sheffield III, director of the Detroit chapter of
Reverend Al Sharpton's National Action Network, wrote,

> The B-Gas Campaign is all about making certain that if the color of our skin
> is not respected, then at least the green that leaves our black hand is. . . . We
> need to demand our respect and better treatment and accept nothing less. We
> need to STOP spending our money in places and with people who mistreat
> us, display disdain for us and who openly disrespect us. . . . Will you Black
> Detroiters—let this community and this country now know—that we finally
> mean business and that our business is to operate on the basis of our interests
> not others?[35]

In response, several Arab American gas station owners complained that the
boycott was unjust, since their entire group was being punished for the bad
behavior of a few businesses that happened to be owned by coethnics.[36]

The Africa Town Project

Perhaps the most extensive and controversial solution for the low rates of
black business ownership in Detroit is reflected in the approval of a resolution favoring the creation of the Detroit Capital Development Corporation
(DCDC; often described as the Africa Town proposal) by the Detroit city
council on July 15, 2004.

The DCDC was to be supported by thirty million dollars from funds collected from newly opened Detroit casinos and would be supplemented by
an additional one million dollars annually from gambling revenues. These
funds would be used to establish a low-interest, revolving loan fund for the
creation or expansion of businesses owned by "the City's majority under-
served population" (African Americans) within the boundaries of the city
of Detroit.[37]

The DCDC plan was spelled out in a report entitled "A Powernomics
Economic Development Plan for Detroit's Under-Served Majority Population" written by Claud Anderson, a Detroit native and author of several
books about black economic development. For preparing the report, Anderson was paid more than one hundred thousand dollars by Detroit's city

council. The report received a nonbinding endorsement from seven of the nine city council members, even though several expressed reservations about some sections of the report.[38] For example, council president pro tem Kenneth Cockrel said he didn't support the rhetoric in the plan but voted for it anyway because he wanted to find ways to increase black wealth and entrepreneurship.[39]

While the council's endorsement lacked legal standing, the proposal was nevertheless vetoed by Mayor Kilpatrick on July 27, 2004. The mayor reasoned that the creation of the DCDC violated the Michigan Constitution. He further asserted that allocating funds strictly according race was illegal.[40]

The plan emphasized that, since African Americans are the overwhelming majority of the population of Detroit, they should act accordingly, by unflinchingly advocating policies that are directed toward, and beneficial to, African Americans. "As the clear majority of the population, blacks should logically own and control a greater percentage of the city's businesses, industries, land, downtown buildings, public contracts, and jobs. But they do not. Blacks may be an official minority in the nation, but in the city of Detroit, the Black under-served is the numerical majority. They must learn to behave accordingly."[41] In addition to suggesting the creation of a loan fund, the proposal outlined the establishment of a black business district in Detroit that would compete with other local ethnic enclaves including Mexicantown and Greektown in Detroit, and nearby Arabtown (the report's name for the Arab American community in Dearborn).

It also suggested the creation of a variety of wholesome, black-oriented economic activities, ranging from culture-related enterprises to restaurants, a beverage bottling company, and a fish farm that would market goods and services to the local population. Finally, the report recommended that Detroit use its access to the city airport, Great Lakes shipping lanes, and nearby border with Canada to establish itself as an international center for Pan-African commerce linking Africa, the Caribbean, and Latin America.

The proposal did not mince words about its intentions to develop black businesses in Detroit. While acknowledging the skills of nonblack entrepreneurs in Detroit, it emphasized the negative impact of their activities on black residents, decried immigrants' eligibility for affirmative action benefits that should be reserved for blacks, and emphasized black opposition to and victimization by immigrants. To quote the report,

> Race and immigration are fundamental societal issues that are sometimes contentious. Raising and discussing these issues does not mean the author or the City Council are against any group. It does mean that they have accepted the challenge to examine the facts for the good of the City. . . .

As a group, [black Americans] own and control little of value and when they try to build their own Black communities or Black businesses they are called segregationists, racists, or charged with practicing "reverse discrimination." When American Indians, Arabs, Asians or Hispanics aggregate and pool their resources, establish organization and institutions in their own best interests, it is accepted without challenge.[42]

Toward the goal of maximizing and retaining Detroit's wealth and business resources for black people, the report rejected economic development activities that sought to strengthen Detroit's economic links with the larger society. For example, the plan ruled out gentrification, regional development initiatives, and the establishment of chain stores within the city. While such programs are generally regarded as conducive to economic growth and as contributing to the quality of life as well as employment opportunities for Detroit residents, the report rejected these schemes because they provide nonblacks with greater access to Detroit's resources, consumers, and physical environment (such as its riverfront and water system).[43]

The veto of this program by Mayor Kilpatrick notwithstanding, it enjoyed considerable popular endorsement. The *Detroit Free Press*, for example, quoted upbeat responses from several stylists employed by an African American business—Nelson's Praise Him Beauty Barber and Nail Salon. "It's about time someone tries to help black entrepreneurs—We need it the most," said Pam Morrel, a hairstylist. "Blacks are the only people who do not have businesses in their own community." Sandra Nelson, who opened the shop in 2003 without bank loans or a business plan, concurred. "I need the help. I would love to get one of those grants."[44]

Some respondents commend the Africa Town proposal's assertion that immigrants unfairly benefit from government-provided financial resources. For example, in discussing the ability of recently arrived immigrants to open businesses soon after arrival while the native born could not, a college student referred to an urban myth circulated among both whites and blacks: that the prevalence of businesses opened by recent immigrants can be traced to the special loans and tax credits that they receive.[45]

Well I don't know this as a fact, because I haven't done my own research, but through conversations with individuals and various sources, [I have heard that] there are opportunities allotted for people, non-blacks, that allow them to have these opportunities to open up businesses. For instance, it has been told to me that many people from other countries are able to establish a business and not pay taxes for up to seven years, during that establishing. . . . And so as a result, native born Americans are not allotted those same opportunities and it is difficult [for us].

In addition to grassroots endorsements, well-known religious leaders also supported the Africa Town plan. Longtime civil rights activist Reverend C. T. Vivian's approval was quoted in the *New York Times*. "Establishing a loan fund exclusively for blacks would help remove 'psychological barriers' to their success. 'What we're really talking about is accumulation of capital, which African-Americans have never been able to get in this country,' Mr. Vivian said. 'To vote against that is to vote against our future as black people.'"[46]

Similarly, Minister Farrakhan of the Nation of Islam endorsed the proposal in a Detroit speech:

> I was fascinated by the concept of Africa Town because, if anything can be done by black people, it should be done in Detroit. Suppose we had an Africa Town, wherein black architects can show their genius, black construction people can show their ability, and black entrepreneurs can open businesses. We can show that we, too, can do for ourselves as others are doing. We ought to do it for ourselves! New York is watching; Chicago is looking; Baltimore, which is 85 percent black with a White mayor—is looking. If Detroit does it, then Detroit will set an example for the rest of America.[47]

Despite its being vetoed, supporters of the project continue to work toward its implementation. For example, in 2008 (some four years after the proposal was turned down), the city's Harmonie Park Entertainment District was renamed the Paradise Valley Entertainment District, in honor of a black business district from years gone by. As of this writing, over 17 million dollars had been spent on the project with an additional 7.5 million more allocated for its completion. Emphasizing their commitment to Anderson's concept, two city councilwomen asserted, "The new district will serve as Africa Town, even though it is not going to be called that."[48]

Finally, while the Detroit mayor vetoed the DCDC plan, apparently he could not resist the political benefits yielded by appealing to the popular resentment against nonblack entrepreneurs that animated it. This can be seen in his calling for the enforcement of food safety laws among minimarts and groceries, which are owned almost exclusively by Chaldeans and other nonblack merchants, at the same time that he also sought to expand business development activities directed at diverse interests as part of his economic agenda.[49]

DETROIT AS A MULTIRACIAL PLACE

The most prominent alternative to the racial solidarity approach to business development in Detroit emphasized the city's municipal rather than racial boundaries.[50] While identifying the lack of black-owned businesses as a major problem, adherents of this place-defined perspective encouraged the participation of anyone willing to contribute to the city's growth.

For example, despite the history of conflict between African Americans and Chaldean entrepreneurs in Detroit, when the American Chaldean Council (ACC) engaged in a series of revitalization efforts on Seven Mile Road that provided needed services to both African Americans and recently arrived Middle Eastern immigrants and drove prostitutes and drug dealers from the area, residents and politicians expressed their gratitude. The ACC's projects included a 3.8 million-dollar Youth Leadership and Education Center attended by more than three hundred African American and immigrant members of the community, a facility for the mentally ill, and a proposed 2.2 million-dollar adult learning center.

About the project, Mayor Kilpatrick's spokesman Matt Allen stated, "It's a wonderful story to be told. . . . In the last few years they have made substantial efforts to rebuild and redevelop that neighborhood and in the most African-American city in the country, we are seeing new immigrants' stories and new tales from an ethnic melting pot being told. It is obviously welcomed by the city."[51]

Acceptance of Nonblack Entrepreneurs

Given that much of the city's retail sector is dominated by nonblacks, both business development personnel and entrepreneurs who held the place-based view suggested that the impact of immigrant and ethnic entrepreneurs could be positive. Consequently, such merchants should not be regarded simply as exploiters or impediments to the development of black enterprises. The African American director of the Detroit branch of a privately funded, nonprofit organization that provides minority entrepreneurs with corporate contracts and business assistance describes the role of nonblack entrepreneurs in the city:

A lot of less wealthy black neighborhoods have always been prime, predatory targets for any number of people [ethnic groups] who have business models. Because of limited access, whether it's the transportation or any number of things, [business owners] have been able to exploit and charge lower-income people, especially lower-income black people, a premium for services. You know, we can see the proliferation of the rent-to-own stores, the check cashing, payday loans. . . .

I've worked with the folks who own the grocery stores, and I know the folks who own the beauty supply [shops], the Koreans and Chaldeans and other [groups], and I don't necessarily fault them. I think they're making a sound business decision. [The local community] can't lock anyone out of the market. I think a lot of the anger toward them is really misplaced, and I don't blame them for it. There's a viable market that you tap into. I think someone would be foolish not to tap into a viable market when it's neglected.

Small grocery stores, you know, are able to charge substantial premiums for their service. So it is a lucrative market. People who are strong in that market, like any other business market, do what they can to discourage competition.

While acknowledging that nonblacks own a disproportionate share of Detroit's retail businesses, respondents refrained from describing them in a hostile manner. Rather, they often commented on the high level of business skill and community organization upon which nonblack entrepreneurs relied to fulfill consumer demand. Their disagreement with racially exclusive business development activities is revealed in their opposition to the Africa Town project and by their endorsement of interracial collaboration. In the following excerpt, the director of a minority business development program acknowledges the strengths of ethnic entrepreneurs in Detroit.

[Other] cultures [groups involved in self-employment], they have a business model. When they come here—and I know this for a fact—they have dealt with someone that has a business, and they've refined the model. Like some of these beauty supply places, [they have] a huge demand, but their inventory's always stocked. You can go in there, and they're never out of product[s]. They have some distribution model in place where they can source that product and keep it, and they're doing fantastic. Whereas if you don't have any resources outside of your area, and you're trying to do that volume purchasing, you won't be as successful. It's just the lack of connectedness outside of your area that keeps many black business owners from being able to compete.

Several of the African American business development staff members we interviewed felt that Detroit, like other urban centers in the United States and abroad, would benefit from increased ethnic diversity and by having access to goods and service provided by a multiethnic business community.

Even though it's great for the city of Detroit to be 70 percent, 80 percent minority, it's a detriment as well and, that is, it lacks diversity. Diversity is the key. In my travels all over the country in promoting entrepreneurship, one thing you don't have, and that is there needs to be more diversity of ethnic groups in the Detroit area.

I believe for a city to truly be great—to be a community—ethnicity and cultural mixes are important. I enjoy Asian food. I enjoy receiving other types of cultural types of products and services. That's why we [my business development program] have been endorsed by the Arab American Chamber of Commerce. We work closely with the Hispanic Business Alliance, and the Asian Pacific Chamber of Commerce, and things of that nature. What I truly believe in is that, as this city moves forward, we have to work together.

Taking a similar view, Michael Goodin, the senior editor of the *Michigan Chronicle* (one of Detroit's two major African American newspapers), wrote a 1999 editorial about Detroit's retail situation:

> I support Black economics as much as anyone, but I don't support fanning African American and Arab tensions in the city. Yes, I'd like to see more Black youth work at all these convenience stores and I'd like to see fewer beer and wine stores and more substantial kinds of retail projects such as modern strip malls. But until we see a cadre of entrepreneurs with the willingness to build a Black-owned retail base that can meet the needs of Detroit shoppers, the city's diverse business community will continue to provide a valuable service.[52]

A *New York Times* article about the Africa Town proposal quoted Bill Ross, the president of Detroit's Booker T. Washington Business Association, one of the oldest organizations involved in the promotion of African American entrepreneurship. Ross said his group supported the development of black-owned businesses but also asserted, "We do not believe you do it by trampling on the rights and spirits of others."[53]

Several respondents who emphasized the notion of place over race highlighted the fact that, while various ethnic groups ran businesses in Detroit, African Americans constituted the overwhelming majority of the local population. As such, they felt that immigrant and ethnic entrepreneurs should not pose a threat to a mobilized community of African American business owners and customers. In the words of a business developer,

> African Americans are the majority. And I think once folks have the types of resources and capital they need to help them move forward, they will. Especially in a city that is 80 plus percent African American. No matter how you look at it, there's going to always be a large percentage of black folks in the city. Even if gentrification is a process that may be happening right now, it's not easy to get rid of eight hundred thousand to a million black folks. It's just not going to happen overnight.
>
> Black folks are used to losing jobs and moving after the house forecloses, going down the street and living with Grandma until the air clears again. You know, and then they move right back into the house that got foreclosed. So I think folks are going to be here, so you're going to have a marketing demographic available to you. I think once we mobilize ourselves, I think once we're able to help businesses upgrade their services and products and standards, then will we be able to be competitive on a global level.

We have to be more inclusive in doing things with Asians who hold a large percentage of businesses in African American neighborhoods [and] Arab Americans who own a large percentage and extract major economic dollars from the African American community via liquor or convenience stores— things of that nature that used to be African American owned—so we all have a common entrepreneurial mindset, and I think, once we all get to a level of equal knowledge, we'll be able to do business on a higher level.

Seeking Chain Stores

Rather than referring to the negative impact of nonblack economic actors and protesting their presence, a number of respondents sought their collaboration in the city's economic life by enlisting their cooperation in business development activities. For example, while the proponents of the Africa Town project seek to limit the number of corporate businesses in Detroit because of the competition that they generate for black merchants, advocates of the place-based approach decried the city's lack of chain stores and high-quality retail outlets. In their view, even if such businesses are white owned, they offer a host of benefits—desirable goods and services, convenience, employment opportunities, tax revenues, and a means of drawing customers to adjacent, black-owned businesses.

A successful, nonretail entrepreneur, who resides in Detroit, articulates this position. In her view, since Detroit residents patronize suburban chain stores, the firms owning them are obliged to invest in the city. They refuse to do so because of racial stereotypes. She believes that, if more corporate businesses would locate in Detroit, this would not only yield increased profits for the firms but also provide Detroit residents with both economic opportunities and prestige. However, cognizant of corporate reluctance to allocate resources to communities of color, she believes there won't be significant corporate investment in Detroit until its white population increases.

> Detroit has a committed black, middle-class population. Why do they disperse to the suburbs? Because [of] the Catch-22 that we are talking about. You know, where are the services?
> I go to Royal Oak [a suburb] to the grocery store. When I go out to Holiday Market in Royal Oak, I see a lot of people from the city of Detroit. If you look at the customers that shop at these suburban stores, I think you'll find a disproportionate number of Detroiters actually shopping there. And it is because we don't have the services in Detroit. These people [who run the businesses] know that. Because they know that the demographics [of Detroit] would support a lot of these things [businesses].

I think there is a sufficient number of customers to support any type of business within the city of Detroit. But, I think there has been a conscious decision [by corporate business interests] that "we'll just keep the store out in the suburbs, because they are going to come out here [to shop] anyway."

I mean at some point, I think that it is going to take people who are recognizing it as being a problem that we don't have stores. We don't have retail. When are these [corporate business] people going to come into our town?

But, without anybody really addressing the direct/indirect issues that come up, nobody is going to tell you, "Okay, I'm not building a store in Detroit because the city is predominantly black." When it is predominantly black, people assume there is going to be shrinkage, theft, whatever they want to call it. And so, therefore, [they conclude,] "We don't want to be there or it is not the image that we want to have. We don't want to be in a predominantly black area." Nobody is going to tell you that. But that's the reality of it. Until you can actually address that and say, "Okay, that's why you are not coming," you know. What do you do about that?

I think that the [business development] people that are here [in Detroit] are doing a yeoman's job in terms of making that case. I think the people that have made the decision to come here are doing well. I think it took a lot for them to get that Hard Rock Cafe here, but from what I understand, it is the best performing [location] in the chain and that generally is what happens. I'm very pleased with the positive changes that I've seen, particularly in the downtown area. I think that the current mayor's [Kilpatrick] administration is largely responsible for that, because they do have a very good team of people that are able to implement plans. But you still see empty storefronts on the street. Many of the stores that you do see are basically owned by young black entrepreneurs.

I think that is the answer because there is nobody that is going to come in and save Detroit, unless Detroit changes. And part of that is the demographic change. I think for folks, it is based on race. If Detroit's numbers start changing and it becomes a sixty/forty population [black/white], I think you'll start seeing some renewed interest in national retailers coming in or even regional retailers coming to town. But, until that happens, I don't see them really expressing much of an interest, and I see that as the only way that you actually will get retail.

In contrast to the racially focused group who seek to exclude corporate businesses, the respondent is adamant about the need for such interests to be involved in and contribute to the city's economic life. In her view, advancement will be produced through corporate investment in Detroit.

A business developer echoes the previously quoted entrepreneur's perspective about winning back chain stores to the city.

BUSINESS DEVELOPER: One of the first reasons [for the poor retail environment] is the negative perception of the city of Detroit, and I think that we're moving past that negative perception now. I mean, after the Super Bowl I think we're some-how getting over that hurdle. I think it has to do with the fact that retailers might overlook our city. However, we know that we have the economic base because . . . our people are going out to the suburban locations to those retail stores.

John and I were just at a community meeting last night where they're say-ing, "Why aren't these retailers coming to our city?" And so we're saying that we need to put the demand on these retailers. But if we're going out to the suburbs, then we're really not demanding that they come to our city because we're getting on the freeway or whatever and we're going to support them in their suburban locations. I think that negative image or perception is one of the main reasons why we don't have the retail population that we need to start up businesses here.

Despite her frustration with the reluctance of corporations to invest, the entrepreneur quoted above felt that certain forms of confrontation used in the past might not yield a desired outcome today. "From time to time, people have called for boycotts of institutions or of businesses or even sub-urban areas. But I think, at this point, that is seen as sort of an outdated way of dealing with things."

In sum, while advocates of the race-based approach rejected making deals with white corporations, the advocates of the place-based approach reasoned that forms of investment and economic development, even if controlled by white corporations, would yield sizeable benefits for African American merchants and residents. Consequently, their goal was not to exclude such interests but rather to encourage their presence in the city.

IMMIGRANT ENTREPRENEURS DEFEND THEIR PRESENCE

Well aware that a fraction of African American activists and residents paint them as self-serving exploiters, ethnic entrepreneurs defend their commitment to the city where they spend their lives, invest their savings, contend with crime, and pay taxes. Accordingly, they emphasized their ties to the place, even if many do not live there and are not members of its racial majority.

Following the endorsement of the Africa Town project by the Detroit city council, members of Detroit's Latino, Asian, and Arab communities engaged in a street protest and demanded a public apology.[54] While Jeffrey Roby, whose family has run a shoe store in Detroit for over thirty years, approved of Africa Town as an advertising strategy, he worried that the initiative might result in longtime business owners like himself, who are not black, getting pushed out.[55]

Challenging the Africa Town proposal's characterization of immigrant entrepreneurs as receiving more rewards than blacks, Latinos point out that they have suffered discrimination in Detroit—in the 1930s, 90 percent of the city's Mexican population was deported—and as a tiny minority, they continue to lack power. "Detroiters of Hispanic descent say that even though Latinos, mainly Mexicans, have been settling in Detroit since the 1800s, they remain an invisible community and have no elected representation in a city where 82 percent of the population is black."[56]

It is true that Latinos in Detroit lack political representation. Despite this, however, they have achieved a commendable record of entrepreneurship. In 2002, blacks owned 19,530 total firms, which resulted in a business participation rate of 25.17. In contrast, Latino-owned firms numbered 955, which resulted in a BPR of 20.25. Among persons working in sole proprietor firms, African Americans outstripped Latinos. However, when firms with paid employees are examined, Latinos did better. Only 6.1 percent of all black-owned firms had paid employees, compared to 15.3 percent of all Latino-owned firms. Blacks had 1,199 firms for a BPR of 1.55. In contrast, Latinos had 146 firms for a BPR of 3.10, twice the black BPR.[57]

Chaldean Perspectives on Relations with Customers

Because they have been merchants in Detroit since the early twentieth century and currently own a large fraction of Detroit's retail businesses, Chaldeans feel very connected to the city, even as they have been embroiled in conflicts with local residents and increasingly live beyond the city limits.[58]

In both personal interviews and communal publications, Chaldeans emphasize the great personal cost of running a business in Detroit. The sacrifices they most commonly mention are the incredibly long hours that they spend in their shops (and away from their families) and the frequent violence and even death that they suffer in the course of robberies. In addition, Chaldean entrepreneurs point out that, as a tiny but visible minority, they have been subject to harsh treatment, discrimination, and abuse.

Chaldeans object to overworked Detroit police officers being used to crack down on food safety violations in ethnic shops at the same time that merchants must deal with frequent and violent robberies. As a case in point, the *Chaldean News* quoted Brenda Murad, whose husband was killed in a drive-by shooting at his Detroit car lot.

"Our image of Detroit is that it has a long way to go in regards to safety, economy and the well-being of the people who live and/or work in Detroit," said Brenda Murad. "The elected officials have taken their focus off of major crime in the city and have shifted their attention to minor problems like raiding stores that have a few expired items on their shelves or who are not following the city's sign ordinance. Instead of organizing six officers to make sure a store is in compliance, these officers can be on the street showing a presence and solving crimes. We pray that this city can rise once again to the prestige that it used to have."[59]

In the following quotes, Chaldean entrepreneurs describe their experience in Detroit and how they believe African American customers see them. Lastly, they describe measures that they have taken to improve relations with customers.

We Chaldeans immediately moved to Detroit [when we entered the United States]. We lived around the State Fair area. We taught ourselves capitalism. We self-taught ourselves, eking out prosperity. We taught ourselves that. We didn't have anybody. We bought stores from the Jews, from other Chaldeans, we started some from scratch, and we bought franchises that went under.

For example, the Krogers and the Farmer Jacks [chain groceries] in the city were going belly up. We were the only ones that could make a success of those stores 'cause our profit margins were better. Because our overhead was lower. We don't have union cost. We don't have a huge national franchise [with] unknown types of expenses.

INTERVIEWER: How about relations between the two [black and Chaldean] communities?

RESPONDENT: Well, a lot of it comes from a lack of understanding between us. And major prejudices [happen] when you walk into a community that you don't live in. From the perspective of an African American living in Detroit who is probably poor, who basically has no one to mentor them, [they see] these foreigners [that] come from nowhere. They come with nothing in their pocket . . . and all they know is to work twenty-four hours a day. They are putting in an average [of] eighteen hours a day, these people. Never seeing their family, my father never saw us grow up. He never went to a football game, baseball game, ballet, school meetings, PTA meetings. He never did one thing. But that was because he had to make a living for us. So he sacrificed those things for us. So he could become an economic success. In the neighborhoods that we served, which is Detroit, we would go in, work our butt off, make all this money, and then we would just leave. Go back to the suburbs.

So they saw us as outsiders, coming into their neighborhoods, taking all their money, and then going and living in big, beautiful houses in Southfield and West Bloomfield. So there is that lack of understanding. The way we acted is just like anybody of any ethnic race. Once they are successful, they are going to move up the ranks. Whether it be where they live, what kind of car they drive, or what kind of schools their kids go to. So again, there is that sense of envy. And especially Chaldeans have a reputation for being successful. This is not true. The majority of Chaldeans are poor. We are not wealthy people. The majority of Chaldeans are low- to middle-class people.

We examined the accuracy of this statement by checking the 2000 Census of Population and Housing. Although the census does not provide detailed socioeconomic data for Chaldeans, it does reveal information on immigrants from Iraq, their country of origin. According to the 2000 Census, Iraqis living in the city of Detroit had a median household income of 10,387 dollars compared to a black median household income of 29,647 dollars. Also, 69 percent of Iraqis were living in poverty compared to 22 percent of blacks in the city in 2000.[60] Detroit Iraqis' extremely low incomes are associated with their status as recently arrived refugees who entered the United States in the wake of the Gulf War.[61]

However, an overwhelming majority (91 percent) of Iraqis do not live in the city of Detroit, although many who are self-employed may have businesses there. In the Detroit metropolitan area, which includes the suburbs of Detroit, the median household income of Iraqis was 33,352 dollars compared to 31,945 dollars for blacks. Moreover, the percent of Iraqis in poverty was 25 compared to 20 percent of blacks.[62]

Generational Change in Customer Relations Several younger Chaldean entrepreneurs claimed that the older generation was sometimes hostile toward customers. According to these respondents, over time, the U.S.-raised generation has learned to emphasize civility and worked to establish better rapport:

We finally figured it out, that you know what? You have to put into the system to get out of the system later. Plus, that sense of responsibility is on the forefront. Because we [the second generation] are more educated than the older generation. We don't have that mentality anymore. Every ethnic group goes through that when they come here. When we first came here, it was like every immigrant that comes into this country. They don't understand democracy. They don't understand the makeup of a capitalist society. They saw it as all greed. They didn't really realize that the harder you worked, the more you're going to keep and make. But also, the more you are going to contribute to the greater good of society. And that is where we are today. That is how we are, intellectually.

Every nationality comes here with fear, fear that like my parents came with. The first fear [is] that we are going to assimilate too much, that we are going to lose our heritage. The second fear is how are we going to survive in this country? How are we going to make our money in this country? Capitalism is so intimidating 'cause we don't understand it. [Fear number] three is how am I going to provide an education for my kids so that they have a fair chance, a fighting chance, with my neighbor who is Jewish, Polish, Irish, and African American? Once those fears are alleviated, then you find that the pessimism, the distrust, starts to go away.

In response to those fears, we never reached out to the communities and supported the communities in which we are making money. Chaldeans were not very. . . . We are better today. We were not good at reaching out to the African American community. And instead, we became an isolationist community in this country. And all we cared about was ourselves and making money.

And not to be derogatory of my community, but we didn't reach out to them [black Americans] to say, "We are your neighbors. We work in your community, no we don't live side by side with you, but we are going to support this community that we work in to make it look good, to make it act good, to make it function good."

You know, we are the ones paying all the taxes in the city of Detroit. We are the outsiders paying, getting taxed two and three times. Because we are not Detroit residents; we are the tax base. We are the ones paying for all that. You have property taxes, you have to pay city of Detroit taxes, you have to pay corporate taxes, [and] you have to pay personal income taxes. You have to pay payroll taxes, social security taxes. The list goes on and on.

INTERVIEWER: Did things get better?

RESPONDENT: We have been very cooperative with local government, city government. We have created associations, neighborhood associations; we have worked together with churches, with associated food dealers, which are a trade organization which deals almost strictly with grocery stores, or food industry. We have created alliances and cooperative agreements with the City of Detroit, with the local Wayne County executive. We have created programs, baseball programs, church programs, school programs; we have come a long, long, long, long way. It's not perfect.

INTERVIEWER: What was the turning point?

RESPONDENT: It was proving to the community that I served that we are not there to rape them and go home with their money. We had to prove to them, by making sure that my store is clean all the time, that I care about neighborhoods, that my neighborhood, the neighborhood you live in and I am working in, is clean, that my gardening is done, that my property is clean, that my windows are taken care of, [and] that I contribute to the local Baptist churches around me. Donate to picnics. You know, someone comes to me and wants a fundraiser for a local program; it is very popular with local baseball teams, with no money to buy T-shirts to go and compete against

Catholic Central. You know. "Hey can you give us a hundred dollars?" So hey, you have to prove yourself. Like any other generation, any other society, you have to prove yourself.

In the following excerpt, another second-generation Chaldean describes her efforts to maintain civil relations with customers in her family's store:

LANA: I knew every customer by their first name. I also knew pretty much what they bought, what number they played in the lottery, and I always had their stuff ready when they came in. I would ask them personal questions. And my brothers would talk to them about sports. So they learned about our family.

My parents had a problem with me knowing everybody's name. They asked, "Why do you have to know every man's name?" I said, "You know what? I have a marketing degree. In marketing, you learn that the best way to gain customers is to learn personal stuff about people." And that is what people used to say: "You know us by our first name, you know what we want."

We didn't overcharge people. We never cheated the kids. And that was a big problem in that area, because there are stores on every corner. A lot of store owners felt that it was okay for them to cheat somebody if they could get away with it.

I also did little incentives. Like, I had little kids that used to come in. I'd say, "Okay let me see your report card." And if they improved on their report card, I would give them a bag of chips or a pop just to give them incentive to do well in school. And the kids loved that. And my parents would always give little kids pretzels or bubble gum.

That was the other thing, we always hired. The bottle boys were always kids in the neighborhood. And we paid them a decent amount of money. I had a couple of my employees that I took their money and saved it for them. I had one employee that bought Jordans every single month when they came out. I asked, "Why do you need all those gym shoes? You are fifteen years old. Why don't you save up this money for a car?" So I started taking a percentage of his pay out, with his permission, and putting it away for him. By the time he was sixteen, he was able to buy his own car. I like to teach them how to budget.

In sum, adherents of a place-based view of communal membership in Detroit endorsed the collaboration of various groups in the city's economy. Well aware of the city's black majority and the need to increase rates of black business ownership, they also valued nonblacks' contribution. Accordingly, they included corporate chains and ethnic entrepreneurs in their plans to expand Detroit's economy. Ethnic entrepreneurs' extensive commitments to the city made them identify with this perspective. Admitting that some first-generation merchants had been disrespectful to black customers, second-generation owners described their efforts to maintain civil relations by treating residents with kindness, providing employment, and contributing to communal causes.

CLASS CONFLICTS AMONG BUSINESSES OWNERS

The African American community, unified by shared racial oppression, has long been stratified by class.[63] Patterns of differentiation have expanded since the 1960s, as the contradictory influences of civil rights reforms and deindustrialization have provided a fraction of blacks with new opportunities while denying others a chance for stable employment. Reflecting these trends, observers have debated the fate of black solidarity within a population that includes both an expanding number of educated and professional persons as well as a lower class whose access to the basic necessities of survival is increasingly difficult.[64]

One perspective on class stratification in the black community regards the middle class as natural leaders—the so-called talented tenth—who have the skills, insight, and connections to ensure the advancement of the entire community.[65]

However, another take on class polarization among African Americans asserts that the middle class accepts rewards from whites for manipulating the larger black population.[66] To some critics, the black middle class's race allows them to make appeals to poorer blacks that would be rejected out of hand if advanced by members of other racial groups.

Social differentiation is revealed in a growing literature that documents class conflict in black neighborhoods. Several studies address gentrification, wherein middle-class African Americans move into low-income black neighborhoods, revitalize aging row houses and transforming the neighborhood into an environment conducive to their own lifestyles and aspirations, often to the displeasure of the lower class around whom communal patterns formerly revolved.[67]

Documenting a similar conflict, Wilson and Richard Taub describe how black middle-class communities adjacent to poorer enclaves seek to preserve property values and the middle-class way of life by ensuring the continued exclusion of less-affluent and less-educated African Americans. In either case, studies reveal how middle-class blacks cultivate an ambiance reflective of their own tastes but alien to that of the rank and file.[68]

A business development specialist for a public/private agency that is directed toward profitable established firms describes class stratification in the black community.

> RESPONDENT: The Detroit population is very bimodal. You've got the gap in between the two groups.
>
> If you plot African Americans' income versus the other ethnic groups' income, you've got more of a continuum with other ethnicities, but a bimodal thing with African Americans. There is a gap. There is a huge gap, and that exists not only here but across the nation.
>
> It's the haves and the trickle down. There is really a small trickle down to the group because of that gap. I guess, this is the best thing I can liken it to, when the Order for Affirmative Action opened up, and a certain number of people made it through, and then you start seeing the door close a little bit.
>
> And you say, "Well, why don't they get skills?" But it's like, they're so busy trying to survive. Hey, it's like, where do you put your focus, on your long-term dream or some immediate need to eat?

Class and Soft Skills   Some middle-class interviewees believed that poor people lacked the skills that were required for advancement. They saw this deficit as a major obstacle to the development of black entrepreneurship. This was evident as Ruth, a manager, and Virginia, the owner of a Detroit-based manufacturing business, described what they regard as the lack of self-presentation skills among a certain group of Detroit residents.[69]

> RUTH: I mean, we as a people, and I'm an African American female, we have to truly step it up. Step up our game. It's not about being black. It's about handling business professionally with a positive attitude. [You have to] think about how you would want to be treated as a customer. . . .
>
> VIRGINIA: A lot of these people that are not working or employed, they never had the opportunity [to learn how to present themselves] and that is real. Still nowadays, these people are stereotyped, but then again, they deserve to be stereotyped because they put themselves in that position.
>
> INTERVIEWER: You're saying that they put themselves in it willingly or due to circumstances beyond their control?
>
> VIRGINIA: I don't know if they know better, but, for example, if someone comes to work, or they come to apply for a job and they have their pants hanging half down on their hips, I'm not looking for that type of person. So I think it's their overall attitude, or maybe they don't know better or what, but I'm not going to hire them and neither would you want them representing your school, you know. I would never send them . . . to make a sales call. I don't know if they know better or not. But still, they can buy clothes that fit. Or they can borrow some. . . .

I'm not sure if they're not aware or they don't care or they think that a lot of people dress like that. It's just their attitude toward their job. I just think they follow. There's a lazy guy out there, he could be the leader and lead a whole lot of guys down the wrong path.

In order to make up for these deficits, the interviewees described their involvement in a variety of volunteer activities intended to assist low-income Detroiters.

Class Conflict and Business Development Programs

Class conflicts among black entrepreneurs are sometimes exacerbated by business development programs that are directed toward established entrepreneurs with a proven track record.[70] While established businesses are much more viable than start-up operations, aspiring entrepreneurs often feel that programs that fund established and profitable businesses rather than their own projects are unfair.

A staff member of a joint public/private business development organization describes the relatively affluent target market of her agency.

Our office is targeted at minority businesses that are currently making five hundred thousand dollars in annual revenue up to fifteen million dollars. The reason why the Department of Commerce or the Minority Business Agency has targeted that group is because they can make the greatest economic impact in terms of creating jobs and generating revenue, so they've passed their start-up phase, they've already got their feet wet, and they're ready to contribute to the economy.

Because we're a small office, we can't be all things, as they say in marketing; you can't be all things to all people. So we have to target those areas where we can help out most, give the greatest impact.

In the following exchange, the director of the Detroit branch of a privately funded, nonprofit organization that provides minority entrepreneurs with corporate contracts and business assistance describes class conflict among entrepreneurs:

INTERVIEWER: There are obviously class differences in Detroit between the downtown with the casinos, the stadiums, and the rest of the city. Some of the discussion suggests that, even among minority or African American entrepreneurs, there's a difference between the more well-connected, well-heeled types who have access to some of that growth, and the more kind of mom-and-pop entrepreneurs that are struggling; that don't benefit so much from the All Star game, the Super Bowl, things like that. Is that a kind of issue that you're aware of?

RESPONDENT: It's true, it's accurate, and I hear it all the time. I think those are concerns that are raised with my organization. I had a meeting with the Detroit Black Chamber of Commerce, and I said, "You guys only help these large businesses. You only help the affluent, talented tenth." But that's not entirely true. Those folks do dominate our membership, and their presence is hard to ignore, but I do think it's true that in part the needs of those businesses are very, very different. We have some folks who are small retailers, but their needs are very different than the needs of somebody like a Dave Bing [former NBA star and major entrepreneur elected mayor of Detroit in spring 2009], both in terms of capital, in terms of strategic things that we do with them, [and] in terms of the time we spend interfacing with our corporate members.

I think there is a difference between a small entrepreneur versus somebody larger. Larger businesses have access to folks at the bank that they may know, a senior VP at Chase or Comerica [banks], as opposed to the [small business] person that may know someone at the branch.

And maybe that's where some of the class comes in because so much of the stuff is still business down on the golf course, and a number of our larger minority-owned businesses play the game of business much as you would see with a majority business—the golf course, the networking, those types of things, in terms of building, developing business relationships, and partnerships, to kind of drive their business forward. The smaller businesses have a different set of challenges. And I don't know how well their needs are being met across the continuum of folks who provide services.

A city program intended to improve the appearance of downtown buildings prior to the Super Bowl epitomized issues of inequality inherent in the provision of public benefits to Detroit businesses. Over two million dollars was spent on "some of the most prestigious and best-kept buildings in downtown Detroit" despite the fact that most were outside the program's original boundaries. Meanwhile, many decrepit storefronts near the stadium remained in disrepair even though they were in the program's original target area.

While city officials were aware of the issue, they felt that any improvement to the city's business environment was a positive step. They explained that the owners of vacant and decaying properties often lacked access to the financing required to put up the 50 percent share needed to access matching funds. Following a very poor response to the program when it was first announced, the Downtown Development Authority revised the original boundaries and accepted applications from throughout downtown Detroit. George Jackson Jr., who administers the program, explained the policy: "We can't shut down or deny the benefits to the people who have stepped up and done the right thing. I think that would send the wrong message."[71]

In order to obtain more resources and call attention to their plight, a group of mostly small, neighborhood-based entrepreneurs formed the Independent Retailers Association (IRA). Many members complained that major city-sponsored events, such as the All-Star Baseball Game of 2005 and the Super Bowl of 2006, which were celebrated in downtown Detroit's new stadiums, provided very few opportunities for small start-up business owners.[72]

"I did not even get a chance to bid on what would have been a perfect match for my company," said Gwen Thomas, who heads Promotion Unlimited 2000. "A Troy-based company, Entech Staffing, was awarded the contract."

"That is the same thing that happened during the All Star Game," claimed Tony Davis, who owns a transportation company. "Most of the cab services they used were not African American and some were not Detroit-based."[73]

While the largest and most resource-rich business development programs in Detroit *are* directed toward large minority-owned firms with a proven record, at the same time, however, several initiatives also assist smaller entrepreneurs like those who belonged to the IRA. For example, a privately funded program called Bizdom U provides entrepreneurial training and a stipend to help college graduates create Detroit-based businesses.[74]

A microloan program directed toward a similar constituency was created by the City of Detroit and Wayne County. Gloria and Sarah, two of its directors, described their activities in a 2006 interview.[75]

GLORIA: We just wrote out the Small Business Detroit Microloan Program. It really is based on the understanding that there is a lot of interest in becoming an entrepreneur and owning your own business. Lack of access to capital is a huge barrier in the African American community, and so the Small Business Detroit Microloan Program provides microenterprise loans for people who want to start or expand businesses here in the city of Detroit. The loan amounts range from five to thirty-five thousand dollars, and really it's for those companies who are not yet what we call bankable.

SARAH: And the idea's that they open with a less stringent demand for profit. We do have underwriting requirements that do have to go through credit checks and have collateral and all those things.

I think that is definitely a situation where we're willing to make loans to someone that might be a little too risky for a professional lending institution, so maybe after getting one loan, or two loans through the Microloan Program, then they would be able to go on to a conventional lending source. So our philosophy is not only that they should be able to pay the loan back. We offer them technical assistance in conjunction with the loan. But also, we want them to be a sustainable business here in the city of Detroit. We don't want them to fold down two years after they pay the loan back. We want them to be here for the long run so that the dollars can circulate here in our city.

People have been attending loan orientations, which is a requirement for those who have less than three years business experience, a two-hour loan orientation. We've had almost five hundred people go to that loan orientation, and like I said, we have about twenty loan applications ready to go before the loan goes to the city for approval. This is just the first time that the city of Detroit has had a microloan program for our small business community to help them stay in business and grow.

Gloria and Sarah elaborate on their program's constituency:

GLORIA: We're the counterpart for Michigan Minority Business Council. I think, what we're talking about trying to put in a grocery store that does two hundred thousand dollars a year in sales, is able to pull forty or fifty thousand dollars to support the owner, and make two jobs in the neighborhood.

There *are* business associations. They just don't have any juice. We've visited some of them where they might have three to five people show up [at a meeting] because they don't have any carrot.

SARAH: They have lots of juice and not any meat. There's lots of names on the members' list, but they're not really doing, digging down, and I think Gloria hit it on the head where she said there has to be community buy-in as well.

And that, again, goes back to the trust factor, engaging people and keeping them engaged by really delivering. What is happening is that people come up with these really great ideas, they formulate these concepts and form these organizations and work really hard at developing the infrastructure, and then they hit a brick wall because they can't get access to the resources.

You've got a mother who lost her son in gang violence. She doesn't want that to happen anymore, and she's created a neighborhood association, but she really doesn't have the political connections in order to really change the economic front of the community so that the drug dealers know they can't be in there, so it's all sort of connected.

I think the environment plays a huge part in it, and let us not forget that the city of Detroit has a long history of distrust at the political level, at the city level, at the county level. You know, there's the suburban flight that took place, there's a feeling of abandonment, and there's abuses by the people who were in leadership.[76]

Most recently, the Ewing Marion Kauffman Foundation of Kansas City created a program called "FastTrac to the Future," which will spend 9.5 million dollars to save automotive jobs in Detroit. Endorsed by the White

House and with funding from several local foundations, the program is intended to create 1,200 new businesses in Southeast Michigan. It includes a component called the Urban Entrepreneur Partnership, which is directed toward displaced minority workers. This program will evaluate these workers and then provide them with needed training, skills, and mentorship from a team of experienced business owners.[77]

Given the complexity of economic issues in Detroit, class conflicts are likely to be an enduring issue among Detroit's entrepreneurs. This is especially the case as numbers of persons lose jobs in existing firms and seek to create businesses as a means of supporting themselves despite their lack of business skill and economic resources. In an effort to assist novice entrepreneurs while also bridging some of the social distance between them and owners of established enterprises, several business development programs work to link experienced entrepreneurs as mentors to fledgling business owners.

BASES FOR OPTIMISM

Seeing the positive impact of business training and development programs, several of our respondents believed that Detroit has the potential to foster a significant level of black self-employment. A staff member of a business development program looked forward to the achievement of such goals:

> So I think all the folks who seek economic growth will follow Quincy Jones's famous line "We're gonna check our egos at the door and see if we can work together." It needs to be about the bigger goal and not about any of the organizations or about the leadership or about the credit. It needs to be about building wealth in this community—intergenerational wealth—and hoping that some of that wealth can stay in the community.
>
> I understand folks are gonna move and buy their big mansion in West Bloomfield (an affluent suburb), but in terms of investing sustainable wealth into the community, that can be accomplished if we can have the data, and get people focused on one thing with some solid leadership.

Economic Change as Fostering Black Entrepreneurship

Several respondents asserted that the dire economic conditions currently confronted by the region might have a silver lining because they could foster creativity and innovation. For example, a city official explained how layoffs among white-collar workers in the auto industry would yield a supply of individuals endowed with the skills and resources required to start viable businesses.

> Downsized ex-corporate employees . . . make entrepreneurs that start from ground zero and move up very quickly. Their credit is usually intact, so they can get working capital, loans. They've already made those connections in corporate environments. They got the skills. All they do is get a partner, and they just jump right in there and take off. So you do see some people moving into the realm.

In addition, one respondent asserted that the declining city budget means that, while the city will no longer provide certain services directly, it will allocate dollars to the private sector in order to do so. This will provide increased opportunities to local entrepreneurs.

> In our administration, the mayor's [Kilpatrick] thinking out of the box about what we can do to create employment opportunities. He's pushing this entrepreneurial idea because we've gotta go in different directions. We've gotta hope that the small business owner begins to employ some of those unemployed people in this city.
>
> We're suggesting to our city workers employed in the Department of Public Works or things of that nature, where we run into a situation where the city can't provide that service to the degree we used to provide it anymore, that they can take over.
>
> So we're encouraging these folks to go and start their own companies and to come back and get these contracts, and if they don't know what they're doing, then we show them how to get certified, we train them in the area that they need to be trained in to get their business up and running, and help the city continue to move forward. Now, we've got employers, we['ve] got employees, and they are making a living again, doing something that they might not have even thought of doing prior to this time.

Finally, the business development staff and local entrepreneurs that we interviewed described having a very high level of commitment to improving black self-employment in particular and social conditions more generally in Detroit. Accordingly, they were extensively involved in leadership development, mentoring, philanthropy, and a variety of other community service activities directed toward improving the local social and economic environment.

CONCLUSIONS

As the largest black majority city in the United States, Detroit's situation suggests contrasting prospects for self-determination via the development of black entrepreneurship. Given the larger society's recent economic troubles as well as its long-standing reluctance to allocate sufficient resources to improve the lot of urban and African American communities, it appears likely that resources for betterment will remain scarce, and the city will continue to suffer.

At the same time, however, because of the city's demographic composition, Detroiters also have the potential to strive toward shared goals in an atmosphere of racial solidarity, relatively free from the coercive influence of whites and other groups—at least on the local level. In this environment, a dedicated, engaged, and passionate collectivity works in cooperation with foundations, business leaders, political activists, and academics to foster the creation of businesses that provide residents with the goods, quality of service, and economic benefits that they desire.

In our review, we found ample evidence of both tendencies. Detroit does have significant resources that are deployed to support the growth of a black ethnic economy. It sustains a higher fraction of black-owned businesses than any other major city in the United States. Unfortunately, however, Detroit remains a very poor city in a region of the United States that is struggling economically. Its residents must contend with terrible economic and social problems. Even the corporate elite of Detroit—the Big Three of the American auto industry—are struggling. If this were not enough of an obstacle, the ability of policy makers to assist business development among African Americans, women, and other racial-ethnic groups is heavily restricted by a recently enacted anti–affirmative action law (Proposal 2) passed in November 2006.[78] It prohibits "preferential treatment to any individual or group on the basis of race, sex, color, ethnicity or national origin in the operation of public employment, public education or public contracting." Accordingly, due to dire social and economic conditions and limited policy options, the number of jobs and the amount of income generated by Detroit's black businesses is far below that required to resolve the city's myriad problems.

Detroit residents share many views about their city's economic condition and the reasons for its relatively low rates of black entrepreneurship. No respondents, for example, condemned capitalism. Rather, they believed that Detroit needed more black businesses. Further, they asserted that a history of discriminatory policies by both big business and government contributed to the city's problems generally and the underdevelopment of black entrepreneurship in particular. While holding larger social institutions responsible for the city's condition, residents also faulted African American politicians, merchants, and consumers for failing to emphasize cooperation and self-reliance in a manner that would nurture a black economy.

While residents shared many basic assumptions about conditions in Detroit, our analysis suggests that subgroups within the community also diverge in their opinions about black business development. One group sees Detroit primarily in racial terms. It considers nonblack merchants and corporate chains to be exploitative competitors who should be denied access to the city's resources and customers. In contrast, another group understands Detroit as a locality rather than a racial community. Acknowledging the city's black majority and the need to increase the number of black-owned businesses therein, advocates of this position welcome beneficial investments from chain stores and ethnic merchants. While the management of chain stores appears to be relatively uninterested in the faction's welcome, non-black ethnic entrepreneurs often endorse this position, which acknowledges their contributions to the city in which they earn a living.

Finally, perspectives on business development in Detroit are fragmented along class lines. By virtue of their access to skills and financial and political resources, established business owners are favored by nonprofits, government, and corporations as the entrepreneurs most likely to generate jobs and economic growth. Because of their proven competence and financial capacity, they are able to take advantage of contracts and matching funds directed toward underrepresented groups. In contrast, the most numerous and needy members of the minority business community generally lack the extensive skills, resources, and connections required to benefit from loans, directed purchasing arrangements, and other forms of assistance that are allocated to those who can demonstrate a record of business success. Because such fledgling businesspersons seek to establish very small enterprises in an environment of high unemployment and massive layoffs, they are poor risks.

Despite the fact that sound financial reasons warrant investing in established and profitable firms rather than start-ups, many members of the public chafe at the government's subsidizing multi-million-dollar firms while denying resources to impoverished individuals struggling to survive. In an attempt to bring a measure of equality to the differential allocation of resources among Detroit's large and small business owners, government, educational institutions, nonprofit organizations, and established merchants direct services and mentorship to would-be entrepreneurs.

The ideological conflicts and difficult economic conditions they face notwithstanding, many Detroiters remain passionately committed to the city and its status as a symbol of African American life. They hope that, through ethnic solidarity, perseverance, and a new emphasis on entrepreneurship, African Americans might be able to establish a viable black ethnic economy.

Residents of America's largest black majority city may have relatively more local political power at their disposal to address the limited retail options and the dearth of black merchants. Despite this advantage, however, their ability to resolve such issues is not very different than it is in cities where African Americans remain in the numerical minority.[79] While residents resent the poor state of the city's retail businesses and the low representation of African Americans among merchants, neither the political consensus nor the practical means of solving these long-standing problems have been discovered.[80] As a consequence, popular opinions regarding black business development remain diverse and reflect many of the ideological, class, and generational differences that exist among members of the larger society.

9

SOCIAL INEQUALITY AND
MERCHANT-CUSTOMER CONFLICTS

Conflicts between ethnic entrepreneurs and their customers have been a subject of concern for academics, policy makers, journalists, and social activists. While the resulting accounts are richly detailed, they are narrow and often focus upon especially volatile incidents associated with major "race riots" and involving a limited number of groups located in major cities during the 1960s and the 1990s. Existing literature largely ignores events involving other groups, locations, and time periods, as well as a wider spectrum of contributing factors, most notably those associated with the larger social structure.

In this book, I have taken a more comparative approach, which includes a wider array of groups, conflicts, and settings. This view acknowledges that, over the course of the last century, the nature of urban communities has changed, as have the customers and merchants who carry on economic relations within them as well as the legal and informal codes through which our society defines and reacts to racial and ethnic differences. Further, my perspective emphasizes that a variety of government policies—ranging from housing to urban renewal, to microenterprise development, welfare reform, and affirmative action—intended to address urban inequalities have been implemented, evaluated, and often abandoned. Yet, despite these many changes, conflicts between merchants and customers continue to occur.

While the group-specific, local, and contextual issues highlighted as causes in existing literature certainly contribute to merchant-customer conflicts, such disputes are also significantly shaped by social, economic, and political concerns originating in and involving the larger society and over which neither merchants nor customers have much control. Accordingly, conflicts between entrepreneurs and customers are more often the consequence of broader patterns of inequality, urban policy, and racial-ethnic interaction in American society than the cause of them.

SUMMARY OF FINDINGS

This review shows that the incidence of conflict between immigrant entrepreneurs and their customers in impoverished areas varies over time and social context. Such conflicts have taken place during periods of economic growth, like the mid-1940s and mid-1960s, as well as during eras of decline, such as the mid-1930s and early 1990s. Events have occurred within liberal political climates associated with expanding welfare benefits—as was the case during the 1930s, 1940s, and 1960s—as well as during times of political conservatism and shrinking public spending, such as the 1980s and 1990s. Finally, conflicts have persisted even as social norms regarding racial and ethnic inequality have evolved from the epoch of Jim Crow, restrictive covenants, and openly stated ethnic preferences in want ads, to the era of equal opportunity, affirmative action, and cultural pluralism.

My examination begins with a description of African Americans' long commitment to the development of an ethnic economy as well as their involvement in many forms of scholarship and activism directed toward this goal. Prior to the Great Migration and until the Depression Era, African Americans had small but noteworthy ethnic economies, initially serving consumers of all racial backgrounds and then directed toward black consumers when patterns of segregation reduced their ability to do business with nonblacks. Because of systematic patterns of legal and informal discrimination that were greater than those confronted by other groups, African Americans' ability to be self-employed was limited. Nevertheless, this group has continued to work toward the expansion of a black ethnic economy in a manner that has supported members of the community and emphasized economic self-determination.

Much research on entrepreneur-customer conflict characterizes African American customers and activists as the aggressors in confrontations with European or Asian entrepreneurs. However, in analyzing the history of such imbroglios, we find that white mobs often attacked black-owned businesses (and white-owned businesses serving blacks) in the South and Midwest prior to 1920. In addition, in northern, midwestern, and western cities before the Great Migration, when only minuscule black populations resided in these locations, merchant-customer conflicts most commonly occurred among European-origin groups, including both immigrants and their American-born descendants. Large numbers of African Americans did not play a major role in disputes with ethnic merchants until much later—generally in the 1930s and 1940s—when significant populations had moved to northern cities. During the 1930s and 1940s, and again since the 1970s, white communities, politicians, workers, and entrepreneurs also engaged in hostile actions against immigrant and ethnic merchants.

The assumption that merchant-customer conflicts involve only impoverished, uneducated, and socially marginal groups such as immigrants, minorities, and workers is found wanting. While persons of low social standing did confront immigrant entrepreneurs, the scapegoating of ethnic merchants—and immigrant groups more generally—was publicized and sanctioned by members of the social elite, including politicians, journalists, clergymen, industrialists, and academics, who provided sophisticated, often scientific, justifications for ethnocentric assertions and behavior. Paradoxically, when such sentiments were codified into national law in the Johnson-Reed Immigration Act of 1924, an unintended consequence was to increase the migration of African Americans into northern and western cities, where they found jobs in factories, developed their own ethnic economies, and provided sizeable consumer markets for immigrant and ethnic merchants.

However, most of the early cases of interaction among immigrant shop owners and native blacks occurred in the South, where U.S.-born white shop owners' unwillingness to trade with African Americans provided immigrant merchants with many opportunities to service their consumer needs. Moreover, because southern norms emphasized black/white differences above others, nonblack ethnic merchants, like Jews, Italians, Greeks, and Chinese often found more opportunity in the South than in the North and West, where Protestant elites highlighted and racialized religious, national, and linguistic differences between themselves and others.[1]

A comparison of disputes between different groups of immigrant merchants and customers on the east and west coasts during the Depression reveals the significant role that political power had in such conflicts. In the East and Midwest, blacks involved in the "Don't Shop Where You Can't Work" campaign used boycotts and protests to demand jobs and better treatment from businesses owned by Jews and other European-origin merchants. On the West Coast, whites used the wartime political climate to eliminate competition from Japanese American entrepreneurs.

Despite Jews' and blacks' low standing in the larger society, factions of both groups, which gained political power through the New Deal coalition, were able to reduce intergroup conflicts and engage in actions to expand social, political, and economic opportunities. In contrast, after the attack on Pearl Harbor, the entirety of the highly entrepreneurial Japanese community on the U.S. mainland—who were denied the most basic political rights including voting and land ownership—was interned for the duration of World War II. Whites' desire to eliminate competition from Japanese merchants is made apparent by the fact that the leaders of Hawaii decided that the sizeable Japanese-origin population there (which had low rates of self-employment but was a source of essential agricultural labor) did not warrant incarceration.

Government policy was also vital to determining relations between immigrant merchants and minority customers during the postwar decades. While the era was one of both economic growth and a gradual expansion of social, political, and economic opportunities for blacks, Latinos, Asians, and white ethnics, it was also a period of planned urban transformation. During this time, a series of local, state, and federal laws governing housing, urban renewal, and highway construction expanded the size of urban ghettos. These programs subsidized the movement of whites—and, with them, economic and communal institutions—away from urban centers and into segregated suburbs. They increased residential segregation and concentrated poverty to a degree far beyond anything that had existed previously. Consequently, the massive black ghettos in which most merchant-customer conflicts have occurred since midcentury were not the result of unanticipated circumstances. Rather, they are the outcome of deliberate policy making.

There were relatively few conflicts between immigrant entrepreneurs and their customers from the late 1940s until the mid-1960s. However, 1964 through 1969 saw an unprecedented period of urban uprisings that exacted a significant toll on the social and political landscape from which many neighborhoods, and even entire cities like Detroit and Newark, have yet to recover.[2] During these uprisings, thousands of persons—the majority of them African American—were injured and killed. At the same time, a wide variety of businesses, owned by corporate chains, ethnic merchants, and African Americans were looted and burned. Many would never open again. These events brought increased attention to the plight of urban America. Reactions were diverse and far reaching and included both the expansion of civil rights and economic opportunities as well as the implementation of law and order regimes that sought to punish transgression.

Since the late 1960s, the United States has been the destination of millions of immigrants, most with non-European origins and including subpopulations characterized by both high and low levels of skill. These recent arrivals have become customers and entrepreneurs in urban locations. At the same time, this period saw considerable economic restructuring, whereby well-paid manufacturing jobs became scarce while both unskilled and professional positions in service industries became key sources of employment.

As a consequence of these demographic and economic transformations, conflicts between entrepreneurs and customers have become much more complex in their causes and effects than in previous years. The most destructive of these occurred in Miami and Los Angeles, locations where large numbers of international migrants settled in or near traditionally African American neighborhoods, with the result being enhanced competition for jobs, business ownership, government services, housing, and political power.

The years of economic growth during the 1990s yielded economic improvements in the inner-city neighborhoods of many coastal, sunbelt, and gateway cities. Patterns of gentrification made urban regions (once left to impoverished minority residents and the immigrant merchants who serve them) desirable to ambitious real estate developers, well-capitalized merchants, and urban pioneers seeking affordable housing options. Such transformations brought a wide range of new merchants and residents to areas that had been formerly characterized by tense relations between established residents and embedded entrepreneurs. At the same time, economic growth displaced both the residents and entrepreneurs who formerly made lives there. Urban gentrification did not, however, affect all regions of the country equally during and after the 1990s. Few improvements were evident in rustbelt cities where established patterns of stagnation, disinvestment, and population decline persisted.

In order to justify reductions in social spending and absolve the larger society of responsibility for a range of urban problems, a group of pundits, politicians, and researchers has contrasted the indigence of impoverished groups including native minorities, undocumented immigrants, and unskilled refugees with the accomplishments of entrepreneurial immigrant and ethnic groups. Their moralistic accounts emphasize the former collectives' low rates of business ownership and vindictive conflicts with immigrant merchants as evidence of their dysfunctional behavior and retrograde values.

Such characterizations, however, are generally inaccurate because they ignore the many forms of *informal* self-employment that residents of impoverished neighborhoods engage in to survive discrimination, welfare reform, undocumented status, deindustrialization, and rising prices. What distinguishes their entrepreneurship from that of classic middlemen is not the propensity to run businesses, per se. Rather, it is the fact that informal businesses are not included in official enumerations. By acknowledging impoverished immigrant and minority group members' extensive involvement in informal self-employment, we realize that conflicts between them and ethnic merchants are not simply malicious. Rather, these struggles often embody disadvantaged groups' desire to challenge the social, legal, and economic advantages of formal entrepreneurs so that they too can establish and maintain an ethnic economy.

Finally, our case study of contemporary Detroit considers the extent to which the political and demographic power available to residents of the largest black majority city in the United States can facilitate the creation of a black ethnic economy. It finds that Motown does have a higher rate of black-owned businesses than any other American city. Despite this, however, Detroit's terrible economic conditions mean that black-owned businesses are incapable of creating anywhere near an adequate number of jobs for its residents. Respondents cite an array of factors to explain the underdevelopment of black business. These include a legacy of racism, the unwillingness of corporate businesses and banks to invest in the city, and years of hard times for the city's major employers. African Americans place a significant amount of blame on their own community for not patronizing coethnic shops and for abandoning the legacy of black entrepreneurship in favor of well-paid blue- and white-collar employment in the auto industry.

Despite these widely shared views, Detroit residents also disagree about how to enhance entrepreneurship. One faction emphasizes Detroit's racial identity. They endorse programs that reserve economic opportunities for African Americans and seek to exclude suburbanites, corporations, and nonblack ethnic entrepreneurs (who now control the city's retail sector). In contrast, another faction identifies Detroit as a multiethnic municipality and welcomes members of all groups as long as they make positive contributions. Detroit residents' views on the development of black business also vary according to class, with ambitious but inexperienced neighborhood entrepreneurs complaining about the privileged position that established and well-connected downtown firms enjoy in obtaining benefits from public, private, and nonprofit development programs.

In sum, this book finds the popular conception that conflicts between merchants and customers most commonly involve violent acts between Jews, Koreans, and blacks residing in ghettos to be mistaken. In addition to being wrong, this outlook also reinforces inaccurate assumptions about how American society functions. For if violent and unethical business transactions are seen as confined to and determined by racial and ethnic groups, then the larger society and its majority of citizens are not responsible for such disputes, do not profit from them, and are incapable of reducing their frequency or intensity.

Popular stereotypes and strident editorials often condemn racial minorities for their hostility to ethnic entrepreneurs.[3] In fact, the most powerful forms of restriction and vengeance imposed on immigrant and ethnic entrepreneurs—including the exclusion of black businesses from nonblack neighborhoods at the dawn of the twentieth century and the wholesale internment of West Coast Japanese Americans during World War II—have come not from the hands of ghetto teenagers but rather from the social, economic, and legal actions of society's power holders, leading companies, majority voters, and ruling institutions.

RACIAL AND ETHNIC FACTORS AND MERCHANT-CUSTOMER CONFLICT

I have argued throughout this book that research on conflicts between immigrant entrepreneurs and their customers places excessive emphasis on the role of racial differences in such interactions and often focuses on disputes involving African Americans (who are often depicted in a monolithic fashion) to the exclusion of other incidents of conflict. This contention notwithstanding, racial and ethnic categories are vital to understanding the nature of such conflicts and the way they are explained in American society.

Racial and ethnic categories are implicated on at least two levels in conflicts between merchants and customers. The first involves the forms of personal and institutional discrimination, including residential segregation, that are encountered by such groups. While patterns of racialization vary over time and place, these factors consistently limit immigrant and native minority merchants' and customers' political rights and opportunities and restrict their geographic and social mobility. As a consequence, racialized groups wind up living in and running businesses in environments characterized by isolation and neglect. Because members of minority groups are often compelled to reside in segregated communities, the homes that they purchase do not appreciate in value to the same degree as those in white neighborhoods. This results in blacks and other minorities having much less wealth than whites and, consequently, restricts their access to the investment capital required to start a business or otherwise improve their economic status.[4]

At the same time, the racial and ethnic identification of the groups involved in conflicts affects the larger society's perception of these events. While there is some evidence of increased hostility being directed toward big business since the economic crash of 2008, white entrepreneurs like Bill Gates, Sam Walton, Donald Trump, and Warren Buffett continue to be celebrated as economic heroes.[5] In contrast, the accomplishments of ethnic and racial groups are often described as undeserved and socially detrimental.[6]

White Protestants' amassing of wealth is often credited to their hard work, organizational skill, and the ability to take advantage of undiscovered opportunities. In contrast, business success of minority and immigrant entrepreneurs may be linked to unfair advantages acquired through scheming, exploitation, bribes, clannishness, cutting corners, and government subsidies (including affirmative action and kickbacks). Even when ethnic groups' achievements in business are acknowledged, they may be attributed to abilities innate to nerdy overachievers rather than to intelligence and hard work.[7]

Further, when ethnic and racial groups are determined to have low rates of entrepreneurship, many observers assign their poor record to inherent pathologies like a deficient business aptitude, insufficient work ethic, limited intelligence, and malevolent communities, rather than to the poor economic conditions, lack of resources, or discrimination that are known to constrain business success among any group.[8] In reality, however, few if any groups characterized by poverty and low education are successful in self-employment. In an ambitious study of impoverished urban communities, political scientist Paul Jargowsky evaluated the importance of cultural versus economic factors and found that opportunity was crucial.

> The conclusion I draw is that neighborhood poverty is not primarily the product of "the people who live there" or "ghetto culture" that discourages upward mobility, but the predictable result of the economic status of minority communities and the degree to which minorities are residentially segregated from whites and from each other by income. Neighborhood effects may well exist, and pathologies in the poor neighborhoods may well be destructive to people living in there. But such phenomena, I would argue, are more like symptoms than root causes.[9]

Ethnic entrepreneurs and native minority groups are both subject to racial and ethnic stereotypes. However, native minorities, especially African Americans, have received the most enduring and negative characterizations. So much so that pundits and scholars often cite examples of immigrant success as a rhetorical means of castigating African Americans' lack of mobility.[10] As a case in point, since the ethnic revivals of the 1970s, immigrant groups' collaboration to build ethnic economies has been increasingly celebrated as ethnic solidarity, cooperation, selfless dedication to a common cause, and the mobilization of communal social capital, even if such activities are known to exploit employees, exclude outgroup members, and vex customers.[11] In contrast, African Americans' working together to develop political power, improve their economic standing. or exert control over the communities in which they reside is frequently condemned as Black Nationalism, which is defined as an undemocratic strategy based on prejudice, chauvinism, and thuggish intimidation.[12] Upon reflection, the most significant difference between "commendable" ethnic cooperation and "reprehensible" Black Nationalism is neither the activities undertaken nor the goal of seeking group advantage. Rather, it would appear to be the racial-ethnic identity of the group involved.

As shown in chapters 3, 5, and 6, members of the European American community, including immigrants and members of the native-born working and middle class, have their own history of disputes with immigrant merchants. Moreover, white Protestants have systematically excluded immigrants and racial and ethnic minorities from access to jobs, educational institutions, neighborhoods, private clubs, and job-finding networks. Historically, white elites created and benefitted from the patterns of racial and ethnic inequality that can be traced back to the very origins of the United States.[13] Yet this history is infrequently linked to contemporary urban conflicts. These are much more likely to be attributed to the actions of immigrants and native minorities who live in such communities and certainly didn't establish the context within which they find themselves.

Accordingly, not only does racial and ethnic membership deprive groups so labeled of opportunities and resources and compel them to live and work together in poorly served, impoverished neighborhoods. It also encourages members of the larger society to regard these groups and their interactions as fundamentally unlike those of mainstream Americans. This is the case, even though the economic and political actions of the larger society—as represented by the decisions of major corporations; the economic, urban, and welfare policies of the government; and a host of social practices with regard to how immigrants and minorities are treated—play significant roles in creating the environments where such conflicts take place.

ETHNIC ENTREPRENEURSHIP IN AMERICAN LIFE

While this book describes problems associated with ethnic self-employment, it is not my intention to condemn entrepreneurship as a viable means of economic survival and advancement. Business ownership has provided an otherwise unavailable conduit into the middle class for many individuals and groups while also improving urban environments and allowing for the creation of viable and self-sustaining communities.[14] That does not mean, however, that all of our economic problems can be solved by business formation. The failure rate of small business is high under normal conditions and further elevated during hard economic times. A large fraction of small businesses have no employees, and even employer firms tend to create few well-paid and secure jobs. Moreover, failed entrepreneurs, along with their dependents, continue to require an economic safety net.[15] Increasing the

number of failed entrepreneurs who lack other options may foster desperation and increase antisocial behavior, including violence directed toward
successful merchants.

In recent years, we have noted the rapid growth of self-employment
among disadvantaged groups, just as St. Clair Drake and Horace Cayton
did in their study of Chicago's Bronzeville during the Great Depression.[16]
Indeed, according to the U.S. Census, the rates of self-employment among
minority groups and women for 1997–2002 have grown much faster than
those for the entire U.S. population. This suggests that assertions of minorities' reluctance to take advantage of the opportunities afforded by entrepreneurship are overstated. However, while the sheer number of businesses
created by women and minorities are growing fast, earnings are increasing
at a much slower rate than for the country at large.[17] For these women and
minority entrepreneurs, the promised benefits of self-employment have yet
to be seen. (See table 9.1.)

Given the current state of the U.S. economy, many of these recently
created enterprises might be considered survivalist businesses that were
opened because other employment opportunities were unavailable. Small
business will be most beneficial to America's economic growth when those
who seek to become self-employed are well prepared to do so, with training, experience, adequate financing, and sound business plans. Fostering an
increase in the number of survivalist enterprises opened due to economic
desperation is not a promising means of achieving this goal.

I have argued that community-based hostility toward ethnic merchants
among customers is not as pervasive or calculated as it is sometimes
described. Nevertheless, in some cases, residents of impoverished communities do scapegoat and menace merchants and steal or destroy their
property. While ethnic merchants may receive accolades from politicians
and pundits for their hard work, determination, and willingness to make
risky investments, they pay dearly when their businesses are intentionally
or inadvertently harmed when the neighborhoods in which they do business
explode in disorder. When such disturbances occur, ethnic merchants generally receive little compensation for the damages that their businesses suffer, even when attacks are the consequence of issues like police brutality.[18]
Their contributions to urban communities—providing goods and services,
donations, jobs, and taxes in settings that are rejected as irredeemable by
more established merchants—generally go unappreciated and may even be
disparaged. Demonstrating the undesirability of this niche, few individuals
or groups remain in the role of inner-city merchant for long. Rather, they
abandon the activity as soon as they can afford to do so.[19]

Table 9.1. Changes in the Number of Businesses and Their Receipts for All of United States, by Women and Minority Groups

	All firms in 2002		All firms in 1997		Change from 1997 to 2002			
	Firms (Number)	Sales and Receipts ($1,000,000)	Firms (Number)	Sales and Receipts ($1,000,000)	Net Change in Firm Count	Firms (Percent)	Net Change in Receipts	Sales and Receipts (Percent)
United States	22,977,164	22,634,870	20,821,934	18,553,243	2,155,230	10	4,081,627	22
Black owned	1,197,567	88,642	823,499	71,215	374,068	45	17,427	24
Hispanic owned	1,574,159	226,468	1,199,896	186,275	374,263	31	40,193	22
Asian owned	1,105,329	343,322	893,590	302,795	211,739	24	40,527	13
Women owned	6,492,795	950,600	5,417,034	818,669	1,075,761	20	131,931	16
American Indian and Alaska Native owned	206,125	26,396	197,300	34,344	8,825	4	−79,848	−23
Native Hawaiian and other Pacific Islander owned	32,299	5,221	19,370	4,138	12,929	67	1,082	26

Source: Mike Bergman and Mark Tolbert, "Minority Groups Increasing Business Ownership at Higher Rates than National Average. Census Bureau Reports," U.S. Census Bureau, July 28, 2005.

POLICY SUGGESTIONS

Research suggests that public and private business development programs as well as broader policy agendas that assist members of impoverished communities to improve their education, income, and work histories are likely to increase successful involvement in entrepreneurship.[20] In the current political environment, such programs are unpopular. Nevertheless, they are still among the more viable options for advancing both mobility and self-employment among disadvantaged groups. Given the magnitude of U.S. economic problems and the reality that even the country's largest corporations need government bailouts, it is unrealistic to assume that small entrepreneurs can survive and prosper without assistance.

Because informal entrepreneurship has the potential to serve as an economic lifeboat for disadvantaged populations, it might be worthwhile for policy makers to identify means by which the positive impact of such enterprises could be expanded while minimizing their negative features and outcomes. Informal enterprises have the potential to generate income, deliver needed services, and provide benefits to businesses in the formal economy and can have positive effects on neighborhoods. The expansion of socially benign forms of informal enterprise could improve the quality of life and standard of living in impoverished areas. In addition, such activities have the potential to supply owners with the experience and funds that can help them to eventually run conventional firms.[21]

Finally, the complexity surrounding business ownership and merchant-customer conflicts needs to be acknowledged. Because of the symbolic and economic importance of self-employment, how well a group appears to do with regard to business ownership is a volatile topic in American political discourse, closely related to divergent notions about merit and opportunity and mired in racial-ethnic stereotypes. Accordingly, the expression of simplistic and one-sided interpretations of rates of entrepreneurship and causes of conflict between immigrant merchants and customers—while offering tempting sound bites for ideologues—can be corrosive to both constructive policy making as well as an impartial understanding of these contentious issues.

NOTES

CHAPTER I

1. Jean Ann Scarpaci, "Italian Immigrants in Louisiana's Sugar Parishes: Recruitment, Labor Conditions, and Community Relations, 1880–1910" (PhD diss., Department of History, Rutgers University, 1972), 211.

2. Alfred McClung Lee and Norman D. Humphrey, *Race Riot: Detroit, 1943*, with a new introductory essay by Alfred McClung Lee (New York: Octagon Books, 1968), 28.

3. Pyong Gap Min, *Caught in the Middle: Korean Communities in New York and Los Angeles* (Berkeley: University of California Press, 1996); Seth Mydans, "Criticism Grows Over Aliens Seized during Riots," *New York Times*, May 29, 1992.

4. Ruby L. Bailey, "Tensions between Arab and Black Communities Fuel Protest against Reopening Gas Station Where Man Was Killed," *Detroit Free Press*, October 5, 1999.

5. Steven J. Gold, "The Migrant Economy" (in Swedish), *Axess* 4, May 2005, 14–17.

6. Ivan Light and Steven J. Gold, *Ethnic Economies* (San Diego: Academic Press, 2000).

7. John Sibley Butler, *Entrepreneurship and Self-help among Black Americans* (Albany: State University of New York Press, 1991); Juliette Walker, *The History of Black Business in America: Capitalism, Race, Entrepreneurship* (New York: Macmillan Library Reference, 1998).

8. Gina Holland, "Poll: Blacks Want to Run Businesses," *Los Angeles Times*, July 21, 2001; Charles Choy Wong, "Black and Chinese Grocery Stores in Los Angeles' Black Ghetto," *Urban Life* 5, no. 4 (1977): 460.

9. Amy Elizabeth Ansel, *New Right, New Racism: Race and Reaction in the United States and Britain* (New York: New York University Press, 1997), 111; cited in Henry Giroux, *The Terror of Neoliberalism* (Boulder, Colo.: Paradigm, 2004), 63.

10. George Lipsitz, "The Possessive Investment in Whiteness: Racial Social Democracy and the 'White' Problem in American Studies," *American Quarterly* 47, no. 3 (1995): 369–87.

11. Edna Bonacich, "A Theory of Middleman Minorities," *American Sociological Review* 38, no. 5 (October 1973): 583–94; Walter P. Zenner, *Minorities in the Middle: A Cross-cultural Analysis* (Albany: State University of New York Press, 1991).

12. Charles Tilly, *The Politics of Collective Violence* (New York: Cambridge University Press, 2003), 9.

13. Stephen Cornell and Douglas Hartmann, *Ethnicity and Race: Making Identities in a Changing World*, 2nd ed. (Thousand Oaks, Calif.: Pine Forge Press, 2007), 19.

14. Richard A. Schermerhorn, *Comparative Ethnic Relations: A Framework for Theory and Research*, with a new preface (Chicago: University of Chicago Press, 1978), 12.

15. Cornell and Hartmann, *Ethnicity and Race*, 25.

16. Cornell and Hartmann, *Ethnicity and Race*, 25–26; Michael Omi and Howard Winant, *Racial Formation in the United States: From the 1960s to the 1990s* (New York: Routledge, 1994), 55.

17. Louis Coser, *The Functions of Social Conflict* (New York: Free Press, 1956), 7–8.

18. Ronald H. Bayor, *Neighbors in Conflict: The Irish, Germans, Jews and Italians of New York City, 1929–1941* (Baltimore: Johns Hopkins University Press, 1978).

19. Susan Olzak, *The Dynamics of Ethnic Competition and Conflict* (Stanford, Calif.: Stanford University Press, 1992).

20. Jennifer Lee, *Civility in the City: Blacks, Jews, and Koreans in Urban America* (Cambridge, Mass.: Harvard University Press, 2002), 9.

21. Donald Horowitz, *Ethnic Conflict* (Berkeley: University of California Press, 1985).

22. Lee, *Civility in the City*.

23. Horowitz, *Ethnic Conflict*.

24. Frederick D. Sturdivant, ed., *The Ghetto Marketplace* (New York: Free Press, 1969); In Jin Yoon, *On My Own: Korean Businesses and Race Relations in America* (Chicago: University of Chicago Press, 1997); Min, *Caught in the Middle*.

25. Michael D. Woodard, *Black Entrepreneurs in America: Stories of Struggle and Success* (New Brunswick, N.J.: Rutgers University Press, 1997); Joe T. Darden and Steven J. Gold, "The Impact of Proposal 2 on the Survival of Minority- and Women-Owned New Firms in Michigan," *Michigan Applied Public Policy Research Report*, East Lansing, July 2008.

26. Anny Bakalian and Mehdi Borzorgmehr, *Backlash 911* (Berkeley: University of California Press, 2009).

27. Jonathan J. Bean, "'Burn, Baby Burn': Small Business in the Urban Riots of the 1960s," *Independent Review* 5, no. 2 (2000): 165–87; Edward C. Banfield, *The Unheavenly City Revised: A Revision of the Unheavenly City* (Boston: Little, Brown, 1974).

28. Sidney Fine, *Violence in the Model City: The Cavanaugh Administration, Race Relations, and the Detroit Riot of 1967* (Ann Arbor: University of Michigan Press, 1989).

29. Yoon, *On My Own*.

30. Timothy Bates, *Race, Self-Employment and Upward Mobility: An Illusive American Dream* (Baltimore: John Hopkins University Press, 1997).

31. Ivan Light, *Cities in World Perspective* (New York: Macmillan, 1983); Alejandro Portes and William Haller, "The Informal Economy," in *The Handbook of Economic Sociology*, ed. Neil J. Smelser and Richard Swedberg, 403–25, 2nd ed. (Princeton, N.J.: Princeton University Press, 2005).

32. Light and Gold, *Ethnic Economies*; Roger Waldinger, *Still the Promised City? African-Americans and New Immigrants in Postindustrial New York* (Cambridge, Mass.: Harvard University Press, 1996); Alejandro Portes and Robert Bach, *Latin Journey: Cuban and Mexican Immigrants in the United States* (Berkeley: University of California Press,

1985); Ivan Light and Carolyn Rosenstein, *Race, Ethnicity and Entrepreneurship in Urban America* (New York: Aldine De Gruyter, 1995); Robert Fairlie and Alicia M. Robb, *Race and Entrepreneurial Success: Black-, Asian-, and White-Owned Businesses in the United States* (Cambridge, Mass.: MIT Press, 2008).

33. Ivan Light, "Immigrant and Ethnic Enterprise in North America," *Ethnic and Racial Studies* 17, no. 2 (1984): 195–216; Light and Gold, *Ethnic Economies*.

34. Max Weber, *The Protestant Ethic and the Spirit of Capitalism*, trans. T. Parsons (New York: Scribners, 1958), 39.

35. Bonacich, "A Theory of Middleman Minorities"; Zenner, *Minorities in the Middle*.

36. Light and Gold, *Ethnic Economies*.

37. Illsoo Kim, *New Urban Immigrants: The Korean Community in New York* (Princeton, N.J.: Princeton University Press, 1981); Ivan Light and Edna Bonacich, *Immigrant Entrepreneurs* (Berkeley: University of California Press, 1988); Yoon, *On My Own*; Min, *Caught in the Middle*.

38. Min, *Caught in the Middle*; Pyong Gap Min, *Ethnic Solidarity for Economic Survival* (New York: Russell Sage Foundation, 2008).

39. Alejandro Portes and Rubén G. Rumbaut, *Immigrant America: A Portrait*, 3rd ed. (Berkeley: University of California Press, 2006), 82; Yoon, *On My Own*, 20.

40. Donald W. Light, "The Migrant Enclaves to Mainstream: Reconceptualizing Informal Economic Behavior," *Theory and Society* 33 (2004): 705–37; Portes and Haller, "The Informal Economy"; Marta Tienda and Rebeca Raijman, "Immigrants' Income Packaging and Invisible Labor Force Activity," *Social Science Quarterly* 81, no. 1 (2000): 291–311; Betty Lou Valentine, *Hustling and Other Hard Work* (New York: Free Press, 1978); Christian Zlolniski, *Janitors, Street Vendors, and Activists: The Lives of Mexican Immigrants in Silicon Valley* (Berkeley: University of California Press, 2006).

41. Portes and Bach, *Latin Journey*.

CHAPTER 2

1. Ivan Light, *Ethnic Enterprise in America: Business and Welfare among Chinese, Japanese and Blacks* (Berkeley: University of California Press, 1972); E. Franklin Frazier, *The Negro in the United States*, 2nd ed. (New York: MacMillan, 1957); Thomas Sowell, *Ethnic America* (New York: Basic Books, 1981); Nathan Glazer and Daniel Patrick Moynihan, *Beyond the Melting Pot* (Cambridge, Mass.: MIT Press, 1963); Jennifer Lee, *Civility in the City: Blacks, Jews, and Koreans in Urban America* (Cambridge, Mass.: Harvard University Press, 2002).

2. Robert Fairlie and Alicia M. Robb, *Race and Entrepreneurial Success: Black-, Asian-, and White-Owned Businesses in the United States* (Cambridge, Mass.: MIT Press, 2008), 9.

3. Glazer and Moynihan, *Beyond the Melting Pot*, 30.

4. Glazer and Moynihan, *Beyond the Melting Pot*, 34.

5. John Sibley Butler, *Entrepreneurship and Self-Help among Black Americans* (Albany: State University of New York Press, 1991), xiii, 35.

6. W. E. B. Du Bois, *The Negro in Businesses* (Atlanta: Atlanta University Press, 1898); W. E. B. Du Bois, *Economic Co-operation among Negro Americans* (Atlanta: Atlanta University Press, 1907); Joseph A. Pierce, *Negro Business and Business Education: Their Present and Prospective Development* (New York: Harper & Brothers, 1947); Abram Lincoln Harris,

The Negro as Capitalist: A Study of Banking and Business among American Negroes (Philadelphia: American Academy of Political and Social Science, 1936).

7. Frazier, *The Negro in the United States*, 393.

8. Juliette Walker, *The History of Black Business in America: Capitalism, Race, Entrepreneurship* (New York: Macmillan Library Reference, 1998), 183.

9. Quoted in Walker, *The History of Black Business in America*, 183.

10. Walker, *The History of Black Business in America*, 183–85; Butler, *Entrepreneurship and Self-Help*, 64–65.

11. Booker T. Washington, *The Negro in Business* (Chicago: Hertel, Jenkins, 1907), 14–15, cited in Butler, *Entrepreneurship and Self-Help*, 67.

12. Quoted in Walker, *The History of Black Business in America*, 216.

13. Robert Blauner, "Internal Colonialism and Ghetto Revolt," *Social Problems* 16, no. 4 (1969): 393–408.

14. Ralph J. Bunche, "Conceptions and Ideologies of the Negro Problem" (unpublished manuscript prepared for the Carnegie-Myrdal Study, *An American Dilemma: The Negro Problem and Modern Democracy*, New York, 1940), 122–24, cited in Gunnar Myrdal, *An American Dilemma* (New York: McGraw Hill, 1964), 804.

15. Earl Ofari Hutchinson, "Black Capitalism: Self-Help or Self-Delusion?" in *Race and Ethnic Conflict: Contending Views on Prejudice, Discrimination and Ethnoviolence*, ed. Fred L. Pincus and Howard J. Ehrlich, 264–71 (Boulder, Colo.: Westview, 1994).

16. E. Franklin Frazier, *Black Bourgeoisie* (Glencoe, Ill.: Free Press, 1957).

17. William K. Tabb, *The Political Economy of the Black Ghetto* (New York: Norton, 1970).

18. Ivan Light and Steven J. Gold, *Ethnic Economies* (San Diego: Academic Press, 2000).

19. John S. Butler and Kenneth L. Wilson, "Entrepreneurial Enclaves: An Exposition into the Afro-American Experience," *National Journal of Sociology* 2 (1989): 127–66.

20. Harris, *The Negro as Capitalist*; Butler, *Entrepreneurship and Self-Help*; Michael D. Woodard, *Black Entrepreneurs in America: Stories of Struggle and Success* (New Brunswick, N.J.: Rutgers University Press, 1997).

21. Walker, *The History of Black Business in America*, xix.

22. Manning Marable, *How Capitalism Underdeveloped Black America: Problems in Race, Political Economy and Society* (Boston: South End Press, 1983), 141.

23. Woodard, *Black Entrepreneurs in America*.

24. Butler, *Entrepreneurship and Self-Help*.

25. A survey of American blacks conducted by the Urban League in 2001 found that two-thirds want to run their own business and would prefer self-employment to joining a law firm, medical practice, or established corporation. Gina Holland, "Poll: Blacks Want to Run Businesses," *Los Angeles Times*, July 21, 2001.

26. Frazier, *The Negro in the United States*, 403.

27. Butler, *Entrepreneurship and Self-Help*, 72.

28. W. E. B. DuBois, *The Philadelphia Negro* (New York: Schocken, 1967 [1899]), cited in Butler, *Entrepreneurship and Self-Help*, 145.

29. Kenneth L. Kusmer, *A Ghetto Takes Shape: Black Cleveland, 1870–1930* (Urbana: University of Illinois Press, 1976), 81.

30. Carter G. Woodson, *The Negro Professional Man and the Community, with Special Emphasis on the Physician and the Lawyer* (New York: Negro Universities Press, 1934); Myrdal, *An American Dilemma*, 322.

31. Walker, *The History of Black Business in America*.

557433454454234334323232321

32. Walker, *The History of Black Business in America*, 168–69, 193.

33. Walker, *The History of Black Business in America*, 193.

34. Margaret Levenstein, "African American Entrepreneurship: The View from the 1910 Census," in *Immigrant and Minority Entrepreneurship: The Continuous Rebirth of American Communities*, ed. John Sibley Butler and Groge Kozmetsky, 1–17 (Westport, Conn.: Praeger, 2004).

35. Levenstein, "African American Entrepreneurship," 2–3.

36. Levenstein, "African American Entrepreneurship," 9.

37. Glazer and Moynihan, *Beyond the Melting Pot*, 34.

38. Walker, *The History of Black Business in America*, 163.

39. Walker, *The History of Black Business in America*, 163.

40. Levenstein, "African American Entrepreneurship," 11.

41. Woodard, *Black Entrepreneurs in America*, 16. Several studies (and the 1947 film *Gentleman's Agreement*) suggest that hotels and other public establishments did exclude some of these ethnic groups until the 1960s. However, the extent and pervasiveness of segregation was below that experienced by blacks. Leonard Dinnerstein, Roger L. Nichols, and David M. Riemers, *Natives and Strangers: Blacks, Indians and Immigrants in America*, 2nd ed. (New York: Oxford University Press, 1990).

42. E. Digby Baltzell, *Philadelphia Gentlemen: The Making of a National Upper Class* (New York: Free Press, 1957); John Higham, "Anti-Semitism in the Gilded Age: A Reinterpretation," *Mississippi Valley Historical Review* 43, no. 4 (March 1957): 559–78; George Lipsitz, "The Possessive Investment in Whiteness: Racial Social Democracy and the 'White' Problem in American Studies," *American Quarterly* 47, no. 3 (1995): 369–87.

43. Frazier, *The Negro in the United States*, 413.

44. Lawrence H. Fuchs, "The Reactions of Black Americans to Immigration," in *Immigration Reconsidered: History, Sociology and Politics*, ed. Virginia Yans-McLaughlin, 293–314 (New York: Oxford University Press, 1990), 294–95.

45. Fuchs, "The Reactions of Black Americans to Immigration," 294.

46. Kusmer, *A Ghetto Takes Shape*, 103.

47. Fuchs, "The Reactions of Black Americans to Immigration," 295.

48. Kusmer, *A Ghetto Takes Shape*, 76.

49. Kusmer, *A Ghetto Takes Shape*, 76.

50. Kusmer, *A Ghetto Takes Shape*, 76.

51. Fuchs, "The Reactions of Black Americans to Immigration," 295.

52. Myrdal, *An American Dilemma*, 311.

53. Myrdal, *An American Dilemma*, 312.

54. W. E. B. Du Bois, *The Philadelphia Negro* (New York: Schocken, 1967 [1899]), 120, cited in Myrdal, *An American Dilemma*, 311.

55. Myrdal, *An American Dilemma*, 311.

56. Sheila E. Henry, *Cultural Persistence and Socio-economic Mobility: A Comparative Study of Assimilation among Armenians and Japanese in Los Angeles* (San Francisco: R&E Research Associates, 1978); Leonard Pitt and Dale Pitt, "African Americans," in *Los Angeles A to Z: An Encyclopedia of the City and County*, 4–5 (Berkeley: University of California Press, 1997), 5.

57. Fuchs, "The Reactions of Black Americans to Immigration," 295.

58. Fuchs, "The Reactions of Black Americans to Immigration," 295–96.

59. Fuchs, "The Reactions of Black Americans to Immigration," 296.

60. Blacks support open immigration and refugee resettlement to an extent that far exceeds whites. Survey data collected among African Americans in New York and Los Angeles during the peak years of what some have called the "Black/Korean Conflict" of the 1980s and 1990s showed low levels of support for boycotts and other anti-Korean activities. Similarly, in-depth interviews conducted in 2006 and 2007 with African American business development staff, entrepreneurs, and residents in Detroit, where a very large fraction of retail businesses are owned by immigrants, revealed little hostility toward immigrants. Pyong Gap Min, *Caught in the Middle: Korean Communities in New York and Los Angeles* (Berkeley: University of California Press, 1996), chap. 7.

61. Thomas Gibson, "The Anti-Negro Riots in Atlanta," *Harper's Weekly*, October 13, 1906, 1457ad–1459ac.

62. Gibson, "The Anti-Negro Riots in Atlanta."

63. Light and Gold, *Ethnic Economies*; Butler, *Entrepreneurship and Self-Help*.

64. St. Clair Drake and Horace Cayton, *Black Metropolis* (Chicago: University of Chicago Press, 1945).

65. Drake and Cayton, *Black Metropolis*, 434.

66. Ronald Takaki, *A Different Mirror: A History of Multicultural America* (Boston: Little, Brown, 1993).

67. Takaki, *A Different Mirror*, 343.

68. Ray Stannard Baker, "The Negro Goes North," *World's Work* 34 (July 1917): 315, cited in Takaki, *A Different Mirror*, 342–43.

69. Takaki, *A Different Mirror*, 345.

70. Drake and Cayton, *Black Metropolis*, 80–81.

71. Walker, *The History of Black Business in America*, 183.

72. Drake and Cayton, *Black Metropolis*, 434.

73. Butler, *Entrepreneurship and Self-Help*, 71.

74. Walker, *The History of Black Business in America*, 186.

75. Walker, *The History of Black Business in America*, 186.

76. Butler, *Entrepreneurship and Self-Help*.

77. Walker, *The History of Black Business in America*, 193–95.

78. Walker, *The History of Black Business in America*, 195–96.

79. Pierce, *Negro Business and Business Education*, 193–94, cited in Frazier, *The Negro in the United States*, 407.

80. Drake and Cayton, *Black Metropolis*, 459.

81. Drake and Cayton, *Black Metropolis*, 464.

82. Walker, *The History of Black Business in America*, 208, 210–11.

83. Walker, *The History of Black Business in America*, 210–11; Robert Mark Silverman, *Doing Business in Minority Markets: Black and Korean Entrepreneurs in Chicago's Ethnic Beauty Aids Industry* (New York: Garland, 2000); Adia Harvey Wingfield, *Doing Business with Beauty: Black Women, Hair Salons, and the Racial Enclave Economy* (Lanham, Md.: Rowman & Littlefield, 2007).

84. Drake and Cayton, *Black Metropolis*, 438; Myrdal, *An American Dilemma*, 307.

85. Mayor's Commission on Conditions in Harlem, "The Negro in Harlem: A Report on Social and Economic Conditions Responsible for the Outbreak of March 19, 1935" (New York, 1936), 23–24, cited in Frazier, *The Negro in the United States*, 406–7.

86. Steven J. Gold, "Immigrant Entrepreneurs and Customers throughout the 20th Century," in *Not Just Black and White: Historical and Contemporary Perspectives on Immigration, Race and Ethnicity in the United States*, ed. Nancy Foner and George M. Fredrickson,

315–40 (New York: Russell Sage Foundation, 2004); Silverman, *Doing Business in Minority Markets*.

87. Myrdal, *An American Dilemma*, 323.
88. Myrdal, *An American Dilemma*, 324.
89. Myrdal, *An American Dilemma*.
90. Kusmer, *A Ghetto Takes Shape*.
91. U.S. Census 1940, cited in Myrdal, *An American Dilemma*, 307.
92. U.S. Census 1941, cited in Frazier, *The Negro in the United States*, 402.
93. Drake and Cayton, *Black Metropolis*, 436.
94. Drake and Cayton, *Black Metropolis*, 454.
95. Drake and Cayton, *Black Metropolis*, 436.
96. Kusmer, *A Ghetto Takes Shape*, 83.
97. Kusmer, *A Ghetto Takes Shape*, 83.

CHAPTER 3

1. Bill McGraw, "Today's Detroit Has Little to Do with 1967: What If Riot Never Happened? City Was Still Headed for Slide," *Detroit Free Press*, July 20, 2007.

2. Jonathan Rieder, *Canarsie: The Jews and Italians of Brooklyn against Liberalism* (Cambridge, Mass.: Harvard University Press, 1985), 25.

3. U.S. Census; Josef J. Barton, *Peasants and Strangers: Italians, Rumanians and Slovaks in an American City, 1890–1950* (Cambridge, Mass.: Harvard University Press, 1975); St. Clair Drake and Horace Cayton, *Black Metropolis* (Chicago: University of Chicago Press, 1945), 8; Nathan Glazer and Daniel Patrick Moynihan, *Beyond the Melting Pot* (Cambridge, Mass.: MIT Press, 1963), 318.

4. Theodore Saloutos, *The Greeks in the United States* (Cambridge, Mass.: Harvard University Press, 1964); Ronald Takaki, *Strangers from a Different Shore: A History of Asian Americans* (Boston: Little, Brown, 1989).

5. Stanford M. Lyman, "Stranger in the Cities: The Chinese on the Urban Frontier," in *Ethnic Conflict in California History*, ed. Charles Wollenberg, 61–100, Letters and Science Extension Series, University of California, Berkeley (Los Angeles: Tinnon-Brown, 1970); Erika Lee, *At America's Gates: Chinese Immigration during the Exclusion Era, 1882–1943* (Chapel Hill: University of North Carolina Press, 2003).

6. Stanford M. Lyman, *Chinese Americans* (New York: Random House, 1974), 73, 57.

7. Ronald H. Bayor, *Neighbors in Conflict: The Irish, Germans, Jews and Italians of New York City, 1929–1941* (Baltimore: Johns Hopkins University Press, 1978); John P. Diggins, *Mussolini and Fascism: The View from America* (Princeton, N.J.: Princeton University Press, 1972).

8. Sidney Bolkosky, *Harmony and Dissonance: Voices of Jewish Identity in Detroit, 1914–1967* (Detroit: Wayne State University Press, 1991); Jean Ann Scarpaci, "Italian Immigrants in Louisiana's Sugar Parishes: Recruitment, Labor Conditions, and Community Relations, 1880–1910," (PhD diss., Department of History, Rutgers University, 1972).

9. Irving Howe, with Kenneth Libo, *World of Our Fathers* (New York: Harcourt Brace Jovanovich, 1976), 129; John Higham, "Anti-Semitism in the Gilded Age: A Reinterpretation," *Mississippi Valley Historical Review* 43, no. 4 (March 1957): 559–78.

10. Thomas A. Guglielmo, "Rethinking Whiteness Historiography: The Case of Italians in Chicago, 1890–1945," in *White Out: The Continuing Significance of Racism*, ed. Ashley W.

Doane, and Eduardo Bonilla-Silva, 35–48 (New York: Routledge, 2003); Scarpaci, "Italians Immigrants"; David R. Roediger, *Colored White: Transcending the Racial Past* (Berkeley: University of California Press, 2002); George Lipsitz, "The Possessive Investment in White-ness: Racial Social Democracy and the 'White' Problem in American Studies," *American Quarterly* 47, no. 3 (1995): 369–87.

11. Saloutos, *The Greeks in the United States*, 266.

12. Irish, Jews, and blacks had connections to sizeable coethnic communities and influen-tial allies in the United States.

13. Saloutos, *The Greeks in the United States*, 164.

14. Scarpaci, "Italian Immigrants," 198, 253.

15. John Modell, "Japanese-Americans: Some Costs of Group Achievement," in *Ethnic Conflict in California History*, ed. Charles Wollenberg, 101–19, Letters and Science Exten-sion Series, University of California, Berkeley (Los Angeles: Tinnon-Brown, 1970), 109–12.

16. Lyman, "Stranger in the Cities," 97–98.

17. Saloutos, *The Greeks in the United States*, 64.

18. *Crisis*, November 1910, cited in Scarpaci, "Italians Immigrants," 251.

19. Steven J. Gold and Bruce A. Phillips, "Mobility and Continuity among Eastern Euro-pean Jews," in *Origins and Destinies: Immigration, Race and Ethnicity in America*, ed. Silvia Pedraza and Rubén G. Rumbaut, 182–94 (Belmont, Calif.: Wadsworth, 1996).

20. Ronald Takaki, *A Different Mirror: A History of Multicultural America* (Boston: Little, Brown, 1993), 162; D. P. Clark, "The Expansion of the Public Sector and Irish Economic Development," in *Self-Help in Urban America: Patterns of Minority Business Enterprise*, ed. S. Cummings (Port Washington, N.Y.: Kennikat Press, 1980).

21. John Bodnar, *The Transplanted: A History of Immigrants in Urban America* (Bloom-ington: University of Indiana Press, 1985).

22. Saloutos, *The Greeks in the United States*, 55.

23. Jack Katz, *Seductions of Crime* (New York: Basic Books, 1988); Ivan Light, "The Eth-nic Vice Industry, 1880–1944," *American Sociological Review* 42 (1977): 464–79; Martin San-chez-Jankowski, *Islands in the Street* (Berkeley: University of California Press, 1992), 124.

24. Morrison Wong, "Chinese Americans," in *Asian Americans: Contemporary Trends and Issues*, ed. Pyong Gap Min, 110–45, 2nd ed. (Thousand Oaks, Calif.: Pine Forge Press, 2006); Huping Ling, "Governing 'Hop Alley': On Leong Chinese Merchants and Laborers Associa-tion, 1906–1966," *Journal of American Ethnic History* 23, no. 2 (winter 2004): 50–84.

25. Lyman, *Chinese Americans*, 52.

26. Dominic A. Pacyga, *Polish Immigrants and Industrial Chicago: Workers on the South Side, 1880–1922* (Columbus: Ohio State University Press, 1991).

27. Hadassa Kosak, "Tailors and Troublemakers: Jewish Militancy in the New York Gar-ment Industry, 1899–1920," in *A Coat of Many Colors: Immigration, Globalization and Reform in New York's Garment Industry*, ed. Daniel Soyer, 115–40 (New York: Fordham University Press, 2005), 128–30; Nancy L. Green, ed., *Jewish Workers in the Modern Dias-pora* (Berkeley: University of California Press, 1998), 120–22.

28. Kosak, "Tailors and Troublemakers," 130, 132.

29. Joan S. Wang, "Race, Gender, and Laundry Work: The Roles of Chinese Laundrymen and American Women in the United States, 1850–1950," *Journal of American Ethnic History* 24, no. 1 (fall 2004): 81.

30. Alejandro Portes and Robert D. Manning, "The Immigrant Enclave: Theory and Em-pirical Examples," in *Ethnicity: Structure and Process*, ed. J. Nagel and S. Olzak, 47–68 (New York: Academic Press, 1986).

31. Light, "The Ethnic Vice Industry."

32. Immigration Commission, *Immigrants in Cities: A Study of the Population of Selected Districts in New York, Chicago, Philadelphia, Boston, Cleveland, Buffalo and Milwaukee*, vol. 1 (Washington, D.C.: Government Printing Office, 1911), tabs. 73, 74.

33. Roger Waldinger, "When the Melting Pot Boils Over: The Irish, Jews, Blacks and Koreans of New York," Department of Sociology, University of California, Los Angeles, 1992; Robert L. Boyd, "Ethnicity, Niches, and Retail Enterprise in Northern Cities, 1900," *Sociological Perspectives* 44, no. 1 (2001): 89–110; Saloutos, *The Greeks in the United States*.

34. Boyd, "Ethnicity, Niches, and Retail Enterprise," 97.

35. Modell, "Japanese-Americans," 107–8; Ivan Light, *Ethnic Enterprise in America: Business and Welfare among Chinese, Japanese and Blacks* (Berkeley: University of California Press, 1972); Daisuke Akiba, "Japanese Americans," in *Asian Americans: Contemporary Trends and Issues*, ed. Pyong Gap Min, 148–77, 2nd ed. (Thousand Oaks, Calif.: Pine Forge Press, 2006).

36. Light, *Ethnic Enterprise in America*, 10.

37. Saloutos, *The Greeks in the United States*, 49, 263, 267.

38. Stanley Lieberson, *A Piece of the Pie: Blacks and White Immigrants since 1880* (Berkeley: University of California Press, 1980).

39. Gary Ross Mormino, *Immigrants on the Hill: Italian-Americans in St. Louis, 1882–1982* (Urbana: University of Illinois Press, 1986); Barton, *Peasants and Strangers*, 94.

40. Mormino, *Immigrants on the Hill*, 248–50.

41. Light, *Ethnic Enterprise in America*; Lyman, *Chinese Americans*.

42. Samuel Joseph, *Jewish Immigration to the United States from 1881 to 1910* (New York: Arno Press and New York Times, 1914); Gold and Phillips, "Mobility and Continuity."

43. Thomas Sowell, *Ethnic America* (New York: Basic Books, 1981); Joel Kotkin, *Tribes: How Race, Religion and Identity Determined Success in the New Global Economy* (New York: Random House, 1992).

44. Saloutos, *The Greeks in the United States*, 258–59; Ivan Light and Steven J. Gold, *Ethnic Economies* (San Diego: Academic Press, 2000). A similar case involves that of Koreans during the late twentieth century. Those settled in the United States have significant rates of self-employment, while those in Japan do not.

45. Pacyga, *Polish Immigrants*, 117–18.

46. Louis Wirth, *The Ghetto* (Chicago: University of Chicago Press, 1928), 229.

47. Pacyga, *Polish Immigrants*, 224; Arnold R. Hirsch, "E. Pluribus Duo? Thoughts on 'Whiteness' and Chicago's 'New' Immigration as a Transient Third Tier," *Journal of American Ethnic History* 23, no. 4 (summer 2004): 16.

48. Robert A. Rockaway, *The Jews of Detroit: From the Beginning, 1762–1914* (Detroit: Wayne State University Press, 1986), 20, 90–91.

49. Saloutos, *The Greeks in the United States*; John J. Bukowczyk, "The Transformation of Working-Class Ethnicity: Corporate Control, Americanization, and the Polish Immigrant Middle Class in Bayonne, New Jersey, 1915–1925," *Labor History* 25, no. 1 (winter 1984): 70–71.

50. Lyman, "Stranger in the Cities," 94–95; Lyman, *Chinese Americans*, 74.

51. Betty Lee Sung, *The Story of the Chinese in America* (New York: Collier Books, 1971), 44–45, cited in Wong, "Chinese Americans," 124.

52. Wong, "Chinese Americans," 125.

53. Lyman, "Stranger in the Cities," 96–97; Lyman, *Chinese Americans*, 80; Wong, "Chinese Americans," 123; Wang, "Race, Gender, and Laundry Work."

54. Quoted in Higham, "Anti-Semitism in the Gilded Age," 573.

55. Higham, "Anti-Semitism in the Gilded Age," 575.

56. Higham, "Anti-Semitism in the Gilded Age," 576–78.

57. Saloutos, *The Greeks in the United States*, 269.

58. Saloutos, *The Greeks in the United States*, 69, 264–67.

59. Saloutos, *The Greeks in the United States*, 164–65.

60. Philip M. Kayal and Joseph M. Kayal, *The Syrian-Lebanese: A Study in Religion and Assimilation* (Boston: Twayne Publishers, 1975); Rhonda F. Levine, *Class, Networks and Identity: Replanting Jewish Lives from Nazi Germany to Rural New York* (Lanham, Md.: Rowman & Littlefield, 2001); Mormino, *Immigrants on the Hill*; Lyman, "Stranger in the Cities."

61. Scarpaci, "Italian Immigrants," 222.

62. Scarpaci, "Italian Immigrants," 193, 211.

63. James W. Loewen, *The Mississippi Chinese: Between Black and White* (Cambridge, Mass.: Harvard University Press, 1971), 32–33.

64. Wang, "Race, Gender, and Laundry Work," 78–79.

65. Robert G. Weisbrod and Arthur Stein, *Bittersweet Encounter: The Afro-American and the American Jew* (Westport, Conn.: Negro Universities Press, 1970), 31.

66. John Dollard, *Caste and Class in a Southern Town*, 3rd ed. (Garden City, N.Y.: Doubleday Anchor, 1957), 129.

67. Scarpaci, "Italian Immigrants," 212.

68. Scarpaci, "Italian Immigrants"; Loewen, *The Mississippi Chinese*, 52.

69. Thomas Gibson, "The Anti-Negro Riots in Atlanta," *Harper's Weekly*, October 13, 1906, 1457ad–1459ac.

70. Gibson, "The Anti-Negro Riots in Atlanta."

71. Cheryl Lynn Greenberg, *Troubling the Waters: Black-Jewish Relations in the American Century* (Princeton, N.J.: Princeton University Press, 2006), 208.

72. Loewen, *The Mississippi Chinese*, 183.

73. Evan Friss, "Blacks, Jews, and Civil Rights Law in New York, 1895–1913," *Journal of American Ethnic History* 24, no. 4 (summer 2004): 71, 79.

74. In 1900, there were approximately 240,000 foreign-born Jews in New York and about 61,000 African Americans. Glazer and Moynihan, *Beyond the Melting Pot*, 318.

75. Edwin Emerson, "The New Ghetto," *Harper's Weekly*, January 9, 1897, 44.

76. Wirth, *The Ghetto*, 230.

77. Kenneth L. Kusmer, *A Ghetto Takes Shape: Black Cleveland, 1870–1930* (Urbana: University of Illinois Press, 1976); Rockaway, *The Jews of Detroit*.

78. Wirth, *The Ghetto*, 129.

79. Drake and Cayton, *Black Metropolis*; Loewen, *The Mississippi Chinese*; Jennifer Lee, *Civility in the City: Blacks, Jews, and Koreans in Urban America* (Cambridge, Mass.: Harvard University Press, 2002).

80. Mormino, *Immigrants on the Hill*; Lee, *Civility in the City*.

81. Pyong Gap Min, *Ethnic Solidarity for Economic Survival* (New York: Russell Sage Foundation, 2008); Michael B. Katz, "Why Don't American Cities Burn Very Often," *Journal of Urban History* 34 (2008): 185–208.

CHAPTER 4

1. New Deal economic programs assisted black Americans even though the Roosevelt administration "did not seriously tackle the problems of racial discrimination and segregation"

for fear of losing support of southern Democrats. Leonard Dinnerstein, Roger L. Nichols, and David M. Riemers, *Natives and Strangers: Blacks, Indians and Immigrants in America*, 2nd ed. (New York: Oxford University Press, 1990), 301; Dalton Conley, *Being Black, Living in the Red: Race, Wealth and Social Policy in America* (Berkeley: University of California Press, 1999), 135.

2. Cheryl Lynn Greenberg, *Troubling the Waters: Black-Jewish Relations in the American Century* (Princeton, N.J.: Princeton University Press, 2006); Ronald Takaki, *A Different Mirror: A History of Multicultural America* (Boston: Little, Brown, 1993).

3. Kenneth L. Kusmer, *A Ghetto Takes Shape: Black Cleveland, 1870–1930* (Urbana: University of Illinois Press, 1976).

4. Kusmer, *A Ghetto Takes Shape*.

5. Gary Jerome Hunter, "Don't Buy from Where You Can't Work: Black Urban Boycott Movements during the Depression, 1929–1941" (PhD diss., Department of History, University of Michigan, 1977); *Chicago Defender*, "Court Rules Boycott Not Fair to Race," October 8, 1927, 3.

6. St. Clair Drake and Horace Cayton, *Black Metropolis* (Chicago: University of Chicago Press, 1945).

7. *New York Times*, "Bias against Negro on Relief Charged," January 14, 1932.

8. Mary Ross, "Negro City in Harlem Is a Race Capital," *New York Times*, March 1, 1925.

9. Gunnar Myrdal, *An American Dilemma* (New York: McGraw Hill, 1964); Roi Ottley, *New World a-Coming* (New York: Arno Press and New York Times, 1968 [1943]), 74.

10. Kusmer, *A Ghetto Takes Shape*, 228.

11. Ottley, *New World a-Coming*; Juliette Walker, *The History of Black Business in America: Capitalism, Race, Entrepreneurship* (New York: Macmillan Library Reference, 1998).

12. Cheryl Lynn Greenberg, *Or Does It Explode? Black Harlem in the Great Depression* (New York: Oxford University Press, 1991), 94.

13. In the early 1950s, studies of the job markets in Los Angeles and Chicago found that between 17 percent and 20 percent of all job openings requested non-Jewish applicants. Lois Waldman, "Employment Discrimination against Jews in the United States—1955," *Jewish Social Studies* 18 (1956): 208–16; Sidney Bolkosky, *Harmony and Dissonance: Voices of Jewish Identity in Detroit, 1914–1967* (Detroit: Wayne State University Press, 1991).

14. Shelly Tenenbaum, *A Credit to Their Community: Jewish Loan Societies in the United States, 1880–1945* (Detroit: Wayne State University Press, 1993), 64.

15. Hasia R. Diner, *The Jews of the United States* (Berkeley: University of California Press, 2004), 210.

16. Ronald H. Bayor, *Neighbors in Conflict: The Irish, Germans, Jews and Italians of New York City, 1929–1941* (Baltimore: Johns Hopkins University Press, 1978), 100–102.

17. Bayor, *Neighbors in Conflict*, 100–102.

18. Diner, *The Jews of the United States*, 210–12; J. J. Goldberg, *Jewish Power: Inside the American Jewish Establishment* (Reading, Mass.: Addison-Wesley, 1996), 116–19; Rita J. Simon, *In the Golden Land: A Century of Russian and Soviet Jewish Immigration in America* (Westport, Conn.: Praeger, 1997), 21.

19. Greenberg, *Troubling the Waters*, 55.

20. E. Franklin Frazier, *The Negro in the United States*, 2nd ed. (New York: MacMillan, 1957), 226.

21. Drake and Cayton, *Black Metropolis*; Greenberg, *Or Does It Explode?*; Greenberg, *Troubling the Waters*; Ottley, *New World a-Coming*; Frazier, *The Negro in the United*

States; Nathan Glazer and Daniel Patrick Moynihan, *Beyond the Melting Pot* (Cambridge, Mass.: MIT Press, 1963); Irving Spiegel, "Survey Finds Blacks Own Most Harlem Stores," *New York Times*, September 16, 1968; Frederick D. Sturdivant, "Better Deal for Ghetto Shoppers," in *The Ghetto Marketplace*, ed. Frederick D. Sturdivant, 142–57 (New York: Free Press, 1969).

22. Joseph A. Pierce, *Negro Business and Business Education: Their Present and Prospective Development* (New York: Harper & Brothers, 1947), 23.

23. Hunter, "Don't Buy from Where You Can't Work"; Ottley, *New World a-Coming*.

24. John P. Diggins, *Mussolini and Fascism: The View from America* (Princeton, N.J.: Princeton University Press, 1972); William R. Scott, "Black Nationalism and the Italo-Ethiopian Conflict, 1934–1936," *Journal of Negro History* 63, no. 2 (1978): 118–34; *New York Times*, "Police End Harlem Riot; Mayor Starts Inquiry; Dodge Sees a Red Plot," March 21, 1935; Greenberg, *Troubling the Waters*, 85. Because of Mussolini's ties to Hitler, Jews were also involved in entrepreneurial conflicts with Italian Americans—for example, denying Italian American garment firms access to jobbers. Bayor, *Neighbors in Conflict*, 98.

25. Drake and Cayton, *Black Metropolis*, 432.

26. Hunter, "Don't Buy from Where You Can't Work," 187.

27. Ottley, *New World a-Coming*, 53–55.

28. Charles Choy Wong, "Black and Chinese Grocery Stores in Los Angeles' Black Ghetto," *Urban Life* 5, no. 4 (1977): 439–64; Scott Kurashige, *The Shifting Ground of Race: Black and Japanese Americans in the Making of Multiethnic Los Angeles* (Princeton, N.J.: Princeton University Press, 2008).

29. Alan Raucher, "Dime Store Chains: The Making of Organization Men, 1880–1940," *Business History Review* 65, no. 1 (1991): 130–63; *Chicago Defender*, "Detroit Residents Push Plans to Get Chain Store Clerks," January 30, 1932, 3.

30. Greenberg, *Troubling the Waters*, 61.

31. Drake and Cayton, *Black Metropolis*; Frazier, *The Negro in the United States*; Myrdal, *An American Dilemma*; Hunter, "Don't Buy from Where You Can't Work."

32. Kelly Miller, "The Harvest of Race Prejudice," *Survey Graphic* 6, no. 6 (March 1925): 682–83, 711–12.

33. Kusmer, *A Ghetto Takes Shape*, 170–171.

34. Jazz Age Chicago, "South Center," July 3, 2000, at http://chicago.urban-history.org/ven/dss/socenter.shtml (accessed April 15, 2010).

35. Ottley, *New World a-Coming*.

36. Glazer and Moynihan, *Beyond the Melting Pot*, 71; Myrdal, *An American Dilemma*, 308.

37. Years later, Harlem congressman Adam Clayton Powell urged residents to quit numbers gambling, which enriched Jewish and Italian racketeers, despite the fact that, during police crackdowns, only blacks were arrested. Emanuel Perlmutter, "Powell Demands Numbers Inquiry," *New York Times*, January 11, 1960; Greenberg, *Troubling the Waters*.

38. Steven J. Gold and Bruce A. Phillips, "Mobility and Continuity among Eastern European Jews," in *Origins and Destinies: Immigration, Race and Ethnicity in America*, ed. Silvia Pedraza and Rubén G. Rumbaut, 182–94 (Belmont, Calif.: Wadsworth, 1996).

39. Ottley, *New World a-Coming*, 128

40. Drake and Cayton, *Black Metropolis*, 432.

41. David Caplovitz, *The Poor Pay More* (New York: Free Press, 1967); Frederick D. Sturdivant and Walter T. Wilhelm, "Poverty, Minorities, and Consumer Exploitation," in *The Ghetto Marketplace*, ed. Frederick D. Sturdivant, 108–17 (New York: Free Press, 1969).

42. Sturdivant, "Better Deal for Ghetto Shoppers," 145.

43. Quoted in Greenberg, *Troubling the Waters*, 95.

44. Greenberg, *Troubling the Waters*; Ottley, *New World a-Coming*.

45. Kenneth B. Clark, "Candor about Negro-Jewish Relations," in *Anti-Semitism in the United States*, ed. Leonard Dinnerstein, 116–24 (New York: Holt, Rinehart and Winston, 1971).

46. James Baldwin, "Negroes Are Anti-Semitic Because They're Anti-White," *New York Times*, April 9, 1967.

47. Robert G. Weisbrod and Arthur Stein, *Bittersweet Encounter: The Afro-American and the American Jew* (Westport, Conn.: Negro Universities Press, 1970); Greenberg, *Troubling the Waters*.

48. For example, during the World War II era, both black and Jewish activists linked racial and ethnic discrimination with Nazism in order to discredit it. The implication of such efforts is that discrimination itself was not seen as wrong by significant parts of the American population and would only be subject to condemnation by associating it with the enemy. Greenberg, *Troubling the Waters*; Robert E. Weems Jr., *Black Business in the Black Metropolis: The Chicago Metropolitan Assurance Company, 1925–1985* (Bloomington: Indiana University Press, 1996); Drake and Cayton, *Black Metropolis*.

49. Greenberg, *Or Does It Explode?*, 117.

50. One exception was Chicago's Regal Theater. Initially opened in 1928 by the Lubliner and Trinz movie theater chain to serve the African American market, almost all of the theater's management staff, cashiers, ushers, and house musicians were black. Jazz Age Chicago, "Regal Theater," July 3, 2000, at http://chicago.urban-history.org/ven/ths/regal.shtml (accessed April 15, 2010).

51. Hunter, "Don't Buy from Where You Can't Work," 249.

52. Hunter, "Don't Buy from Where You Can't Work," 86.

53. Hunter, "Don't Buy from Where You Can't Work," 91.

54. Hunter, "Don't Buy from Where You Can't Work."

55. Abram Lincoln Harris, *The Negro as Capitalist: A Study of Banking and Business among American Negroes* (Philadelphia: American Academy of Political and Social Science, 1936), x; Hunter, "Don't Buy from Where You Can't Work," 286.

56. *Chicago Defender*, "Detroit Residents Push Plans to Get Chain Store Clerks," January 30, 1932, 3; W. E. B. DuBois predicted this possibility. Christopher Robert Reed, *The Chicago NAACP and the Rise of Black Professional Leadership, 1910–1966* (Bloomington: Indiana University Press, 1997), 82.

57. Hunter, "Don't Buy from Where You Can't Work."

58. The *Chicago Defender* included frequent small articles supportive of boycotts. *Chicago Defender*, "Shun Business Places that Draw Color Line," November 3, 1928, 7; *Chicago Defender*, "Plan to Boycott Stores Refusing Employment," December 1, 1928, 2.

59. *New York Times*, "Harlem's Hitler Brought to Court," October 9, 1934.

60. Hunter, "Don't Buy from Where You Can't Work," 189; Ottley, *New World a-Coming*.

61. Hunter, "Don't Buy from Where You Can't Work," 183; Ottley, *New World a-Coming*, 119.

62. Ottley, *New World a-Coming*, 119–21.

63. Hunter, "Don't Buy from Where You Can't Work," 191.

64. *New York Times*, "Police End Harlem Riot."

65. Ottley, *New World a-Coming*, 152.

66. Hunter, "Don't Buy from Where You Can't Work," 192.

67. Quoted in Hunter, "Don't Buy from Where You Can't Work," 194; Ottley, *New World a-Coming*, 153.

68. Greenberg, *Troubling the Waters*, 213.

69. Ottley, *New World a-Coming*, 115.

70. Hunter, "Don't Buy from Where You Can't Work," 278.

71. Jacqueline Jones, *Labor of Love, Labor of Sorrow: Black Women, Work and Family from Slavery to the Present* (New York: Basic Books, 1985), 215.

72. Hunter, "Don't Buy from Where You Can't Work," 284.

73. Frazier, *The Negro in the United States*, 406.

74. Greenberg, *Troubling the Waters*, 60–61.

75. Greenberg, *Troubling the Waters*, 95.

76. Ottley, *New World a-Coming*, 133.

77. *New York Times*, "Liebowitz Asks Truce of Negroes and Jews," August 22, 1939.

78. L. D. Reddick, "Anti-Semitism among Negroes," *Negro Quarterly* 1, no. 2 (summer 1942): 119.

79. Greenberg, *Or Does It Explode?* 200.

80. Walker, *The History of Black Business*.

81. Eleanor Paperno Wolf, Alvin D. Loving, and Donald C. Marsh, *Negro-Jewish Relationships* (Detroit: Wayne State University Press, 1944), 5.

82. Alfred McClung Lee and Norman D. Humphrey, *Race Riot: Detroit, 1943*, with a new introductory essay by Alfred McClung Lee (New York: Octagon Books, 1968).

83. Vivian Baulch and Patricia Zacharias, "The 1943 Detroit Race Riots," *Detroit News*, n.d.

84. Bolkosky, *Harmony and Dissonance*, 1991.

85. Joseph Lelyveld, "Riots Viewed against History of Clashes Almost as Old as US," *New York Times*, September 11, 1964.

86. Greenberg, *Or Does It Explode?*

87. Harold L. Sheppard, "The Negro Merchant: A Study of Negro Anti-Semitism," *American Journal of Sociology* 53, no. 2 (September 1947): 97–98.

88. Louis Coser, *The Functions of Social Conflict* (New York: Free Press, 1956), 121–28.

89. Tomás Almaguer, *Racial Fault Lines: The Historical Origins of White Supremacy in California* (Berkeley: University of California Press, 1994), 210.

90. John Modell, *The Economics and Politics of Racial Accommodation: The Japanese of Los Angeles, 1900–1942* (Urbana: University of Illinois Press, 1977), 5.

91. Modell, *The Economics and Politics*, 10–11.

92. Modell, *The Economics and Politics*, 59.

93. Modell, *The Economics and Politics*, 66.

94. Ronald Takaki, *Strangers from a Different Shore: A History of Asian Americans* (Boston: Little, Brown, 1989), 204, 390; Leonard Bloom and Ruth Riemer, *Removal and Return: The Socio-Economic Effects of the War on Japanese Americans*, University of California Publications in Culture and Society 4 (Berkeley: University of California Press, 1949).

95. Takaki, *Strangers from a Different Shore*, 206; *New York Times*, "Japanese Will Quit California Farms," December 16, 1923.

96. Ivan Light, *Ethnic Enterprise in America: Business and Welfare among Chinese, Japanese and Blacks* (Berkeley: University of California Press, 1972).

97. *New York Times*, "Japanese Will Quit California Farms"; Robert M. Jiobu, "Ethnic Hegemony and the Japanese of California," *American Sociological Review* 53, no. 3 (1988): 359; Light, *Ethnic Enterprise in America*.

98. Modell, *The Economics and Politics*.
99. Modell, *The Economics and Politics*, 175.
100. Takaki, *Strangers from a Different Shore*, 389.
101. Takaki, *A Different Mirror*, 381–90.
102. Takaki, *A Different Mirror*, 382.
103. Modell, *The Economics and Politics*, 45.
104. Thomas J. Sugrue, *The Origins of the Urban Crisis: Race and Inequality in Postwar Detroit*, with a new preface by the author (Princeton, N.J.: Princeton University Press, 2005), 10; Takaki, *A Different Mirror*, 369.

CHAPTER 5

1. Max Herman, "The Newark and Detroit 'Riots' of 1967," at www.67riots.rutgers.edu/introduction.html (accessed April 10, 2010); Tom Hayden, "A Special Supplement: The Occupation of Newark," *New York Review of Books*, August 24, 1967; Sidney Fine, *Violence in the Model City: The Cavanaugh Administration, Race Relations, and the Detroit Riot of 1967* (Ann Arbor: University of Michigan Press, 1989), 300.
2. Arnold R. Hirsch, *Making the Second Ghetto: Race and Housing in Chicago, 1940–1960* (Cambridge: Cambridge University Press, 1983); Kenneth T. Jackson, *Crabgrass Frontier: The Suburbanization of the United States* (New York: Oxford University Press, 1985); Douglas S. Massey and Nancy A. Denton, *American Apartheid: Segregation and the Making of the Underclass* (Cambridge, Mass.: Harvard University Press, 1993).
3. Shannon Harper and Barbara Reskin, "Affirmative Action at School and on the Job," *Annual Review of Sociology* 31 (2005): 357–79; Leslie Fulbright, "Connerly Gearing Up for Wider Crusade: Affirmative Action Foe Considers Launching Campaigns in 9 States," *San Francisco Chronicle*, December 14, 2006.
4. William J. Wilson, *The Declining Significance of Race* (Chicago: University of Chicago Press, 1978).
5. Hirsch, *Making the Second Ghetto*; Jackson, *Crabgrass Frontier*; Massey and Denton, *American Apartheid*; George Lipsitz, "The Possessive Investment in Whiteness: Racial Social Democracy and the 'White' Problem in American Studies," *American Quarterly* 47, no. 3 (1995): 369–87.
6. By 2006, "the FHA and the U.S. Department of Housing and Urban Development had insured over 34 million home mortgages and 47,205 multifamily project mortgages since 1934." U.S. Department of Housing and Urban Development (HUD), "The Federal Housing Administration," September 6, 2006, at www.hud.gov/offices/hsg/fhahistory.cfm (accessed April 16, 2010).
7. Douglas S. Massey, "Origins of Economic Disparities: The Historical Role of Housing Segregation," in *Segregation: The Rising Costs for America*, ed. James H. Carr and Nandinee K. Kutty, 39–80 (New York: Routledge, 2008), 63.
8. Kenneth L. Kusmer, *A Ghetto Takes Shape: Black Cleveland, 1870–1930* (Urbana: University of Illinois Press, 1976).
9. Robert C. Weaver, "Class, Race and Urban Renewal," in *Racial and Ethnic Relations*, ed. Bernard E. Segal. 2nd ed. (New York: Crowell, 1966), 341.
10. Massey, "Origins of Economic Disparities," 64.
11. Jackson, *Crabgrass Frontier*, 201.
12. Massey, "Origins of Economic Disparities," 72.

13. Ron French, "New Segregation: Races Accept the Divide," *Detroit News*, January 13, 2002.

14. Massey, "Origins of Economic Disparities," 72.

15. Weaver, "Class, Race and Urban Renewal," 335.

16. Massey, "Origins of Economic Disparities," 93.

17. Dalton Conley, *Being Black, Living in the Red: Race, Wealth and Social Policy in America* (Berkeley: University of California Press, 1999), 37; Campbell Gibson and Kay Jung, "Historical Census Statistics on Population Totals by Race, 1790 to 1990, and by Hispanic Origin, 1970 to 1990, for the United States, Regions, Divisions, and States," Working Paper Series No. 56 (Population Division, U.S. Census Bureau, Washington, D.C., September 2002).

18. August Meier and Elliot Rudwick, *From Plantation to Ghetto*, rev. ed. (New York: Hill and Wang, 1970), 282–83.

19. Massey and Denton, *American Apartheid*, 56.

20. D. Bradford Hunt, "What Went Wrong with Public Housing in Chicago? A History of the Robert Taylor Homes," *Journal of the Illinois State Historical Society* (spring 2001), at http://findarticles.com/p/articles/mi_qa3945/is_200104/ai_n8939181/pg_5 (accessed April 10, 2010).

21. Nathan Glazer and Daniel Patrick Moynihan, *Beyond the Melting Pot* (Cambridge, Mass.: MIT Press, 1963); Ivan Light, *Ethnic Enterprise in America: Business and Welfare among Chinese, Japanese and Blacks* (Berkeley: University of California Press, 1972); John Sibley Butler, *Entrepreneurship and Self-help among Black Americans* (Albany: State University of New York Press, 1991); Francis Fukuyama, *Trust: The Social Virtues and the Creation of Prosperity* (New York: Free Press, 1995); Otto Kerner, *Report of the National Advisory Commission on Civil Disorders* (New York: Bantam Books, 1968).

22. "There has been a tendency to view Afro-Americans as another ethnic group not basically different in experience from previous ethnics and whose 'immigration' condition in the North would in time follow their upward course. The inadequacy of this model is now clear. Even the Kerner Report devotes a chapter to criticizing this analogy." Robert Blauner, "Internal Colonialism and Ghetto Revolt," *Social Problems* 16, no. 4 (1969): 394.

23. Massey, "Origins of Economic Disparities," 52; Thomas Philpott, *The Slum and the Ghetto: Neighborhood Deterioration and Middle Class Reform, Chicago, 1880–1930* (New York: Oxford University Press, 1978), 139–41.

24. Gary Ross Mormino, *Immigrants on the Hill: Italian-Americans in St. Louis, 1882–1982* (Urbana: University of Illinois Press, 1986).

25. Massey, "Origins of Economic Disparities," 52.

26. St. Clair Drake and Horace Cayton, *Black Metropolis* (Chicago: University of Chicago Press, 1945).

27. Massey, "Origins of Economic Disparities," 53; Wilson, *The Declining Significance of Race*.

28. Butler, *Entrepreneurship and Self-help*, 268.

29. Massey and Denton, *American Apartheid*; Roi Ottley, *New World a-Coming* (New York: Arno Press and New York Times, 1968 [1943]).

30. William J. Wilson, *When Work Disappears: The World of the New Urban Poor* (New York: Knopf, 1996), 35.

31. Michael D. Woodard, *Black Entrepreneurs in America: Stories of Struggle and Success* (New Brunswick, N.J.: Rutgers University Press, 1997).

32. Joe T. Darden, Richard Hill, June Thomas, and Richard Thomas, *Detroit: Race and Uneven Development* (Philadelphia: Temple University Press, 1987), 170.

33. California Newsreel, *Race: The Power of an Illusion*, 2003, at www.pbs.org/race/000_ General/000_00-Home.htm (accessed April 16, 2010).

34. Richard F. Weingroff, "The Battle of Its Life," *Public Roads* 69, no. 6 (May/June 2006): 26–38.

35. Massey, "Origins of Economic Disparities," 74.

36. Jackson, *Crabgrass Frontier*, 217.

37. Drake and Cayton, *Black Metropolis*; William J. Wilson and Richard P. Taub, *There Goes the Neighborhood: Racial, Ethnic and Class Tensions in Four Chicago Neighborhoods and Their Meanings for America* (New York: Knopf, 2006).

38. Manning Marable, *How Capitalism Underdeveloped Black America: Problems in Race, Political Economy and Society* (Boston: South End Press, 1983); Butler, *Entrepreneurship and Self-help*; Jennifer L. Hochschild, "Rich and Poor African Americans," in *Multiculturalism in the United States: Current Issues, Contemporary Voices*, ed. Peter Kivisto and Georganne Rundblad, 193–207 (Thousand Oaks, Calif.: Pine Forge Press, 2000).

39. Roger Waldinger, *Still the Promised City? African-Americans and New Immigrants in Postindustrial New York* (Cambridge, Mass.: Harvard University Press, 1996); Minority Business Development Agency (MBDA), "Minority Business and Entrepreneurship," at ftp://ftp.mbda.gov/ntrepp.pdf.

40. John A. Williams, "Harlem Nightclubs," in *Harlem: A Community in Transition*, ed. John Henrik Clarke, 167–79 (New York: Citadel Press, 1964).

41. Massey and Denton, *American Apartheid*, 135.

42. Fine, *Violence in the Model City*; Kerner, *Report of the National Advisory Commission*.

43. Marta Tienda and Rebeca Raijman, "Immigrants' Income Packaging and Invisible Labor Force Activity," *Social Science Quarterly* 81, no. 1 (2000): 291–311; Massey and Denton, *American Apartheid*, 137; Steven J. Gold, "Chinese-Vietnamese Entrepreneurs in California," in *The New Asian Immigration in Los Angeles and Global Restructuring*, ed. Paul Ong, Edna Bonacich and Lucy Cheng, 196–226 (Philadelphia: Temple University Press, 1994).

44. Mary J. Fischer and Douglas S. Massey, "Residential Segregation and Ethnic Enterprise in U.S. Metropolitan Areas," *Social Problems* 47, no. 3 (August 2000): 416; Mario Luis Small and Monica McDermott, "The Presence of Organizational Resources in Poor Urban Neighborhoods: An Analysis of Average and Contextual Effects," *Social Forces* 84, no. 3 (2006): 1716.

45. Drake and Cayton, *Black Metropolis*, 434; Marable, *How Capitalism Underdeveloped Black America*.

46. Fischer and Massey, "Residential Segregation," 408.

47. Howard Aldrich and Albert J. Reiss Jr., "The Effect of Civil Disorders on Small Business in the Inner City," *Journal of Social Issues* 26, no. 1 (1970): 205.

48. Jennifer Lee, *Civility in the City: Blacks, Jews, and Koreans in Urban America* (Cambridge, Mass.: Harvard University Press, 2002).

49. Gary David, "Behind the Bulletproof Glass: Iraqi Chaldean Store Ownership in Metropolitan Detroit," in *Arab Detroit: From Margins to Mainstream*, ed. Nabeel Abraham and Andrew Shryock, 151–78 (Detroit: Wayne State University Press, 2000).

50. Ivan Light, *Ethnic Enterprise in America*, 2; Bruce Porter and Marvin Dunn, *The Miami Riot of 1980: Crossing the Bounds* (Lexington, Mass.: D.C. Heath, 1984), 175.

51. Darden et al., *Detroit*, 72.

52. Light, *Ethnic Enterprise in America*, 2.

53. Morris Janowitz, "Collective Racial Violence: A Contemporary History," in *Violence in America: Historical and Comparative Perspectives*, ed. Hugh Davis Graham and Ted Robert Gurr, 261–86, rev. ed. (Beverly Hills, Calif.: Sage, 1979).

54. Jonathan J. Bean, "'Burn, Baby Burn': Small Business in the Urban Riots of the 1960s," *Independent Review* 5, no. 2 (2000): 169.

55. CNN, "Mayor Pleads Innocent in 1969 Race Riot Death," July 24, 2001, at http://archives.cnn.com/2001/LAW/07/23/race.riot.hearing/index.html (accessed April 9, 2010).

56. James W. Loewen, *The Mississippi Chinese: Between Black and White* (Cambridge, Mass.: Harvard University Press, 1971), 174–75.

57. Bean, "'Burn, Baby Burn.'"

58. Gary T. Marx, "Two Cheers for the National Riot (Kerner) Commission Report," in *Black American*, ed. J. F. Szwed, 77–95 (New York: Basic Books, 1970).

59. Fine, *Violence in the Model City*, 300; Herman, "The Newark and Detroit 'Riots.'"

60. Hayden, "A Special Supplement."

61. Associated Press, "White Man Gets Life Term for Slaying Detroit Negro," *Miami News*, February 12, 1969, 29.

62. Edward C. Banfield, *The Unheavenly City Revised: A Revision of the Unheavenly City* (Boston: Little, Brown, 1974); Sears 2000; David O. Sears, "Urban Rioting in Los Angeles: A Comparison of 1965 with 1992," in *The Los Angeles Riots: Lessons for the Urban Future*, ed. Mark Baldassare, 237–55 (Boulder: Westview, 1994); Robert Blauner, *Racial Oppression in America* (New York: Harper & Row, 1972); Walter C. Farrell Jr. and James H. Johnson Jr., "Structural Violence as an Inducement to African American and Hispanic Participation in the Los Angeles Civil Disturbances of 1992," *Journal of Human Behavior in the Social Environment* 4, no. 4 (2001): 337–59; Fine, *Violence in the Model City*.

63. Hayden, "A Special Supplement"; Blauner, "Internal Colonialism."

64. Fine, *Violence in the Model City*; *New York Times*, "Excerpts from a Study to Determine the Characteristics of Negro Rioters," July 2, 1968; InChul Choi, "The South Side: The End of Korean Frontier?" in *Koreans in the Windy City: 100 Years of Korean Americans in the Chicago Area*, ed. Hyock Chun, Kwang Chung Kim, and Shin Kim, 109–33 (New Haven, Conn.: East Rock Institute, 2005).

65. Michael J. Rosenfeld, "Celebration, Politics, Selective Looting and Riots: A Micro Level Study of the Bulls Riot of 1992 in Chicago," *Social Problems* 44, no. 4 (1997): 483–502; Susan Olzak and Suzanne Shanahan, "Deprivation and Race Riots: An Extension of Spilerman's Analysis," *Social Force* 74, no. 3 (1996): 931–61; Stanley Lieberson and Arnold R. Silverman, "The Precipitants and Underlying Conditions of Race Riots," *American Sociological Review* 30, no. 6 (December 1965): 887–98; Fine, *Violence in the Model City*.

66. Olzak and Shanahan, "Deprivation and Race Riots," 942.

67. Aldrich and Reiss, "The Effect of Civil Disorders"; Alejandro Portes and Alex Stepick, *City on the Edge* (Berkeley: University of California Press, 1993); Fine, *Violence in the Model City*, 295–96; Rosenfeld, "Celebration, Politics," 485.

68. Fine, *Violence in the Model City*, 292.

69. Fine, *Violence in the Model City*, 295.

70. Fine, *Violence in the Model City*, 42, 293.

71. Fine, *Violence in the Model City*, 292; Richard A. Berk, "The Role of Ghetto Merchants in Civil Disorders" (PhD diss., Johns Hopkins University, 1970), 48, 163, 179.

72. Aldrich and Reiss, "The Effect of Civil Disorders," 203, 206.

73. Fine, *Violence in the Model City*, 352; Jeffrey M. Page, "Collective Violence and the Culture of Subordination: A Study of Participants in the July 1967 Riots in Newark and Detroit" (PhD diss., University of Michigan, 1968), 33, 47–48.

74. Edward T. Chang and Jeannette Diaz-Veizades, *Ethnic Peace in the American City: Building Communities in Los Angeles and Beyond* (New York: New York University Press, 1999), 26; Victor Merina, "A Story of Refugee Success Ended Tragically in Riots," *Los Angeles Times*, August 17, 1992.

75. Portes and Stepick, *City on the Edge*; Rosenfeld, "Celebration, Politics."

76. Fine, *Violence in the Model City*, 348–49; Herman, "The Newark and Detroit 'Riots'"; *New York Times*, "Excerpts from a Study."

77. Olzak and Shanahan, "Deprivation and Race Riots," 953.

78. Civil disorders recently taking place in the large public housing projects of France involving police brutality, unemployment, concentrated poverty, and racism are environmentally very similar to those that occurred in U.S. ghettos during the 1960s, even though conflict with merchants is not a major part of the French uprisings and other historical, economic, and cultural factors are quite different. Bernard Salanié, "The Riots in France: An Economist's View," June 11, 2006, at http://riotsfrance.ssrc.org/Salanie (accessed April 11, 2010).

79. Robert G. Weisbrod and Arthur Stein, *Bittersweet Encounter: The Afro-American and the American Jew* (Westport, Conn.: Negro Universities Press, 1970), 81.

80. Aldrich and Reiss, "The Effect of Civil Disorders," 198.

81. William J. Wilson, *The Truly Disadvantaged* (Chicago: University of Chicago Press, 1987), 40.

82. James H. Johnson Jr., Cloyzelle K. Jones, Walter C. Farrell Jr., and Melvin L. Oliver, "The Los Angeles Rebellion: A Retrospective View," *Economic Development Quarterly* 6, no. 4 (November 1992): 359, 362; Fine, *Violence in the Model City*, 458; Wilson, *The Truly Disadvantaged*.

83. Farrell and Johnson, "Structural Violence."

84. M. Waters, *Black Identities* (New York: Russell Sage Foundation and Harvard University Press, 1999); Roger Waldinger and Michael I. Lichter, *How the Other Half Works: Immigration and the Social Organization of Labor* (Berkeley: University of California Press, 2003); Farrell and Johnson, "Structural Violence."

85. Wilson, *The Truly Disadvantaged*; Wilson, *When Work Disappears*.

86. Camillo Jose Vergara, *The New American Ghetto* (New Brunswick, N.J.: Rutgers University Press, 1997).

87. Cheryl Lynn Greenberg, *Troubling the Waters: Black-Jewish Relations in the American Century* (Princeton, N.J.: Princeton University Press, 2006); Weisbrod and Stein, *Bittersweet Encounter*.

88. Waldinger, *Still the Promised City?*

89. Judd L. Teller, "Negroes and Jews: A Hard Look," *Conservative Judaism* 21, no. 1 (fall 1966): 13–20; Max Geltman, "The Negro-Jewish Confrontation," *National Review*, June 28, 1966, 621–23; Weisbrod and Stein, *Bittersweet Encounter*, 81.

90. Waldinger, *Still the Promised City?*

91. Herman, "The Newark and Detroit 'Riots.'"

92. Jonathan Rieder, *Canarsie: The Jews and Italians of Brooklyn against Liberalism* (Cambridge, Mass.: Harvard University Press, 1985); Maria C. Lizzi, "'My Heart Is as Black as Yours': White Backlash, Racial Identity and Italian American Stereotypes in New York City's 1969 Mayoral Campaign," *Journal of American Ethnic History* 27, no. 3 (2008): 43–80;

Bean, "'Burn, Baby Burn'"; Aldrich and Reiss, "The Effect of Civil Disorders," 201. For example, during the early 1960s, Norman Podhoretz—who would go on to be a leader of the neoconservative movement—wrote openly about his fear and resentment of blacks in an essay called "My Negro Problem—and Ours" (*Commentary*, February 1963, 93–101).

93. Aldrich and Reiss, "The Effect of Civil Disorders," 193–94.

94. Illsoo Kim, *New Urban Immigrants: The Korean Community in New York* (Princeton, N.J.: Princeton University Press, 1981); Robert Mark Silverman, *Doing Business in Minority Markets: Black and Korean Entrepreneurs in Chicago's Ethnic Beauty Aids Industry* (New York: Garland, 2000); Pyong Gap Min, *Caught in the Middle: Korean Communities in New York and Los Angeles* (Berkeley: University of California Press, 1996); Mary C. Sengstock, *Chaldean-Americans: Changing Conceptions of Ethnic Identity*, 2nd ed. (Staten Island, N.Y.: Center for Migration Studies, 1999).

95. Raphael J. Sonenshein, "The Battle over Liquor Stores in South Central Los Angeles: Management of an Interminority Conflict," *Urban Affairs Review* 31, no. 6 (1996): 710–37; Min, *Caught in the Middle*; Kim, *New Urban Immigrants*. "Our own field observations showed that Chinese grocers tended to be more often rude [to black customers] than black grocers." Charles Choy Wong, "Black and Chinese Grocery Stores in Los Angeles' Black Ghetto," *Urban Life* 5, no. 4 (1977): 454.

96. Min, *Caught in the Middle*; Kim, *New Urban Immigrants*.

97. Robert Fairlie and Alicia M. Robb, *Race and Entrepreneurial Success: Black-, Asian-, and White-Owned Businesses in the United States* (Cambridge, Mass.: MIT Press, 2008), 182–88.

98. Conley, *Being Black*, 140.

99. Conley, *Being Black*, 140. One exception to this trend was musicians. Producers like Berry Gordy and artists like James Brown escaped from the control of white producers and record companies (many of whom where members of the same ethnic groups as ghetto entrepreneurs) in an attempt to achieve economic independence. Blues artists including Chester Burnett (Howlin' Wolf) and Willie Dixon successfully sued producers for millions of dollars' worth of royalties. Brian Ward, *Just My Soul Responding: Rhythm and Blues, Black Consciousness, and Race Relation* (Berkeley: University of California Press, 1998).

100. William K. Tabb, *The Political Economy of the Black Ghetto* (New York: Norton, 1970).

101. Marable, *How Capitalism Underdeveloped Black America*, 166–67.

102. Butler, *Entrepreneurship and Self-help*, 274.

103. Juliette Walker, *The History of Black Business in America: Capitalism, Race, Entrepreneurship* (New York: Macmillan Library Reference, 1998); Conley, *Being Black*.

104. Rick Perlstein, *Nixonland: The Rise of a President and the Fracturing of America* (New York: Scribners, 2008).

105. John T. Woolley and Gerhard Peters, "Richard Nixon: Statement About a National Program for Minority Business Enterprise," American Presidency Project, University of California–Santa Barbara, March 5, 1969, at www.presidency.ucsb.edu/ws/index.php?pid=1943 (accessed April 11, 2010).

106. Timothy Bates, *Race, Self-Employment, and Upward Mobility: An Illusive American Dream* (Baltimore: Johns Hopkins University Press, 1997); Woodard, *Black Entrepreneurs in America*.

107. The Equal Opportunity Loan (EOL) program provided loans directly to entrepreneurs that were "socially and economically" disadvantaged. The SBA 7(a) program guaranteed bank loans made to small minority and nonminority businesses and is credited with

giving black business owners access to commercial bank loans for the first time. In contrast to the EOL program, which was directed toward very small-scale businesses, the 7(a) program "targeted larger and more promising businesses, such as manufacturing, wholesale and large retail enterprises." Unfortunately, both programs were marked by high failure rates: 26.4 percent for 7(a) and over 50 percent for EOL. A third SBA program, the Minority Enterprise Small Business Investment Companies (MESBIC), involved a series of government-funded but privately owned and managed venture capital corporations that offered ethnic entrepreneurs investment capital, loan guarantees, and management assistance. It too suffered from limited resources and had little impact. Woodard, *Black Entrepreneurs in America*, 26.

108. Ivan Light and Edna Bonacich, *Immigrant Entrepreneurs* (Berkeley: University of California Press, 1988), 267.

109. Bates, *Race, Self-Employment*, 173.

110. Hugh Davis Graham, *Collision Course: The Strange Convergence of Affirmative Action and Immigration Policy in America* (New York: Oxford University Press, 2002), 89.

111. Woodard, *Black Entrepreneurs in America*, 29.

112. Woodard, *Black Entrepreneurs in America*, 28.

113. MBDA, "Minority Business and Entrepreneurship," 6.

114. Fairlie and Robb discuss the cost and the controversy associated with these business development programs: "Relatively little is known" about the effectiveness of set-aside programs, and "more research is clearly needed." Fairlie and Robb, *Race and Entrepreneurial Success*, 184.

115. Waldinger, *Still the Promised City?*

116. Waldinger, *Still the Promised City?*; Timothy Bates, "The Urban Development Potential of Black-Owned Businesses," *Journal of the American Planning Association* 72, no. 2 (2006): 227–37; Harper and Reskin, "Affirmative Action at School."

117. Timothy Bates, William E. Jackson III, and James H. Johnson Jr., "Advancing Research on Minority Entrepreneurship," *Annals of the American Academy of Political and Social Science* 613 (September 2007): 10–17.

118. Philip Kasinitz, *Caribbean New York: Black Immigrants and the Politics of Race* (Ithaca, N.Y.: Cornell University Press, 1992).

119. By 1980, a majority of black college graduates "held jobs tied to federal government spending." M. D. Pohlmann, *Black Politics in Conservative America* (New York: Longman, 1990), 45. "In Los Angeles, as in all cities across America, African Americans have been overrepresented in government employment. About one-fourth of all black men and nearly one-third of all black women in the Los Angeles region worked for the government in 1970, 1980, and 1990." By 1990, these jobs were highly professionalized and well paid, employing a third of college-educated black men and 43 percent of college-educated black women. Government was unable to offer many opportunities for less educated blacks because the public sector has little need of workers lacking a high school diploma. Oliver Grant and James 1996, 398–400.

120. Timothy Bates, "Minority Business Access to Mainstream Markets," *Journal of Urban Affairs* 23, no. 1 (2001): 41–56.

121. CBS Chicago, "Mayor Daley Names New Contract Overseer," January 2, 2008, at http://cbs2chicago.com/politics/chief.procurement.officer.2.621857.html (accessed April 16, 2010).

122. Fran Spielman, "Public Building Chief Is in Line for New Job: Gayles Boosted Minority Participation," *Chicago Sun-Times*, October 3, 2007.

123. Bates, "The Urban Development Potential," 235.

124. Michigan Minority Supplier Development Council, home page, at www.mmbdc.com/.

125. Marilyn Gittell, Kathe Newman, Janice Bockmeyer, and Robert Lindsay, "Expanding Civic Opportunity: Urban Empowerment Zones," *Urban Affairs Review* 33, no. 4 (1998): 530–31.

126. HUD User, "Interim Assessment of the Empowerment Zones and Enterprise Communities (EZ/EC) Program," U.S. Department of Housing and Urban Development, Washington, D.C., 2005, at www.huduser.org/.

127. HUD User, "Interim Assessment."

128. Bates, "The Urban Development Potential," 234.

129. Bárbara J. Robles and Héctor Cordero-Guzmán, "Latino Self-Employment and Entrepreneurship in the United States: An Overview of the Literature and Data Sources," *Annals of the American Academy of Political and Social Science* 613 (2007): 18–31; Bates, "The Urban Development Potential"; Bates, Jackson, and Johnson, "Advancing Research."

130. Cedric Herring, Hayward D. Horton, and Melvin E. Thomas, "Inner-City Entrepreneurship: Is Self-Employment a Cure for Poverty?" in *The New Politics of Race: From Du Bois to the 21st Century*, ed. Marlese Durr, 89–111 (Westport, Conn.: Praeger, 2002), 108.

131. Bates, "The Urban Development Potential," 231.

132. Bates, "The Urban Development Potential," 231.

133. Bates, "The Urban Development Potential"; Bates, Jackson, and Johnson, "Advancing Research."

134. Harper and Reskin, "Affirmative Action at School," 361.

135. Harper and Reskin, "Affirmative Action at School," 361.

136. Ellis Cose, "A Decade of Proposition 209: Debate Sidelines the Real Issue," *San Francisco Chronicle*, November 6, 2006.

137. Discrimination Research Center, "Free to Compete," Berkeley, Calif., 2006, 4.

138. Woodard, *Black Entrepreneurs in America*, 27.

139. Boston Consulting Group, "The New Agenda for Minority Business Development," 2005, at www.kauffman.org/uploadedfiles/minority_entrep_62805_report.pdf (accessed April 9, 2010), 7.

140. Insight Center for Community Economic Development, "The Evolution of Affirmative Action: An Executive Summary of the Research Series: Best Practices, Imperfections, and Challenges in State Inclusive Business Programs," Oakland, Calif., November 2007, at www.insightcced.org/uploads/publications/assets/The%20Evolution%20of%20Affirmative%20Action.pdf (accessed April 10, 2010), 3.

141. Boston Consulting Group, "The New Agenda," 7; Mike Bergman and Mark Tolbert, "Minority Groups Increasing Business Ownership at Higher Rates than National Average, Census Bureau Reports," U.S. Census Bureau, July 28, 2005.

142. Fulbright, "Connerly Gearing Up."

143. Harry Stein, "Racial-Preference Ballots Go National: Initiatives in Four States Could Shape the Presidential Election," *City Journal*, April 16, 2008.

144. Peter Schmidt, "Michigan Overwhelmingly Adopts Ban on Affirmative-Action Preferences," *Chronicle of Higher Education*, November 17, 2006; Stein, "Racial-Preference Ballots."

145. William J. Wilson, *The Bridge over the Racial Divide: Rising Inequality and Coalition Politics* (Berkeley: University of California Press and Russell Sage Foundation, 1999), 20.

146. Discrimination Research Center, "Free to Compete," 3.

147. Insight Center for Community Economic Development, "The Evolution of Affirmative Action," 4.

148. Harper and Reskin, "Affirmative Action at School."

149. Insight Center for Community Economic Development, "The Evolution of Affirmative Action," 4.

150. Conley, *Being Black*, 138.

151. Conley, *Being Black*, 143.

CHAPTER 6

1. James H. Johnson Jr., Cloyzelle K. Jones, Walter C. Farrell Jr., and Melvin L. Oliver, "The Los Angeles Rebellion: A Retrospective View," *Economic Development Quarterly* 6, no. 4 (November 1992): 356–72.

2. Steven J. Gold, "Immigrant Entrepreneurs and Customers throughout the 20th Century," in *Not Just Black and White: Historical and Contemporary Perspectives on Immigration, Race and Ethnicity in the United States*, ed. Nancy Foner and George M. Fredrickson, 315–40 (New York: Russell Sage Foundation, 2004).

3. Ivan Light, *Deflecting Immigration: Networks, Markets and Regulation in Los Angeles* (New York: Russell Sage Foundation, 2006); Nancy Foner, *From Ellis Island to JFK: New York's Two Great Waves of Immigration* (New Haven, Conn.: Yale University Press, 2000).

4. Nancy Gibbs, "Shades of Difference," *Time*, November 18, 1991; Light, *Deflecting Immigration*; J. Horton, with J. Calderon, M. Pardo, L. Saito, L. Shaw, and Y. Tseng, *The Politics of Diversity: Immigration, Resistance, and Change in Monterey Park, California* (Philadelphia: Temple University Press, 1995); Anh K. Tran, "Economic Base of the Vietnamese Community in the Los Angeles and Orange County Area," Department of Asian-American Studies, University of California, Los Angeles, 1986.

5. Otto Friedrich, "The Changing Face of America," *Time*, July 8, 1985.

6. Ali Stanton, "Koreans Open BBQ Business in Harlem," *Amsterdam News*, April 27, 1985, 36.

7. Nathan Caplan, Marcella H. Choy, and John K. Whitmore, "Indochinese Refugee Families and Academic Achievement," *Scientific American* 266, no. 2 (February 1992): 36–42.

8. Andrew Greeley, *Ethnicity in the U.S.* (New York: Wiley, 1974).

9. Nancy Foner, Rubén G. Rumbaut, and Steven J. Gold, "Immigration and Immigration Research in the United States," in *Immigration Research for a New Century: Multidisciplinary Perspectives*, ed. Nancy Foner, Rubén G. Rumbaut, and Steven J. Gold, 1–19 (New York: Russell Sage Foundation, 2000).

10. Accordingly, during these periods, the government was ready to address conditions in inner-city neighborhoods, promote equality, and provide entrepreneurs' and customers' groups with educational and career opportunities beyond running small businesses in ghettos.

11. Bruce Porter and Marvin Dunn, *The Miami Riot of 1980: Crossing the Bounds* (Lexington, Mass.: D.C. Heath, 1984), 175.

12. Alejandro Portes and Robert D. Manning, "The Immigrant Enclave: Theory and Empirical Examples," in *Ethnicity: Structure and Process*, ed. J. Nagel and S. Olzak, 47–68 (New York: Academic Press, 1986); Ivan Light and Steven J. Gold, *Ethnic Economies* (San Diego: Academic Press, 2000); Roger Waldinger, Howard Aldrich, Robin Ward, et al., *Ethnic Entrepreneurs: Immigrant Business in Industrial Societies* (Newbury Park, Calif.: Sage, 1990).

13. Pyong Gap Min, *Ethnic Solidarity for Economic Survival* (New York: Russell Sage Foundation, 2008); In Jin Yoon, *On My Own: Korean Businesses and Race Relations in America* (Chicago: University of Chicago Press, 1997).

14. William J. Wilson and Richard P. Taub, *There Goes the Neighborhood: Racial, Ethnic and Class Tensions in Four Chicago Neighborhoods and Their Meanings for America* (New York: Knopf, 2006).

15. Raphael J. Sonenshein, "The Battle over Liquor Stores in South Central Los Angeles: Management of an Interminority Conflict," *Urban Affairs Review* 31, no. 6 (1996): 710–37; Jennifer Lee, *Civility in the City: Blacks, Jews, and Koreans in Urban America* (Cambridge, Mass.: Harvard University Press, 2002).

16. Ivan Light, Hadas Har-Chvi, and Kenneth Kan, "Black/Korean Conflict in Los Angles," in *Managing Divided Cities*, ed. Seamus Dunn, 74–87 (Keele, UK: Keele University Press, 1994).

17. Claire Jean Kim, *Bitter Fruit: The Politics of Black-Korean Conflict in New York City* (New Haven, Conn.: Yale University Press, 2000); Patrick D. Joyce, *No Fire Next Time: Black-Korean Conflicts and the Future of America's Cities* (Ithaca, N.Y.: Cornell University Press, 2003); John Lie, "The Black-Asian Conflict?" in *Not Just Black and White: Historical and Contemporary Perspectives on Immigration, Race and Ethnicity in the United States*, ed. Nancy Foner and George M. Fredrickson, 301–14 (New York: Russell Sage Foundation, 2004).

18. William J. Wilson, *When Work Disappears: The World of the New Urban Poor* (New York: Knopf, 1996); Reynolds Farley, Sheldon Danziger, and Harry J. Holzer, *Detroit Divided: A Volume in the Multi-City of Urban Inequality* (New York: Russell Sage Foundation, 2000).

19. Sam Roberts, "White Flight Reversed," *New York Times*, September 23, 2008.

20. While population growth is often associated with some degree of affluence, Miami and El Paso appears to be an exception to this trend as these cities exhibit both significant increases in population and are among the ten poorest large cities in the United States. Light, *Deflecting Immigration*; Min, *Ethnic Solidarity*.

21. Frank D. Bean and Gillian Stevens, *America's Newcomers and the Dynamics of Diversity*, American Sociological Association's Rose Series in Sociology (New York: Russell Sage Foundation, 2003).

22. Julia Preston, "Decline Seen in Numbers of People Here Illegally," *New York Times*, July 31, 2008.

23. A significant fraction of refugees placed elsewhere became secondary migrants as they relocated to major points of coethnic concentration soon after arrival. Gold 1992.

24. William J. Wilson, *The Truly Disadvantaged* (Chicago: University of Chicago Press, 1987); Roger Waldinger and Mehdi Bozorgmehr, eds., *Ethnic Los Angeles* (New York: Russell Sage Foundation, 1996).

25. Roger Waldinger and Michael I. Lichter, *How the Other Half Works: Immigration and the Social Organization of Labor* (Berkeley: University of California Press, 2003); M. Waters, *Black Identities* (New York: Russell Sage Foundation and Harvard University Press, 1999).

26. Philip Kasinitz, *Caribbean New York: Black Immigrants and the Politics of Race* (Ithaca, N.Y.: Cornell University Press, 1992); Steven J. Gold and Ivan Light, "Ethnic Economies and Social Policy," *Research in Social Movements, Conflicts and Change* 22 (summer 2000): 165–91.

27. Roger Waldinger, *Still the Promised City? African-Americans and New Immigrants in Postindustrial New York* (Cambridge, Mass.: Harvard University Press, 1996).

28. Marc Ballon, "A Hole in Their Dreams: Ambitious Immigrants Found Success with Doughnut Shops, but Now Big Chains Are Eating Away Their Profits," *Los Angeles Times*, April 7, 2002.

29. Victoria Malkin, "Who's behind the Counter? Retail Workers in New York City," in *Becoming New Yorkers: Ethnographies of the New Second Generation*, ed. Philip Kasinitz, John H. Mollenkopf, and Mary C. Waters, 115–53 (New York: Russell Sage Foundation, 2004).

30. Robert Mark Silverman, *Doing Business in Minority Markets: Black and Korean Entrepreneurs in Chicago's Ethnic Beauty Aids Industry* (New York: Garland, 2000).

31. Steven J. Gold, "Chinese-Vietnamese Entrepreneurs in California," in *The New Asian Immigration in Los Angeles and Global Restructuring*, ed. Paul Ong, Edna Bonacich, and Lucy Cheng, 196–226 (Philadelphia: Temple University Press, 1994); Pyong Gap Min, *Caught in the Middle: Korean Communities in New York and Los Angeles* (Berkeley: University of California Press, 1996).

32. Timothy P. Fong, *The Contemporary Asian American Experience: Beyond the Model Minority* (Upper Saddle River, N.J.: Prentice Hall, 1998), 52.

33. Min, *Caught in the Middle*; Bean and Stevens, *America's Newcomers*; Bernard Wong, *Ethnicity and Entrepreneurship: The New Chinese Immigrants in the San Francisco Bay Area* (Boston: Allyn & Bacon, 1998).

34. Richard Lacayo, "Immigration: Give Me Your Rich, Your Lucky . . . ," *Time*, October 14, 1991.

35. Johanna Lessinger, *From the Ganges to the Hudson: Indian Immigrants in New York City* (Boston: Allyn & Bacon, 1996); Portes and Manning, "The Immigrant Enclave."

36. Alejandro Portes, "The Social Origins of the Cuban Enclave Economy of Miami," *Sociological Perspectives* 30, no. 4 (1987): 340–72.

37. These underlie ethnic growth machines that draw on both U.S.-based and international resources to develop ethnic business districts like those in Little Saigon, Monterey Park, Little India, and Koreatown in Los Angeles; Flushing and Jackson Heights in New York City; Devon in Chicago; Dearborn, Michigan; and other areas.

38. Light, *Deflecting Immigration*.

39. Min, *Ethnic Solidarity*; Dae Young Kim, "Leaving the Ethnic Economy: The Rapid Integration of Second-Generation Korean Americans in New York," in *Becoming New Yorkers: Ethnographies of the New Second Generation*, ed. Philip Kasinitz, John H. Mollenkopf, and Mary C. Waters, 154–88 (New York: Russell Sage Foundation, 2004).

40. Sumi K. Cho, "Korean Americans vs. African Americans: Conflicts and Construction," in *Reading Rodney King, Reading Urban Uprising*, ed. Robert Gooding-Williams, 196–211 (New York: Routledge, 1993); Gary David, "Behind the Bulletproof Glass: Iraqi Chaldean Store Ownership in Metropolitan Detroit," in *Arab Detroit: From Margins to Mainstream*, ed. Nabeel Abraham and Andrew Shryock, 151–78 (Detroit: Wayne State University Press, 2000); Steven J. Gold and Mehdi Bozorgmehr, "Middle East and North Africa," in *The New Americans: A Guide to Immigration since 1965*, ed. Mary Waters and Reed Ueda with Helen B. Marrow, 518–33 (Cambridge, Mass.: Harvard University Press, 2007).

41. Irving Spiegel, "Survey Finds Blacks Own Most Harlem Stores," *New York Times*, September 16, 1968; Cain 1985.

42. Min, *Caught in the Middle*, 67; Silverman, *Doing Business*, 95.

43. InChul Choi, "The South Side: The End of Korean Frontier?" in *Koreans in the Windy City: 100 Years of Korean Americans in the Chicago Area*, ed. Hyock Chun, Kwang Chung Kim, and Shin Kim, 109–33 (New Haven, Conn.: East Rock Institute, 2005), 111.

44. Yoon, *On My Own*; Min, *Caught in the Middle*.

45. Gary David, "Intercultural Relations across the Counter: An Interactional Analysis of In Situ Service Encounters" (unpublished PhD diss., Wayne State University, Department of Sociology, 1999); David, "Behind the Bulletproof Glass."

46. Mary C. Sengstock, *Chaldean-Americans: Changing Conceptions of Ethnic Identity*, 2nd ed. (Staten Island, N.Y.: Center for Migration Studies, 1999), 49; Sidney Fine, *Violence in the Model City: The Cavanaugh Administration, Race Relations, and the Detroit Riot of 1967* (Ann Arbor: University of Michigan Press, 1989).

47. Porter and Dunn, *The Miami Riot of 1980*, 195–96.

48. Paul Ong, Kye Y. Park, and Y. Tong, "Korean-Black Conflict and the State," in *The New Asian Immigration in Los Angeles and Global Restructuring*, ed. Paul Ong, Edna Bonacich, and Lucie Cheng, 264–94 (Philadelphia: Temple University Press, 1994), 267.

49. Choi, "The South Side," 113.

50. Yoon, *On My Own*, 119.

51. Illsoo Kim, *New Urban Immigrants: The Korean Community in New York* (Princeton, N.J.: Princeton University Press, 1981).

52. Yoon, *On My Own*, 121.

53. Lee, *Civility in the City*, 18.

54. Min, *Ethnic Solidarity*, 85.

55. Kim, *Bitter Fruit*, 196; Lee, *Civility in the City*.

56. Lee, *Civility in the City*; David, "Behind the Bulletproof Glass."

57. "Koreans exploit blacks, they reduce blacks' opportunities to own their own businesses, their presence constitutes an "economic invasion" of the black community and drain blacks' resources." Min, *Caught in the Middle*, 111, tab. 10.

58. Elijah Anderson, *Streetwise* (Chicago: University of Chicago Press, 1990), 61.

59. David H. Kaplan and Bessie House-Soremekun, "Race, Space, Crime, and the African American Entrepreneur: Business Owner Attitudes, Business Success, and the Neighborhood Context," in *Landscapes of the Ethnic Economy*, ed. David H. Kaplan and Wei Lei, 67–82 (Lanham, Md.: Rowman & Littlefield, 2006); Lee, *Civility in the City*.

60. Rudy Cain, "Black Community under Siege," *New York Amsterdam News*, May 16, 1987, 13.

61. Concerning this, Harold Cruse wrote, "When we speak of Negro social disabilities under capitalism . . . we refer to the fact that he does not own anything—even what is ownable in his own community. Thus to fight for Black liberation is to fight for his right to own." Quoted in Robert Blauner, *Racial Oppression in America* (New York: Harper & Row, 1972), 86–87.

62. Manning Marable, *The Great Wells of Democracy: The Meaning of Race in American Life* (New York: Basic Civitas Books, 2002), 205.

63. During the period of the boycott, the offending clothing store was set on fire, with the flames spreading to a black- and a Korean-owned shop as well. Worried that bad relations with customers put all Korean entrepreneurs at risk, the owner of the new store went out of business and was compensated by fellow Korean business owners. Yoon, *On My Own*, 176–77.

64. Wilbert A. Tatum, "Editorials: Blacks, Jews—A Turning Point," *New York Amsterdam News*, October 5, 1985, 12.

65. Cain, "Black Community under Siege"; John Sibley Butler, *Entrepreneurship and Self-help among Black Americans* (Albany: State University of New York Press, 1991); Marable, *The Great Wells of Democracy*; Walker 2005.

66. Porter and Dunn, *The Miami Riot of 1980*; Fine, *Violence in the Model City*; Lee, *Civility in the City*.

67. Thomas Sowell, *Black Rednecks and White Liberals* (San Francisco: Encounter Books, 2005); Jonathan J. Bean, "'Burn, Baby Burn': Small Business in the Urban Riots of the 1960s," *Independent Review* 5, no. 2 (2000): 165–87; Max Arthur Herman, *Fighting in the Streets: Ethnic Succession and Urban Unrest in Twentieth Century America* (New York: Peter Lang, 2005).

68. Marlon T. Riggs, *Ethnic Notions*, videorecording (San Francisco: California Newsreel, 1987).

69. Regina Freer, "Black-Korean Conflict," in *The Los Angeles Riots: Lessons for the Urban Future*, edited by Mark Baldassare, 175–204 (Boulder, Colo.: Westview, 1994), 191, cited in Bean, "'Burn, Baby Burn,'" 180–81.

70. David O. Sears, "Urban Rioting in Los Angeles: A Comparison of 1965 with 1992," in *The Los Angeles Riots: Lessons for the Urban Future*, ed. Mark Baldassare, 237–55 (Boulder, Colo.: Westview, 1994).

71. Choi, "The South Side"; Lee, *Civility in the City*.

72. For example, in their analysis of residents in neighborhoods associated with the Miami riots of 1980, Robert Ladner and colleagues found that, while more that 85 percent of local residents thought that police brutality was a serious problem, only about half as many (48 percent or fewer) thought that anger with local businessmen was a problem. Robert A. Ladner, Barry J. Schwartz, Sandra J. Roker, and Loretta S. Titterud, "The Miami Riots of 1980: Antecedent Conditions, Community Responses and Participant Characteristics," *Research in Social Movements, Conflict and Change* 4 (1981): 195, tab. 9. Similarly, from surveys conducted in New York City in 1992, Min found that African Americans' support for boycotts of Korean stores was below 27 percent. Min, *Caught in the Middle*.

73. Alison Mitchell, "The Crown Heights Report: From Earliest Hours, Calls Were Ignored," *New York Times*, July 21, 1993.

74. Unlike the recent riots in Los Angeles, the disturbances in Washington Heights produced little significant damage to businesses, other than the Hongs' and a handful of smaller shops. No federal declaration of disaster has been issued, and no emergency assistance is available. Jane Fritsch, "Looters' Booty: A Dream; Korean Immigrants' Harlem Store Is Plundered," *New York Times*, July 18, 1992; CNN, "Protesters Loot, Set Fires in Cincinnati," April 11, 2001, at http://archives.cnn.com/2001/US/04/10/cincinnati.protest.04 (accessed April 19, 2010); Michael B. Katz, "Why Don't American Cities Burn Very Often," *Journal of Urban History* 34 (2008): 185–208.

75. See, for example, Anti-Defamation League, "Farrakhan in His Own Words: On Jews," at www.adl.org/special_reports/farrakhan_own_words2/on_jews.asp (accessed April 19, 2010). Anti-Semitic activists apply the same technique to the denigration of Jews. See http://radioislam.com; Marable, *The Great Wells of Democracy*; Kim, *Bitter Fruit*.

76. Marable, *The Great Wells of Democracy*, 216.

77. Min, *Caught in the Middle*; Min, *Ethnic Solidarity*; Light, Har-Chvi, and Kan, "Black/Korean Conflict"; Herman, *Fighting in the Streets*, 170–72.

78. Kim, *Bitter Fruit*, 7.

79. Alejandro Portes and Robert Bach, *Latin Journey: Cuban and Mexican Immigrants in the United States* (Berkeley: University of California Press, 1985); Light and Gold, *Ethnic Economies*; Waldinger et al., *Ethnic Entrepreneurs*.

80. Sonenshein, "The Battle over Liquor Stores"; Yoon, *On My Own*; Min, *Caught in the Middle*; David, "Intercultural Relations"; Marable, *The Great Wells of Democracy*.

81. Joel Kurth and Delores Patterson, "Boycott Targets Arabs," *Detroit News*, August 1, 2001.

82. Marable, *The Great Wells of Democracy*, 208–9.

83. Marable, *The Great Wells of Democracy*; Kurth and Patterson, "Boycott Targets Arabs."

84. Min, *Ethnic Solidarity*, 76.

85. Min, *Ethnic Solidarity*; Silverman, *Doing Business*.

86. Min, *Ethnic Solidarity*; Tran, "Economic Base of the Vietnamese"; Gold and Bozorg-mehr, "Middle East."

87. Kim, *New Urban Immigrants*, 118.

88. Paul James Rutledge, *The Vietnamese Experience in America* (Bloomington: Indiana University Press, 1992).

89. Claiming the proposition to be unconstitutional, the mayor publically tore it up. Tran, "Economic Base of the Vietnamese."

90. Horton et al., *The Politics of Diversity*, 85.

91. Foner, *From Ellis Island to JFK*.

92. Gold and Bozorgmehr, "Middle East."

93. Min, *Ethnic Solidarity*.

94. Greta Guest and Victoria Turk, "The Quality of Urban Life: Food Violations Higher in Detroit, Buyers Face a Commute for Groceries," *Detroit Free Press*, October 24, 2004.

95. Joe T. Darden and Steven J. Gold, "The Impact of Proposal 2 on the Survival of Minority- and Women-Owned New Firms in Michigan," *Michigan Applied Public Policy Research Report*, East Lansing, July 2008.

96. Edward T. Chang and Jeannette Diaz-Veizades, *Ethnic Peace in the American City: Building Communities in Los Angeles and Beyond* (New York: New York University Press, 1999), 81; Ken Ellington and K. Connie Kang, "A Student, a Shopkeeper and a Moment of Tragedy Slaying," *Los Angeles Times*, November 23, 1996.

97. Lucie Cheng and Yen Le Espiritu, "Korean Business in Black and Hispanic Neighbor-hoods: A Study of Intergroup Relations," *Sociological Perspectives* 32, no. 4 (1989): 521–34.

98. During the Los Angeles Riot of 1992, more immigrants—mostly Latinos—were arrested for violence and looting than were blacks. However, this number may not reflect actual rates of criminality. Rather, observers suggested that police were reluctant to arrest African Americans because, as English-speaking U.S. citizens, they were more likely to resist the criminal justice system than undocumented Latinos who had few options for recourse. Joan Petersilia and Allan Abrahamse, "A Profile of Those Arrested," in *The Los Angeles Ri-ots: Lessons for the Urban Future*, ed. Mark Baldassare, 135–47 (Boulder, Colo.: Westview, 1994); Yoon, *On My Own*; Min, *Caught in the Middle*; Sears, "Urban Rioting in Los Angeles"; Ewa Morawska, "Immigrant-Black Dissension in American Cities: An Argument for Multiple Explanations," in *Problem of the Century: Racial Stratification in the United States*, ed. Eli-jah Anderson and Douglas Massey, 47–96 (New York: Russell Sage Foundation, 2001); Lee, *Civility in the City*.

99. Herbert Blumer, "Race Relations as a Sense of Group Position," *Pacific Sociologi-cal Review* 1 (1958): 3–7. Lawrence Bobo and Vincent L. Hutchings, "Perceptions of Racial Competition in a Multiracial Setting," *American Sociological Review* 61 (December 1996): 951–72.

100. Steven J. Gold, "Patterns of Economic Cooperation among Israeli Immigrants in Los Angeles," *International Migration Review* 28, no. 105 (1994): 114–35; Gold, "Chinese-Vietnamese Entrepreneurs"; Dae Young Kim, "Beyond Coethnic Solidarity: Mexican and Ecuadorian Employment in Korean-Owned Businesses in New York City," *Racial and Ethnic Studies* 22, no. 3 (1999): 581–605; Waldinger and Lichter, *How the Other Half Works*.

101. Nathan Glazer and Daniel Patrick Moynihan, *Beyond the Melting Pot* (Cambridge, Mass.: MIT Press, 1963); Alex Stepick, *Pride against Prejudice: Haitians in the United States* (Boston: Allyn & Bacon, 1998); L. E. Guarnizo, "The Mexican Ethnic Economy in Los Angeles: Capitalist Accumulation, Class Restructuring, and the Transnationalization of Migration" (working paper, California Communities Program, University of California, Davis, 1998); Cheikh Anta Mbacke Babou, "Brotherhood Solidarity, Education and Migration: The Role of the Dahira in the Economy of the Murid Immigrant Community of New York," *Les Journées de l'IISM, "l'Internationalisation du religieux, Réseaux et politiques de l'Islam Africain,"* Ecoles des Hautes Etudes en Sciences Sociales, Paris, 1, 2, 3, mars., 2001; Marta Tienda and Rebeca Raijman, "Immigrants' Income Packaging and Invisible Labor Force Activity," *Social Science Quarterly* 81, no. 1 (2000): 291–311.

102. Light, Har-Chvi, and Kan, "Black/Korean Conflict"; Jack Katz, *Seductions of Crime* (New York: Basic Books, 1988); Martin Sanchez-Jankowski, *Islands in the Street* (Berkeley: University of California Press, 1992); Light and Gold, *Ethnic Economies*; Alejandro Portes and Alex Stepick, *City on the Edge* (Berkeley: University of California Press, 1993).

103. Janny Scott, "Rethinking Segregation beyond Black and White," *New York Times*, July 29, 2001, sec. 4, 1; Massey and Denton 1993.

104. Francois Nielsen, "Towards a Theory of Ethnic Solidarity in Modern Societies," *American Sociological Review* 50, no. 2 (1985): 133–49.

105. José A. Cobas and Jorge Duany, *Cubans in Puerto Rico: Ethnic Economy and Cultural Identity* (Gainesville: University Press of Florida, 1997), 43–44.

106. Margaret M. Chin, *Sewing Women: Immigrants and the New York City Garment Industry* (New York: Columbia University Press, 2005), 149.

107. Robert C. Smith, "Transnational Migrants and Community Formation," Social Science History Association Annual Meeting, Chicago, November 16, 1995; Portes and Stepick, *City on the Edge*.

108. Cain, "Black Community under Siege," 13; Min, *Caught in the Middle*; Stepick, *Pride against Prejudice*; Waters, *Black Identities*.

109. Sameer Y. Abraham and Nabeel Abraham, eds., *Arabs in the New World* (Detroit: Wayne State University Center for Urban Studies, 1983).

110. Norman Sinclair, "Gas Price War Turns Deadly in Detroit: Owner of Station Killed Rival Who Cut Price by 3 Cents a Gallon, Cops Say," *Detroit News*, November 17, 2007.

111. Steven Gold, "Ethnic Boundaries and Ethnic Entrepreneurship: A Photoelicitation Study," *Visual Sociology* 6, no. 2 (1991): 9–22.

112. Gold, "Chinese-Vietnamese Entrepreneurs."

113. Monica Trieu, "Intra-national Ethnic Identities in Flux: Identity Construction among the Chinese-Vietnamese and Vietnamese Second Generation" (unpublished PhD diss., Department of Sociology, University of California, Irvine, 2008).

114. Trieu, "Intra-national Ethnic Identities."

115. Angie Y. Chung, *Legacies of Struggle: Conflict and Cooperation in Korean American Politics* (Stanford, Calif.: Stanford University Press, 2007), 94.

116. Chung, *Legacies of Struggle*, 92.

117. Ong, Park, and Tong, "Korean-Black Conflict."

118. David, "Behind the Bulletproof Glass," 174.

119. Min, *Ethnic Solidarity*, 39.

120. Min, *Caught in the Middle*; Kim, *Bitter Fruit*; Min, *Ethnic Solidarity*; Yoon, *On My Own*; Chung, *Legacies of Struggle*.

121. Chung, *Legacies of Struggle*; Min, *Caught in the Middle*.

122. Chung, *Legacies of Struggle*, 96.

123. Chung, *Legacies of Struggle*, 98.

124. Chung, *Legacies of Struggle*, 98.

125. Chung, *Legacies of Struggle*, 99.

126. Min, *Caught in the Middle*; Min, *Ethnic Solidarity*; Chung, *Legacies of Struggle*; Arlene Dallalfar, "Iranian Women as Immigrant Entrepreneurs," *Gender and Society* 8, no. 4 (1994): 541–61.

127. Suzette Hackney, "Tension Runs High over Man's Death: Two Suspects Are Denied Bail; Task Force Looks for Healing," *Detroit Free Press*, May 18, 1999; Lekan Oguntoyinbo, "Program Aims to Keep Peace for Merchants: Harmony Project Could Lessen Racial Tensions with Customers," *Detroit Free Press*, July 6, 1999.

128. Portes and Stepick, *City on the Edge*, 199.

129. Min, *Ethnic Solidarity*, 91.

130. Min, *Ethnic Solidarity*; John Hartigan Jr., *Racial Situations: Class Predicaments of Whiteness in Detroit* (Princeton, N.J.: Princeton University Press, 1999); Sharon Zukin, *Naked City: The Death and Life of Authentic Urban Places* (New York: Oxford University Press, 2009); Emmanuel David, "Signs of Resistance: Marking Public Space through a Renewed Cultural Activism," in *Visual Research Methods: Image, Society and Representation*, ed. Gregory C. Stanczak, 225–54 (Los Angeles: Sage, 2007); Sam Roberts, "As Population Shifts in Harlem, Blacks Lose Their Majority," *New York Times*, January 6, 2010.

131. Zukin, Sharon, Valerie Trujillo, Peter Frase, Danielle Jackson, Tim Recuber, and Abraham Walker. "New Retail Capital and Neighborhood Change: Boutiques and Gentrification in New York City." Graduate Program in Sociology. City University of New York, 2009, p. 7.

132. Nicholas Riccardi, "Shops Under Siege," *Los Angeles Times*, November 27, 1996.

133. Michael Hudson ed., *Merchants of Misery: How Corporate America Profits from Poverty* (Monroe, Maine: Common Courage Press, 1996); Michael Hudson, "Fringe Banks that Exploit the Poor," in *Real World Banking*, ed. Mark Breslow, Jim Campen, Ellen Frank, John Miller, and Abby Scher, 46–52, 3rd ed. (Somerville, Mass.: Dollars and Sense, 1997); Michael Hudson, "Robbin' the Hood: How Wall Street Takes from the Poor and Gives to the Rich," *Mother Jones*, July/August 1994.

134. Manning Marable, *How Capitalism Underdeveloped Black America: Problems in Race, Political Economy and Society* (Boston: South End Press, 1983), 164, italics in original.

135. Kami Pothukuchi, *The Detroit Food System: A Handbook for Community Planners* (Detroit: Wayne State University Press, 2003); Guest and Turk, "The Quality of Urban Life."

136. Ong, Park, and Tong, "Korean-Black Conflict"; Abelman and Lie 1994; David, "Intercultural Relations"; Porter and Dunn, *The Miami Riot of 1980*.

137. Calvin Goldscheider and Francis E. Kobrin, "Ethnic Continuity and the Process of Self-Employment," *Ethnicity* 7 (1980): 256–78; Min, *Ethnic Solidarity*; Kim, "Leaving the Ethnic Economy"; Waldinger, *Still the Promised City?*

138. Marable, *The Great Wells of Democracy*, 217.

CHAPTER 7

1. Luciano Mangiafico, *Contemporary American Immigrants: Patterns of Filipino, Korean, and Chinese Settlement in the United States* (New York: Praeger, 1988).

2. Nathan Glazer and Daniel Patrick Moynihan, *Beyond the Melting Pot* (Cambridge, Mass.: MIT Press, 1963); Thomas Sowell, *Ethnic America* (New York: Basic Books, 1981); Herbert Gans, "Second Generation Decline: Scenarios for the Economic and Ethnic Futures of the Post-1965 American Immigrants," *Ethnic and Racial Studies* 15, no. 2 (1992): 173–92; Joel Kotkin, *Tribes: How Race, Religion and Identity Determined Success in the New Global Economy* (New York: Random House, 1992).

3. Dinesh D'Souza and Tony Brown, "Work and the African American," *American Enterprise* 6, no. 5 (1995): 33.

4. Alejandro Portes and Robert Bach, *Latin Journey: Cuban and Mexican Immigrants in the United States* (Berkeley: University of California Press, 1985), 186, 193–95, 240.

5. Claire Jean Kim, *Bitter Fruit: The Politics of Black-Korean Conflict in New York City* (New Haven, Conn.: Yale University Press, 2000), 38.

6. Nathan Caplan, Marcella H. Choy, and John K. Whitmore, "Indochinese Refugee Families and Academic Achievement," *Scientific American* 266, no. 2 (February 1992): 36–42; Min Zhou and Carl Bankston III, *Growing Up American: How Vietnamese Children Adapt to Life in the United States* (New York: Russell Sage Foundation, 1998).

7. Edward C. Banfield, *The Unheavenly City Revised: A Revision of the Unheavenly City* (Boston: Little, Brown, 1974); Jonathan J. Bean, "'Burn, Baby Burn': Small Business in the Urban Riots of the 1960s," *Independent Review* 5, no. 2 (2000): 165–87.

8. St. Clair Drake and Horace Cayton, *Black Metropolis* (Chicago: University of Chicago Press, 1945).

9. Roi Ottley, *New World a-Coming* (New York: Arno Press and New York Times, 1968 [1943]), 154; Jacqueline Jones, *Labor of Love, Labor of Sorrow: Black Women, Work and Family from Slavery to the Present* (New York: Basic Books, 1985), 214–15.

10. Carol Stack, *All Our Kin* (New York: Harper & Row, 1974); Elliot Liebow, *Tally's Corner: A Study of Negro Streetcorner Men* (Boston: Little, Brown, 1967).

11. Betty Lou Valentine, *Hustling and Other Hard Work* (New York: Free Press, 1978), 23–24.

12. Elijah Anderson, "The Community Consequences of Welfare Reform" (paper presented at the National Poverty Center's Qualitative Research on Urban Poverty symposium, Ann Arbor, Mich., June 14, 2004), at www.npc.umich.edu/news/events/anderson.pdf (accessed April 20, 2010); Ivan Light, *Cities in World Perspective* (New York: Macmillan, 1983); Jan E. Losby, Marcia E. Kingslow, and John F. Else, *The Informal Economy: Experiences of African Americans* (Washington, D.C.: Institute for Social and Economic Development Solutions, 2003); Elaine L. Edgcomb and Maria Medrano Armington, *The Informal Economy: Latino Enterprises at the Margins* (Washington, D.C.: FIELD (Microenterprise Fund for Innovation, Effectiveness and Dissemination), Aspen Institute, 2003); Pascale Joassart Marcelli and Daniel Flaming, "Workers without Rights: The Informal Economy in Los Angeles" (Economic Roundtable Briefing Paper, Los Angeles, 2002).

13. Sudhir Alladi Venkatesh, *Off the Books: The Underground Economy of the Urban Poor* (Cambridge, Mass.: Harvard University Press, 2006), 17, 92–93.

14. Marta Tienda and Rebeca Raijman, "Immigrants' Income Packaging and Invisible Labor Force Activity," *Social Science Quarterly* 81, no. 1 (2000): 291–311.

15. Venkatesh, *Off the Books*, 100.

16. Light, *Cities in World Perspective*, 380.

17. Tienda and Raijman, "Immigrants' Income Packaging."

18. As Robert Merton notes, "legitimate" and "illegitimate" businesses are virtually identical in that both provide goods and services for which there is a demand. Robert K.

Merton, *Social Theory and Social Structure*, rev. and enlarged ed. (Glencoe, N.Y.: Free Press, 1957), 79.

19. Banfield, *The Unheavenly City Revised*; Bean, "'Burn, Baby Burn'"; Ivan Light, "The Ethnic Vice Industry, 1880–1944," *American Sociological Review* 42 (1977): 464–79.

20. Louis Coser, *The Functions of Social Conflict* (New York: Free Press, 1956), 48–55.

21. Regina Austin, "'An Honest Living': Street Vendors, Municipal Regulation and the Black Public Sphere," *Yale Law Journal* 103, no. 8 (1994): 2119–131; Juliette Walker, *The History of Black Business in America: Capitalism, Race, Entrepreneurship* (New York: Macmillan Library Reference, 1998), xix–xx.

22. Donald W. Light, "The Migrant Enclaves to Mainstream: Reconceptualizing Informal Economic Behavior," *Theory and Society* 33 (2004): 710.

23. Jennifer Lee, *Civility in the City: Blacks, Jews, and Koreans in Urban America* (Cambridge, Mass.: Harvard University Press, 2002).

24. Clifford Geertz, "The Rotating Credit Association: A 'Middle Rung' in Development," *Economic Development and Cultural Change* 10, no. 3 (April 1962): 241–63.

25. John C. Cross and Alfonso Morales, "Introduction: Locating Street Markets in the Modern/Postmodern World," in *Street Entrepreneurs: People, Place, and Politics in Local and Global Perspective*, ed. John C. Cross and Alfonso Morales, 1–14 (New York: Routledge, 2007); Edna Bonacich and John Modell, *The Economic Basis of Ethnic Solidarity: Small Business in the Japanese-American Community* (Berkeley: University of California Press, 1980).

26. Joseph P. Gaughan and Louis A. Ferman, "Toward an Understanding of the Informal Economy," *Annals of the American Academy of Political and Social Science* 493 (1987): 24.

27. Saskia Sassen, *Cities in a World Economy* (Thousand Oaks, Calif.: Pine Forge Press, 1994), 1–7.

28. Alejandro Portes and William Haller, "The Informal Economy," in *The Handbook of Economic Sociology*, ed. Neil J. Smelser and Richard Swedberg, 403–25, 2nd ed. (Princeton, N.J.: Princeton University Press, 2005); S. M. Miller, "The Pursuit of Informal Economies," *Annals of the American Academy of Political and Social Science* 493 (1987): 26–35.

29. Light, "The Migrant Enclaves"; Saskia Sassen, "The Informal Economy," in *Dual City: Restructuring New York*, ed. J. H. Mollenkopf and M. Castells, 79–101 (New York: Russell Sage Foundation, 1991).

30. Edna Bonacich and Richard P. Appelbaum, *Behind the Label: Inequality in the Los Angeles Apparel Industry* (Berkeley: University of California Press, 2000).

31. Manuel Castells and Alejandro Portes, "World Underneath: The Origins, Dynamics, and Effects of the Informal Economy," in *The Informal Economy: Studies in Advanced and Less Developed Countries*, ed. Alejandro Portes, Manuel Castells, and Lauren A. Benton, 11–37 (Baltimore: Johns Hopkins University Press, 1989).

32. Sassen defines the informal economy as "income-generating activities that take place outside the framework of public regulation, where similar activities are regulated." Sassen, "The Informal Economy," 79. Most people in the informal economy are self-employed. Ivan Light and Steven J. Gold, *Ethnic Economies* (San Diego: Academic Press, 2000).

33. Losby, Kingslow, and Else, *The Informal Economy*, 20.

34. Robert Fairlie, "Drug Dealing and Legitimate Self-Employment," *Journal of Labor Economics* 20, no. 3 (July 2002): 538–67.

35. Light and Gold, *Ethnic Economies*; Howard Becker, *Outsiders: Studies in the Sociology of Deviance* (New York: Free Press, 1963).

36. Portes and Haller, "The Informal Economy," tab. 1.

37. Barry Molefsky, "America's Underground Economy" (Report No. 81-181E, Congressional Research Service, Library of Congress, Washington, D.C., 1981), 25, cited in Portes and Haller, "The Informal Economy."

38. Portes and Haller, "The Informal Economy," 413.

39. Kevin McCrohan, James D. Smith, and Terry K. Adams, "Consumer Purchases in Informal Markets: Estimates for the 1980s, Prospects for the 1990s," *Journal of Retailing* 67, no. 1 (1991): 37, cited in Portes and Haller, "The Informal Economy," 416.

40. U.S. Bureau of Labor Statistics, "Contingent and Alternative Employment Arrangements," Technical Note, U.S. Department of Labor, Washington, D.C., February 2001, cited in Abel Valenzuela Jr., "Day Labor Work," *Annual Review of Sociology* 29 (2003): 307–33.

41. Beth Barrett, "Los Angeles County, California, Cash Economy Threatens Wages," *Los Angeles Daily News*, May 6, 2002.

42. Marcelli and Flaming, "Workers without Rights," 6.

43. Abel Valenzuela Jr., "Day Labourers as Entrepreneurs?" *Journal of Ethnic and Migration Studies* 27, no. 2 (2001): 335–52.

44. Deborah Sontag, "Émigrés in New York: Work Off the Books," *New York Times*, June 13, 1993.

45. Edgcomb and Armington, *The Informal Economy*, 7, 24–25; Tienda and Raijman found that Mexican immigrant households in Chicago with one or more members involved in the informal economy derived 19 percent of their family income from such activities. Tienda and Raijman, "Immigrants' Income Packaging."

46. Losby, Kingslow, and Else, *The Informal Economy*.

47. Valenzuela, "Day Labourers as Entrepreneurs?" 347–48.

48. Edgcomb and Armington, *The Informal Economy*, 21.

49. Daniel Bell, *The End of Ideology: On the Exhaustion of Political Ideas in the Fifties* (New York: Collier, 1961).

50. Merton, *Social Theory*, 77, italics in original.

51. Austin, "'An Honest Living,'" 2119.

52. Nation's Restaurant News, "Calif.'s 'Little Saigon' Operators Seek Food-Temperature Variance," February 14, 2000.

53. Austin, "'An Honest Living,'" 2119.

54. Peggy Levitt, "A Todos Les Llamo Primo (I Call Everyone Cousin): The Social Basis for Latin Small Businesses," in *New Migrants in the Marketplace: Boston's Ethnic Entrepreneurs*, ed. M. Halter, 120–40 (Amherst: University of Massachusetts Press, 1995).

55. Anderson, "The Community Consequences," 16–17.

56. Venkatesh, *Off the Books*; Stack, *All Our Kin*.

57. Robert Mark Silverman, *Doing Business in Minority Markets: Black and Korean Entrepreneurs in Chicago's Ethnic Beauty Aids Industry* (New York: Garland, 2000), 84.

58. William J. Wilson, *When Work Disappears: The World of the New Urban Poor* (New York: Knopf, 1996), 36.

59. Anderson, "The Community Consequences," 1.

60. Colin C. Williams, "The Nature of Entrepreneurship in the Informal Sector: Evidence from England," *Journal of Developmental Entrepreneurship* 12, no. 2 (2007): 239–54.

61. Mario Luis Small and Monica McDermott, "The Presence of Organizational Resources in Poor Urban Neighborhoods: An Analysis of Average and Contextual Effects," *Social Forces* 84, no. 3 (2006): 1716.

62. John Sibley Butler, *Entrepreneurship and Self-Help among Black Americans* (Albany: State University of New York Press, 1991).

63. Valenzuela, "Day Labourers as Entrepreneurs?" 347–48; Pierrette Hondagneu-Sotelo, *Doméstica: Immigrant Workers Cleaning and Caring in the Shadows of Affluence* (Berkeley: University of California Press, 2001). An exception to this trend is the resale of tickets for sports events and concerts. African Americans involved in this enterprise often ply their trade in largely white environments. D. Keith Mano, "Scalping," *National Review*, August 28, 1987.

64. Austin, "'An Honest Living.'"

65. Kathy A. Kaufman, "Outsourcing the Hearth: The Impact of Immigration on Labor Allocation in American Families," in *Immigration Research for a New Century: Multidisciplinary Perspectives*, ed. Nancy Foner, Rubén G. Rumbaut, and Steven J. Gold, 345–68 (New York: Russell Sage Foundation, 2000).

66. Austin, "'An Honest Living,'" 2121.

67. Venkatesh, *Off the Books*, 98.

68. Austin, "'An Honest Living,'" 2127.

69. Christian Zlolniski, *Janitors, Street Vendors, and Activists: The Lives of Mexican Immigrants in Silicon Valley* (Berkeley: University of California Press, 2006), 80–83.

70. Theodore Saloutos, *The Greeks in the United States* (Cambridge, Mass.: Harvard University Press, 1964).

71. Valenzuela, "Day Labor Work," 322.

72. Austin, "'An Honest Living,'" 2131.

73. Isabel Wilkerson, "A Great Escape: A Dwindling Legacy," *New York Times*, February 15, 1998; James Segrest and Mark Hoffman, *Moanin' at Midnight: The Life and Times of Howlin' Wolf* (New York: Pantheon, 2004).

74. Light, "The Migrant Enclaves," 723.

75. Kevin Kelly, "Where Music Will Be Coming From," *New York Times Magazine*, March 30, 2002.

76. Adia Harvey Wingfield, *Doing Business with Beauty: Black Women, Hair Salons, and the Racial Enclave Economy* (Lanham, Md. Rowman & Littlefield, 2007); Silverman, *Doing Business in Minority Markets*.

77. Daniel Melero Malpica, "Making a Living in the Streets of Los Angeles: An Ethnographic Study of Day Laborers," *Migraciones Internacionales* 1, no. 3 (2002): 124–48.

78. Valenzuela, "Day Labor Work."

79. Steven J. Gold, "Patterns of Economic Cooperation among Israeli Immigrants in Los Angeles," *International Migration Review* 28, no. 105 (1994): 114–35.

80. Steven J. Gold, *Israeli Diaspora* (Seattle: University of Washington Press, 2002), 82.

81. Gold, *Israeli Diaspora*, 87.

82. Gold, *Israeli Diaspora*, 77.

83. Steven J. Gold, *Refugee Communities* (Newbury Park, Calif.: Sage, 1992).

84. John K. Leba, *The Vietnamese Entrepreneurs in the U.S.A.* (Houston: Zieleks, 1985).

85. Losby, Kingslow, and Else, *The Informal Economy*.

86. Mark Arax, "Refugees Called Victims and Perpetrators of Fraud," *Los Angeles Times*, February 9, 1987, 3.

87. Venkatesh, *Off the Books*, 94–95.

88. Williams, "The Nature of Entrepreneurship."

89. Natalie Y. Moore, "Party Store Tickets Hit 1,300," *Detroit News*, March 1, 2004; Frederick D. Sturdivant and Walter T. Wilhelm, "Poverty, Minorities, and Consumer Exploitation," in *The Ghetto Marketplace*, ed. Frederick D. Sturdivant, 108–17 (New York: Free Press, 1969).

90. Valenzuela, "Day Labourers as Entrepreneurs?" 339.

91. Harvey Wingfield, *Doing Business with Beauty*, 21, 71–72.

92. Austin, "'An Honest Living,'" 2124–126.

93. Valenzuela, "Day Labourers as Entrepreneurs?" 342.

94. Michael D. Woodard, *Black Entrepreneurs in America: Stories of Struggle and Success* (New Brunswick, N.J.: Rutgers University Press, 1997); Steven Greenhouse, "New Support but Few Gains for Urban Enterprise Zones," *New York Times*, May 25, 1992; Debbie Gruenstein, Scott Hebert, Franklin James, Greg Mills, and Avis Vidal, "Interim Assessment of the Empowerment Zones and Enterprise Communities (EZ/EC) Program: A Progress Report" (U.S. Department of Housing and Urban Development, Washington, D.C., November 2001); Cross and Morales, "Introduction."

95. Edgcomb and Armington, *The Informal Economy*.

96. Portes and Haller, "The Informal Economy," 420.

97. Leslie Wayne, "Congress to Debate Greater Oversight of Hedge Funds," *New York Times*, October 1, 1998.

98. Gregg W. Kettles, "Legal Responses to Sidewalk Vending: The Case of Los Angeles, California," in *Street Entrepreneurs: People, Place, and Politics in Local and Global Perspective*, ed. John C. Cross and Alfonso Morales, 58–78 (New York: Routledge, 2007).

99. Cross and Morales, "Introduction," 9.

100. Anderson, "The Community Consequences."

CHAPTER 8

1. Nathan Glazer and Daniel Patrick Moynihan, *Beyond the Melting Pot* (Cambridge, Mass.: MIT Press, 1963); St. Clair Drake and Horace Cayton, *Black Metropolis* (Chicago: University of Chicago Press, 1945); Steven J. Gold, "Immigrant Entrepreneurs and Customers throughout the 20th Century," in *Not Just Black and White: Historical and Contemporary Perspectives on Immigration, Race and Ethnicity in the United States*, ed. Nancy Foner and George M. Fredrickson, 315–40 (New York: Russell Sage Foundation, 2004); Ivan Light and Edna Bonacich, *Immigrant Entrepreneurs* (Berkeley: University of California Press, 1988).

2. Pyong Gap Min, *Caught in the Middle: Korean Communities in New York and Los Angeles* (Berkeley: University of California Press, 1996); Raphael J. Sonenshein, "The Battle over Liquor Stores in South Central Los Angeles: Management of an Interminority Conflict," *Urban Affairs Review* 31, no. 6 (1996): 710–37.

3. Frank D. Bean, Jennifer Van Hook, and Mark A. Fossett, "Immigration, Spatial and Economic Change, and African American Employment," in *Immigration and Opportunity: Race, Ethnicity and Employment in the U.S.*, ed. Frank D. Bean and Stephanie Bell-Rose, 31–63 (New York: Russell Sage Foundation, 1999), 56.

4. Reynolds Farley, "Detroit in 2000: Racial, Economic and Geographic Trends in a Polarized Metropolis," in *Racial Liberalism and the Politics of Urban America*, ed. Curtis Stokes and Theresa Melendez, 295–324 (East Lansing: Michigan State University Press, 2003), 297.

5. Joe T. Darden, Richard Hill, June Thomas, and Richard Thomas, *Detroit: Race and Uneven Development* (Philadelphia: Temple University Press, 1987), 202–18.

6. Timothy Bates, *Race, Self-Employment and Upward Mobility: An Elusive American Dream* (Baltimore: John Hopkins University Press, 1997), 174; Michael D. Woodard, *Black*

Entrepreneurs in America: Stories of Struggle and Success (New Brunswick, N.J.: Rutgers University Press, 1997).

7. Reynolds Farley, Sheldon Danziger, and Harry J. Holzer, *Detroit Divided: A Volume in the Multi-City of Urban Inequality* (New York: Russell Sage Foundation, 2000).

8. Farley, "Detroit in 2000," 305; Darden et al., *Detroit*, 258–60.

9. Jonathan Mahler, "G.M., Detroit and the Fall of the Black Middle Class," *New York Times Magazine*, June 24, 2009.

10. Darden et al., *Detroit*; Thomas J. Sugrue, *The Origins of the Urban Crisis: Race and Inequality in Postwar Detroit*, with a new preface by the author (Princeton, N.J.: Princeton University Press, 2005); Farley et al., *Detroit Divided*.

11. M. J. Stephey, "Kwame Kilpatrick," *Time*, October 28, 2008, at www.time.com/time/politics/article/0,8599,1854335,00.html (accessed July 4, 2009).

12. Joel J. Smith and Nathan Hurst, "Grocery Closings Hit Detroit Hard," *Detroit News*, July 5, 2007.

13. Gary David, "Behind the Bulletproof Glass: Iraqi Chaldean Store Ownership in Metropolitan Detroit," in *Arab Detroit: From Margins to Mainstream*, ed. Nabeel Abraham and Andrew Shryock, 151–78 (Detroit: Wayne State University Press, 2000); Mary C. Sengstock, *Chaldean-Americans: Changing Conceptions of Ethnic Identity*, 2nd ed. (Staten Island, N.Y.: Center for Migration Studies, 1999).

14. J. H. Lowry, *Realizing the New Agenda for Minority Business Development* (Boston: Boston Consulting Group, 2005); Joe T. Darden and Steven J. Gold, "The Impact of Proposal 2 on the Survival of Minority- and Women-Owned New Firms in Michigan," *Michigan Applied Public Policy Research Report*, East Lansing, July 2008.

15. Sarah Ryley, "Black Businesses Flourish in Mich.," *Detroit News*, June 20, 2006.

16. U.S. Census Bureau, "Black-Owned Firms: 2002," 2002 Economic Census, Survey of Business Owners, Company Statistics Series, August 2006, at www.census.gov/prod/ec02/sb0200csblk.pdf (accessed April 11, 2010).

17. Ryley, "Black Businesses."

18. U.S. Census Bureau, "Black-Owned Firms."

19. John Iceland, *Where We Live Now: Immigration and Race in the United States* (Berkeley: University of California Press, 2009).

20. Alfred McClung Lee and Norman D. Humphrey, *Race Riot: Detroit, 1943*, with a new introductory essay by Alfred McClung Lee (New York: Octagon Books, 1968); Eleanor Paperno Wolf, Alvin D. Loving, and Donald C. Marsh, *Negro-Jewish Relationships* (Detroit: Wayne State University Press, 1944); Sidney Fine, *Violence in the Model City: The Cavanaugh Administration, Race Relations, and the Detroit Riot of 1967* (Ann Arbor: University of Michigan Press, 1989); Darden et al., *Detroit*; David, "Behind the Bulletproof Glass."

21. Darden et al., *Detroit*; Sugrue, *The Origins of the Urban Crisis*; Fine, *Violence in the Model City*; Sengstock, *Chaldean-Americans*; Sidney Bolkosky, *Harmony and Dissonance: Voices of Jewish Identity in Detroit, 1914–1967* (Detroit: Wayne State University Press, 1991); Robert Fairlie and Alicia M. Robb, *Race and Entrepreneurial Success: Black-, Asian-, and White-Owned Businesses in the United States* (Cambridge, Mass.: MIT Press, 2008); Bates, *Race, Self-Employment*.

22. Mahler, "G.M., Detroit."

23. Drake and Cayton, *Black Metropolis*.

24. William J. Wilson and Richard P. Taub, *There Goes the Neighborhood: Racial, Ethnic and Class Tensions in Four Chicago Neighborhoods and Their Meanings for America* (New York: Knopf, 2006).

25. Smith and Hurst, "Grocery Closings."

26. Jennifer Lee, *Civility in the City: Blacks, Jews, and Koreans in Urban America* (Cambridge, Mass.: Harvard University Press, 2002).

27. Charles Choy Wong, "Black and Chinese Grocery Stores in Los Angeles' Black Ghetto," *Urban Life* 5, no. 4 (1977): 452.

28. Adia Harvey Wingfield, *Doing Business with Beauty: Black Women, Hair Salons, and the Racial Enclave Economy* (Lanham, Md.: Rowman & Littlefield, 2007).

29. W. E. B. Du Bois, *The Philadelphia Negro* (New York: Schocken, 1967 [1899]); Drake and Cayton, *Black Metropolis*; E. Franklin Frazier, *Black Bourgeoisie* (Glencoe, Ill.: Free Press, 1957); William J. Wilson, *More than Just Race: Being Black and Poor in the Inner City* (New York: Norton, 2009); Mary Pattillo, *Black on the Block: The Politics of Race and Class in the City* (Chicago: University of Chicago Press, 2007).

30. Darden et al., *Detroit*; Wolf, Loving, and Marsh, *Negro-Jewish Relationships*.

31. Darden et al., *Detroit*, 202.

32. Armand Gebert, "Store Slayings Fuel Tensions," *Detroit News*, October 26, 1980; Suzette Hackney, "Blacks, Arabs, Split on Motive in Killing," *Detroit Free Press*, May 21, 1999.

33. Ronald Marshall Jr., "Store Makes Turn Around," *Michigan Citizen*, July 16, 1997.

34. Ruby L. Bailey, "Tensions between Arab and Black Communities Fuel Protest against Reopening Gas Station Where Man Was Killed," *Detroit Free Press*, October 5, 1999; Lekan Oguntoyinbo, "Program Aims to Keep Peace for Merchants: Harmony Project Could Lessen Racial Tensions with Customers," *Detroit Free Press*, July 6, 1999.

35. Horace L. Sheffield, "Our Interests or Others'," *Michigan Citizen*, September 8, 2001, A8.

36. Cecil Angel, "Gasoline Boycott Initiated," *Detroit Free Press*, August 1, 2001.

37. Claud Anderson, "A Powernomics Economic Development Plan for Detroit's Under-Served Majority Population" (prepared for Detroit City Council, Bethesda, Md., Powernomics Corporation of American, n.d.).

38. Marisol Bello, "Official Pushes to Rescind Plan for African Town," *Detroit Free Press*, September 30, 2004.

39. Marisol Bello, "Remedy or Racist? Detroit Council Plan Aims to Increase Black Businesses," *Detroit Free Press*, September 27, 2004.

40. Kwame M. Kilpatrick, mayor, City of Detroit, press release, July 27, 2004.

41. Anderson, "A Powernomics Economic Development Plan," 19.

42. Anderson, "A Powernomics Economic Development Plan," 6, 11.

43. Darden et al., *Detroit*; Farley et al., *Detroit Divided*.

44. Bello, "Remedy or Racist?"

45. Lee, *Civility in the City*.

46. Stephen Kinzer and Jeremy W. Peters, "Debating a Plan for a Blacks-Only Fund to Finance an 'Africa Town' in Detroit," *New York Times*, October 13, 2004.

47. Louis Farrakhan, "Black Men Taking Responsibility," *Final Call*, November 27, 2004.

48. Santiago Esparza, "Paradise Valley Project to Begin at End of the Month," *Detroit News*, April 1, 2008.

49. City of Detroit, Office of the Mayor, "Mayor Launches Crackdown on Liquor and Beer/Wine Stores," press release, December 10, 2003. Similarly, the *Detroit Free Press* wrote a multipart series on how the State Department of Agriculture developed an inspection program heavily focused upon violations of food safety laws by Detroit groceries, a market

niche characterized by virtually no grocery chains or African American owners and heavily controlled by Middle Eastern entrepreneurs. Greta Guest and Victoria Turk, "The Quality of Urban Life: Food Violations Higher in Detroit, Buyers Face a Commute for Groceries," *Detroit Free Press*, October 24, 2004.

50. Thomas Gieryn, "A Space for Place in Sociology," *Annual Review of Sociology* 26 (2000): 463–96.

51. Gregg Krupa, "Revival Revs on Seven Mile: Group Helps Area Thrive by Bringing Needed Resources In," *Detroit News*, July 26, 2007.

52. Michael Goodin, "Retail Blues in Detroit," *Michigan Chronicle*, September 28, 1999.

53. Kinzer and Peters, "Debating a Plan."

54. Marisol Bello, "Ethnics Protest Detroit's Plan for African Town," *Detroit Free Press*, September 29, 2004.

55. Bello, "Remedy or Racist?"

56. Bello, "Ethnics Protest Detroit's Plan."

57. U.S. Census Bureau, "Black-Owned Firms"; U.S. Census Bureau, "Hispanic-Owned Firms: 2002," 2002 Economic Census, Survey of Business Owners, Company Statistics Series, August 2006, at www.census.gov/prod/ec02/sb0200cshisp.pdf (accessed April 11, 2010); U.S. Census Bureau, *2000 Census of Population and Housing: Summary File 3 (SF3)* (Washington, D.C.: Data User Services, 2002).

58. David, "Behind the Bulletproof Glass"; Sengstock, *Chaldean-Americans*.

59. Vanessa Denha-Garmo, "Deadly Detroit: Chaldeans Dying for the American Dream," *Chaldean News*, June 1, 2005.

60. U.S. Census Bureau, *2000 Census of Population and Housing: Summary File 4 (SF4)* (Washington, D.C.: Data User Services, 2004).

61. Louise Cainkar, "Immigration to the United States," in *Arab American Encyclopedia*, ed. Michelle Lee (Detroit: Gale Group, 2000).

62. U.S. Census Bureau, *2000 Census . . . (SF4)*.

63. Drake and Cayton, *Black Metropolis*.

64. Derrick Bell, *Faces at the Bottom of the Well: The Permanence of Racism* (New York: Harper Collins, 1992).

65. Kenneth L. Kusmer, *A Ghetto Takes Shape: Black Cleveland, 1870–1930* (Urbana: University of Illinois Press, 1976).

66. Pattillo, *Black on the Block*, 122.

67. Sharon Zukin, *Naked City: The Death and Life of Authentic Urban Places* (New York: Oxford University Press, 2009); Pattillo, *Black on the Block*; Derek S. Hyra, *The New Urban Renewal: The Economic Transformation of Harlem and Bronzeville* (Chicago: University of Chicago Press, 2008).

68. Wilson and Taub, *There Goes the Neighborhood*.

69. Philip Moss and Chris Tilly, "'Soft' Skills and Race: An Investigation of Black Men's Employment Problems," *Work and Occupations* 23 (1996): 252–76.

70. Woodard, *Black Entrepreneurs*.

71. Paul Egan, "Super Bowl XL: Posh Spots Get Fix-up Cash," *Detroit News*, December 23, 2005.

72. Jonah Nadir Omowale, "Black Business Unites," *Michigan Citizen*, June 4, 2006.

73. Bankole Thompson, "Super Bowl Blackout," *Michigan Citizen*, January 8, 2006.

74. Bizdom U, "What Is Bizdom U?" at www.bizdom.com/ (accessed April 22, 2010).

75. Because the program enlisted clients on geographical criteria rather than on the basis of race, ethnicity, or gender, it continued to function after the passage of Proposal 2, the statewide anti–affirmative action proposal.

76. By 2008, the city had approved over twenty microloans and distributed six hundred thousand dollars of the three million dollars allocated for the program. City of Detroit, Office of the Mayor, news release, October 31, 2008.

77. Kauffman Foundation, "White House Expresses Support for Kauffman–New Economy Initiative to Revitalize Detroit," June 24, 2009, at www.kauffman.org/newsroom/white-house-expresses-support-for-kauffman-new-economy-initiative-to-revitalize-detroit.aspx (accessed July 6, 2009).

78. Michigan Constitution, Article 1, Section 26, 2007.

79. Dennis Judd and Todd Swanstrom, *City Politics: Private Power and Public Policy*, 2nd ed. (New York: Longman, 1998); Paul Lawless, "Power and Conflict in Pro-Growth Regimes: Tensions in Economic Development in Jersey City and Detroit," *Urban Studies* 39, no. 8 (2002): 1329–346.

80. Lawless, "Power and Conflict."

CHAPTER 9

1. David R. Roediger, *Colored White: Transcending the Racial Past* (Berkeley: University of California Press, 2002); Ronald H. Bayor, *Neighbors in Conflict: The Irish, Germans, Jews and Italians of New York City, 1929–1941* (Baltimore: Johns Hopkins University Press, 1978).

2. Max Arthur Herman, *Fighting in the Streets: Ethnic Succession and Urban Unrest in Twentieth Century America* (New York: Peter Lang, 2005).

3. Claire Jean Kim, *Bitter Fruit: The Politics of Black-Korean Conflict in New York City* (New Haven, Conn.: Yale University Press, 2000); Edward C. Banfield, *The Unheavenly City Revised: A Revision of the Unheavenly City* (Boston: Little, Brown, 1974); Jonathan J. Bean, "'Burn, Baby Burn': Small Business in the Urban Riots of the 1960s," *Independent Review* 5, no. 2 (2000): 165–87.

4. Melvin Oliver and Thomas Shapiro, *Black Wealth/White Wealth: A New Perspective on Racial Inequality* (New York: Routledge, 1995); Ivan Light and Steven J. Gold, *Ethnic Economies* (San Diego: Academic Press, 2000). In addition, immigrant and minority merchants and customers alike also suffer from disadvantages that are not the product of discrimination per se but limit their opportunity just the same.

5. Jeffrey M. Jones, "Big Gov't. Still Viewed as Greater Threat than Big Business," *Gallup*, April 20, 2009, at www.gallup.com/poll/117739/big-gov-viewed-greater-threat-big-business.aspx (accessed April 10, 2010).

6. Christie Davies, *Ethnic Humor around the World: A Comparative Analysis* (Bloomington: Indiana University Press, 1990); Walter P. Zenner, *Minorities in the Middle: A Cross-cultural Analysis* (Albany: State University of New York Press, 1991).

7. D. B. Qin, N. Way, and M. Rana, "The 'Model Minority' and Their Discontent: Examining Peer Discrimination and Harassment of Chinese American Immigrant Youth," *New Directions for Child and Adolescent Development* 121 (fall 2008): 27–42.

8. Francis Fukuyama, *Trust: The Social Virtues and the Creation of Prosperity* (New York: Free Press, 1995).

9. Paul Jargowsky, *Poverty and Place: Ghettos, Barrios and the American City* (New York: Russell Sage Foundation, 1996), 193.

10. Kim, *Bitter Fruit*; Fukuyama, *Trust*; Thomas Sowell, *Ethnic America* (New York: Basic Books, 1981).

11. Steven J. Gold, "Patterns of Economic Cooperation among Israeli Immigrants in Los Angeles," *International Migration Review* 28, no. 105 (1994): 114–35; Pyong Gap Min, *Ethnic Solidarity for Economic Survival* (New York: Russell Sage Foundation, 2008); M. Waters, *Black Identities* (New York: Russell Sage Foundation and Harvard University Press, 1999).

12. Kim, *Bitter Fruit*; Herman, *Fighting in the Streets*, 170–73.

13. Ronald Takaki, *A Different Mirror: A History of Multicultural America* (Boston: Little, Brown, 1993); G. Fredrickson, *The Arrogance of Race: Historical Perspectives on Slavery, Racism, and Social Inequality* (Middletown, Conn.: Wesleyan University Press, 1988); Andrew Hacker, *Two Nations* (New York: Scribners, 1992).

14. Roger Waldinger, *Still the Promised City? African-Americans and New Immigrants in Postindustrial New York* (Cambridge, Mass.: Harvard University Press, 1996); Light and Gold, *Ethnic Economies*.

15. Scott Shane, "Failure Is a Constant in Entrepreneurship, You're the Boss: The Art of Running a Small Business," *New York Times*, July 15, updated July 17, 2009.

16. St. Clair Drake and Horace Cayton, *Black Metropolis* (Chicago: University of Chicago Press, 1945), 436, 454.

17. Mike Bergman and Mark Tolbert, "Minority Groups Increasing Business Ownership at Higher Rates than National Average, Census Bureau Reports," U.S. Census Bureau, July 28, 2005.

18. Illsoo Kim, *New Urban Immigrants: The Korean Community in New York* (Princeton, N.J.: Princeton University Press, 1981); Pyong Gap Min, *Caught in the Middle: Korean Communities in New York and Los Angeles* (Berkeley: University of California Press, 1996); Min, *Ethnic Solidarity*; Angie Y. Chung, *Legacies of Struggle: Conflict and Cooperation in Korean American Politics* (Stanford, Calif.: Stanford University Press, 2007); Kim, *Bitter Fruit*; Bean, "'Burn, Baby Burn'"; Robert G. Weisbrod and Arthur Stein, *Bittersweet Encounter: The Afro-American and the American Jew* (Westport, Conn.: Negro Universities Press, 1970); Cheryl Lynn Greenberg, *Or Does It Explode? Black Harlem in the Great Depression* (New York: Oxford University Press, 1991).

19. Min, *Ethnic Solidarity*; Waldinger, *Still the Promised City?*; Steven J. Gold, Ivan Light, and M. Francis Johnston, "The Second Generation and Self-Employment," *Migration Information Source*, October 1, 2006, at www.migrationinformation.org/Feature/display.cfm?id=447 (accessed April 9, 2010).

20. Robert Fairlie and Alicia M. Robb, *Race and Entrepreneurial Success: Black-, Asian-, and White-Owned Businesses in the United States* (Cambridge, Mass.: MIT Press, 2008); Timothy Bates, William E. Jackson III, and James H. Johnson Jr., "Advancing Research on Minority Entrepreneurship," *Annals of the American Academy of Political and Social Science* 613 (September 2007): 10–17.

21. Marta Tienda and Rebeca Raijman, "Immigrants' Income Packaging and Invisible Labor Force Activity," *Social Science Quarterly* 81, no. 1 (2000): 291–311; John C. Cross and Alfonso Morales, "Introduction: Locating Street Markets in the Modern/Postmodern World," in *Street Entrepreneurs: People, Place, and Politics in Local and Global Perspective*, ed. John C. Cross and Alfonso Morales, 1–14 (New York: Routledge, 2007).

BIBLIOGRAPHY

Abraham, Sameer Y., and Nabeel Abraham, eds. *Arabs in the New World*. Detroit: Wayne State University Center for Urban Studies, 1983.

Akiba, Daisuke. "Japanese Americans." In *Asian Americans: Contemporary Trends and Issues*, edited by Pyong Gap Min, 148–77. 2nd ed. Thousand Oaks, Calif.: Pine Forge Press, 2006.

Aldrich, Howard, and Albert J. Reiss Jr. "The Effect of Civil Disorders on Small Business in the Inner City." *Journal of Social Issues* 26, no. 1 (1970): 187–206.

Almaguer, Tomás. *Racial Fault Lines: The Historical Origins of White Supremacy in California*. Berkeley: University of California Press, 1994.

Anderson, Claud. "A Powernomics Economic Development Plan for Detroit's Under-Served Majority Population." Prepared for Detroit City Council. Bethesda, Md., Powernomics Corporation of America, n.d.

Anderson, Elijah. "The Community Consequences of Welfare Reform." Paper presented at the National Poverty Center's Qualitative Research on Urban Poverty symposium, Ann Arbor, Mich., June 14, 2004. www.npc.umich.edu/news/events/anderson.pdf (accessed April 20, 2010).

———. *Streetwise*. Chicago: University of Chicago Press, 1990.

Angel, Cecil. "Gasoline Boycott Initiated." *Detroit Free Press*, August 1, 2001.

Ansel, Amy Elizabeth. *New Right, New Racism: Race and Reaction in the United States and Britain*. New York: New York University Press, 1997.

Anti-Defamation League. "Farrakhan in His Own Words: On Jews." www.adl.org/special_reports/farrakhan_own_words2/on_jews.asp (accessed April 19, 2010).

Arax, Mark. "Refugees Called Victims and Perpetrators of Fraud." *Los Angeles Times*, February 9, 1987.

Arellano, Amber. "Police, Store Owners to Meet: Arab-Owned Businesses Seek Better Protection." *Detroit Free Press*, February 1, 2000.

Associated Press. "White Man Gets Life Term for Slaying Detroit Negro." *Miami News*, February 12, 1969.

Austin, Regina. "'An Honest Living': Street Vendors, Municipal Regulation and the Black Public Sphere." *Yale Law Journal* 103, no. 8 (1994): 2119–131.

Babou, Cheikh Anta Mbacke. "Brotherhood Solidarity, Education and Migration: The Role of the Dahira in the Economy of the Murid Immigrant Community of New York." *Les Journées de l'IISM, "l'Internationalisation du religieux, Réseaux et politiques de l'Islam Africain."* Ecoles des Hautes Etudes en Sciences Sociales, Paris, 1, 2, 3, mars., 2001.

Bailey, Ruby L. "Tensions between Arab and Black Communities Fuel Protest against Reopening Gas Station Where Man Was Killed." *Detroit Free Press*, October 5, 1999.

Bakalian, Anny, and Mehdi Bozorgmehr. *Backlash 911.* Berkeley: University of California Press, 2009.

Baker, Ray Stannard. "The Negro Goes North." *World's Work* 34 (July 1917): 315.

Baldwin, James. "Negroes Are Anti-Semitic Because They're Anti-White." *New York Times*, April 9, 1967.

Ballon, Marc. "A Hole in Their Dreams: Ambitious Immigrants Found Success with Doughnut Shops, but Now Big Chains Are Eating Away Their Profits." *Los Angeles Times*, April 7, 2002.

Baltzell, E. Digby. *Philadelphia Gentlemen: The Making of a National Upper Class.* New York: Free Press, 1957.

Banfield, Edward C. *The Unheavenly City Revised: A Revision of the Unheavenly City.* Boston: Little, Brown, 1974.

Barrett, Beth. "Los Angeles County, California, Cash Economy Threatens Wages." *Los Angeles Daily News*, May 6, 2002.

Barton, Josef J. *Peasants and Strangers: Italians, Rumanians and Slovaks in an American City, 1890–1950.* Cambridge, Mass.: Harvard University Press, 1975.

Bates, Timothy. "Minority Business Access to Mainstream Markets." *Journal of Urban Affairs* 23, no. 1 (2001): 41–56.

———. *Race, Self-Employment and Upward Mobility: An Elusive American Dream.* Baltimore: John Hopkins University Press, 1997.

———. "The Urban Development Potential of Black-Owned Businesses." *Journal of the American Planning Association* 72, no. 2 (2006): 227–37.

Bates, Timothy, William E. Jackson III, and James H. Johnson Jr. "Advancing Research on Minority Entrepreneurship." *Annals of the American Academy of Political and Social Science* 613 (September 2007): 10–17.

Baulch, Vivian, and Patricia Zacharias. "The 1943 Detroit Race Riots." *Detroit News*, n.d.

Bayor, Ronald H. *Neighbors in Conflict: The Irish, Germans, Jews and Italians of New York City, 1929–1941.* Baltimore: Johns Hopkins University Press, 1978.

Bean, Frank D., and Gillian Stevens. *America's Newcomers and the Dynamics of Diversity.* American Sociological Association's Rose Series in Sociology. New York: Russell Sage Foundation, 2003.

Bean, Frank D., Jennifer Van Hook, and Mark A. Fossett. "Immigration, Spatial and Economic Change, and African American Employment." In *Immigration and Opportunity: Race, Ethnicity and Employment in the U.S.*, edited by Frank D. Bean and Stephanie Bell-Rose, 31–63. New York: Russell Sage Foundation, 1999.

Bean, Jonathan J. "'Burn, Baby Burn': Small Business in the Urban Riots of the 1960s." *Independent Review* 5, no. 2 (2000): 165–87.

Becker, Howard. *Outsiders: Studies in the Sociology of Deviance*. New York: Free Press, 1963.

Bell, Daniel. *The End of Ideology: On the Exhaustion of Political Ideas in the Fifties*. New York: Collier, 1961.

Bell, Derrick. *Faces at the Bottom of the Well: The Permanence of Racism*. New York: Harper Collins, 1992.

Bello, Marisol. "Ethnics Protest Detroit's Plan for African Town." *Detroit Free Press*, September 29, 2004.

———. "Official Pushes to Rescind Plan for African Town." *Detroit Free Press*, September 30, 2004.

———. "Remedy or Racist? Detroit Council Plan Aims to Increase Black Businesses." *Detroit Free Press*, September 27, 2004.

Bergman, Mike, and Mark Tolbert. "Minority Groups Increasing Business Ownership at Higher Rates than National Average, Census Bureau Reports." U.S. Census Bureau, July 28, 2005.

Berk, Richard A. "The Role of Ghetto Merchants in Civil Disorders." PhD diss., Johns Hopkins University, 1970.

Biggart, Homer. "Baldwin Leaves Negro Monthly." *New York Times*, February 28, 1967.

Bizdom U. "What Is Bizdom U?" www.bizdom.com (accessed April 22, 2010).

Blauner, Robert. "Internal Colonialism and Ghetto Revolt." *Social Problems* 16, no. 4 (1969): 393–408.

———. *Racial Oppression in America*. New York: Harper & Row, 1972.

Bloom, Leonard, and Ruth Riemer. *Removal and Return: The Socio-Economic Effects of the War on Japanese Americans*. University of California Publications in Culture and Society 4. Berkeley: University of California Press, 1949.

Blumer, Herbert. "Race Relations as a Sense of Group Position." *Pacific Sociological Review* 1 (1958): 3–7.

Bobo, Lawrence, and Vincent L. Hutchings. "Perceptions of Racial Competition in a Multiracial Setting." *American Sociological Review* 61 (December 1996): 951–72.

Bodnar, John. *The Transplanted: A History of Immigrants in Urban America*. Bloomington: University of Indiana Press, 1985.

Bodnar, John, R. Simon, and M. P. Weber. *Lives of Their Own: Blacks, Italians and Poles in Pittsburgh, 1900–1960*. Urbana: University of Illinois Press, 1982.

Bolkosky, Sidney. *Harmony and Dissonance: Voices of Jewish Identity in Detroit, 1914–1967*. Detroit: Wayne State University Press, 1991.

Bonacich, Edna. "A Theory of Middleman Minorities." *American Sociological Review* 38, no. 5 (October 1973): 583–94.

Bonacich, Edna, and Richard P. Appelbaum. *Behind the Label: Inequality in the Los Angeles Apparel Industry*. Berkeley: University of California Press, 2000.

Bonacich, Edna, and John Modell. *The Economic Basis of Ethnic Solidarity: Small Business in the Japanese-American Community*. Berkeley: University of California Press, 1980.

Boston Consulting Group. "The New Agenda for Minority Business Development." 2005. www.kauffman.org/uploadedfiles/minority_entrep_62805_report.pdf (accessed April 9, 2010).

Boyd, Robert L. "Black Enterprise in the Retail Trade during the Early Twentieth Century." *Sociological Focus* 34, no. 3 (August 2001): 241–50.

———. "Ethnicity, Niches, and Retail Enterprise in Northern Cities, 1900." *Sociological Perspectives* 44, no. 1 (2001): 89–110.

Brush, Candida, Daniel Monti, Andrea Ryan, and Amy M. Gannon. "Building Ventures through Civic Capitalism." *Annals of the American Academy of Political and Social Science* 613 (September 2007): 155–77.

Bukowczyk, John J. "The Transformation of Working-Class Ethnicity: Corporate Control, Americanization, and the Polish Immigrant Middle Class in Bayonne, New Jersey, 1915–1925." *Labor History* 25, no. 1 (winter 1984): 53–82.

Bunche, Ralph J. "Conceptions and Ideologies of the Negro Problem." Unpublished manuscript prepared for the Carnegie-Myrdal Study, *An American Dilemma: The Negro Problem and Modern Democracy*, New York, 1940.

Butler, John Sibley. *Entrepreneurship and Self-help among Black Americans*. Albany: State University of New York Press, 1991.

Butler, John S., and Kenneth L. Wilson. "Entrepreneurial Enclaves: An Exposition into the Afro-American Experience." *National Journal of Sociology* 2 (1989): 127–66.

Cain, Rudy. "Black Community under Siege." *New York Amsterdam News*, May 16, 1987.

Cainkar, Louise. "Immigration to the United States." In *Arab American Encyclopedia*, edited by Michelle Lee. Detroit: Gale Group, 2000.

California Newsreel. *Race: The Power of an Illusion*, 2003. www.pbs.org/race/000_General/000_00-Home.htm (accessed April 16, 2010).

Camarota, Steven A. "Immigrants in the United States—2000: A Snapshot of America's Foreign-Born Population." Center for Immigration Studies, December 2000.

Caplan, Nathan, Marcella H. Choy, and John K. Whitmore. "Indochinese Refugee Families and Academic Achievement." *Scientific American* 266, no. 2 (February 1992): 36–42.

Caplovitz, David. *The Poor Pay More*. New York: Free Press, 1967.

Castells, Manuel, and Alejandro Portes. "World Underneath: The Origins, Dynamics, and Effects of the Informal Economy." In *The Informal Economy: Studies in Advanced and Less Developed Countries*, edited by Alejandro Portes, Manuel Castells, and Lauren A. Benton, 11–37. Baltimore: Johns Hopkins University Press, 1989.

CBS Chicago. "Mayor Daley Names New Contract Overseer." January 2, 2008. http://cbs2chicago.com/politics/chief.procurement.officer.2.621857.html (accessed April 16, 2010).

Chang, Edward T., and Jeannette Diaz-Veizades. *Ethnic Peace in the American City: Building Communities in Los Angeles and Beyond*. New York: New York University Press, 1999.

Cheng, Lucie, and Yen Le Espiritu. "Korean Business in Black and Hispanic Neighborhoods: A Study of Intergroup Relations." *Sociological Perspectives* 32, no. 4 (1989): 521–34.

Chicago Defender. "Court Rules Boycott Not Fair to Race." October 8, 1927.

———. "Detroit Residents Push Plans to Get Chain Store Clerks." January 30, 1932.

———. "Plan to Boycott Stores Refusing Employment." December 1, 1928.

———. "Shun Business Places that Draw Color Line." November 3, 1928.

———. "Women Opposed Picketing and Boycott of Business Places." March 6, 1932.

Chin, Margaret M. *Sewing Women: Immigrants and the New York City Garment Industry*. New York: Columbia University Press, 2005.

Cho, Sumi K. "Korean Americans vs. African Americans: Conflicts and Construction." In *Reading Rodney King, Reading Urban Uprising*, edited by Robert Gooding-Williams, 196–211. New York: Routledge, 1993.

Choi, InChul. "The South Side: The End of Korean Frontier?" In *Koreans in the Windy City: 100 Years of Korean Americans in the Chicago Area*, edited by Hyock Chun, Kwang Chung Kim, and Shin Kim, 109–33. New Haven, Conn.: East Rock Institute, 2005.

Chung, Angie Y. *Legacies of Struggle: Conflict and Cooperation in Korean American Politics.* Stanford, Calif.: Stanford University Press, 2007.

City of Detroit, Office of the Mayor. "Mayor Launches Crackdown on Liquor and Beer/Wine Stores." Press release, December 10, 2003.

———. News release, October 31, 2008.

Clark, D. P. "The Expansion of the Public Sector and Irish Economic Development." In *Self-Help in Urban America: Patterns of Minority Business Enterprise*, edited by S. Cummings. Port Washington, N.Y.: Kennikat Press, 1980.

Clark, Kenneth B. "Candor about Negro-Jewish Relations." In *Anti-Semitism in the United States*, edited by Leonard Dinnerstein, 116–24. New York: Holt, Rinehart and Winston, 1971.

CNN. "Mayor Pleads Innocent in 1969 Race Riot Death." July 24, 2001. http://archives.cnn .com/2001/LAW/07/23/race.riot.hearing/index.html (accessed April 9, 2010).

———. "Protesters Loot, Set Fires in Cincinnati." April 11, 2001. http://archives.cnn .com/2001/US/04/10/cincinnati.protest.04 (accessed April 19, 2010).

Cobas, José A., and Jorge Duany. *Cubans in Puerto Rico: Ethnic Economy and Cultural Identity.* Gainesville: University Press of Florida, 1997.

Conley, Dalton. *Being Black, Living in the Red: Race, Wealth and Social Policy in America.* Berkeley: University of California Press, 1999.

Cornell, Stephen, and Douglas Hartmann. *Ethnicity and Race: Making Identities in a Changing World.* 2nd ed. Thousand Oaks, Calif.: Pine Forge Press, 2007.

Cose, Ellis. "A Decade of Proposition 209: Debate Sidelines the Real Issue." *San Francisco Chronicle*, November 6, 2006.

Coser, Louis. *The Functions of Social Conflict.* New York: Free Press, 1956.

Cross, John C., and Alfonso Morales. "Introduction: Locating Street Markets in the Modern/Postmodern World." In *Street Entrepreneurs: People, Place, and Politics in Local and Global Perspective*, edited by John C. Cross and Alfonso Morales, 1–14. New York: Routledge, 2007.

Cruse, Harold. *Rebellion or Revolution.* New York: Morrow, 1968.

Dallalfar, Arlene. "Iranian Women as Immigrant Entrepreneurs." *Gender and Society* 8, no. 4 (1994): 541–61.

Daniels, Roger. *The Politics of Prejudice.* 2nd ed. Berkeley: University of California Press, 1977.

Darden, Joe T., and Steven J. Gold. "The Impact of Proposal 2 on the Survival of Minority- and Women-Owned New Firms in Michigan." *Michigan Applied Public Policy Research Report*, East Lansing, July 2008.

Darden, Joe T., Richard Hill, June Thomas, and Richard Thomas. *Detroit: Race and Uneven Development.* Philadelphia: Temple University Press, 1987.

David, Emmanuel. "Signs of Resistance: Marking Public Space through a Renewed Cultural Activism." In *Visual Research Methods: Image, Society and Representation*, edited by Gregory C. Stanczak, 225–54. Los Angeles: Sage, 2007.

David, Gary. "Behind the Bulletproof Glass: Iraqi Chaldean Store Ownership in Metropolitan Detroit." In *Arab Detroit: From Margins to Mainstream*, edited by Nabeel Abraham and Andrew Shryock, 151–78. Detroit: Wayne State University Press, 2000.

———. "Intercultural Relations across the Counter: An Interactional Analysis of In Situ Service Encounters." Unpublished PhD diss., Wayne State University, Department of Sociology, 1999.

Davies, Christie. *Ethnic Humor around the World: A Comparative Analysis*. Bloomington: Indiana University Press, 1990.

Denha-Garmo, Vanessa. "Deadly Detroit: Chaldeans Dying for the American Dream." *Chaldean News*, June 1, 2005.

Detroit News. "The Activists" (Malik Shabazz). January 32, 1996.

Diggins, John P. *Mussolini and Fascism: The View from America*. Princeton, N.J.: Princeton University Press, 1972.

Diner, Hasia R. *The Jews of the United States*. Berkeley: University of California Press, 2004.

Dinnerstein, Leonard, Roger L. Nichols, and David M. Riemers. *Natives and Strangers: Blacks, Indians and Immigrants in America*. 2nd ed. New York: Oxford University Press, 1990.

Discrimination Research Center. "Free to Compete." Berkeley, Calif., 2006.

Dollard, John. *Caste and Class in a Southern Town*. 3rd ed. Garden City, N.Y.: Doubleday Anchor, 1957.

Drake, St. Clair, and Horace Cayton. *Black Metropolis*. Chicago: University of Chicago Press, 1945.

D'Souza, Dinesh, and Tony Brown. "Work and the African American." *American Enterprise* 6, no. 5 (1995): 33–34.

DuBois, W. E. B. *Economic Co-operation among Negro Americans*. Atlanta: Atlanta University Press, 1907.

———. *The Negro in Businesses*. Atlanta: Atlanta University Press, 1898.

———. *The Philadelphia Negro*. New York: Schocken, 1967 [1899].

Edgcomb, Elaine L., and Maria Medrano Armington. *The Informal Economy: Latino Enterprises at the Margins*. Washington, D.C.: FIELD (Microenterprise Fund for Innovation, Effectiveness and Dissemination), Aspen Institute, 2003.

Egan, Paul. "Super Bowl XL: Posh Spots Get Fix-up Cash." *Detroit News*, December 23, 2005.

Ellington, Ken, and K. Connie Kang. "A Student, a Shopkeeper and a Moment of Tragedy Slaying." *Los Angeles Times*, November 23, 1996.

Emerson, Edwin. "The New Ghetto." *Harper's Weekly*, January 9, 1897.

Esparza, Santiago. "Paradise Valley Project to Begin at End of the Month." *Detroit News*, April 1, 2008.

Fairlie, Robert. "Drug Dealing and Legitimate Self-Employment." *Journal of Labor Economics* 20, no. 3 (July 2002): 538–67.

Fairlie, Robert, and Alicia M. Robb. *Race and Entrepreneurial Success: Black-, Asian-, and White-Owned Businesses in the United States*. Cambridge, Mass.: MIT Press, 2008.

Farley, Reynolds. "Detroit in 2000: Racial, Economic and Geographic Trends in a Polarized Metropolis." In *Racial Liberalism and the Politics of Urban America*, edited by Curtis Stokes and Theresa Melendez, 295–324. East Lansing: Michigan State University Press, 2003.

Farley, Reynolds, Sheldon Danziger, and Harry J. Holzer. *Detroit Divided: A Volume in the Multi-City of Urban Inequality*. New York: Russell Sage Foundation, 2000.

Farrakhan, Louis. "Black Men Taking Responsibility." *Final Call*, November 27, 2004. www.finalcall.com/artman/publish/Minister_Louis_Farrakhan_9/Black_men_taking_responsibility_1660.shtml (accessed April 9, 2010).

Farrell, Walter C., Jr., and James H. Johnson Jr. "Structural Violence as an Inducement to African American and Hispanic Participation in the Los Angeles Civil Disturbances of 1992." *Journal of Human Behavior in the Social Environment* 4, no. 4 (2001): 337–59.

Fine, Sidney. *Violence in the Model City: The Cavanaugh Administration, Race Relations, and the Detroit Riot of 1967.* Ann Arbor: University of Michigan Press, 1989.

Fischer, Mary J., and Douglas S. Massey. "Residential Segregation and Ethnic Enterprise in U.S. Metropolitan Areas." *Social Problems* 47, no. 3 (August 2000): 408–24.

Foley, Eugene P. "The Negro Businessman: In Search of a Tradition." In *The Negro American,* edited by Talcott Parsons and Kenneth B. Clark, 555–92. Boston: Houghton Mifflin, 1966.

Foner, Nancy. *From Ellis Island to JFK: New York's Two Great Waves of Immigration.* New Haven, Conn.: Yale University Press, 2000.

Foner, Nancy, Rubén G. Rumbaut, and Steven J. Gold. "Immigration and Immigration Research in the United States." In *Immigration Research for a New Century: Multidisciplinary Perspectives,* edited by Nancy Foner, Rubén G. Rumbaut, and Steven J. Gold, 1–19. New York: Russell Sage Foundation, 2000.

Fong, Timothy P. *The Contemporary Asian American Experience: Beyond the Model Minority.* Upper Saddle River, N.J.: Prentice Hall, 1998.

Frazier, E. Franklin. *Black Bourgeoisie.* Glencoe, Ill.: Free Press, 1957.

———. *The Negro in the United States.* 2nd ed. New York: MacMillan, 1957.

Fredrickson, G. *The Arrogance of Race: Historical Perspectives on Slavery, Racism, and Social Inequality.* Middletown, Conn.: Wesleyan University Press, 1988.

Freer, Regina. "Black-Korean Conflict." In *The Los Angeles Riots: Lessons for the Urban Future,* edited by Mark Baldassare, 175–204. Boulder, Colo.: Westview, 1994.

French, Ron. "New Segregation: Races Accept the Divide." *Detroit News,* January 13, 2002.

Frey, William H. "The New Great Migration: Black Americans' Return to the South, 1965–2000." Metropolitan Policy Program, Brookings Institution, Washington, D.C., May 2004. www.brookings.edu/reports/2004/05demographics_frey.aspx (accessed April 9, 2010).

Friedrich, Otto. "The Changing Face of America." *Time,* July 8, 1985.

Friss, Evan. "Blacks, Jews, and Civil Rights Law in New York, 1895–1913." *Journal of American Ethnic History* 24, no. 4 (summer 2004): 70–99.

Fritsch, Jane. "Looters' Booty: A Dream; Korean Immigrants' Harlem Store Is Plundered." *New York Times,* July 18, 1992.

Fuchs, Lawrence H. "The Reactions of Black Americans to Immigration." In *Immigration Reconsidered: History, Sociology and Politics,* edited by Virginia Yans-McLaughlin, 293–314. New York: Oxford University Press, 1990.

Fukuyama, Francis. *Trust: The Social Virtues and the Creation of Prosperity.* New York: Free Press, 1995.

Fulbright, Leslie. "Connerly Gearing Up for Wider Crusade: Affirmative Action Foe Considers Launching Campaigns in 9 States." *San Francisco Chronicle,* December 14, 2006.

Gans, Herbert. "Second Generation Decline: Scenarios for the Economic and Ethnic Futures of the Post-1965 American Immigrants." *Ethnic and Racial Studies* 15, no. 2 (1992): 173–92.

Gaughan, Joseph P., and Louis A. Ferman. "Toward an Understanding of the Informal Economy." *Annals of the American Academy of Political and Social Science* 493 (1987): 15–25.

Gebert, Armand. "Store Slayings Fuel Tensions." *Detroit News,* October 26, 1980.

Geertz, Clifford. "The Rotating Credit Association: A 'Middle Rung' in Development." *Economic Development and Cultural Change* 10, no. 3 (April 1962): 241–63.

Geltman, Max. "The Negro-Jewish Confrontation." *National Review,* June 28, 1966.

Gibbs, Nancy. "Shades of Difference." *Time,* November 18, 1991.

Gibson, Campbell, and Kay Jung. "Historical Census Statistics on Population Totals by Race, 1790 to 1990, and by Hispanic Origin, 1970 to 1990, for the United States, Regions, Divisions, and States." Working Paper Series No. 56. Population Division, U.S. Census Bureau, Washington, D.C., September 2002.

Gibson, Thomas. "The Anti-Negro Riots in Atlanta." *Harper's Weekly*, October 13, 1906.

Gieryn, Thomas. "A Space for Place in Sociology." *Annual Review of Sociology* 26 (2000): 463–96.

Giroux, Henry. *The Terror of Neoliberalism*. Boulder, Colo.: Paradigm, 2004.

Gittell, Marilyn, Kathe Newman, Janice Bockmeyer, and Robert Lindsay. "Expanding Civic Opportunity: Urban Empowerment Zones." *Urban Affairs Review* 33, no. 4 (1998): 530–58.

Glazer, Nathan, and Daniel Patrick Moynihan. *Beyond the Melting Pot*. Cambridge, Mass.: MIT Press, 1963.

Gold, Steven J. "Chinese-Vietnamese Entrepreneurs in California." In *The New Asian Immigration in Los Angeles and Global Restructuring*, edited by Paul Ong, Edna Bonacich, and Lucy Cheng, 196–226. Philadelphia: Temple University Press, 1994.

———. "Ethnic Boundaries and Ethnic Entrepreneurship: A Photoelicitation Study." *Visual Sociology* 6, no. 2 (1991): 9–22.

———. "From Nationality to Peoplehood: Adaptation and Identity Formation in the Israeli Diaspora." *Diaspora* 13, no. 2/3 (fall/winter 2004): 331–58.

———. "Immigrant Entrepreneurs and Customers throughout the 20th Century." In *Not Just Black and White: Historical and Contemporary Perspectives on Immigration, Race and Ethnicity in the United States*, edited by Nancy Foner and George M. Fredrickson, 315–40. New York: Russell Sage Foundation, 2004.

———. *Israeli Diaspora*. Seattle: University of Washington Press, 2002.

———. "The Migrant Economy" (in Swedish). *Axess* 4, May 2005.

———. "Patterns of Economic Cooperation among Israeli Immigrants in Los Angeles." *International Migration Review* 28, no. 105 (1994): 114–35.

———. *Refugee Communities*. Newbury Park, Calif.: Sage, 1992.

Gold, Steven J., and Mehdi Bozorgmehr. "Middle East and North Africa." In *The New Americans: A Guide to Immigration since 1965*, edited by Mary Waters and Reed Ueda with Helen B. Marrow, 518–33. Cambridge, Mass.: Harvard University Press, 2007.

Gold, Steven J., and Joe T. Darden. "Black Entrepreneurship in a Black Majority Environment: The Case of Detroit and Other Selected Central Cities." Michigan Applied Public Policy Research Report. Michigan State University, East Lansing, June 2007.

Gold, Steven J., and Ivan Light. "Ethnic Economies and Social Policy." *Research in Social Movements, Conflicts and Change* 22 (summer 2000): 165–91.

Gold, Steven J., Ivan Light, and M. Francis Johnston. "The Second Generation and Self-Employment." *Migration Information Source*, October 1, 2006. www.migrationinformation. org/Feature/display.cfm?id=447 (accessed April 9, 2010).

Gold, Steven J., and Bruce A. Phillips. "Mobility and Continuity among Eastern European Jews." In *Origins and Destinies: Immigration, Race and Ethnicity in America*, edited by Silvia Pedraza and Rubén G. Rumbaut, 182–94. Belmont, Calif.: Wadsworth, 1996.

Goldberg, J. J. *Jewish Power: Inside the American Jewish Establishment*. Reading, Mass.: Addison-Wesley, 1996.

Goldscheider, Calvin, and Francis E. Kobrin. "Ethnic Continuity and the Process of Self-Employment." *Ethnicity* 7 (1980): 256–78.

Goodin, Michael. "Retail Blues in Detroit." *Michigan Chronicle*, September 28, 1999.

Graham, Hugh Davis. *Collision Course: The Strange Convergence of Affirmative Action and Immigration Policy in America*. New York: Oxford University Press, 2002.

Greeley, Andrew. *Ethnicity in the U.S.* New York: Wiley, 1974.

Green, Nancy L., ed. *Jewish Workers in the Modern Diaspora*. Berkeley: University of California Press, 1998.

Greenberg, Cheryl Lynn. *Or Does It Explode? Black Harlem in the Great Depression*. New York: Oxford University Press, 1991.

——. *Troubling the Waters: Black-Jewish Relations in the American Century*. Princeton, N.J.: Princeton University Press, 2006.

Greenhouse, Steven. "New Support but Few Gains for Urban Enterprise Zones." *New York Times*, May 25, 1992.

Gruenstein, Debbie, Scott Hebert, Franklin James, Greg Mills, and Avis Vidal. "Interim Assessment of the Empowerment Zones and Enterprise Communities (EZ/EC) Program: A Progress Report." U.S. Department of Housing and Urban Development, Washington, D.C., November 2001.

Guarnizo, L. E. "The Mexican Ethnic Economy in Los Angeles: Capitalist Accumulation, Class Restructuring, and the Transnationalization of Migration." Working paper, California Communities Program, University of California, Davis, 1998.

Guest, Greta, and Victoria Turk. "The Quality of Urban Life: Food Violations Higher in Detroit, Buyers Face a Commute for Groceries." *Detroit Free Press*, October 24, 2004.

Guglielmo, Thomas A. "Rethinking Whiteness Historiography: The Case of Italians in Chicago, 1890–1945." In *White Out: The Continuing Significance of Racism*, edited by Ashley W. Doane and Eduardo Bonilla-Silva, 35–48. New York: Routledge, 2003.

Hacker, Andrew. *Two Nations*. New York: Scribners, 1992.

Hackney, Suzette. "Blacks, Arabs, Split on Motive in Killing." *Detroit Free Press*, May 21, 1999.

——. "Tension Runs High over Man's Death: Two Suspects Are Denied Bail; Task Force Looks for Healing." *Detroit Free Press*, May 18, 1999.

Hall, Charles E. *Negros in the United States, 1920–1932*. New York: Arno Press and New York Times, 1969 [1935].

Harper, Shannon, and Barbara Reskin. "Affirmative Action at School and on the Job." *Annual Review of Sociology* 31 (2005): 357–79.

Harris, Abram Lincoln. *The Negro as Capitalist: A Study of Banking and Business among American Negroes*. Philadelphia: American Academy of Political and Social Science, 1936.

Hartigan, John, Jr. *Racial Situations: Class Predicaments of Whiteness in Detroit*. Princeton, N.J.: Princeton University Press, 1999.

Harvey Wingfield, Adia. *Doing Business with Beauty: Black Women, Hair Salons, and the Racial Enclave Economy*. Lanham, Md.: Rowman & Littlefield, 2007.

Hayden, Tom. "A Special Supplement: The Occupation of Newark." *New York Review of Books*, August 24, 1967.

Henry, Sheila E. *Cultural Persistence and Socio-economic Mobility: A Comparative Study of Assimilation among Armenians and Japanese in Los Angeles*. San Francisco: R&E Research Associates, 1978.

Herman, Max. "The Newark and Detroit 'Riots' of 1967." www.67riots.rutgers.edu/introduction.html (accessed April 10, 2010).

———. *Fighting in the Streets: Ethnic Succession and Urban Unrest in Twentieth Century America*. New York: Peter Lang, 2005.

Herring, Cedric, Hayward D. Horton, and Melvin E. Thomas. "Inner-City Entrepreneurship: Is Self-Employment a Cure for Poverty?" In *The New Politics of Race: From Du-Bois to the 21st Century*, edited by Marlese Durr, 89–111. Westport, Conn.: Praeger, 2002.

Higham, John. "Anti-Semitism in the Gilded Age: A Reinterpretation." *Mississippi Valley Historical Review* 43, no. 4 (March 1957): 559–78.

Hirsch, Arnold R. "E. Pluribus Duo? Thoughts on 'Whiteness' and Chicago's 'New' Immigration as a Transient Third Tier." *Journal of American Ethnic History* 23, no. 4 (summer 2004): 7–44.

———. *Making the Second Ghetto: Race and Housing in Chicago, 1940–1960*. Cambridge: Cambridge University Press, 1983.

Hochschild, Jennifer L. "Rich and Poor African Americans." In *Multiculturalism in the United States: Current Issues, Contemporary Voices*, edited by Peter Kivisto and Georganne Rundblad, 193–207. Thousand Oaks, Calif.: Pine Forge Press, 2000.

Holland, Gina. "Poll: Blacks Want to Run Businesses." *Los Angeles Times*, July 21, 2001.

Hondagneu-Sotelo, Pierrette. *Doméstica: Immigrant Workers Cleaning and Caring in the Shadows of Affluence*. Berkeley: University of California Press, 2001.

Horowitz, Donald. *Ethnic Conflict*. Berkeley: University of California Press, 1985.

Horton, J., with J. Calderon, M. Pardo, L. Saito, L. Shaw, and Y. Tseng. *The Politics of Diversity: Immigration, Resistance, and Change in Monterey Park, California*. Philadelphia: Temple University Press, 1995.

Howe, Irving, with Kenneth Libo. *World of Our Fathers*. New York: Harcourt Brace Jovanovich, 1976.

Hudson, Michael. "Fringe Banks that Exploit the Poor." In *Real World Banking*, edited by Mark Breslow, Jim Campen, Ellen Frank, John Miller, and Abby Scher, 46–52. 3rd ed. Somerville, Mass.: Dollars and Sense, 1997.

———, ed. *Merchants of Misery: How Corporate America Profits from Poverty*. Monroe, Maine: Common Courage Press, 1996.

———. "Robbin' the Hood: How Wall Street Takes from the Poor and Gives to the Rich." *Mother Jones*, July/August 1994.

HUD User. "Interim Assessment of the Empowerment Zones and Enterprise Communities (EZ/EC) Program." U.S. Department of Housing and Urban Development, Washington, D.C., 2005. www.huduser.org/.

Hunt, D. Bradford. "What Went Wrong with Public Housing in Chicago? A History of the Robert Taylor Homes." *Journal of the Illinois State Historical Society* (spring 2001). http://findarticles.com/p/articles/mi_qa3945/is_200104/ai_n8939181/pg_5 (accessed April 10, 2010).

Hunter, Gary Jerome. "Don't Buy from Where You Can't Work: Black Urban Boycott Movements during the Depression, 1929–1941." PhD diss., Department of History, University of Michigan, 1977.

Hutchinson, Earl Ofari. "Black Capitalism: Self-Help or Self-Delusion?" In *Race and Ethnic Conflict: Contending Views on Prejudice, Discrimination and Ethnoviolence*, edited by Fred L. Pincus and Howard J. Ehrlich, 264–71. Boulder, Colo.: Westview, 1994.

Hyra, Derek S. *The New Urban Renewal: The Economic Transformation of Harlem and Bronzeville*. Chicago: University of Chicago Press, 2008.

Iceland, John. *Where We Live Now: Immigration and Race in the United States.* Berkeley: University of California Press, 2009.

Immigration Commission. *Immigrants in Cities: A Study of the Population of Selected Districts in New York, Chicago, Philadelphia, Boston, Cleveland, Buffalo and Milwaukee.* Vol. 1. Washington, D.C.: Government Printing Office, 1911.

Insight Center for Community Economic Development. "The Evolution of Affirmative Action: An Executive Summary of the Research Series: Best Practices, Imperfections, and Challenges in State Inclusive Business Programs." Oakland, Calif., November 2007. www.insightcced.org/uploads/publications/assets/The%20Evolution%20of%20Affirmative%20Action.pdf (accessed April 10, 2010).

———. "The Impact of State Procurement Policies on Minority- and Women-Owned Businesses in Five States." Oakland, Calif., October 26, 2007. www.policyarchive.org/handle/10207/bitstreams/5666.pdf (accessed April 10, 2010).

———. "State Policies and Programs for Minority- and Women-Business Development." Oakland, Calif., December 14, 2007. www.insightcced.org/uploads///publications/assets/50%20state%20inclusive%20business%20policy%20scan.pdf (accessed April 10, 2010).

Jackson, Kenneth T. *Crabgrass Frontier: The Suburbanization of the United States.* New York: Oxford University Press, 1985.

Janowitz, Morris. "Collective Racial Violence: A Contemporary History." In *Violence in America: Historical and Comparative Perspectives*, edited by Hugh Davis Graham and Ted Robert Gurr, 261–86. Rev. ed. Beverly Hills, Calif.: Sage, 1979.

Jargowsky, Paul. *Poverty and Place: Ghettos, Barrios and the American City.* New York: Russell Sage Foundation, 1996.

Jaynes, Gerald D., and Robin M. Williams Jr., eds. *A Common Destiny: Blacks and American Society.* Washington, D.C.: National Academies Press, 1989.

Jazz Age Chicago. "Regal Theater." July 3, 2000. http://chicago.urban-history.org/ven/ths/regal.shtml (accessed April 15, 2010).

———. "South Center." July 3, 2000. http://chicago.urban-history.org/ven/dss/socenter.shtml (accessed April 15, 2010).

Jiobu, Robert M. "Ethnic Hegemony and the Japanese of California." *American Sociological Review* 53, no. 3 (1988): 353–67.

Johnson, James H., Jr., Cloyzelle K. Jones, Walter C. Farrell Jr., and Melvin L. Oliver. "The Los Angeles Rebellion: A Retrospective View." *Economic Development Quarterly* 6, no. 4 (November 1992): 356–72.

Johnson, James H., and Melvin L. Oliver. "Interethnic Minority Conflict in Urban America: The Effect of Economic and Social Dislocations." In *Race and Ethnic Conflict: Contending Views on Prejudice, Discrimination and Ethnoviolence*, edited by Fred L. Pincus and Howard J. Ehrlich, 194–205. Boulder, Colo.: Westview, 1994.

Jones, Jacqueline. *Labor of Love, Labor of Sorrow: Black Women, Work and Family from Slavery to the Present.* New York: Basic Books, 1985.

Jones, Jeffrey M. "Big Gov't. Still Viewed as Greater Threat than Big Business." *Gallup*, April 20, 2009. www.gallup.com/poll/117739/big-gov-viewed-greater-threat-big-business.aspx (accessed April 10, 2010).

Joseph, Samuel. *Jewish Immigration to the United States from 1881 to 1910.* New York: Arno Press and New York Times, 1914.

Joyce, Patrick D. *No Fire Next Time: Black-Korean Conflicts and the Future of America's Cities.* Ithaca, N.Y.: Cornell University Press, 2003.

Judd, Dennis, and Todd Swanstrom. *City Politics: Private Power and Public Policy*. 2nd ed. New York: Longman, 1998.

Kaplan, David H., and Bessie House-Soremekun. "Race, Space, Crime, and the African American Entrepreneur: Business Owner Attitudes, Business Success, and the Neighborhood Context." In *Landscapes of the Ethnic Economy*, edited by David H. Kaplan and Wei Lei, 67–82. Lanham, Md.: Rowman & Littlefield, 2006.

Kasinitz, Philip. *Caribbean New York: Black Immigrants and the Politics of Race*. Ithaca, N.Y.: Cornell University Press, 1992.

Katz, Jack. *Seductions of Crime*. New York: Basic Books, 1988.

Katz, Michael B. "Why Don't American Cities Burn Very Often." *Journal of Urban History* 34 (2008): 185–208.

Kauffman Foundation. "White House Expresses Support for Kauffman–New Economy Initiative to Revitalize Detroit." June 24, 2009. www.kauffman.org/newsroom/white-house-expresses-support-for-kauffman-new-economy-initiative-to-revitalize-detroit.aspx (accessed July 6, 2009).

Kaufman, Kathy A. "Outsourcing the Hearth: The Impact of Immigration on Labor Allocation in American Families." In *Immigration Research for a New Century: Multidisciplinary Perspectives*, edited by Nancy Foner, Rubén G. Rumbaut, and Steven J. Gold, 345–68. New York: Russell Sage Foundation, 2000.

Kayal, Philip M., and Joseph M. Kayal. *The Syrian-Lebanese: A Study in Religion and Assimilation*. Boston: Twayne Publishers, 1975.

Kelly, Kevin. "Where Music Will Be Coming From." *New York Times Magazine*, March 30, 2002.

Kerner, Otto. *Report of the National Advisory Commission on Civil Disorders*. New York: Bantam Books, 1968.

Kettles, Gregg W. "Legal Responses to Sidewalk Vending: The Case of Los Angeles, California." In *Street Entrepreneurs: People, Place, and Politics in Local and Global Perspective*, edited by John C. Cross and Alfonso Morales, 58–78. New York: Routledge, 2007.

Kilpatrick, Kwame M., mayor, City of Detroit. Press release, July 27, 2004.

Kim, Claire Jean. *Bitter Fruit: The Politics of Black-Korean Conflict in New York City*. New Haven, Conn.: Yale University Press, 2000.

Kim, Dae Young. "Beyond Coethnic Solidarity: Mexican and Ecuadorian Employment in Korean-Owned Businesses in New York City." *Racial and Ethnic Studies* 22, no. 3 (1999): 581–605.

———. "Leaving the Ethnic Economy: The Rapid Integration of Second-Generation Korean Americans in New York." In *Becoming New Yorkers: Ethnographies of the New Second Generation*, edited by Philip Kasinitz, John H. Mollenkopf, and Mary C. Waters, 154–88. New York: Russell Sage Foundation, 2004.

Kim, Illsoo. *New Urban Immigrants: The Korean Community in New York*. Princeton, N.J.: Princeton University Press, 1981.

Kinzer, Stephen, and Jeremy W. Peters. "Debating a Plan for a Blacks-Only Fund to Finance an 'Africa Town' in Detroit." *New York Times*, October 13, 2004.

Kosak, Hadassa. "Tailors and Troublemakers: Jewish Militancy in the New York Garment Industry, 1899–1920." In *A Coat of Many Colors: Immigration, Globalization and Reform in New York's Garment Industry*, edited by Daniel Soyer, 115–40. New York: Fordham University Press, 2005.

Kotkin, Joel. *Tribes: How Race, Religion and Identity Determined Success in the New Global Economy*. New York: Random House, 1992.

Krupa, Gregg. "Revival Revs on Seven Mile: Group Helps Area Thrive by Bringing Needed Resources In." *Detroit News*, July 26, 2007.

Kurashige, Scott. *The Shifting Ground of Race: Black and Japanese Americans in the Making of Multiethnic Los Angeles*. Princeton, N.J.: Princeton University Press, 2008.

Kurth, Joel, and Delores Patterson. "Boycott Targets Arabs." *Detroit News*, August 1, 2001.

Kusmer, Kenneth L. *A Ghetto Takes Shape: Black Cleveland, 1870–1930*. Urbana: University of Illinois Press, 1976.

Lacayo, Richard. "Immigration: Give Me Your Rich, Your Lucky . . ." *Time*, October 14, 1991.

Ladner, Robert A., Barry J. Schwartz, Sandra J. Roker, and Loretta S. Titterud. "The Miami Riots of 1980: Antecedent Conditions, Community Responses and Participant Characteristics." *Research in Social Movements, Conflict and Change* 4 (1981): 171–214.

Lawless, Paul. "Power and Conflict in Pro-Growth Regimes: Tensions in Economic Development in Jersey City and Detroit." *Urban Studies* 39, no. 8 (2002): 1329–346.

Leba, John K. *The Vietnamese Entrepreneurs in the U.S.A.* Houston: Zieleks, 1985.

Lee, Alfred McClung, and Norman D. Humphrey. *Race Riot: Detroit, 1943*, with a new introductory essay by Alfred McClung Lee. New York: Octagon Books, 1968.

Lee, Erika. *At America's Gates: Chinese Immigration during the Exclusion Era, 1882–1943*. Chapel Hill: University of North Carolina Press, 2003.

Lee, Jennifer. *Civility in the City: Blacks, Jews, and Koreans in Urban America*. Cambridge, Mass.: Harvard University Press, 2002.

———. "From Civil Relations to Racial Conflict: Merchant-Customer Interactions in Urban America." *American Sociological Review* 67 (February 2002): 77–98.

Lelyveld, Joseph. "Riots Viewed against History of Clashes Almost as Old as US." *New York Times*, September 11, 1964.

Lessinger, Johanna. *From the Ganges to the Hudson: Indian Immigrants in New York City*. Boston: Allyn & Bacon, 1996.

Levenstein, Margaret. "African American Entrepreneurship: The View from the 1910 Census." In *Immigrant and Minority Entrepreneurship: The Continuous Rebirth of American Communities*, edited by John Sibley Butler and Groge Kozmetsky, 1–17. Westport, Conn.: Praeger, 2004.

Levine, Rhonda F. *Class, Networks and Identity: Replanting Jewish Lives from Nazi Germany to Rural New York*. Lanham, Md.: Rowman & Littlefield, 2001.

Levitt, Peggy. "A Todos Les Llamo Primo (I Call Everyone Cousin): The Social Basis for Latin Small Businesses." In *New Migrants in the Marketplace: Boston's Ethnic Entrepreneurs*, edited by M. Halter, 120–40. Amherst: University of Massachusetts Press, 1995.

Lie, John. "The Black-Asian Conflict?" In *Not Just Black and White: Historical and Contemporary Perspectives on Immigration, Race and Ethnicity in the United States*, edited by Nancy Foner and George M. Fredrickson, 301–14. New York: Russell Sage Foundation, 2004.

Lieberson, Stanley. *A Piece of the Pie: Blacks and White Immigrants since 1880*. Berkeley: University of California Press, 1980.

Lieberson, Stanley, and Arnold R. Silverman. "The Precipitants and Underlying Conditions of Race Riots." *American Sociological Review* 30, no. 6 (December 1965): 887–98.

Liebow, Elliot. *Tally's Corner: A Study of Negro Streetcorner Men*. Boston: Little, Brown, 1967.

Light, Donald W. "The Migrant Enclaves to Mainstream: Reconceptualizing Informal Economic Behavior." *Theory and Society* 33 (2004): 705–37.

Light, Ivan. *Cities in World Perspective*. New York: Macmillan, 1983.

———. *Deflecting Immigration: Networks, Markets and Regulation in Los Angeles*. New York: Russell Sage Foundation, 2006.

———. *Ethnic Enterprise in America: Business and Welfare among Chinese, Japanese and Blacks*. Berkeley: University of California Press, 1972.

———. "The Ethnic Vice Industry, 1880–1944." *American Sociological Review* 42 (1977): 464–79.

———. "Immigrant and Ethnic Enterprise in North America." *Ethnic and Racial Studies* 17, no. 2 (1984): 195–216.

———. "Numbers Gambling among Blacks: A Financial Institution." *American Sociological Review* 42 (1977): 892–904.

Light, Ivan, and Edna Bonacich. *Immigrant Entrepreneurs*. Berkeley: University of California Press, 1988.

Light, Ivan, and Steven J. Gold. *Ethnic Economies*. San Diego: Academic Press, 2000.

Light, Ivan, Hadas Har-Chvi, and Kenneth Kan. "Black/Korean Conflict in Los Angles." In *Managing Divided Cities*, edited by Seamus Dunn, 74–87. Keele, UK: Keele University Press, 1994.

Light, Ivan, and Carolyn Rosenstein. *Race, Ethnicity and Entrepreneurship in Urban America*. New York: Aldine De Gruyter, 1995.

Ling, Huping. "Governing 'Hop Alley': On Leong Chinese Merchants and Laborers Association, 1906–1966." *Journal of American Ethnic History* 23, no. 2 (winter 2004): 50–84.

Lipsitz, George. "The Possessive Investment in Whiteness: Racial Social Democracy and the 'White' Problem in American Studies." *American Quarterly* 47, no. 3 (1995): 369–87.

Lizzi, Maria C. "'My Heart Is as Black as Yours': White Backlash, Racial Identity and Italian American Stereotypes in New York City's 1969 Mayoral Campaign." *Journal of American Ethnic History* 27, no. 3 (2008): 43–80.

Loewen, James W. *The Mississippi Chinese: Between Black and White*. Cambridge, Mass.: Harvard University Press, 1971.

Losby, Jan E., Marcia E. Kingslow, and John F. Else. *The Informal Economy: Experiences of African Americans*. Washington, D.C.: Institute for Social and Economic Development Solutions, 2003.

Lowry, J. H. *Realizing the New Agenda for Minority Business Development*. Boston: Boston Consulting Group, 2005.

Lyman, Stanford M. *Chinese Americans*. New York: Random House, 1974.

———. "Stranger in the Cities: The Chinese on the Urban Frontier." In *Ethnic Conflict in California History*, edited by Charles Wollenberg, 61–100. Letters and Science Extension Series, University of California, Berkeley. Los Angeles: Tinnon-Brown, 1970.

Mahler, Jonathan. "G.M., Detroit and the Fall of the Black Middle Class." *New York Times Magazine*, June 24, 2009.

Mahler, Sarah J. *Salvadorans in Suburbia: Symbiosis and Conflict*. Boston: Allyn & Bacon, 1995.

Malkin, Victoria. "Who's behind the Counter? Retail Workers in New York City." In *Becoming New Yorkers: Ethnographies of the New Second Generation*, edited by Philip Kasinitz, John H. Mollenkopf, and Mary C. Waters, 115–53. New York: Russell Sage Foundation, 2004.

Malpica, Daniel Melero. "Making a Living in the Streets of Los Angeles: An Ethnographic Study of Day Laborers." *Migraciones Internacionales* 1, no. 3 (2002): 124–48.

Mangiafico, Luciano. *Contemporary American Immigrants: Patterns of Filipino, Korean, and Chinese Settlement in the United States*. New York: Praeger, 1988.

Mano, D. Keith. "Scalping." *National Review*, August 28, 1987.

Marable, Manning. *The Great Wells of Democracy: The Meaning of Race in American Life*. New York: Basic Civitas Books, 2002.

———. *How Capitalism Underdeveloped Black America: Problems in Race, Political Economy and Society*. Boston: South End Press, 1983.

Marcelli, Pascale Joassart, and Daniel Flaming. "Workers without Rights: The Informal Economy in Los Angeles." Economic Roundtable Briefing Paper, Los Angeles, 2002.

Marshall, Ronald, Jr. "Store Makes Turn Around." *Michigan Citizen*, July 16, 1997.

Marx, Gary T. *Protest and Prejudice: A Study of Belief in the Black Community*. New York: Harper & Brothers, 1967.

———. "Two Cheers for the National Riot (Kerner) Commission Report." In *Black American*, edited by J. F. Szwed, 77–95. New York: Basic Books, 1970.

Massey, Douglas S. "Origins of Economic Disparities: The Historical Role of Housing Segregation." In *Segregation: The Rising Costs for America*, edited by James H. Carr and Nandinee K. Kutty, 39–80. New York: Routledge, 2008.

Massey, Douglas S., and Nancy A. Denton. *American Apartheid: Segregation and the Making of the Underclass*. Cambridge, Mass.: Harvard University Press, 1993.

Mayor's Commission on Conditions in Harlem. "The Negro in Harlem: A Report on Social and Economic Conditions Responsible for the Outbreak of March 19, 1935." New York, 1936.

McCrohan, Kevin, James D. Smith, and Terry K. Adams. "Consumer Purchases in Informal Markets: Estimates for the 1980s, Prospects for the 1990s." *Journal of Retailing* 67, no. 1 (1991): 22–50.

McGraw, Bill. "Today's Detroit Has Little to Do with 1967: What If Riot Never Happened? City Was Still Headed for Slide." *Detroit Free Press*, July 20, 2007.

Meier, August, and Elliot Rudwick. *From Plantation to Ghetto*. Rev. ed. New York: Hill and Wang, 1970.

Merina, Victor. "A Story of Refugee Success Ended Tragically in Riots." *Los Angeles Times*, August 17, 1992.

Merton, Robert K. *Social Theory and Social Structure*. Rev. and enlarged ed. Glencoe, N.Y.: Free Press, 1957.

Michigan Constitution. Article 1, Section 26. 2007.

Michigan Minority Supplier Development Council. Home page. www.mmbdc.com/.

Miller, Kelly. "The Harvest of Race Prejudice." *Survey Graphic* 6, no. 6 (March 1925): 682–83, 711–12.

Miller, S. M. "The Pursuit of Informal Economies." *Annals of the American Academy of Political and Social Science* 493 (1987): 26–35.

Min, Pyong Gap. *Caught in the Middle: Korean Communities in New York and Los Angeles*. Berkeley: University of California Press, 1996.

———. *Ethnic Business Enterprise: Korean Small Business in Atlanta*. Staten Island, N.Y.: Center for Migration Studies, 1988.

———. *Ethnic Solidarity for Economic Survival*. New York: Russell Sage Foundation, 2008.

Minority Business Development Agency (MBDA). "Minority Business and Entrepreneurship." http://www.mbda.gov.

Mitchell, Alison. "The Crown Heights Report: From Earliest Hours, Calls Were Ignored." *New York Times*, July 21, 1993.

Modell, John. *The Economics and Politics of Racial Accommodation: The Japanese of Los Angeles, 1900–1942*. Urbana: University of Illinois Press, 1977.

———. "Japanese-Americans: Some Costs of Group Achievement." In *Ethnic Conflict in California History*, edited by Charles Wollenberg, 101–19. Letters and Science Extension Series, University of California, Berkeley. Los Angeles: Tinnon-Brown, 1970.

Molefsky, Barry. "America's Underground Economy." Report No. 81-181E. Congressional Research Service, Library of Congress, Washington, D.C., 1981.

Moore, Natalie Y. "Party Store Tickets Hit 1,300." *Detroit News*, March 1, 2004.

Morawska, Ewa. "Immigrant-Black Dissension in American Cities: An Argument for Multiple Explanations." In *Problem of the Century: Racial Stratification in the United States*, edited by Elijah Anderson and Douglas Massey, 47–96. New York: Russell Sage Foundation, 2001.

Mormino, Gary Ross. *Immigrants on the Hill: Italian-Americans in St. Louis, 1882–1982*. Urbana: University of Illinois Press, 1986.

Moss, Philip, and Chris Tilly. "'Soft' Skills and Race: An Investigation of Black Men's Employment Problems." *Work and Occupations* 23 (1996): 252–76.

Mydans, Seth. "Criticism Grows Over Aliens Seized during Riots." *New York Times*, May 29, 1992.

Myrdal, Gunnar. *An American Dilemma*. New York: McGraw Hill, 1964.

Nation's Restaurant News. "Calif.'s 'Little Saigon' Operators Seek Food-Temperature Variance." February 14, 2000.

New York Times. "Bias against Negro on Relief Charged." January 14, 1932.

———. "Excerpts from a Study to Determine the Characteristics of Negro Rioters." July 28, 1968.

———. "Harlem's Hitler Brought to Court." October 9, 1934.

———. "Japanese Will Quit California Farms." December 16, 1923.

———. "Liebowitz Asks Truce of Negroes and Jews." August 22, 1939.

———. "Police End Harlem Riot; Mayor Starts Inquiry; Dodge Sees a Red Plot." March 21, 1935.

Nielsen, Francois. "Towards a Theory of Ethnic Solidarity in Modern Societies." *American Sociological Review* 50, no. 2 (1985): 133–49.

Office of Refugee Resettlement (ORR). "Annual Report to Congress—2005." U.S. Department of Health and Human Services, Administration for Children and Families, 2007. www.acf.hhs.gov/programs/orr/data/05arc7.htm#2 (accessed April 10, 2010).

Oguntoyinbo, Lekan. "More Black Business Ownership Promoted: Group Plans to Issue Certificates of Approval." *Detroit Free Press*, June 21, 1999.

———. "Program Aims to Keep Peace for Merchants: Harmony Project Could Lessen Racial Tensions with Customers." *Detroit Free Press*, July 6, 1999.

Oliver, Melvin, and Thomas Shapiro. *Black Wealth/White Wealth: A New Perspective on Racial Inequality*. New York: Routledge, 1995.

Olzak, Susan. *The Dynamics of Ethnic Competition and Conflict*. Stanford, Calif.: Stanford University Press, 1992.

Olzak, Susan, and Suzanne Shanahan. "Deprivation and Race Riots: An Extension of Spilerman's Analysis." *Social Force* 74, no. 3 (1996): 931–61.

Omi, Michael, and Howard Winant. *Racial Formation in the United States: From the 1960s to the 1990s*. New York: Routledge, 1994.

Omowale, Jonah Nadir. "Black Business Unites." *Michigan Citizen*, June 4, 2006.

Ong, Paul, Kye Y. Park, and Y. Tong. "Korean-Black Conflict and the State." In *The New Asian Immigration in Los Angeles and Global Restructuring*, edited by Paul Ong, Edna Bonacich, and Lucie Cheng, 264–94. Philadelphia: Temple University Press, 1994.

Ottley, Roi. *New World a-Coming*. New York: Arno Press and New York Times, 1968 [1943].

Pacyga, Dominic A. *Polish Immigrants and Industrial Chicago: Workers on the South Side, 1880–1922*. Columbus: Ohio State University Press, 1991.

Page, Jeffrey M. "Collective Violence and the Culture of Subordination: A Study of Participants in the July 1967 Riots in Newark and Detroit." PhD diss., University of Michigan, 1968.

Pattillo, Mary. *Black on the Block: The Politics of Race and Class in the City*. Chicago: University of Chicago Press, 2007.

Perlmutter, Emanuel. "Powell Demands Numbers Inquiry." *New York Times*, January 11, 1960.

Perlstein, Rick. *Nixonland: The Rise of a President and the Fracturing of America*. New York: Scribners, 2008.

Petersilia, Joan, and Allan Abrahamse. "A Profile of Those Arrested." In *The Los Angeles Riots: Lessons for the Urban Future*, edited by Mark Baldassare, 135–47. Boulder, Colo.: Westview, 1994.

Philpott, Thomas. *The Slum and the Ghetto: Neighborhood Deterioration and Middle Class Reform, Chicago, 1880–1930*. New York: Oxford University Press, 1978.

Pierce, Joseph A. *Negro Business and Business Education: Their Present and Prospective Development*. New York: Harper & Brothers, 1947.

Pitt, Leonard, and Dale Pitt. "African Americans." In *Los Angeles A to Z: An Encyclopedia of the City and County*, 4–5. Berkeley: University of California Press, 1997.

Podhoretz, Norman. "My Negro Problem—and Ours." *Commentary*, February 1963.

Pohlmann, M. D. *Black Politics in Conservative America*. New York: Longman, 1990.

Porter, Bruce, and Marvin Dunn. *The Miami Riot of 1980: Crossing the Bounds*. Lexington, Mass.: D.C. Heath, 1984.

Portes, Alejandro. "The Social Origins of the Cuban Enclave Economy of Miami." *Sociological Perspectives* 30, no. 4 (1987): 340–72.

Portes, Alejandro, and Robert Bach. *Latin Journey: Cuban and Mexican Immigrants in the United States*. Berkeley: University of California Press, 1985.

Portes, Alejandro, and William Haller. "The Informal Economy." In *The Handbook of Economic Sociology*, edited by Neil J. Smelser and Richard Swedberg, 403–25. 2nd ed. Princeton, N.J.: Princeton University Press, 2005.

Portes, Alejandro, and Robert D. Manning. "The Immigrant Enclave: Theory and Empirical Examples." In *Ethnicity: Structure and Process*, edited by J. Nagel and S. Olzak, 47–68. New York: Academic Press, 1986.

Portes, Alejandro, and Rubén G. Rumbaut. *Immigrant America: A Portrait*. 3rd ed. Berkeley: University of California Press, 2006.

Portes, Alejandro, and Alex Stepick. *City on the Edge*. Berkeley: University of California Press, 1993.

Pothukuchi, Kami. *The Detroit Food System: A Handbook for Community Planners*. Detroit: Wayne State University Press, 2003.

Preston, Julia. "Decline Seen in Numbers of People Here Illegally." *New York Times*, July 31, 2008.

Qin, D. B., N. Way, and M. Rana. "The 'Model Minority' and Their Discontent: Examining Peer Discrimination and Harassment of Chinese American Immigrant Youth." *New Directions for Child and Adolescent Development* 121 (fall 2008): 27–42.

Raucher, Alan. "Dime Store Chains: The Making of Organization Men, 1880–1940." *Business History Review* 65, no. 1 (1991): 130–63.

Reddick, L. D. "Anti-Semitism among Negroes." *Negro Quarterly* 1, no. 2 (summer 1942): 112–22.

Reed, Christopher Robert. *The Chicago NAACP and the Rise of Black Professional Leadership, 1910–1966*. Bloomington: Indiana University Press, 1997.

Riccardi, Nicholas. "Shops Under Siege." *Los Angeles Times*, November 27, 1996.

Rieder, Jonathan. *Canarsie: The Jews and Italians of Brooklyn against Liberalism*. Cambridge, Mass.: Harvard University Press, 1985.

Riggs, Marlon T. *Ethnic Notions*. Videorecording. San Francisco: California Newsreel, 1987.

Roberts, Sam. "As Population Shifts in Harlem, Blacks Lose Their Majority." *New York Times*, January 6, 2010.

———. "White Flight Reversed." *New York Times*. September 23, 2008.

Robles, Bárbara J., and Héctor Cordero-Guzmán. "Latino Self-Employment and Entrepreneurship in the United States: An Overview of the Literature and Data Sources." *Annals of the American Academy of Political and Social Science* 613 (2007): 18–31.

Rockaway, Robert A. *The Jews of Detroit: From the Beginning, 1762–1914*. Detroit: Wayne State University Press, 1986.

Roediger, David R. *Colored White: Transcending the Racial Past*. Berkeley: University of California Press, 2002.

Rosenfeld, Michael J. "Celebration, Politics, Selective Looting and Riots: A Micro Level Study of the Bulls Riot of 1992 in Chicago." *Social Problems* 44, no. 4 (1997): 483–502.

Ross, Mary. "Negro City in Harlem Is a Race Capital." *New York Times*, March 1, 1925.

Rutledge, Paul James. *The Vietnamese Experience in America*. Bloomington: Indiana University Press, 1992.

Ryley, Sarah. "Black Businesses Flourish in Mich." *Detroit News*, June 20, 2006.

Salanié, Bernard. "The Riots in France: An Economist's View." June 11, 2006. http://riots-france.ssrc.org/Salanie (accessed April 11, 2010).

Saloutos, Theodore. *The Greeks in the United States*. Cambridge, Mass.: Harvard University Press, 1964.

Sanchez-Jankowski, Martin. *Islands in the Street*. Berkeley: University of California Press, 1992.

Sassen, Saskia. *Cities in a World Economy*. Thousand Oaks, Calif.: Pine Forge Press, 1994.

———. "The Informal Economy." In *Dual City: Restructuring New York*, edited by J. H. Mollenkopf and M. Castells, 79–101. New York: Russell Sage Foundation, 1991.

Scarpaci, Jean Ann. "Italian Immigrants in Louisiana's Sugar Parishes: Recruitment, Labor Conditions, and Community Relations, 1880–1910." PhD diss., Department of History, Rutgers University, 1972.

Schermerhorn, Richard A. *Comparative Ethnic Relations: A Framework for Theory and Research*, with a new preface. Chicago: University of Chicago Press, 1978.

Schmidt, Peter. "Michigan Overwhelmingly Adopts Ban on Affirmative-Action Preferences." *Chronicle of Higher Education*, November 17, 2006.

Scott, Janny. "Rethinking Segregation beyond Black and White." *New York Times*, July 29, 2001.

Scott, William R. "Black Nationalism and the Italo-Ethiopian Conflict, 1934–1936." *Journal of Negro History* 63, no. 2 (1978): 118–34.

Sears, David O. "Urban Rioting in Los Angeles: A Comparison of 1965 with 1992." In *The Los Angeles Riots: Lessons for the Urban Future*, edited by Mark Baldassare, 237–55. Boulder, Colo.: Westview, 1994.

Segrest, James, and Mark Hoffman. *Moanin' at Midnight: The Life and Times of Howlin' Wolf*. New York: Pantheon, 2004.

Sengstock, Mary C. *Chaldean-Americans: Changing Conceptions of Ethnic Identity*. 2nd ed. Staten Island, N.Y.: Center for Migration Studies, 1999.

Shane, Scott. "Failure Is a Constant in Entrepreneurship, You're the Boss: The Art of Running a Small Business." *New York Times*, July 15, updated July 17, 2009.

Sheffield, Horace L. "Our Interests or Others'." *Michigan Citizen*, September 8, 2001.

Sheppard, Harold L. "The Negro Merchant: A Study of Negro Anti-Semitism." *American Journal of Sociology* 53, no. 2 (September 1947): 96–99.

Silverman, Robert Mark. "Black Business, Group Resources, and the Economic Detour: Contemporary Black Manufacturers in Chicago's Ethnic Beauty Aids Industry." *Journal of Black Studies* 30, no. 2 (1999): 232–58.

———. *Doing Business in Minority Markets: Black and Korean Entrepreneurs in Chicago's Ethnic Beauty Aids Industry*. New York: Garland, 2000.

Simon, Rita J. *In the Golden Land: A Century of Russian and Soviet Jewish Immigration in America*. Westport, Conn.: Praeger, 1997.

Sinclair, Norman. "Gas Price War Turns Deadly in Detroit: Owner of Station Killed Rival Who Cut Price by 3 Cents a Gallon, Cops Say." *Detroit News*, November 17, 2007.

Singer, Audrey. "The New Geography of United States Immigration." Brookings Immigration Series 3, Brookings Institution, Washington, D.C., July 2009. www.brookings.edu/papers/2009/07_immigration_geography_singer.aspx (accessed April 11, 2010).

Small, Mario Luis, and Monica McDermott. "The Presence of Organizational Resources in Poor Urban Neighborhoods: An Analysis of Average and Contextual Effects." *Social Forces* 84, no. 3 (2006): 1697–1724.

Smith, Joel J., and Nathan Hurst. "Grocery Closings Hit Detroit Hard." *Detroit News*, July 5, 2007.

Smith, Robert C. "Transnational Migrants and Community Formation." Social Science History Association Annual Meeting, Chicago, November 16, 1995.

Sonenshein, Raphael J. "The Battle over Liquor Stores in South Central Los Angeles: Management of an Interminority Conflict." *Urban Affairs Review* 31, no. 6 (1996): 710–37.

Sontag, Deborah. "Émigrés in New York: Work off the Books." *New York Times*, June 13, 1993.

Sowell, Thomas. *Black Rednecks and White Liberals*. San Francisco: Encounter Books, 2005.

———. *Ethnic America*. New York: Basic Books, 1981.

Spiegel, Irving. "Survey Finds Blacks Own Most Harlem Stores." *New York Times*, September 16, 1968.

Spielman, Fran. "Public Building Chief Is in Line for New Job: Gayles Boosted Minority Participation." *Chicago Sun-Times*, October 3, 2007.

Stack, Carol. *All Our Kin*. New York: Harper & Row, 1974.

Stack, John F. *International Conflict in an American City: Boston's Irish, Italian, and Jews, 1935–1944*. Westport, Conn.: Greenwood Press, 1979.

Stanton, Ali. "Koreans Open BBQ Business in Harlem." *Amsterdam News*, April 27, 1985.

Stein, Harry. "Racial-Preference Ballots Go National: Initiatives in Four States Could Shape the Presidential Election." *City Journal*, April 16, 2008.

Stephey, M. J. "Kwame Kilpatrick." *Time*, October 28, 2008. www.time.com/time/politics/article/0,8599,1854335,00.html (accessed July 4, 2009).

Stepick, Alex. *Pride against Prejudice: Haitians in the United States*. Boston: Allyn & Bacon, 1998.

Sturdivant, Frederick D. "Better Deal for Ghetto Shoppers." In *The Ghetto Marketplace*, edited by Frederick D. Sturdivant, 142–57. New York: Free Press, 1969.

———, ed. *The Ghetto Marketplace*. New York: Free Press, 1969.

Sturdivant, Frederick D., and Walter T. Wilhelm. "Poverty, Minorities, and Consumer Exploitation." In *The Ghetto Marketplace*, edited by Frederick D. Sturdivant, 108–17. New York: Free Press, 1969.

Sugrue, Thomas J. *The Origins of the Urban Crisis: Race and Inequality in Postwar Detroit*, with a new preface by the author. Princeton, N.J.: Princeton University Press, 2005.

Sung, Betty Lee. *The Story of the Chinese in America*. New York: Collier Books, 1971.

Tabb, William K. *The Political Economy of the Black Ghetto*. New York: Norton, 1970.

Takaki, Ronald. *A Different Mirror: A History of Multicultural America*. Boston: Little, Brown, 1993.

———. *Strangers from a Different Shore: A History of Asian Americans*. Boston: Little, Brown, 1989.

Tatum, Wilbert A. "Editorials: Blacks, Jews—A Turning Point." *New York Amsterdam News*, October 5, 1985.

Teller, Judd L. "Negroes and Jews: A Hard Look." *Conservative Judaism* 21, no. 1 (fall 1966): 13–20.

Tenenbaum, Shelly. *A Credit to Their Community: Jewish Loan Societies in the United States, 1880–1945*. Detroit: Wayne State University Press, 1993.

Thompson, Bankole. "Super Bowl Blackout." *Michigan Citizen*, January 8, 2006.

Tienda, Marta, and Rebeca Raijman. "Immigrants' Income Packaging and Invisible Labor Force Activity." *Social Science Quarterly* 81, no. 1 (2000): 291–311.

Tilly, Charles. *The Politics of Collective Violence*. New York: Cambridge University Press, 2003.

Tran, Anh K. "Economic Base of the Vietnamese Community in the Los Angeles and Orange County Area." Department of Asian-American Studies, University of California, Los Angeles, 1986.

Trieu, Monica. "Intra-national Ethnic Identities in Flux: Identity Construction among the Chinese-Vietnamese and Vietnamese Second Generation." Unpublished PhD diss., Department of Sociology, University of California, Irvine, 2008.

U.S. Bureau of Labor Statistics. "Contingent and Alternative Employment Arrangements." Technical Note. U.S. Department of Labor, Washington, D.C., February 2001.

U.S. Census Bureau. "Black-Owned Firms: 2002." 2002 Economic Census, Survey of Business Owners, Company Statistics Series. August 2006. www.census.gov/prod/ec02/sb0200csblk.pdf (accessed April 11, 2010).

———. "Hispanic-Owned Firms: 2002." 2002 Economic Census, Survey of Business Owners, Company Statistics Series. August 2006. www.census.gov/prod/ec02/sb0200cshisp.pdf (accessed April 11, 2010).

———. "Minority- and Women-Owned Businesses." 1997 Economic Census, 2002 Economic Census, Survey of Business Owners, Company Statistics Series. August 2006.

———. *2000 Census of Population and Housing: Summary File 3 (SF3)*. Washington, D.C.: Data User Services, 2002.

———. *2000 Census of Population and Housing: Summary File 4 (SF4)*. Washington, D.C.: Data User Services, 2004.

U.S. Department of Housing and Urban Development (HUD). "The Federal Housing Administration." September 6, 2006. www.hud.gov/offices/hsg/fhahistory.cfm (accessed April 16, 2010).

Valentine, Betty Lou. *Hustling and Other Hard Work*. New York: Free Press, 1978.

Valenzuela, Abel, Jr. "Day Labor Work." *Annual Review of Sociology* 29 (2003): 307–33.

———. "Day Labourers as Entrepreneurs?" *Journal of Ethnic and Migration Studies* 27, no. 2 (2001): 335–52.

Venkatesh, Sudhir Alladi. *Off the Books: The Underground Economy of the Urban Poor*. Cambridge, Mass.: Harvard University Press, 2006.

Vergara, Camillo Jose. *The New American Ghetto*. New Brunswick, N.J.: Rutgers University Press, 1997.

Wainright, Jon S. *Racial Discrimination and Minority Business Enterprise: Evidence from the 1990 Census*. New York: Garland, 2000.

Waldinger, Roger. *Still the Promised City? African-Americans and New Immigrants in Postindustrial New York*. Cambridge, Mass.: Harvard University Press, 1996.

———, ed. *Strangers at the Gates: New Immigrants in Urban America*. Berkeley: University of California Press, 2001.

———. "When the Melting Pot Boils Over: The Irish, Jews, Blacks and Koreans of New York." Department of Sociology, University of California, Los Angeles, 1992.

Waldinger, Roger, Howard Aldrich, Robin Ward, et al. *Ethnic Entrepreneurs: Immigrant Business in Industrial Societies*. Newbury Park, Calif.: Sage, 1990.

Waldinger, Roger, and Mehdi Bozorgmehr, eds. *Ethnic Los Angeles*. New York: Russell Sage Foundation, 1996.

Waldinger, Roger, and Michael I. Lichter. *How the Other Half Works: Immigration and the Social Organization of Labor*. Berkeley: University of California Press, 2003.

Waldman, Lois. "Employment Discrimination against Jews in the United States—1955." *Jewish Social Studies* 18 (1956): 208–16.

Walker, Juliette. *The History of Black Business in America: Capitalism, Race, Entrepreneurship*. New York: Macmillan Library Reference, 1998.

Wang, Joan S. "Race, Gender, and Laundry Work: The Roles of Chinese Laundrymen and American Women in the United States, 1850–1950." *Journal of American Ethnic History* 24, no. 1 (fall 2004): 59–99.

Ward, Brian. *Just My Soul Responding: Rhythm and Blues, Black Consciousness, and Race Relations*. Berkeley: University of California Press, 1998.

Washington, Booker T. *The Negro in Business*. Chicago: Hertel, Jenkins, 1907.

Waters, M. *Black Identities*. New York: Russell Sage Foundation and Harvard University Press, 1999.

Wayne, Leslie. "Congress to Debate Greater Oversight of Hedge Funds." *New York Times*, October 1, 1998.

Weaver, Robert C. "Class, Race and Urban Renewal." In *Racial and Ethnic Relations*, edited by Bernard E. Segal. 2nd ed. New York: Crowell, 1966.

Weber, Max. *The Protestant Ethic and the Spirit of Capitalism*. Translated by T. Parsons. New York: Scribners, 1958.

Weems, Robert E., Jr. *Black Business in the Black Metropolis: The Chicago Metropolitan Assurance Company, 1925–1985*. Bloomington: Indiana University Press, 1996.

———. *Desegregating the Dollar: African American Consumerism in the Twentieth Century*. New York: New York University Press, 1998.

Weingroff, Richard F. "The Battle of Its Life." *Public Roads* 69, no. 6 (May/June 2006): 26–38.

Weisbrod, Robert G., and Arthur Stein. *Bittersweet Encounter: The Afro-American and the American Jew.* Westport, Conn.: Negro Universities Press, 1970.

Wilkerson, Isabel. "A Great Escape: A Dwindling Legacy." *New York Times,* February 15, 1998.

Williams, Colin C. "The Nature of Entrepreneurship in the Informal Sector: Evidence from England." *Journal of Developmental Entrepreneurship* 12, no. 2 (2007): 239–54.

Williams, John A. "Harlem Nightclubs." In *Harlem: A Community in Transition,* edited by John Henrik Clarke, 167–79. New York: Citadel Press, 1964.

Wilson, William J. *The Bridge over the Racial Divide: Rising Inequality and Coalition Politics.* Berkeley: University of California Press and Russell Sage Foundation, 1999.

———. *The Declining Significance of Race.* Chicago: University of Chicago Press, 1978.

———. *More than Just Race: Being Black and Poor in the Inner City.* New York: Norton, 2009.

———. *The Truly Disadvantaged.* Chicago: University of Chicago Press, 1987.

———. *When Work Disappears: The World of the New Urban Poor.* New York: Knopf, 1996.

Wilson, William J., and Richard P. Taub. *There Goes the Neighborhood: Racial, Ethnic and Class Tensions in Four Chicago Neighborhoods and Their Meanings for America.* New York: Knopf, 2006.

Wirth, Louis. *The Ghetto.* Chicago: University of Chicago Press, 1928.

Wolf, Eleanor Paperno, Alvin D. Loving, and Donald C. Marsh. *Negro-Jewish Relationships.* Detroit: Wayne State University Press, 1944.

Wong, Bernard. *Ethnicity and Entrepreneurship: The New Chinese Immigrants in the San Francisco Bay Area.* Boston: Allyn & Bacon, 1998.

Wong, Charles Choy. "Black and Chinese Grocery Stores in Los Angeles' Black Ghetto." *Urban Life* 5, no. 4 (1977): 439–64.

Wong, Morrison. "Chinese Americans." In *Asian Americans: Contemporary Trends and Issues,* edited by Pyong Gap Min, 110–45. 2nd ed. Thousand Oaks, Calif.: Pine Forge Press, 2006.

Woodard, Michael D. *Black Entrepreneurs in America: Stories of Struggle and Success.* New Brunswick, N.J.: Rutgers University Press, 1997.

Woodson, Carter G. *The Negro Professional Man and the Community, with Special Emphasis on the Physician and the Lawyer.* New York: Negro Universities Press, 1934.

Woolley, John T., and Gerhard Peters. "Richard Nixon: Statement About a National Program for Minority Business Enterprise." American Presidency Project, University of California, Santa Barbara, March 5, 1969. www.presidency.ucsb.edu/ws/index.php?pid=1943 (accessed April 11, 2010).

Yoon, In Jin. *On My Own: Korean Businesses and Race Relations in America.* Chicago: University of Chicago Press, 1997.

Zenner, Walter P. *Minorities in the Middle: A Cross-cultural Analysis.* Albany: State University of New York Press, 1991.

Zhou, Min, and Carl Bankston III. *Growing Up American: How Vietnamese Children Adapt to Life in the United States.* New York: Russell Sage Foundation, 1998.

Zlolniski, Christian. *Janitors, Street Vendors, and Activists: The Lives of Mexican Immigrants in Silicon Valley.* Berkeley: University of California Press, 2006.

Zukin, Sharon. *Naked City: The Death and Life of Authentic Urban Places.* New York: Oxford University Press, 2009.

INDEX

AFDC. *See* Aid to Families with Dependent Children

affirmative action programs, 115

African Americans: activist outlook of, 135; beauty salons and, 173; business ownership and, 141, 268n99; Chaldean entrepreneurs viewed by, 213–14; city populations of, 96; class polarization of, 217; communal activism by, 136–37; community-building efforts of, 20; community control desire of, 136; Cuban's relationship with, 147; department store employment of, 63–64, 74; disproportionate failure of, 5; education of, 117; entertainment industry and, 260n99, 274n63; entrepreneurship skills lacking of, 5; ethnic economy development concerns by, 20, 230; ethnic succession embraced by, 81; European immigrant competition with, 26; Frazier on, 72; gainful worker records of, 27; ghetto isolation and, 101; goods/services overpayment by, 75; government employment of, 261n119; Great Depression's impact on, 69–70; housing obtainment of, 97–98; immigrant entrepreneurs, in northern U.S., 62–64; immigrant entrepreneurs, in southern U.S., 58–62; immigrant merchant reaction by, 134–37; immigrant merchant underrepresentation of, 20; industrial/ manufacturing jobs and, 191–92; informal economy and, 156–57; Jewish merchant employment of, 74; Jews' willingness to associate with, 73–74; Korean conflict with, 132–33, 266n57; lack of commitment to each other by, 194; as "last hired and first fired," 69; limited business/customer access of, 63–64; lowliest employment positions for, 69, 77, 253n50; low self-employment rates of, 17–18, 191; merchant refusal to hire, 77; mobility lack of, 236; political influence of, 68, 250n1; political power, in Detroit, 182–83, 227, 234; as poor customers, 62; proprietorship view of, 4–5; self-assertion of, 103; self-determination of, 134; self-presentation/ soft skills of, 218–19; as servicemen, 83; social differentiation among, 217; social resources lacking for, 115; solidarity of, 198, 199; unity/self-sufficiency of, 70; victimization of, 60–61; violence

hostility toward, 41, 71–73; influx of, 127, 232–33; jobs accepted by, 41; as proprietors, 129; racial tolerance of, 147; as scapegoats, 67; self-employment rates of, 49; whites' view of, 42

immigrant entrepreneurs: Africa Town Project impact on, 211–12; business associations formed by, 43; business expansion and, 131; businesslike manner of, 141; class origins of, 130–31; conflict bases and, 40–46; crisis/exit/ organization of, 145–47; customer relations in early twentieth century and, 39–65; disadvantages suffering by, 279n4; environment connection felt by, 141; grooming industry and, 129–30; harassment/violence vulnerability of, 41–42; homeland intervention reliance by, 43–45; immigrant customer conflicts and, 139–41; informal/legal discrimination suffering of, 41; inner city departure of, 145–46; native minorities' complaints and, 126; naturalization of, 43; outgroup market advantages for, 52–53; political resources for, 126–27; representation lack of, in Detroit, 212; restriction/vengeance for, 234–35; self-defense of, in Detroit, 211–12; success of, 158, 236

immigrant entrepreneurs, in northern United States: African Americans and, 62–64; Great Migration influencing, 62–63

immigrant entrepreneurs, in southern United States: African Americans and, 58–62; catering to African Americans, 61; desegregation influencing, 61–62; as middlemen, 61; racial differences/norms and, 231; upward mobility of, 58–59

immigrant merchants: African American reactions toward, 134–37; African American underrepresentation of, 20; attack of, 10–11; community control confrontation by, 133–34; conflict response of, 152; nonblack objections to, 137–39; opponents to, 137, 151–52; political power used by, 10; racial change among, 132–33; "shoot first, ask

questions later" self-defense of, 134; social transformations associated with, 137–38

Immigrants: Your Country Needs Them (Legrain), 125

immigration, black objections to, 28–29, 246n60

Immigration and Nationality Act of 1965, 127

Improved Benevolent Protective Order of Elks (IBPOE), 82

Independent Retailers Association (IRA), 221

informal economy, 272n32; African Americans and, 156–57; attractions of, 165–66; banking/credit and, 176; Barnett on, 167–68; benefits of, 177–78; black entrepreneur focus on, 196–97; community context of, 166–69; community control and, 178; consumer markets/color line in, 169; current perspectives on, 160–69; defining characteristics of, 162; demand for, 165, 167; drawbacks of, 179; earnings of, 163–65; formal economy v., 160; forms of, 233; funds/monies spent on purchases in, 163; ghetto impacted by, 168; income concealment and, 165; income generation from, 158, 177, 273n45; legal representation lack and, 172; moral objections to, 161; motives for, 166; mutual survival norms and, 167; ordinances against, 171; potential of, 178, 180, 240; practices of, 157–58; regulation resistance in, 171–72; resistance site provided by, 172; restrictions/prohibition and, 178, 180; self-employment and, 158; services provided by, 161, 171; size measurement of, 162–63; social capital increase by, 167; street vendor as, *164*; success story of, 170–71; temporary, 160–61; underdevelopment linked to, 160; unemployment concealment and, 162; unrealistic optimism and, 179; vital need for, 161; women's involvement in, 164–65. *See also* formal/informal economy

ABOUT THE AUTHOR

Steven J. Gold is professor and graduate program director in the Department of Sociology at Michigan State University. His interests include international migration, ethnic economies, ethnic community development, and visual sociology. As well as being the past chair of the International Migration Section of the American Sociological Association, Gold is also the author, coauthor, or coeditor of five books. Together with Rubén G. Rumbaut, he is the editor of the New Americans book series.